D0372703

"What happens when you bring together one of the most misunderstood subjects (love) and one of the most ignored practices (church membership and discipline) in the church today? A book like this one. Unlike the generation raised on Mr. Spock's child-rearing advice, the Good Shepherd cares for his flock by loving discipline. There is a lot of talk these days about radical discipleship, but what we need today is a lot more ordinary discipleship, where we realize not only in theory but in practice what it means to be conformed to Christ's image. This is the best book I've seen on this subject in a long time."

—Michael Horton, J. Gresham Machen Professor of Systematic Theology and Apologetics, Westminster Seminary California

San Diego Christian College
Library
Santee, CA

The Church and the

SURPRISING OFFENSE

of God's Love

Other IX Marks books published by Crossway

Nine Marks of a Healthy Church, Mark Dever
The Deliberate Church: Building Your Ministry on the Gospel, Mark Dever
    and Paul Alexander
The Gospel and Personal Evangelism, Mark Dever
What Is a Healthy Church? Mark Dever
What Is a Healthy Church Member? Thabiti Anyabwile
It Is Well: Expositions on Substitutionary Atonement, Mark Dever
    and Michael Lawrence
What Is the Gospel? Greg Gilbert
What Does God Want of Us Anyway? A Quick Overview of the Whole Bible,
    Mark Dever

262.8
L485c

The Church and the
SURPRISING
OFFENSE
of God's Love

*Reintroducing the Doctrines of
Church Membership and Discipline*

Jonathan Leeman

:: CROSSWAY

WHEATON, ILLINOIS

The Church and the Surprising Offense of God's Love: Reintroducing the Doctrines of Church Membership and Discipline Copyright © 2010 by 9Marks
Published by Crossway
        1300 Crescent Street
        Wheaton, Illinois 60187

All rights reserved. No part of this publication may be reproduced, stored in a retrieval system, or transmitted in any form by any means, electronic, mechanical, photocopy, recording, or otherwise, without the prior permission of the publisher, except as provided for by USA copyright law.

Cover design: Josh Dennis
First printing 2010
Printed in the United States of America

Unless otherwise indicated, Scripture quotations are from the ESV® Bible (*The Holy Bible, English Standard Version®*), copyright © 2001 by Crossway Bibles, a publishing ministry of Good News Publishers. Used by permission. All rights reserved.

Scripture references marked NIV are from *The Holy Bible: New International Version®*. Copyright © 1973, 1978, 1984 by International Bible Society. Used by permission of Zondervan Publishing House. All rights reserved.

    The "NIV" and "New International Version" trademarks are registered in the United States Patent and Trademark Office by International Bible Society. Use of either trademark requires the permission of International Bible Society.

All emphasis in Scripture quotations have been added by the author.

Trade paperback ISBN: 978-1-4335-0905-6
PDF ISBN: 978-1-4335-0906-3
Mobipocket ISBN: 978-1-4335-0907-0
ePub ISBN: 978-1-4335-2288-8

Library of Congress Cataloging-in-Publication Data
Leeman, Jonathan, 1973-
      The church and the surprising offense of God's love : reintroducing the doctrines
  of church membership and discipline / Jonathan Leeman.
          p. cm.—(IX marks)
      Includes bibliographical references and index.
        ISBN 978-1-4335-0905-6 (tpb)—ISBN 978-1-4335-0906-3—ISBN 978-1-4335-
  0907-0 1. Church discipline. 2. Church membership. I. Title.

    BV740.L39 2010
    262'.8—dc22

                      2009024556
Crossway is a publishing ministry of Good News Publishers

VP		21	20	19	18	17	16	15	14	13	12	11	10
14	13	12	11	10	9	8	7	6	5	4	3	2	

To Mark,
who taught me much of what's here,

and Matt,
who gave me a chance to say it.

CONTENTS

FOREWORD

In a fallen world like ours, Christian love never comes unbidden. It never comes through mere sentiment. As surprising as it may be for us, Christian love involves faith, faith that is impossible for us apart from the miraculous work of the Holy Spirit.

The apostle Paul wrote, "I consider everything a loss compared to the surpassing greatness of knowing Christ Jesus my Lord, for whose sake I have lost all things. I consider them rubbish, that I may gain Christ" (Phil. 3:8 NIV).

Counting everything as loss or rubbish involves effort and self-denial. Surely such considering or counting is the opposite of love.

Love is, for us, pleasure. We associate love with happiness, family, friends, and home. Love is, we think, by its very nature familiar. It is self-evident and immediate. Love by its nature shows itself. In that sense we think that love is simple.

All these notions of love Jonathan Leeman is about to challenge and, my guess is, challenge successfully, if you read through the whole book.

And then there is the notion of offense. We have a mixed relationship with the idea of offense today. We can take offense; we're okay with that. But many people distinctly do not like the idea of God's being offended, and certainly not by us. And we certainly don't associate offense with love.

At this point, Jonathan is leading us into another land—an older land— with commitments and relationships and more defined issues of right and wrong than we today are accustomed to. These once were familiar ideas. I don't know how you deal with new cultures, but there is a cusp of discomfort that many people have to get over when they first move to a new culture. My guess is that some of you will have a similar sensation reading about love and how it can really and truly be offensive, and even how sometimes it needs to be. But the land Jonathan is leading us into is beautiful and fruitful and faithful and biblical, and it reflects God's character.

As we come to understand more of God and his character, we come to see that God's love involves us in self-denial. And sharing God's love with others involves us in discipline, even church discipline. How can we love people and not treat them as Paul treated the self-deceived adulterous man in 1 Corinthians 5? How can we love people who sin against us and not treat them as Jesus instructed in Matthew 18? I'm not saying that this is all easy or uncomplicated (which is why you are holding not just this foreword but an entire book)! But coming to understand what church discipline has to do with love can rock your world. It can even save your soul.

Now, if Jonathan shows us all this, we might not be too surprised to find that as we turn around, we've entered deeply into the Bible's teaching on church membership. "The Bible's teaching on church membership?" you ask. "Where?" And when you're asking that question, I think you're ready to begin reading this book.

Before you is a feast carefully prepared. I've known Jonathan for over a decade. He has encouraged, exasperated, amused, and amazed me. It is one of my joys in life to get to co-labor with him in writing helpful materials for pastors. Jonathan has a restless, inquisitive mind given to him by God, in part to write this book, and so to be able to show us around a world he's been fascinated by and has considered as deeply as anyone I know.

This book is the best thing I have ever read on church membership. I can give you no higher commendation. Read and profit. And thank God for the gift of Jonathan. And for the gift of God's love, which bore his own offense—to our everlasting surprise and delight.

—Mark Dever, Washington DC, July 31, 2009

ACKNOWLEDGMENTS

My wonderful wife, Shannon, supported me in humble, Christlike fashion as I spent many months and long hours either writing this book or walking around the house with my mind stuck in it. She therefore deserves first mention. Thank you, my love, for all your work, prayer, and affection. I'm so grateful for you.

Matt McCullough and Bobby Jamieson read an early draft of the book in its entirety, and Robert Cline and Tom Schreiner both read a couple of chapters. All of you improved it. Thank you, brothers. Thanks also to Josh Coover, my colleague who was encouraging and interested throughout the project and was also patient with me as I repeatedly dropped the ball in other matters at work!

I'm grateful for Al Fisher and Crossway and their willingness to take a chance on first-time authors like me. Thanks also to Lydia Brownback who has been an affirming editor, patient and helpful.

The reader must know that Mark Dever provided the original idea for this book, namely, centering the topic of church membership and discipline on the idea of love. He did the same in a chapter he wrote on church membership.[1] I have simply lifted the theme from him. Thank you for this and so much more, brother.

Tremendous thanks also to Matt Schmucker for his time and patience as I worked through this project. Matt is a humble man who devotes his life to providing opportunities for others. I'm privileged to benefit regularly from his leadership, wisdom, and, best of all, friendship.

Finally, Capitol Hill Baptist Church deserves perhaps the most credit for shaping the heart and mind that would write about the particular matters presented here. My prayer is that this book will be useful for many. To whatever extent it is, the reader must understand that not a page here would have been written apart from this church's instruction and love.

---

[1]Mark Dever, "Regaining Meaningful Church Membership," in *Restoring Integrity in Baptist Churches,* ed. Thomas White, Jason G. Deusing, and Malcolm B. Yarnell III (Grand Rapids: Kregel, 2008), 45–62.

THE MEDIUM IS THE MESSAGE

The medium is the message. Have you heard that phrase? It was first spoken by the Canadian media scholar Marshall McLuhan in 1964, and it means simply that the medium in which a message is communicated affects the content of the message itself. For instance, reading about a foreign battle in the newspaper is different from watching it on television. The first is news; the second is both news and spectacle.

McLuhan's phrase is just another way of describing the symbiotic relationship between form and content. Ask any poet, artist, or architect and they will assure you that the form of something affects its content, and the content affects its form. A room with high, vaulted ceilings, massive pillars, and natural light pouring through stained-glass windows communicates one kind of message, while a room with white plaster walls, a drop-ceiling, florescent lights, and rows of gray cubicles communicates another kind. Sure, these forms and their messages are culturally conditioned, but my point is simply that there is a connection between form and content—in every culture.

An analogous relationship exists within the life of any organization when we compare the purpose for which an organization exists, what we might call the organization's message, and the structure of that organization, or its medium. How does an automobile manufacturer best structure itself to sell cars? How does an army best structure itself to defend a nation? How does a political advocacy group best structure itself to advocate its message? An organization's purpose or message will affect its structure, and its structure will in turn shape its message or purpose.

Suppose then that three Christians sitting down for coffee decide to start an organization for which the purpose is to define God's love for the whole world. That is the organization's message or content. They want it to say to everyone everywhere, "Here is God's love, and this is what it's like." Of course, this message of God's love is nothing other than the gospel of Jesus Christ: "In this is love, not that we have loved God but that he loved us and sent his Son to be the propitiation for our sins" (1 John 4:10).

Now, the three Christians agree that their organization exists for this purpose. And all agree, in principle, that the structure of their organization not only will affect how well they can accomplish this purpose but also has the potential to shape the message itself. For instance, an authoritarian organization that says "God is love" will effectively communicate a different message to the world than an egalitarian organization that says "God is love."

The problem is that the three Christians disagree on how to approach this question of structure. One of them observes that the people in different countries and cultures may require different kinds of structures, so he uses the word "contextualize" a lot and concludes that the organization's structure needs to be flexible and adaptable. The second Christian thinks the conversation about structure is interesting, but she concludes that it's finally not *that* important; what's important is getting the message out. The third Christian, however, thinks that it's extremely important. He insists that the other two effectively dismiss the point with their solutions, even though the other two pay lip service to the fact that a connection exists between form and content. Not only that, but he proposes that God has mandated one structure in the Bible rather than another, that this structure perfectly matches the message itself, almost as if it were an organic outgrowth of the message, like DNA producing a body's skeleton, and that it's precisely this structure that God means to use to accomplish the organization's purpose—to define his love for the world. It is his means for protecting the message, to hold it up on display, to make it attractive, and to put it into action.

Essentially, this book presents the argument of that third Christian. The structure of the church's corporate life together is tightly tied to the content of the gospel, and the content of the gospel is tightly tied to the structure of the church's corporate life together. They shape and implicate one another. This book doesn't try to cover every aspect of church structure. Its focus is principally on the matters of local church membership and discipline.

In language that's popular among evangelicals these days, one could say that the practices of local church membership and discipline are an implication of the gospel. It's not enough to say simply that "the church" is an implication of the gospel. It's the church *in a particular, marked-off form* that's an implication of the message. Membership and discipline are not artificially erected structures. They are not legalistic impositions upon new-covenant grace. They are an organic and inevitable outgrowth of Christ's redemptive work and the gospel call to repentance and faith. Missing local church membership is like missing the fact that Christians are called to pursue good works, or love their neighbors, or care for the poor, or pray to God, or follow in the way of Christ. Submitting oneself to a local church is what a true believer does, just like a true believer pursues good works, loves his or her neighbor, and so forth. Someone who refuses to join—or better, to submit to—a local church is like someone who refuses to pursue a life of righteousness. It calls into question the authenticity of his or her faith.

Insofar as the gospel presents the world with the most vivid picture of God's love, and insofar as church membership and discipline are an implication of the gospel, local church membership and discipline in fact define God's love for the world. That, in one sentence, is the argument of this book. Along the way we will observe that the very things that offend us about church membership root in the things we find offensive about God's love itself.

What's striking, therefore, is how most evangelicals have pushed the question of church structure into the category of nonessential and therefore of non-importance. The gospel is important, even essential, we say. Church structure is neither. And since questions of church structure only divide Christians, like it divided those three individuals sitting down for coffee, it's best to leave it out of the conversation altogether. Right?

What if that's wrong? What if God, in his wisdom, actually revealed both content and form, both a message and a medium, both a gospel and a polity, perfectly suited to one another? Couldn't pushing questions of church structure into the category of "what respectable evangelicals shouldn't hold strong opinions about" eventually undermine the gospel itself?

From God to the Gospel to the Church

What we need, I believe, is a truly systematic theology of church membership and discipline. We need to consider how the practices of local church membership and discipline fit into the larger matters of God's love, God's judgment, God's authority, and the gospel. When thinking or writing about the church, it's easy to err in one direction by sidelining questions of polity. It's also easy to err in the other direction by quickly jumping to our favorite proof-texts about elders and deacons, the Lord's Supper, or church discipline, but doing so in a way that doesn't carefully consider the larger theological context.

A proper doctrine of the church should be informed by everything else we know about God, his love, and his plan of salvation.[1] It should reflect everything we know about God's love and holiness; about humanity as created in God's image but fallen into guilt and corruption; about Christ's sinless life, sacrificial death, victorious resurrection, and the imputation of his own righteousness to sinners; and about life beneath his inaugurated rule through repentance and faith.

---

[1] Kevin Vanhoozer puts it more eloquently: "The evangelical church is a living *summa* of evangelical theology." "Evangelicalism and the Church: The Company of the Gospel," in *The Futures of Evangelicalism: Issues and Prospects*, ed. Craig Bartholomew, Robin Parry, and Andrew West (Grand Rapids: Kregel, 2003), 52.

Though I believe it's theologically problematic to refer to the church as a "continuation of Christ's incarnation,"[2] as some theologians have,[3] I am sympathetic with the impulse to use incarnational language to describe the church: the church is precisely where every doctrine is enfleshed or embodied. The church is where all these doctrines are put into action.

Theologian John Webster captures the spirit of what I'm getting at when he says, "A doctrine of the church is only as good as the doctrine of God which underlies it."[4] You will only understand what or who the church is if you first understand who God is. The same relationship abides between our doctrine of the gospel and our doctrine of the church. Webster also writes, "It is . . . an especial concern for evangelical ecclesiology to demonstrate not only that the church is a necessary implicate of the gospel but also that gospel and church exist in a strict and irreversible order, one in which the gospel precedes and the church follows."[5] In other words, you will only understand what or who the church is if you first understand what God's gospel is.

In a sense, this entire book is an exercise in working out these two comments by Webster. Specifically, it will contend that our understanding of God and the gospel will affect how we view the structural or institutional matters of membership and discipline; and how churches treat these structural matters will, in turn, affect how the world views God's love and God's gospel.

For example, suppose we conceived of God as holy but not very loving. That would have some pretty clear implications for our doctrine of salvation and how human beings should approach God or how he approaches them. Assuming that he called them to some type of corporate life together, there would be further implications for how these humans organized that life. Frankly, my guess is that with this "holy but not loving" God, the structures and rules and lines of authority would become *all* important. It would be a very severe, harsh, legalistic, and Pharisaical religion. A scary picture. Most likely, the world would reject this God and choose to define love on its own.

---

[2]To begin with, it blurs creator/creature distinctions, clouds the uniqueness of the incarnation event, over-identifies Christ and his church, ignores essential differences between sinless Christ and still sinful church, makes too much of this world, and downplays the significance of the Parousia and the church's hope in it. See Michael S. Horton, *People and Place* (Louisville: Westminster John Knox, 2008), 166–70; also, Ronald Y. K. Fung, "Body of Christ," in *Dictionary of Paul and His Letters*, ed. Gerald F. Hawthorne and Ralph P. Martin (Downers Grove, IL: InterVarsity, 1993), 81.

[3]The idea became prominent in both Protestant and Catholic followers of German idealism, beginning with Friedrich Schleiermacher (see Douglas Farrow, *Ascension and Ecclesia* [Edinburgh: T&T Clark, Continuum, 1999], 182–83); J. A. Möhler (see Michael J. Himes, *Ongoing Incarnation: Johann Adam Möhler and the Beginnings of Modern Ecclesiology* [Herder and Herder, 1997]); and Möhler's student Karl Adam. Michael Horton also follows the trail all the way up to the present with writers such as Pope Benedict XVI, Lutheran theologian Robert Jenson, Baptist theologian Stanley Grenz, and the circle of writers known as Radical Orthodoxy such as Graham Ward (http://sites.silaspartners.com/partner/Article_Display_Page/0,,PTID314526|CHID598014|CIID2376346,00.html, accessed January 18, 2008). See also chap. 6 of Horton, *People and Place*, esp. 156–64.

[4]John Webster, "The Church and the Perfection of God," in *The Community of the Word: Toward an Evangelical Ecclesiology*, ed. Mark Husbands and Daniel J. Treier (Downers Grove, IL: InterVarsity, 2005), 78.

[5]Ibid., 76. Cf. Vanhoozer, "Evangelicalism and the Church," 70–77.

Suppose alternatively that God wasn't very holy but that he was very loving. If I had to guess, I expect that a holy-less but loving God would be fairly permissive, whimsical, mercurial, and even dangerous. Salvation would be indiscriminate and not entirely just. And the corporate life of his people would be indistinct from the world. This religion would be increasingly licentious, shallow, meaningless, directionless, and grossly narcissistic. Again, a scary picture. One portion of the world would be only too happy to accept this all-too-human God because he would look just like them. Others, because he looked just like them, would think, "Why bother?"

But what about a God who is both holy and loving? How would such a God relate to humanity? What kind of gospel would his prophets proclaim? What kind of church would his apostles build? Would they draw boundaries and establish lines of authority?

I suspect that most pastors, church leaders, and Christians generally would quickly affirm, "Of course we believe in a God who is both holy and loving." But what if one's understanding of God's love is wrong? What if, in fact, one's understanding of love is downright idolatrous and unholy? How would an idolatrous conception of love affect one's understanding of God, the gospel, and therefore the church?

What's Love Got to Do with It?

In the first instance, therefore, this is a book about church membership and discipline. It's a theology of membership and discipline, and it's an argument for how vital the practices of membership and discipline are to biblical Christianity, to the life of the church, to the church's work of disciple-making, and to the display of God's glory in the world.

But this book is about something more than just membership and discipline. It's also about love. The world thinks it understands love, just like it thinks it loves God. Yet it doesn't. It only understands idolatrous phantoms or fabrications of them, shadows that bear some of the shape but little of the substance. The local church, therefore, is called to be a three-dimensional display of true love. And the practices of church membership and discipline are precisely what help to make the local church visible and clear. They demonstrate love's demands. They help us to know, in the apostle John's phrase, who are the children of God and who are the children of the Devil (see 1 John 3:10). Church membership and discipline give structure or shape to what it means to be a Christian—a person who displays God's love. They help to mark the church off from the world, so that the world can then look and see something *in* but not *of* itself. Can marking off something possibly be a loving thing to do, particularly to the outsiders? I will argue that it can, especially if one of the goals is to give the outsider a hope of its own inclusion into something divinely loving and divinely beautiful.

When the boundary line between church and world gets blurred, God's picture of the loving, forgiving, caring, holy, righteous community becomes less clear. But this blurred line is itself a consequence of another blurred line—the line between holy creator and fallen creature, between loving God and idolatrous man. It's telling that many of the writers today who call for a less "institutionalized" and "boundaried" conception of the local church are the same writers who prefer the immanent God to the transcendent God, the human Jesus to the divine Jesus, and a human Bible instead of a divine one. We reach out with washrags to erase the line between church and world once we are convinced not that we image God but that God images us and have confused our idolatry for his love. Said otherwise, a deficient view of love and the church root finally in a deficient view of God and God's love.

Let me sum up the matter like this: the argument for church membership and discipline is an argument for a clear line between church and world, as clear as the line between the inside of Eden and the outside of Eden, the inside of the ark and the outside of the ark, the inside of the Israelite camp and the outside of the camp, the inside of Jerusalem's walls and the outside of its walls. Yet what stands in the way of our ability—as Christians and churches in the postmodern West—to embrace the biblical call for such a line are our distorted and holy-less, truth-less, wisdom-less conceptions of God and his love. Recovering a biblical understanding of the church and its boundaries, therefore, requires us to reconsider what love is and how it's the very boundaries of the church that help to define love for the world.

A "Love" Story

There are a number of sociological and theological reasons why the first two Christians in my imaginary conversation above responded to the question of organizational structure as they did, one saying that structure needs to be flexible and one saying that it doesn't matter. And since those two responses are both common and deeply ingrained in the Western mindset, it's worth spending some time digging into the assumptions behind them.

I read one love story in high school that, I believe, captures the essence of why it's so difficult for Christians to see the relationship between love and church membership and discipline. In fact, American students have been reading this story for over a century, which indicates something of how well it reflects aspects of our cultural consciousness. This love story opens on a sunny summer's morning with five women standing on a grassy plot outside a town jail. The date is unspecified, but it's somewhere in the seventeenth century. The place is a small Puritan settlement in New England called Boston.

The action begins with a hard-featured woman of fifty offering four other women a piece of her mind:

> Goodwives, I'll tell you a piece of my mind. It would clearly be for the public's benefit, if we women, being of mature age and church-members in good repute, should be given responsibility for handling a malefactress[6] like this Hester Prynne. What think ye, gossips? If the hussy stood up for judgment before us five, would she have come off with such a sentence as the worshipful magistrates have awarded? I think not.[7]

The so-called hussy, Hester Prynne, has committed adultery, a crime proven by the infant daughter cradled in her arms inside the jailhouse. On this particular morning, the town's magistrates have decided that Hester will emerge from her cell, proceed to the town scaffold, and receive several hours of public scorn for her sin. Along the way, and for the remainder of her days, she will be required to don an embroidered scarlet "A"—for adulteress—on her chest.

The scandal has the whole church agog. The church's preacher is aghast. Says a second woman:

> People say that the Reverend Master Dimmesdale, her godly pastor, takes it very grievously to heart that such a scandal should have come on his congregation.

It's not just Hester's sin that scandalizes the good reverend and his town but the fact that her illicit lover, the child's father, remains unknown. A hypocrite is at large, a hard fact to stomach in a "land where iniquity is searched out and punished in the sight of rulers and people."[8] Hester's refusal to reveal the father's identity doubles her guilt, and the gaggle of gossips wants blood. A third matron speaks:

> The town magistrates are God-fearing gentlemen, but too merciful. At the very least, they should have put the brand of a hot iron on Hester Prynne's forehead. Madam Hester would have winced at that, I warrant. But she—the naughty baggage—little will she care what they put upon the bodice of her gown! Why, she may cover it with a brooch or some other heathenish adornment, and so walk the streets as boldly as ever.

Then a fourth matron:

> Ah, but let her cover the mark as she will, the pang of it will be always in her heart.

---

[6]A woman who violates the law.
[7]This quote and those that follow belonging to the same conversation are taken from the copy of Nathaniel Hawthorne, *The Scarlet Letter* that I read in high school (New York: Washington Square Press, 1972), 51–52. I have slightly modernized the language in several places.
[8]Ibid., 62.

Then the fifth:

This woman has brought shame upon us all, and ought to die. Is there no law for it? Truly, there is, both in the Scripture and in the statute-book. Then let the magistrates who have made it of no effect thank themselves if their own daughters and wives go astray.

I read Nathaniel Hawthorne's classic 1850 novel, *The Scarlet Letter*, in my junior-year English class. The entire class was scandalized—not at the tragic heroine Hester but at the townspeople. Did people like this really exist? We glared at them with all the disdain they poured onto Hester. How could they be so self-righteous, cruel, benighted?

Hawthorne's own sympathies in his story are hardly hidden. His descriptions of the five gossips make them look like gargoyles. This last woman he describes as "the ugliest as well as the most pitiless of these self-constituted judges." Compare this woman's portrait with Hawthorne's portrait of the woman she is attacking, Hester. The young Hester

was tall, with a figure of perfect elegance on a large scale. She had dark and abundant hair, so glossy that it threw off the sunshine with a gleam, and a face which, besides being beautiful from regularity of feature and richness of complexion, had the impressiveness belonging to a marked brow and deep black eyes. . . . And never had Hester Prynne appeared more lady-like . . . than as she issued from the prison. Those who had before known her, and had expected to behold her dimmed and obscured by a disastrous cloud, were astonished, and even started to perceive how her beauty shone out, and made a halo of the misfortune and ignominy in which she was enveloped.

The contrast is clear. The reader can sympathize either with ugly and pitiless old women or Hester's shining halo of beauty—not a tough choice for most people. Who wouldn't choose to sympathize with Hester? It seems that employing a beautiful woman to "make the sale" is hardly an innovation of our own marketing-hysterical age.

The reverend mentioned by the gossips, Arthur Dimmesdale, has a character of more complexity. It turns out that he's the secret scoundrel who has impregnated Hester and left her alone to absorb the town's attack. His cowardice is despicable, and his double-facedness deplorable. At the same time, his character is more pitiful than malignant. He and Hester speak several times through the course of the book and at one point plan to run away and begin a new life together. Yet Arthur remains intractably torn between his affections for her and society's hold upon him. Love pulls him in one direction; church law pulls him in the other. All but the most pitiless reader can't help but cheer for his liberation and their reconciliation. Ultimately, he is destroyed by the conflict between heart and mind, soul and society.

Hester's ignominy, ironically, frees her from church convention and social constraint. Never stingy with his symbolism, Hawthorne places her ramshackle shack outside of civilization, out in the wild woods where witches play and Indians have dominion, almost like the unclean Jew or Gentile dog forced outside the ancient Israelite camp. Yet it's out there, beyond the boundaries of respectability, that Hester is freed to love truly and divinely. She can forgive Arthur and her persecutors. She can dream of a different future with him. She can begin her career of caring for the community's poor. She can raise the sprightly daughter who will, in the novel's climactic moment, bend down to kiss her broken father's forehead in an incandescent moment of triumphant grace.

Love and Structure

Though a traditional Christian sitting in a straight-backed church pew, hands folded in lap, might have regarded the late eighteenth- and nineteenth-century Romantics like Hawthorne as working against religion, the Romantics perceived themselves as saving it. They wanted to set God's love and humanity's spiritual impulses free from the tight strictures of Christianized civilization, from the overly scripted formulations of doctrine, from the stranglehold of ecclesiastical structure.

If Hawthorne had lived today, he might have described himself with the well-known mantra "spiritual, not religious." His fictionalized Puritan church codified every conceivable moral transgression and then handed these codes to the magistrate to be enforced. The problem was not the moral or spiritual impulse, per se; it was placing these things inside of a religious structure. It was what we today might call "institutionalism"—treating the various rules and lines of authority within an organization as more important than the people themselves. When spirituality and morality become embedded in the impersonal and authoritative structures of an institution, compliance must be enforced by the institution's keepers. A stark line must be drawn between those on the *inside* and those on the *outside*. Any impulse to individuality or creativity must be suppressed for fear of transgressing code. The men and women who demonstrate a greater ability to abide by the institution's codes tend to calcify into self-righteous postures, while the men and women unable to keep to the straight and narrow receive a slap to the hand or, worse, exclusion from the group. In all of this, grace and mercy vanish, passion is bound, and love and beauty are obliterated.

It's worth noticing how Hawthorne manages to hit all of today's panic buttons: the church has subsumed the state; the private has become public;

religious hate-mongers scorn the young, beautiful, and free. Even the innocent daughter is indirectly made a victim.

So just what kind of love story is *The Scarlet Letter*? It is one that well illustrates the assumptions about love that many people were beginning to make in the nineteenth century when Hawthorne wrote his book, assumptions which I believe are pretty much unquestioned today. It's difficult to succinctly explain those assumptions about love. In fact, I'll use all of chapter 1 to attempt such an explanation. Let me try it briefly here. We assume not that God is love but that love is God. In other words, we don't go before the real creator of the universe and say to him, "Please tell us what *you* are like and therefore how *you* define love." Rather, we begin with our own self-defined concept of love and allow this self-defined concept to play god. When I say it "plays god," I mean that we let it define right and wrong, good and bad, glory-worthy and glory-less, even though such valuations belong to God alone. Love becomes the ultimate idol.

For example, was it "wrong" for Hester to commit adultery? Would it have been wrong for her and Arthur to run away and begin a new life together, despite the fact that she was married to someone else? Or would we say that those vicious townswomen were wasting Hester's life with their self-righteous judgmentalism? The implicit urging of Hawthorne's novel and of everything in our culture today is, "No, it's not wrong because they *love* each other. Or, even if it's kind of wrong, it's justified, because love covers over sin. Love justifies!"

Assumptions about Love

Can you see the assumptions being made about love that play themselves out in *The Scarlet Letter* and which, I would contest, are absolutely unquestioned today? Assumption one is that no boundaries can be placed on love. Rather, love establishes all the boundaries. There is no conception of truth or holiness or wisdom to condition or give a structure to such love. Love runs free, unbound by truth. In fact, it alone constitutes truth, and it's the source of ultimate justification. You can justify anything these days by saying that it's "loving" or "motivated by love."

Consider for a moment what people today mean by "love" when they talk about the love between two homosexual men. What do they mean by love when they use it to justify heterosexual sex before marriage, or outside of marriage, or divorce? What do they mean by love when they spoil their children? What do they mean by love when they move from one church to the next, or never sacrifice themselves for others in their church? It's true that love is the greatest good, and it's true that love justifies, but the question remains what—or who!—defines love.

Assumption two is that love is disassociated in our minds from institutional structures and institutional acts of judgment. At best, the idea of an institution is a cold, impersonal, and bureaucratic idea. Structures have inflexible scaffolding and hard edges. Love, we all know, is flexible, yielding, and personal. At worst, institutions are all about power, not love. And institutional acts of judgment—even if in the rarest of circumstances they are necessary—always indicate a failure of love or a failure to love. They are most certainly not acts of love. What is an institution or an institutionalized church but an impersonal and indiscriminate authority claiming to speak on behalf of God and telling us what is right and wrong when we might know in our gut that love is telling us something else? What are institutions and institutionalized churches other than attempts by a privileged few to grab power? The Romantics of the eighteenth and nineteenth centuries wanted to be guided by love rather than structure, by internal desire rather than external constraint, by spontaneous impulse rather than rationalistic deduction, by feeling rather than fact, by beauty and freedom rather than efficiency and order, by the sweaty wisdom of hardworking days rather than the bloodless ruminations of theology books.[9] Analogous impulses, I believe, characterize the postmodern West. In our minds, the word *love* and the word *institution* could not be further apart.

Assumption three is that *love* and *church* don't go together, particularly a church with sharp boundaries and authoritative pronouncements. Hester wasn't loved by the church. She was persecuted and excommunicated. Say the word *love* and most people's thoughts immediately jump into some other category: maybe the relationship between two lovers, or the relationship between parents and their children, or even the relationship between an individual and God. But how many people today associate love with the relationships that subsist inside the local church? Often, just the opposite is the case. Local churches are better known for bickering, backbiting, and bigotry.

Behind all this is one more assumption the Western mind makes about love: love and authority have nothing to do with one another. Authority restrains. Love frees. Authority exploits. Love empowers. Authority steals life. Love saves life. This disassociation between love and authority is nothing new. They have been divided ever since the Serpent suggested to Adam and Eve that God's love and God's authority were incommensurate. I would contest that the contrast between love and authority has come into even sharper relief with the Enlightenment and the counter-Enlightenment Romantics, who shared all the autonomous individualism of the rationalists and classicists they were reacting against. Love is what we need, they said. Not boundaries. Not structures or institutions. Not

---

[9]For a helpful introduction to the late eighteenth-, early nineteenth-century movement of Romanticism, see Jacques Barzun, *From Dawn to Decadence: 500 Years of Western Cultural Life* (New York: HarperCollins, 2000), 465–89.

authority. Maybe not even churches? These things are the "bad guys" that the Romantics such as Hawthorne and our culture today pit against this greatest good called "love."

Not many Christians today go so far as to say that Christians don't need churches, but for at least two centuries a number of writers have contended that churches need to be de-institutionalized. Liberal Protestants have been calling for "more community" and "less institutional authority" ever since Friedrich Schleiermacher borrowed language from the Romantics to pit religious experience against what he viewed as the Enlightenment's rationalistic formulations of doctrine.[10] About the same time, a Romantic renewal movement began in earnest among Roman Catholic writers as influenced by Schleiermacher and others, a revolution that would eventually culminate in a number of changes made in Vatican II.[11] The mainline Protestants and the Catholics worked within their respective traditions, to be sure, but their doctrines of salvation and the church began to approximate one another, largely because they "share in the same post-Enlightenment Romantic renewal."[12]

Conservative evangelicals have harbored anti-institutional, "essentialist" impulses at least since George Whitefield found the Baptists and Presbyterians in America more amenable to his revival work than his own Anglicans.[13] It crops up, rightly, whenever nominal Christianity and "cheap grace" become a concern within the church.[14]

What's more striking for our purposes is the spate of books released in the last few decades by evangelical and so-called post-evangelical writers within or sympathetic to the emerging church or the missional church that echo this same call for less institution and more community.[15] Not surprisingly, this

---

[10]See Roger Haight, *Christian Community in History, vol. 2: Comparative Ecclesiology* (New York: Continuum, 2005), 312–13.

[11]Among them, Johann Adam Möhler in particular helped inaugurate a "conceptual revolution" in the doctrine of the church among Catholics in the 1820s with his *Unity of the Church*; Haight, *Christian Community*, 355. See also Dennis Doyle's helpful overview, *Communion Ecclesiology* (Maryknoll, NY: Orbis, 2000); and Avery Cardinal Dulles's chapter "The Church as Mystical Communion," in *Models of the Church*, expanded ed. (New York: Image Books, 2002), 39–54. Following after the work of Johann Adam Möhler, key thinkers in the last century of Roman Catholic communion ecclesiology that are commonly cited include Charles Journet, Yves Congar, Henri de Lubac, and Jean-Marie Tillard (see Tillard's *Church of Churches*). Both John Paul II and Benedict XVI also made significant contributions.

[12]Haight, *Christian Community*, 356; Doyle, *Communion Ecclesiology*, 23–37.

[13]A helpful survey of George Whitefield's effect on the evangelical ecclesiological consciousness can be found in Bruce Hindmarsh, "Is Evangelical Ecclesiology an Oxymoron? A Historical Perspective," in *Evangelical Ecclesiology: Reality or Illusion?* ed. John G. Stackhouse (Grand Rapids: Baker, 2003), 15–37.

[14]It's not coincidence that the theologian well known for his criticism of cheap grace in *The Cost of Discipleship*, Dietrich Bonhoeffer, is the same man who would also write, "The whole interpretation of the organizational forms of the Protestant Church as being those of an institution must therefore be dismissed as erroneous"; in Dietrich Bonhoeffer, *Sanctorum Communio* (London: Collins, 1963), 178.

[15]Here is a far from exhaustive sampling of both academic and nonacademic works by evangelicals and post-evangelicals, chronologically listed, which, in varying degrees, call for a greater emphasis on community and less on institution relative to common Protestant practice in the last couple of centuries: Colin Gunton, "The Church on Earth: The Roots of Community," in *On Being the Church: Essays on the Christian Community*, ed. Colin E. Gunton and Daniel W. Hardy (Edinburgh: T&T Clark, 1989), 48–80; Greg Ogden, *Unfinished Business: Returning the Ministry to the People of God* (Grand Rapids: Zondervan, 1990), 62–108; David J.

same Romantic impulse surges through many of these books as well, as does one of their rallying cries: soften the boundary between the church's inside and outside. As one author puts it, "The boundary between those who belong to the church and those who do not should not be drawn too sharply."[16] After all, "the establishment of clear boundaries is usually an act of violence."[17]

IN SEARCH OF A BOTH/AND

Jesus knew that in a fallen world no authority, institutional or otherwise, could be entirely trusted. He knew that in the hands of sinful human beings it always has been and always will be a weapon for the worst acts of exploitation and destruction. Concerning Jesus, the apostle John wrote, "Many believed in his name when they saw the signs that he was doing. But Jesus on his part did not entrust himself to them, because he knew all people and needed no one to bear witness about man, for he himself knew what was in man" (John 2:23–25).

Those are arresting words. He didn't *entrust* himself to them, because he knew what was *in* them. He knew what kinds of appetites ruled even their best actions. In one sense, of course, Jesus did finally entrust himself to the authorities—to the point of death—but never did he entrust his conscience, will, loyalty, or mission to any human authority. Even at the age of twelve he managed to be submissive to his parents while reminding them that his ultimate submission belonged to his Father in heaven (Luke 2:49, 51). Given Jesus' track record with the Pharisees and his less-than-kind comments concerning their traditions, I think we can also safely say, despite the anachronism, that Jesus knew all too well the dangers of institutions and the human temptation to exploit institutional power for selfish gain.

Bosch, *Transforming Mission: Paradigm Shifts in Theology of Mission* (Marynoll, NY: Orbis, 1991), 50–51; Paul G. Hiebert, *Anthropological Reflections on Missiological Issues* (Grand Rapids: Baker Books, 1994), 107–36; 159–72; Kevin Giles, *What on Earth Is the Church: An Exploration in New Testament Theology* (Eugene, OR: Wipf and Stock, 2005; orig. SPCK, 1995), 8–22; *Missional Church: A Vision for the Sending of the Church in North America*, ed. Darrell L. Guder (Grand Rapids: Eerdmans, 1998), 80, 84, 93–94, 221ff; Darrell L. Guder, *The Continuing Conversion of the Church* (Grand Rapids: Eerdmans, 2000), 181–204; Craig Van Gelder, *The Essence of the Church: A Community Created by the Spirit* (Grand Rapids: Baker, 2000), 55–58, 74–75, 125, 157–58; Eddie Gibbs, *Church Next: Quantum Changes in How We Do Ministry* (Downers Grove, IL: InterVarsity, 2000), 65–91; Stanley Grenz, *The Social God and the Relational Self: A Trinitarian Theology of the Imago Dei* (Louisville: Westminster, 2001), 331–36; Doug Pagitt, *Church Re-Imagined: The Spiritual Formation of People in Communities of Faith* (Grand Rapids: Zondervan, 2003), 23–31, 47–48; Stuart Murray, *Church After Christendom* (Milton Keynes, UK: Paternoster, 2004), 135–64; Brian McLaren, *A Generous Orthodoxy* (Grand Rapids: Zondervan, 2004), 62; Reggie McNeal, *The Present Future: Six Tough Questions for the Church* (San Francisco: Jossey-Bass, 2003), 26–27, 34–36; Eddie Gibbs and Ryan K. Bolger, *Emerging Churches: Creating Community in Postmodern Cultures* (Grand Rapids: Baker, 2005), 89–115; Neil Cole, *Organic Church: Growing Faith Where Life Happens* (San Francisco: Jossey-Bass, 2005); *Trinity in Human Community: Exploring Congregational Life in the Image of the Social Trinity* (Milton Keynes, UK: Paternoster, 2006), 1–3; Ray Anderson, *An Emergent Theology for Emerging Churches* (Downers Grove, IL: InterVarsity, 2006), 92; Dan Kimball, *They Like Jesus but Not the Church: Insights from Emerging Generations* (Grand Rapids: Zondervan, 2007), 73–95.
[16] Miroslav Volf, *After Our Likeness* (Grand Rapids: Eerdmans, 1998), 148 n. 84.
[17] Ibid., 151 n. 97.

All this produces something of a dilemma. What if we want the gracious love that Hawthorne embodies in Hester without condoning adultery? What if we want to describe some things as "wrong" and yet remain loving people? What if we want both heart and head, both love and truth, particularly given the fallen state of this world, which often pits these two impulses or two kinds of people against one another, as Hawthorne does? Are we to assume that God calls us to submit to authority only when submission accords with our personal opinions or rational calculations? If so, then what does *submission* really mean? The dilemma is captured in one Anglican writer's statement: "The popular cry is for unequivocal pronouncements from Canterbury—provided they are the ones with which the speaker happens to agree!"[18]

Surely church history is replete with churches falling into this thing called "institutionalism," which can be antithetical to Christianity itself, whether we have in mind the centralization of all authority in the bishop, the commingling of church and state following Constantine, or an over-proliferation of committees in the local Baptist church. The Gospels themselves place no small emphasis on Jesus' opposition to the life-stealing structures the Pharisees established for maintaining Israel's spiritual life. One of the church's perennial temptations has been to allow the institutional elements of its corporate life to be treated as primary;[19] to allow its rules and hierarchies to become more important than the people and their relationships; to let the traditions of men trump the commands of God.[20] Perhaps the wrong rules are enforced. Perhaps the right rules are given a wrong emphasis. Perhaps the institution's keepers simply enjoy having power. These types of things surely can and do happen—often.[21] In fact, so inclined are humans to the abuse of authority and so quick are even Christians to wrongly ground their traditions into the poured-in-concrete foundations of their institutions that it actually feels dangerous to take our eyes for one moment off that impending threat, almost like a jet fighter pilot deciding to turn his radar off even though he hears the beep of his enemy's missile zeroing in on his craft.

Along these lines, I broadly sympathize with significant aspects of recent critiques of "institutionalism" in Western churches, particularly in the missional church literature. Sinful humans in this world—even sinful Christian humans in

---

[18]Paul Avis, *Authority, Leadership, and Conflict in the Church* (Philadelphia: Trinity Press International, 1992), *ix.*

[19]Dulles, *Models of the Church*, 27.

[20]Peter L. Berger and Thomas Luckmann provide a helpful introduction to the idea of institutionalization and its origins in *The Social Construction of Reality: A Treatise in the Sociology of Knowledge* (New York: Anchor Books, 1966), 47–79. "Institutionalization occurs," they say, "whenever there is a reciprocal typification of habitualized actions by types of actors. Put differently, any such typification is an institution," 54. An easier way to say "typification of habitualized actions," I think, is to say "tradition," an idea that is not intrinsically problematic but becomes problematic when, as Jesus said to the Pharisees, "You have let go of the commands of God and are holding on to the traditions of men" (Mark 7:8 NIV). One way we might define "institutionalism" would be to say that our institutions become "institutionalized" whenever our traditions trump the commands of God.

[21]Paul G. Hiebert presents a helpful analysis of the characteristics of a church succumbing to institutionalization as well as some of the dangers of doing so, in *Anthropological Reflections*, 159–64.

churches!—will always want to ensconce their traditions into authoritative structures, and they will do so in ways that ultimately impede loving community.

That said, the threat of institutionalism and the abuse of authority are not what this book is responding to.[22] In fact, it's responding to the opposite error, the error which I think besets more Christians and churches today in light of the anti-institutional, anti-borders, anti-morality, anti-authority worldview and impulses of Western culture. It's responding to the threat of anti-authority boundary-lessness and the threat of un-submissiveness. Properly doing so in a fallen context, of course, requires us to do so without turning our radar screens off. We need to consider what it means to submit to the authority of a local church and its leaders in the very face of the threat of authority being wrongly used.

Implicitly, this book will argue that the dichotomy between love and structure, between authentic community and the structured institution, is a false dichotomy. At the risk of oversimplifying, the Romanticist needs the Classicist; the heart needs the head; creativity needs order; love needs truth and authority. With many such dichotomies we need to take care not to be forced into an *either/or*, but to search for the elusive *both/and*. Emphasizing one against the other yields something less than human because, as we will see later, an overemphasis in either direction yields an image of something less than divine. The mere presence of institutional elements (rules, resources, hierarchies) within a church does not necessarily imply institutionalism, any more than law implies legalism or dogma implies dogmatism.[23]

Church Membership and Discipline

Explicitly, this book will examine the boundary lines of local church membership and discipline—the very things that, in Hawthorne's fictional world, pinned the scarlet "A" to Hester Prynne's bodice and cast her out of the village into the unprotected wilds. Local church membership and discipline, as much as anything, represent the institutional side of religion and church life. Church membership is a line in the dirt, a boundary marker, a wall around the city. It's a list of names. It's an institutional way of saying, "The people on this list are on the *inside*. Everyone else is on the *outside*." Church membership—no doubt about it—is exclusivistic.

---

[22]Miroslav Volf's book *After Our Virtue: The Church as the Image of the Trinity* promotes a relational conception of the local church, but he does so without jettisoning the institutional elements of the church: "According to a view widespread in Protestant circles, the Spirit of God and church institutions stand in contradiction. 'Where the Spirit of the Lord is, there is freedom' (2 Cor. 3:17); by contrast, institutions are perceived as mechanisms of repression. If this view was correct, then resolute 'pneumatic anarchy' would be the only appropriate 'structure' for a charismatic church. This view, however, is prejudiced, and anyone sharing it fails to recognize both the character of ecclesial institutions and the way the Spirit of God acts"; in *After Our Virtue* (Grand Rapids: Eerdmans, 1998), 234.

[23]Dulles, *Models of the Church*, 27; cf. Giles, *What on Earth Is the Church*, 21–22.

Church discipline, then, is the mechanism used to enforce this exclusivistic practice, the pen that writes some names on the list and scratches other names off. It's the bailiff that evicts the imposters. Church membership and discipline are the two sides of the same coin.

Not only will this book examine the practices of church membership and discipline, but also it will argue that God means to use these very structures to help define his love for the onlooking world. That means, just to be clear, it will advocate *in favor* of these exclusivistic practices.

BINDING AND LOOSING

Why would anyone want to do that? Most importantly, because Jesus gave the church this kind of institutional authority. The Gospel writers recorded Jesus' using the word that we translate into English as "church" only twice. It's perhaps ironic then—in light of our own cultural revulsion to anything smacking of institutionalism—that in both those places he grants this gathering of people the authority to "bind and loose."

> I tell you, you are Peter, and on this rock I will build my church, and the gates of hell shall not prevail against it. I will give you the keys of the kingdom of heaven, and whatever you bind on earth shall be bound in heaven, and whatever you loose on earth shall be loosed in heaven. (Matt. 16:18–19)

> Truly, I say to you, whatever you bind on earth shall be bound in heaven, and whatever you loose on earth shall be loosed in heaven. Again I say to you, if two of you agree on earth about anything they ask, it will be done for them by my Father in heaven. For where two or three are gathered in my name, there am I among them. (Matt. 18:18–20)

These passages have been debated by churchmen at least since Matthew wrote them down, and understanding everything about them is not easy. We'll return to an extended discussion of them in chapter 4. For now, it's worth pointing out a couple of matters that, I believe, are fairly straightforward. In this first passage, Jesus describes this power with the metaphor of a key, which is why pastors and theologians throughout church history have referred to the "power of the keys." The metaphor is a simple one. What do keys do? Keys lock doors and unlock doors. Keys allow some people to come inside while keeping other people outside, which is exactly what Jesus intended for this assembly of people gathered in his name to do—regulate who was coming in and who was going out.

Where does Jesus say this key should be used? Where will this binding and loosing take place? Again, his answer is simple and helpful: on earth. Jesus calls this assembly of people gathered in his name to bind and loose people *on earth.* A little less clear is what exactly this binding and loosing on earth signifies in heaven. Roman Catholics say one thing, Protestants another, but just to be clear: this binding and loosing takes place among real flesh and blood people on earth—not among abstract or idealized realities. It necessarily takes place locally because human beings exist locally. Real *gatherings* comprised of real people are granted by Jesus both the power and the obligation to decide whether Euodia or Cyrus or Catherine or Friedrich or McKenzie or Farhod or Jeng is really "one of them"—a Christian, a Christ follower, a disciple. If this real, not-abstract gathering determines that the individual's profession of faith is credible, they will unite the individual to themselves. If not, they won't. How do they exercise their authority to unite? They unite with the two external, visible, institutional mechanisms given to them by Jesus: initiation through baptism and ongoing participation through the new-covenant meal. How do they unbind or loose? They deny the individual the opportunity to participate in this ongoing meal.

It's within this power of binding and loosing for oversight and discipline among real gatherings of Christians on earth that we find the doctrines of church membership and discipline.

The Relevance of This Topic

The topic of church membership and discipline is particularly relevant in our Western postmodern context for at least four reasons.

AN ECCLESIOLOGICAL MESS

First, the pragmatism that has reigned in American churches at least since the twentieth century, especially since the advent of (Donald McGavran-like) church-growth thinking in the middle of the last century, has left our understanding of the church itself fairly doctrine-less, principle-less, structure-less. It's almost as if the wind currents of pragmatism and the barometric pressure of postmodernism came together with the temperature drop of evangelical "essentialism" (the evangelical knack for discarding any doctrine not regarded as essential for salvation) in order to produce the "perfect storm," a storm that left a decimated ability to think seriously and freshly about the local church in its trail.

On the evangelical right are careful thinkers who are absolutely scrupulous in other areas of doctrine but tend to flow with the pragmatic stream in how they lead and structure their churches. When conservatives do write about the church, they usually rehash what the Fathers said about the church being one, holy, universal, and apostolic or what the Reformers described as the two marks of the church. This latter emphasis usually translates into a commitment to preaching and taking the ordinances seriously, which is surely essential, but does not always offer immediately evident guidance in questions facing the contemporary church like the place of programs, small group ministries, multiple services, multiple campuses, pastoring by video feed, relativism, the role of contextualization, the challenges of globalization, a cultural reluctance to commit or join, consumerism, cynicism, contemporary conceptions of tolerance, and much more.

Meanwhile, on the evangelical left interesting new conversations are occurring in how the church relates to the Trinity or how the church's essence is bound up in mission. Yet many of these same writers are building their doctrines of the church upon doctrines of the triune God and the gospel that would prove unsatisfactory to conservatives. The result is something of a mess, with evangelicals across the spectrum building their churches based upon a random mix of tradition, pragmatism, and new ideas that have helpful bits but are premised on inadequate conceptions of God and the gospel.

AN OPPOSITION TO MEMBERSHIP

Second, the topic of church membership and discipline is particularly relevant right now because a growing number of books written for pastors and church leaders in the last several decades explicitly oppose the practice of church membership. Some argue that local church membership is irrelevant, unnecessary, or dated and therefore *can* be dispensed with. Others argue that the exclusivistic boundary line of church membership presents a distorted picture of the gospel and therefore *should* be dispensed with. Among these voices, the words repeated over and over are "less institutionalism" and "more authentic community" or "less structure and more love." As mentioned a few moments ago, certain Roman Catholics and liberal Protestant authors have been saying this since the middle of the nineteenth century and increasingly in the decades before and after Vatican II, but a number of evangelicals and so-called post-evangelicals have been saying this in the last decade or two. It's almost become a mantra: institutionalism, bad; loving community, good.[24]

THE DIMINISHED SIGNIFICANCE OF THE LOCAL CHURCH

These authors and leaders are not thinking in a vacuum, but in the context of deeper culture impulses. This brings us to a third reason for the relevance of the topic of church structure, namely, Western Christians have a weak and anemic conception of the local church and its role in their Christian faith. Evangelical pollster George Barna has testified to that fact:

> While nearly half of the adult population attends religious services during a typical week . . . fewer than one out of every five adults firmly believes that a congregational

---

[24]See n. 15.

church is a critical element in their spiritual growth and just as few strongly contend that participation in some type of community of faith is required for them to achieve their full potential.

Only 17% of adults said that "a person's faith is meant to be developed mainly by involvement in a local church." Even the most devoted church-going groups—such as evangelicals and born again Christians—generally dismissed that notion: only one-third of all evangelicals and one out of five non-evangelical born again adults endorsed the concept. Only one out of every four adults who possesses a biblical worldview (25%) agreed with the centrality of a local church in a person's spiritual growth.

Just as few adults (18%) firmly embraced the idea that spiritual maturity requires involvement in a community of faith.[25]

In my experience as well, asking the average Christian how important committed church membership is to his or her Christianity will yield an answer somewhere in between "Not at all" and "Sort of." Many Christians are happy to attend a particular church indefinitely without formally joining. Others are happy to visit different churches from one month to the next and continue in this pattern for a year or more. Still others don't attend church at all and try to sustain their spiritual lives through a self-directed use of Christian books, fellowship groups, radio stations, or other forms of Christian media. Should you attempt to explain the importance, even necessity, of joining a church to someone with such a mindset, you will probably meet with, at best, a shrug of the shoulders or more likely the charge "That's legalism" or "That's dogmatic" or "That's not loving." Mention the words *church discipline* and you can be pretty confident that these charges will follow.

"AS I HAVE LOVED YOU"

As Christians lose sight of God's call to live out their Christian lives corporately, tragically they lose the ability to define love for the world—a fourth reason why this topic is so relevant. The doctrine of the church, as I said at the beginning, brings the whole of Christian doctrine to bear on how a concrete group of people actually gather and organize their lives.

What evangelicalism needs today is not just a renewed and re-articulated center; it needs boundaries. By that I don't just mean doctrinal boundaries or the "affirmations and denials" signed by the leaders of evangelicalism's various denominations and movements. I mean the boundaries that belong around local

---

[25]From the "Barna Update" entitled, "Americans Have Commitment Issues, New Survey Shows" by The Barna Group, April 18, 2006. The data is based on 1,003 telephone interviews with adults from across the nation. http://www.barna.org/FlexPage.aspx?Page=BarnaUpdate&BarnaUpdateID=235; accessed January 23, 2008.

churches. This is the tool that Christ has given the church on earth to enforce such statements of faith and vibrant doctrinal centers!

This is precisely why the doctrine of the church is most suited to defining love in a way that even the doctrine of salvation or the doctrine of God's love cannot: it prepares God's new-covenant people for displaying God's character, wisdom, and glory to all the universe (Eph. 3:10). This is exactly why Jesus said to his disciples, "A new command I give you: Love one another. As I have loved you, so you must love one another. By this all men will know that you are my disciples, if you love one another" (John 13:34–35 NIV). The world will understand who Christ is and what love is *when* the church defines it for them by loving one another in the gospel—"as I have loved you." But there's the catch—the word "as" in "as I have loved you." Christians are to love one another *as* Christ has loved us. What if, as I said, we have idolatrous conceptions of love—even idolatrous conceptions of Christ's love?

The argument of this book, quite simply, is that God calls the church to draw boundaries, boundaries which mark off these people from those people, boundaries which prevent some individuals from joining while excluding other individuals after they have joined. Not only that, God intends that the church use these boundary markers in order to help define for the world what exactly love is.

The church defines love. It often defines love poorly, mind you, but that's what God calls the church to do—to define love for the world in the very process of including some sinners and excluding others.

Hopefully Relevant for All Polities

My goal in this book is not to make an explicit argument for the form of polity that I personally believe is best—baptistic and congregational. My primary goal, rather, is to argue for two particular aspects of church polity—membership and discipline—that I believe should be applied in every denominational context, even if I would simultaneously maintain that different forms of church government will do better or worse jobs of maintaining these two aspects properly. In other words, I hope to see Baptist, Anglican/Episcopal, Lutheran, Methodist, Pentecostal, Presbyterian, Mennonite, independent but elder-ruled, and all other gospel-preaching congregations practice meaningful church membership and discipline through the mechanisms of their particular polities, even if some of these polities are better suited to doing so than the others.

Therefore, I will attempt to leave some ambiguity in how I define the church "on earth," not because I don't think this is important but because this is not the battle I'm trying to wage here. For example, I would disagree with a Presbyterian who says that the visible church consists "of all those who make profession of their faith in the Lord Jesus Christ, together with their children,"[26] or the Episcopalian who refers to an entity called the Episcopal Church in America.[27] Nonetheless, I believe that a church and its children that take biblical care in binding and loosing Christians on earth is better than one that does not. Yes, I think that including potentially unregenerate children in the church will introduce problems of its own, particularly in the next generation, but my goal here is to consider matters that I hope will benefit both Baptist and Presbyterian churches. Deeper into the book, particularly when I begin to discuss more practical matters, the reader may find more aspects of my congregationalism emerging. And in one or two places I'll even present an argument for why a congregational approach to church polity, along with being biblical, best solves some problems, such as the threat of abuses of authority. I simply ask for the non-congregationalist's patience when I do.

As for disagreements that I as a Baptist might share with non-Baptists over the meaning of baptism or the Lord's Supper, which are two matters that are important to the topics of membership and discipline, the good news for the non-Baptist reader is that most other conservative and moderate Protestant denominations can affirm just about everything a Baptist says on these two topics. On the whole, their disagreements won't typically involve *taking away* from what a Baptist believes; it will involve whether *more should be added* to what a Baptist believes. For that reason, I hope that Presbyterians, Anglicans, Methodists, and others will find themselves able to affirm much of what I will say in relation to the meaning of baptism and the Lord's Supper.

LITERATURE

Also, the reader will notice that I use references to generally well-known works of literature throughout the book, as I have done with *The Scarlet Letter*. I have done this for two reasons. First, it's been fun for me in the writing process. Second, and more importantly, I believe that good literature, with its images and pathos, can better capture a *zeitgeist*—the spirit of the times—than polls can, which is what most books these days seem to employ to characterize the cultural landscape. A good theology must constantly be mindful of how embedded we all are in our own times, and hopefully these literary references will help us become more aware of our presuppositions.

---

[26] "The Book of Church Order of the Presbyterian Church in America," 6th ed.; Office of the Stated Clerk of the General Assembly of the Presbyterian Church in America, as approved by the 35th General Assembly, in Memphis, TN, June 2007: 2–1, 4–1.

[27] E.g., Thomas Witherow, *The Apostolic Church* (1858; repr. Glasgow, Scotland: Free Presbyterian Publications, 2001), 15. On this point, see Miroslav Volf, *After Our Likeness*, 138.

OUR SERVICE PLAN

Finally, here is what's ahead. Chapter 1 begins as a sociological consideration of the cultural factors that inhibit meaningful church membership and discipline. This is another part of my attempt to make theology dialogue with our own time and place. Ultimately, I will argue that these sociological considerations give way to spiritual ones.

Chapters 2 to 5 present one sustained theological argument for church membership and discipline. Chapter 2 attempts to articulate a right understanding of love. Chapter 3 attempts to articulate a godly understanding of authority. I take the time to do both these things for two reasons. First, church membership is a function of God's love and authority exercised among covenanting believers. Second, I believe that most evangelicals have, at best, reductionistic understandings of love and authority. You might almost say that I'm trying to use these two chapters to introduce a new worldview before making the more specific arguments concerning church membership and discipline in chapters 4 and 5. If you're anxious to cut to the chase, however, go straight to chapter 4, where I formally define church membership and discipline, and I defend this definition based on Matthew 16, 18, and 28. Membership, I argue, is a kind of covenant. Chapter 5 then pans the camera in on this covenant and considers what exactly it is in light of the covenants of the Old Testament and the new covenant.

Chapters 6 and 7 are then an attempt to get more practical and "apply" the doctrine developed in the previous four chapters. Chapter 6 walks the reader through the membership and discipline process from the church's perspective. Chapter 7 does the same from the individual Christian's perspective.

PART 1

LOVE MISDEFINED

CHAPTER ONE

THE IDOLATRY OF LOVE

"All you need is love."
—John Lennon

Main Question: How do our common cultural conceptions of love today hinder our acceptance of church membership and discipline?

Main Answer: We have made love into an idol that serves us and so have redefined love into something that never imposes judgments, conditions, or binding attachments.

Step 1: Doing a doctrine of the church requires us to consider our cultural baggage.

The Risky Business of Ecclesiology

Tampering with the doctrine of the church is a risky business. Perhaps more than with any other Christian doctrine, the doctrine of the church—also called "ecclesiology"—is where the variables of personal ambition and vain conceit factor into all the equations. Ecclesiology is the domain of turf wars and political rivalries. It's where the embattled pastor and his ornery deacon board haggle yet again over where the "buck stops"; where the local Episcopal church has to determine what it means to separate from the larger Episcopal communion that has forsaken the gospel; where the presbytery decides whether a member's lifestyle places her outside the community's affirmation of faith.

One might say that it's comparatively easy to debate God's foreknowledge, or whether regeneration precedes conversion, or what the millennium is. Raise one of these topics, and over half the church will shrug their shoulders and claim agnosticism. But raise the topic of who has final say over the church budget, or who chooses a new pastor, or whether the church has the right to discipline the elder's wayward adult son, and you won't find many agnostics here. Sure enough, church history is replete with examples of theologians changing their ecclesiology to suit political circumstance.

In other words, there's a "real worldness" to the doctrine of the church. Deciding who receives baptism and the Lord's Supper and who doesn't is a "political" decision in a way other doctrinal decisions are not. So is deciding who has the final say in decision-making matters. As such, our ideas about ecclesiology will be uniquely affected by the personal experiences we bring to bear, coupled with the ambitions and fears harbored in our hearts. Some writers have speculated that the Scriptures don't have much to say about how Christians should exactly structure their churches, so Christians can fashion and refashion their churches to best suit their missiological contexts. I think it's better—and less speculative about why God did what he did—to remove the normative element from this proposal and say, simply as a matter of sociological description, that our doctrine of the church is at least as likely, if not more likely than other doctrines, to be shaped by our time and place.

After all, is it coincidental that for fifteen hundred years churches moved toward a centralized authority while the world was ruled by Caesars and Charleses? Is it coincidental that democratic revolutions of the eighteenth century and the proliferation of democratic governments that have followed ever since have been roughly matched by a similar proliferation of congregational and other non-connectional forms of church government? Yes, exceptions occurred.[1] But doesn't it stand to reason that, when a culture becomes accustomed to a particular form of government, churches will more likely adopt those same forms? The same is true of business models. It's only natural for people to pattern their church after what works at the office. Committees in the forties and fifties? CEO pastors in the nineties? Multi-campus franchises today? Finally, is it terribly surprising that, in the anti-institutional, anti-boundary, anti-authority postmodern West, Christian leaders today would increasingly call for the de-institutionalization of the church?

For these reasons, it's helpful to consider a writer's context as he or she writes about the doctrine of the church. In the introduction we considered the call for "less institution" and "more community" among many writers today. The theologian Jürgen Moltmann makes this kind of statement in the early pages of his work on ecclesiology, but he does so staring into the "crisis of the national and established churches in 'Christian' countries of long standing," like Germany's state Lutheran church.[2] Given what he's looking at, I'm entirely sympathetic with Moltmann. But what if a writer says the same thing as he is looking at revivalistic and seeker-sensitive Southern Baptist churches, as one Southern Baptist Convention leader does in his popular-level book for pastors?[3] Even though I'm closer to the Baptist author theologically, I'm a little more suspicious.

---

[1] For instance, John Smyth established one of the first Baptist churches before Hobbes wrote the *Leviathan* or Locke wrote the *Two Treatises of Government,* to say nothing of groups like the Waldensians.

[2] Jürgen Moltmann, *The Church in the Power of the Spirit* (Minneapolis: Fortress, 1993; orig. pub. 1975), xx.

[3] Reggie McNeal, *The Present Future: Six Tough Questions for the Church* (San Francisco: Jossey-Bass, 2003), 26–27, 34–36.

So tampering with the doctrine of the church is a risky business because it's particularly susceptible to the realities of enculturation generally and personal ambition specifically. That's why I want to devote an entire chapter to examining some of the forces that most likely affect how we view the matters of church membership and discipline today. We don't come to these topics without cultural baggage. We come with a train full.

A Culturally Counterintuitive Proposal

If the doctrine of the church gets wrapped up with the ambitions and fears of the heart, doing a cultural baggage check is far more involved than asking what presuppositions or opinions we might have about the church. It's a matter of examining fundamental conceptions of love, God, and more. What's more, our understanding of Christian doctrine—especially ecclesiology—ties into every area of our lives. The fact that my wife enjoys romantic comedies on Saturday nights, or that I like watching action-adventure movies, affects how we gather with the church on Sunday mornings more than we realize. Indeed, the very fact that we will watch movies on Saturday evenings instead of sing songs in the old family parlor by lantern light will affect how we give and receive love to other members of our church.

My main argument in this chapter is that our ideas about love are more idolatrous than we realize. To see this, I want to pick up the storyline that we began in the introduction concerning the Romantic impulse latent within postmodern, Western culture against structures, boundaries, or anything reeking of exclusivism. After all, I trust that most Christian readers will find this book's principal proposal—that God intends for the exclusivistic practices of church membership and discipline to help (re)define love and beauty for fallen human beings—deeply counterintuitive. The very elements that comprise the DNA of our Western postmodern culture cause most of us to react against anything remotely suggestive of institutionalism or exclusivism, like white blood cells programmatically responding to foreign bacteria. The one boundary most people agree upon these days is the boundary keeping boundary makers out![4] Most pertinently, it contradicts our ideas about love. We regard love as the very thing that calls us to wield our hammers and knock down the old walls of division rather than build them.

---

[4]Here's one example of this anti-boundary impulse giving shape to how the local church is viewed: Tony Jones, an Emergent church leader, said in an interview, "Statements of faith [in churches] are about drawing borders, which means you have to load your weapons and place soldiers at those borders. You have to check people's passports when they pass at those borders. It becomes an obsession—guarding the borders. That is simply not the ministry of Jesus. It wasn't the ministry of Paul or Peter." Cited in Kevin DeYoung and Ted Kluck, *Why We're Not Emergent* (Chicago: Moody, 2008), 117. Another striking example can be found in Brian McLaren, *A Generous Orthodoxy* (Grand Rapids: Zondervan, 2004), 109.

Why does it feel unloving to draw clear borders around a church? Is it? What do we take "love" to be? Are our notions of love in fact biblical? Many writers today say that Christians in the West are overly (1) individualistic. And along with such individualism, they say, comes (2) consumerism, (3) a reluctance to make commitments generally, and (4) a skepticism toward all absolute truth.

Step 2: Individualism has left us detached, which sends us searching for a love that makes us feel complete. We want churches to do the same.

Individualism

Picture seventeen-year-old Benjamin Franklin, the son of a candle maker who would become a printer, scientist, inventor, author, and ambassador, walking into the city of Philadelphia for the first time not knowing a single soul, tromping up Market Street with nothing more than a Dutch dollar in his pocket, a loaf of bread under each arm, and a third in his hand, and surveying the city in which he would one day help to lead the American colonies through a revolution and into nationhood.[5]

Picture twelve-year-old African-American slave Frederick Douglass, who would one day be the most internationally renowned abolitionist of an era and the occasional counselor to President Abraham Lincoln on matters of slavery, hunched over a piece of cement with a lump of chalk in his fingers teaching himself to write by mimicking the letters he observed shipbuilders mark on pieces of lumber—"L." for larboard side, "S." for starboard side, "L.F." for larboard side forward, "S.A." for starboard side aft.[6]

Picture seven-year-old Amelia Earhart, author, early women's rights advocate, and the first female to fly an airplane unaccompanied across the Atlantic Ocean, standing with bruised lip and torn dress after her homemade rollercoaster, cobbled together from a wooden box and planks propped up against an eight-foot tool shed and greased by lard, spilled her onto the ground, and then exclaiming to her sister, "Oh, Pidge, it's just like flying!"[7]

EVERY ATTACHMENT IS NEGOTIABLE

Remarkable stories like those have presented the American cultural conscience— my own conscience—with a glorious vision of the self-reliant, self-made, self-defining man or woman. Not class, ethnicity, gender, parish, or actual iron

---

[5]Benjamin Franklin, *The Autobiography and Other Writings* (New York: Penguin, 1986), 27.
[6]Frederick Douglass, *Narrative of the Life of Frederick Douglass, An American Slave* (New York: Penguin, 1982), 86–87.
[7]Donald M. Goldstein and Katherine V. Dillon, *Amelia: A Life of the Aviation Legend,* new ed. (Dulles, VA: Brassey's, 1999), 9.

shackles could bind such heroes. To adapt Charles Wesley's hymn, their chains broke off, their hearts were free, they rose, went forth, and followed the proverbial *me*.

Such real life biographies inspired the world of popular fiction, in everything from the Westward ventures of James Fennimore Cooper's *Deerslayer* or *Pioneers* to the upward ventures of Horatio Alger's *Ragged Dick* or *Struggling Upward*. Arising out of such fiction grew up what has been called the myth of the American Adam. Like Adam standing in the garden of Eden, like the first Pilgrims who stepped off the Mayflower at Plymouth Rock, every new generation of Americans has perceived itself as unbounded by national borders or tradition, space or time, as the Western frontier stretched beyond the imagination's reach, offering limitless opportunity to create new worlds.[8] Why is such fiction significant? Because the fiction that a public writes and reads reveals what a public values and despises. Fast-forwarding to our day, one needs only go to the movies to see that the myth of the American Adam remains alive and well, albeit without the hope-inspiring visions of the past. In the 2000s, Jason Bourne, a CIA trained assassin with limitless powers of self-defense and a bad case of amnesia, perhaps embodies it best.[9] And Bourne stands in a long line of Lone Ranger heroes, from Superman in the 1970s, to Indiana Jones in the 1980s, to the Terminator in the 1990s (notice the growing nihilism in this trajectory).

There are so many ways we could tell the history of individualism. I have described it as an English major might. A church historian could go back and tell the story of Luther's Reformation and his doctrine of the priesthood of all believers. This could be followed by the 1555 Peace of Augsburg, which granted the princes of Europe the ability to determine whether their domain would be Protestant or Catholic. This could be followed by the 1648 Peace of Westphalia, which granted the religious minorities of Europe the freedom to decide that question differently from their prince, so long as they remained Roman Catholic, Lutheran, or Reformed. This could be followed by the 1689 Act of Toleration, which granted British citizens the right to gather in their own houses of worship with their own pastors, so long as they remained Trinitarian and Protestant, and this could be followed by the non-establishment clause in the U.S. Bill of Rights. A student of political theory would probably fill his history with characters like King John and the Magna Carta, Thomas Hobbes

---

[8] R. W. B. Lewis famously described this American Adam as "emancipated from history, happily bereft of ancestry, untouched and undefiled by the usual inheritances of family and race; an individual standing alone, self-reliant and self-propelling, ready to confront whatever awaited him with the aid of his own unique and inherent resources . . . and in his newness he was fundamentally innocent." *The American Adam* (Chicago, University of Chicago Press, 1959), 5.

[9] George F. Custen, "Debuting: One Spy, Unshaken," in the *New York Times*, "Week in Review," June 23, 2002; also described in Heather Clark, "The Myth of the American Adam Re-Bourne," an unpublished master's thesis, Fall 2004, Purdue University (http://www.calumet.purdue.edu/engphil/recenttheses.html) accessed January 17, 2008.

and his social contract, John Locke's talk of the "consent of the governed," Rousseau's version of the social contract, the Declaration of Independence, and the head of the king of France resting in the bottom of a bucket in the middle of a cheering throng.

Whatever figures and stories we use to narrate the emerging drama of the Individual, the outcome of the story is the same for the average person in Western culture today: every attachment is negotiable. We are all free agents, and every relationship and life station is a contract that can be renegotiated or canceled, whether we are dealing with the prince, the parents, the spouse, the salesman, the boss, the ballot box, the courtroom judge, or, of course, the local church. I am principally obligated to myself and maximizing my life, liberty, and pursuit of happiness. Among my various relationships, I may choose to identify with another party, but only so long as doing so is demonstrably conducive to personal advantage. I retain veto power over *everything*. When in the course of human events it becomes necessary to dissolve the bands which have connected me to others, I dissolve them.

This ability to negotiate and veto my commitments, of course, stretches all the way to heaven and into eternity. Sociologist Robert Bellah introduced us to the now infamous term "Sheilaism." Sheila Larson was an individual his research team interviewed who felt licensed to cast a religion in her own image by picking and choosing among her favorite religious and moral principles, thereby "transform[ing] external authority into internal meaning"[10]—almost like restaurant customers surveying the salad bar, which is precisely how one Unitarian minister has defined her religion: a salad bowl.[11]

It's true that group identity has been on the rise at least since the 1960s. This has occurred among feminists seeking to carve out an empowered space for individuals belonging to the demographic category called "women" (or "womyn") as well as among some elements of the civil rights movement seeking greater measures of ethnic solidarity. It has also occurred increasingly among "lifestyle enclaves," self-identified cultural blocks not formed around an ethnic, religious, or other traditional form of group identity but around some other type of lifestyle decision such as homosexuality, Harley riding, or hip-hop— movements complete with their own magazines, movies, churches, styles of dress, patterns of speech, and so on.[12] I don't believe that this demographic Balkanization has done anything to undermine or displace the supremacy of the individual. It has simply given him new tools for asserting—or at least attempt- ing to assert—his individual supremacy.

---

[10]Robert Bellah et al., *Habits of the Heart: Individualism and Commitment in American Life* (New York: Harper and Row, 1985), 235, 220.
[11]In Jon D. Levenson, "The Problem with Salad Bowl Religion," in *First Things* 78 (December 1997): 10–12.
[12]Robert Bellah, *Habits of the Heart*, 72–73.

INDIVIDUALISM AND LOVE

What does all this have to do with how we define love today? The growth of individualism over the last several centuries has dramatically affected all areas of Western life, including how Westerners today understand and experience love. As sociologist Anthony Giddens tells the story, most marriages in premodern Europe were entered into not for the sake of love or sexual attraction but for economic reasons. For the poor at least, marriage was a means of organizing labor.[13] When love was spoken of in the context of marriage, it was characterized as the compassionate love between a husband and wife running a household or farm together.[14] Beginning in the late eighteenth century, however, what Giddens calls "romantic love" began to arise amidst a flurry of novels, many authored by women, which situated the love relationship, like a novel, in a narrative of self-discovery and self-expression.[15]

Passionate love itself was nothing new to the late eighteenth and nineteenth centuries. Everything from relics of poetry that have survived from Ancient Egypt to Shakespeare's *Romeo and Juliet* portray an all-consuming, sexual, and passionate love that envelops an individual or a couple, almost like sickness, disrupting their everyday obligations and activities and inspiring them to acts of heroism, sacrifice, or despair. Culturally distinct about the emerging romantic love of the late eighteenth and nineteenth centuries was this narrative of self-realization that involved not just sexual attraction but the discovery of another individual with certain characteristics that would supposedly complete the lone individual. Hence Giddens writes:

> Romantic love presumes some degree of self-interrogation. How do I feel about the other? How does the other feel about me? Are our feelings "profound" enough to support a long-term involvement? Unlike *amour passion* [passionate love], which uproots erratically, romantic love detaches individuals from wider social circumstances in a different way. It provides for a long-term life trajectory, oriented to an anticipated yet malleable future.[16]

Giddens doesn't speculate on the origins or causes of romantic love. Perhaps it was the reaction to the sense people had of feeling adrift as many of their traditional moorings were cut by the rationalistic individualism of the Enlightenment? As much as the Romantics wanted to define themselves against the Enlightenment, they remained derivative of it, in the same way that post-

---

[13] Anthony Giddens, *Transforming Intimacy: Sexuality, Love and Eroticism in Modern Societies* (Palo Alto, CA: Stanford University Press, 1992), 38.
[14] Ibid., 43.
[15] Ibid., 39–40; Bellah, *Habits of the Heart*, 73.
[16] Giddens, *Transforming Intimacy*, 44–45.

modernity is derivative of modernity (simultaneously a reaction against and yet sharing some of its most basic presuppositions).

Interestingly, Giddens characterizes men as the "laggards"[17] in these transforming conceptions of love, since romantic love is "essentially feminised love."[18] Unlike the passive women of medieval tales, the women of the romantic novels are spirited and independent, able to melt the hearts of men originally indifferent or even hostile to them. Giddens doesn't articulate what he means by the feminization of love as clearly as one might hope, but it seems to lie in the fact that the women are the producers of romantic love and the ones responsible for maintaining a marriage on the basis of such love in the face of the continual threat of male infidelity. Men who instigate romantic love are not the masculine men but the "foppish dreamers" who willingly build their entire lives around a particular woman.[19] The feminization of love also seems to be found in its domesticity. He characterizes the household as transformed by the advent of romantic love insofar as children are increasingly perceived as vulnerable and requiring long-term emotional care and maternal compassion. The Victorian man remained the authority of his home, but his authority was increasingly softened by a growing emphasis on emotional warmth between parents and children.[20]

ROMANTIC LOVE VERSUS BIBLICAL LOVE

No doubt, aspects of this romantic love correspond to the yearnings of the lover and beloved in the Song of Solomon, or even elements of the love language between Yahweh and Israel in the Old Testament prophets. Lest any evangelical reader confuse this picture of romantic love with something more wholly biblical, it's worth considering a counterpoint, namely, love and marriage as characterized by the premodern Martin Luther. Luther, like the Romantics, believed strongly that marriages should be founded on love. Criticizing the institution of arranged marriages, Luther wrote, "A fatherly or motherly affection toward children should refuse to tolerate anything but love and delight as the basis of marriage."[21] Not only that, Luther, like the Romantics, personally experienced and testified to the "intoxicating" nature of the beginnings of love: "The first love is ardent, is an intoxication love, so that we are blinded and are drawn to marriage."[22] Yet Luther's conception of marital love was not a matter of individual self-expression and self-realization. It went beyond the

---

[17]Ibid., 59.
[18]Ibid., 43.
[19]Ibid., 43, 59.
[20]Ibid., 42.
[21]Cited in Justin Taylor, "Martin Luther's Reform of Marriage," in *Sex and the Supremacy of Christ*, ed. John Piper and Justin Taylor (Wheaton, IL: Crossway, 2005), 240.
[22]Ibid., 239.

initial intoxication and aspired to something more biblical, something made of the same stuff that comprises the love that Christians should bear for all their neighbors—a wholehearted devotion to the good and holiness of the other:

> After we have slept off our intoxication, sincere love remains in the married life of the godly; but the godless are sorry they ever married. . . . Where conjugal chastity is to be maintained, husband and wife must, above all things, live together in love and harmony, so that one cherishes the other wholeheartedly and with complete fidelity. This wholehearted devotion is one of the chief requirements in the creation of love and desire for chastity.[23]

For Luther, marriage and parenting did not principally exist so that individual humans could realize, complete, and express themselves, or to raise children in cushioned existences that taught them to do the same. Rather, the "ultimate purpose is to obey God, to find aid and counsel against sin; to call upon God; to seek, love, and educate children for the glory of God; to live with one's wife in the fear of God and to bear the cross."[24]

The Romantic love of the late eighteenth and nineteenth centuries differed most fundamentally from Luther's conception and more biblical conceptions of love generally in this way: for the romantic lover, the point of absolute moral reference was an exclusive fidelity to the love relationship and its maximization. All other societal ties—familial, class, religious, professional, etc.—became secondary and, finally, expendable for the sake of preserving this primary human relationship. Giddens does not use the term "idolatrous" to characterize romantic love, but that's what it is. Where Augustine acknowledged that human beings will find complete rest only in God, the romantic lover finds his or her soul's completion in the other. In love! It's not that everything about romantic love is wrong. As I have already suggested, reflections of it can be found in the pages of Scripture. However, romantic love isolates one or two aspects of biblical love—a more complicated, multifaceted thing—and makes those things ultimate, thereby distorting even that which is good in it.

It's not difficult to see how this conception of romantic love, born out of an individual's desire for expression and fulfillment, affects our conceptions of "love" in every sphere of life today. Whether the conversation turns to church services, friendships, or dating, I know that you love me when you let me "be myself" or "express myself" or "be the best person I can be." I love you by allowing you to do the same. So Americans tend to describe churches as "loving" when those churches make us feel relaxed and comfortable, not judged. We can

---

[23]Ibid., 239–40.
[24]Ibid., 231.

be ourselves there. Nonjudgmentalism is important in our friendships too: "I know she's my friend, because she doesn't judge me. I can be real with her."

But is this really love? If that's all such "love" consists of, I myself have become the true object of my affection. I might claim to "love you," but it's really the way that you make me feel that I love. You make me feel accepted, smart, inspired, romantic, tingly, encouraged, special, warm and fuzzy, turned on, attracted, attractive, hot, all that I can be, hardworking, creative, full of life, intellectually edified, spiritually edified, like a hero, empowered, built up, great! As John Piper has said, we call it "love" when people "make much of us."[25]

Like the love of weepy nineteenth-century novels, we employ the idea of love today as the argument that ends all arguments. If an action is motivated by love, it bears all the vindication it needs. It's the ultimate trump card: "But they love each other," or, "That doesn't seem like a loving thing to do," or, "What you're saying might be true, but it's not loving." We know love can be tragic. We know it can be foolish. But love alone is good, and always good. Religious people justify this stance by saying, "God is love." Nonreligious people point to the good of humanity and say—or sing—"All we need is love."

Maybe it's true that love is the ultimate justifier, but if it is true, it would have to be a perfect and divine love that justifies. What if what people call love is not really love? What if it's a shadow or phantom that simply resembles the real thing? Wouldn't it be an idol—a substitute for God—they're using to justify themselves? And what happens when humans use idols to justify their actions and relationships?

SELF-EXPRESSIVE LOVE IN CHURCHES

The question that pastors and church leaders in particular need to ask themselves is, how do Christians relate to their churches when they understand love to be a matter of self-realization and self-expression? For some, the emotive aspects of the church's corporate gatherings takes on undue importance, whether in the style of music or the personality of the preacher. Christians will evaluate a church by whether they can "connect" with the music or the pastor. "Worship wars" will probably follow, because it is through music that we most express ourselves. By this token, their song lyrics do not so much present an opportunity to meditate on God's love for sinners ("When I survey the wondrous cross, on which the prince of glory died") but on repeated expressions of the sinner's love for God ("I could sing of Your love forever, I could sing of your love forever, I could sing . . ."). Both kinds of expressions are biblical, but the latter must always be a response to the former. Is that the case in churches today?

---

[25] John Piper, *God Is the Gospel* (Wheaton, IL: Crossway, 2005), 149–50.

If a church understands love to be a matter of self-expression and self-fulfillment, Sunday school classes, small groups, and other ministries will divide demographically because Christians become more intent on finding people who share their life experiences rather than on finding older people to learn from and younger people to disciple. The ability to integrate ethnically, culturally, or generationally becomes much more difficult. Like the culture at large, entire churches come to represent a city's various cultural enclaves. The "homogenous unit principle" works! Church gatherings feel vibrant and alive, even if an idolatrous conception of love is being worshiped. Preaching becomes "personal counseling on a group basis," as one early twentieth-century pastor put it.

"Spiritual gifts tests" also become popular. Never mind where the church has needs. Never mind where the battle lines need shoring up. "I need to feel fulfilled through my involvement at church, so tell me exactly how God has equipped me personally, and then please assign me a position that allows me to give expression to my own gift set."

When love becomes a matter of self-expression among Christians, the gospel itself—the very heart of Christian love—becomes refashioned for therapeutic purposes. As David Powlison has written:

> In this new gospel, the great "evils" to be redressed do not call for any fundamental change of direction in the human heart. Instead, the problem lies in my sense of rejection from others; in my corrosive experience of life's vanity; in my nervous sense of self-condemnation and diffidence; in the imminent threat of boredom if my music is turned off; in my fussy complaints when a long, hard road lies ahead. These are today's significant felt needs that the gospel is bent to serve. Jesus and the church exist to make you feel loved, significant, validated, entertained, and charged up. This gospel ameliorates distressing symptoms. It makes you feel better. The logic of this therapeutic gospel is a jesus-for-Me who meets individual desires and assuages psychic aches.[26]

God's love in the gospel is all about *me*.

At the same time, churches redolent with this romanticized brand of self-expressive love, liked overly potpourried bathrooms, repel the more masculine clientele, leading many authors to fret over the departure of men from churches.[27] Not everyone enjoys Jane Austen novels or Meg Ryan movies, after all. A number of manly men, therefore, have pulled out their pistols and retaken some evangelical territory. Books, churches, and conferences now explicitly

---

[26]David Powlison, "Therapeutic Gospel," in *Journal of Biblical Counseling* 25 (Summer 2007): 3.
[27]See Leon J. Podles, *The Church Impotent: The Feminization of Christianity* (Dallas: Spence, 1999), 3–4, 57–59; David Murrow, *Why Men Hate Going to Church* (Nashville: Nelson, 2005); Mark Chanski, *Manly Dominion: In a Passive-Purple-Four-Ball-World* (Amityville, NY: Calvary Press, 2004). Remarkably, it's not only recently that this critique has been made of churches; see Cortland Myers, *Why Do Men Not Go to Church?* (New York: Funk and Wagnalls, 1899).

target those more inclined to the action and adventure section of the movie store, stock car racing, mixed martial arts, and any bloak who likes to think of himself as square-jawed and broad-shouldered. Ironically, this entire movement remains enamored with self-expression and self-definition.

What underlying cultural assumptions in the West today keep Christians from taking church membership seriously? Why does the very idea of church membership and discipline have the faint aroma of "unloving" to our contemporary sensibilities? Because we have learned in the democratic, capitalistic West that we are free agents and that the purpose of life is the maximization of individual happiness. Local churches, therefore, are simply one more group vying for our personal allegiance, like political parties, lovers, or grocery stores. And as with political parties, lovers, and grocery stores, we have learned to negotiate and renegotiate our attachment to local churches according to how closely they align to our sense of self and its values. In order to legitimate these contract renegotiations, we have redefined love to accord with this sense of connectedness to another who compliments and affirms our sense of self and its values. "How can you expect me to stay in this marriage? We've grown apart. We don't love each other anymore." If love is no more than self-fulfillment and self-expression, that's a reasonable question.

At the same time, we have learned to dismiss any institutional aspects of a church or organization as the result of a legalistic "intuitionalism." After all, institutions operate by house rules that bind free agents more than they want to be bound.

Step 3: Consumerism has caused us to focus on the desirability of the object of love, rather than the process of loving. We view churches like products which satisfy us or not.

Consumerism

In some ways, we could end our investigation of individualism and its effect on how we understand love here, but at the risk of a little redundancy, I believe we will get a fuller, more helpful understanding of love and the church today if we push deeper into three aspects of individualism: consumerism, a fear of commitment, and skepticism toward all dogma.

If life is a series of negotiating attachments and commitments, then I will do all I can to maximize my purchases. That's what a consumer does. Happiness and rest result from savvy purchases, and unhappiness and anxiety result from poor purchases. The trouble, of course, is that no purchase really closes the deal. The possibility of buyer's remorse always looms. "Should I have purchased the other brand?" "Will a better model be released next month?" "What's the store's exchange policy?"

Salvation has always been a matter of exchange, whether we are exchanging our sin for Christ's righteousness, or the medium-sized shirt for the large. Exchange is not the problem. The problem with the consumeristic society, in the first place, is that people believe something tangible must be exchanged—a shirt, a car, a job, a friendship, a marriage, a lack of education. Redemption is a change of circumstances, which means that salvation is secularized. It's about exchanging something *in this world* for something else *in this world*. We seek our peace and rest and shalom and joy in this world or in this age.

In the second place, the consumeristic society has no idea that the first thing that must be exchanged is the individual's own heart—a stone one for a flesh one, a natural one for a supernatural one. The consumer, by virtue of being a consumer, is working so hard to compare this product against that product that she seldom takes her eyes off the products long enough to interrogate the appetites of the heart. She doesn't ask, "What do my appetites reveal? Am I desiring the right things?" A consumeristic mindset has a misplaced and misleading fixation on the objects of its desires rather than on the faculty of its desiring.

In the past, the boundaries of time and space, tradition and community, worked to restrain and retrain appetite, for better or worse. When the individual is loosed from all tradition and community, the appetite has nothing to guide and shape it other than accident and whim.

CONSUMERISM AND LOVE

As early as the 1940s, sociologist Erich Fromm observed that Western conceptions of love had, in fact, taken a consumeristic turn. Consider how the typical dating process works. A man evaluates his own purchasing power based on what he perceives is valued by women: personality, humor, stature, future prospects, and so forth. Based on this self-appraisal, he makes the best purchase he can according to whichever traits he most values in women, such as intelligence, beauty, or family background. In a market with ample supply, he can be more particular in his demands. It's not just beauty he's looking for; it's a brunette with such-and-such stature. In all of this, Fromm observed that people had shifted their focus from the "faculty" of love to the "objects" of love. We are more concerned about who loves us than we are about loving. He writes, "Two persons thus fall in love when they feel they have found the best object available on the market, considering the limitations of their own exchange values."[28]

---

[28]Erich Fromm, *The Art of Loving* (1956; repr. New York: Harper and Row, 1989), 3.

When we approach love and relationships as consumers, it's the more superficial traits that draw our attention, since the decision-making processes of a consumer rely on externals rather than on deeper, unseen qualities. Beauty counts more than character, income more than constancy, manners more than values, sexual performance more than fidelity. In the romantic love of the nineteenth century, sexuality was regarded as emerging out of true love. By the time the sexual revolution occurred in the latter half of the twentieth century, good sex became a precondition of love. Sex became the test at the beginning of a relationship rather than a prize to be won deep into the relationship. A greater emphasis was then laid on sexual skill and body type.[29] Pornography finds an easier market as the public is easily duped by its fantasies.

CONSUMERISTIC LOVE IN CHURCHES

It is not coincidental that the "loving" church believes that size and performance matter. The best way to love and reach the world is with a good product line. Larger churches have the resources requisite for this type of thing. Smaller churches don't, so smaller churches fade. One pastor recently recounted to another his experience of losing 1,000 of his 2,500 church members to a large seeker-sensitive church when it moved closer to his own (not a smaller church either, admittedly). Remarkably, the church collections didn't drop after the thousand members departed, but actually grew. It seems the consumers left.

When pastors fail to teach Christians that the problem of love begins with the faculty to love rather than with the various objects of love, the critical faculties that Christians develop in the shopping mall transfer to their church lives. They come, listen to the music, listen to the preaching, look around at the other people—"Do they look like me? Will I be comfortable with them?"—and then offer an evaluation of everything they saw on the drive home: "I liked the music, except that one song. The preacher wasn't very funny. Did you see any programs for teenagers?" They evaluate their experience rather than their hearts. They judge the church rather than letting God's Word judge them. In all this they utterly fail to recognize that they are not loving their neighbor as themselves. The question they ask is not "what style of music helps my neighbor praise God?" It's "what style serves me?"

Market-savvy church leaders have figured out that they can employ several services for capturing different market segments. Especially market-savvy church leaders have figured out that they can begin several "campuses," all with the same, reliable franchise brand. They have forgotten—or never been taught—

---

[29]Giddens, *Transforming Intimacy*, 62.

that real love requires personal knowledge, because personal knowledge is a precondition of accountability, discipline, and holiness. With thousands of members spread over several campuses, some sheep will be accounted for, but many will not. Many sheep will wander away looking for a better product, and no one will ever know. Paul couldn't really have meant for the elders to pay careful attention to *all* the flock, right? Just most of them (Acts 20:28).

The name of the game in many churches today is "Your way, right away." Products are not built to last, but obsolescence is planned and expected. A successful church service is one that produces a spiritual high or a mountaintop experience. Growth is counted through decisions made, not through "a long obedience in the same direction," to use Nietzsche's phrase. Statistics and other short-term measurements are all important. When the numbers start to dip on the sigmoid curve, ratchet up the program in order to yield another spurt of growth. Virtues like holiness, self-sacrifice, and faith can't be counted, so never mind. As Mark Dever has said, statistical figures are worshiped more than carved ones.[30]

Step 4: Commitment phobia takes commitment out of love and love becomes about what's advantageous to me. The idea of commitment is removed from our view of churches.

Commitment Phobia

One further outgrowth of individualism and consumerism is a fear of making binding commitments. The drive to pursue happiness in the negotiations and renegotiations of our various contracts means making sure that no contract is too binding. Better yet, it means avoiding contracts altogether while manipulating circumstances in order to yield all the benefits of a contract.

That's a broad generalization that probably does not do justice to the complexities of twenty-first-century urban life. But noteworthy changes in a number of social indicators suggest that people today are generally more reluctant to enter into binding commitments and associations that will limit the options available to them in the future than people were in previous generations.[31] A few concrete examples should make the point, a point which many of us, I think, know from personal experience.

First, Americans today are less likely to join clubs, associations, and civic groups than their historical predecessors. The Frenchman Alexis de Tocqueville may have returned from his famous 1831 trip to the United States with aston-

---

[30]Mark Dever, *What Is a Healthy Church?* (Wheaton, IL: Crossway, 2007), 96.
[31]For a discussion of this phenomenon among younger generations today, especially as it pertains to local churches, see chaps. 2 and 3 of Robert Wuthnow, *After the Baby Boomers: How Twenty- and Thirty-Somethings Are Shaping the Future of American Religion* (Princeton: Princeton University Press, 2007).

ished reports of America's vibrant civic life and associational activity, but recent researchers have dug into over a century's worth of Masonic yearbooks, labor union fee-paying records, Rotary Club statistics, Little League and Boy Scout reports, and even bowling club membership figures to discover that the country de Tocqueville saw has changed.[32] The organizations that ask members for face-to-face involvement and substantial commitments of time have dropped precipitously. On the other hand, national and international organizations like Sierra Club or the National Audubon Society that promise to send the occasional newsletter in exchange for nothing more than an annual membership check are growing.[33]

Second, the more leisurely approach Westerners have been taking to the institution of marriage suggests a greater cultural inability to make binding commitments. Men and women are both marrying at older ages. Cohabitations rates are up. Divorces are more common. Second- and third-marriage statistics are climbing. And it's news to no one that sex outside of marriage is increasingly accepted in the culture at large. By the same token, the continued cultural mandate for abortion on demand suggests a reluctance to the binding commitments of parenthood.

Third, Westerners are changing jobs and careers more often in the course of their working lives than they have in the past. According to 2008 U.S. Department of Labor statistics, the median job tenure for workers of the ages 25 to 34 years is 2.7 years.[34] If an individual begins work at age twenty, he or she will have an average of seven jobs by the age of forty. As with all these statistics, we need to temper the conclusions we draw from this fact with other qualifying factors. For instance, the pace of job change among the average worker over the last century is no doubt also the result of the global economy's increased complexity and efficiencies, which move jobs and make jobs redundant far more rapidly than in the past. Still, whatever the cause, the net effect is less ability to commit to one career for the course of one's days.

Fourth, some commentators have remarked on the ability of conservative evangelical churches to grow their membership roles in comparison to their mainline Protestant counterparts, because the evangelicals "demand more" from their members doctrinally.[35] What this conclusion fails to recognize is the simultaneous trend of evangelical churchgoers to join larger and even megachurches, where the demands of interpersonal involvement, accountability,

---

[32]See Robert Putnam, "Bowling Alone: America's Declining Social Capitol," in *Journal of Democracy* 6 (January 1995): 65–78. Also, Robert Putnam, *Bowling Alone: The Collapse and Revival of American Community* (New York: Simon and Schuster, 2000).

[33]Putnam, *Bowling Alone*, 156.

[34]U.S. Department of Labor, Bureau of Labor Statistics, "News," September 26, 2008, USDL 08-1344 (http://www.bls.gov/news.release/archives/tenure_09262008.pdf).

[35]Roger Finke and Rodney Stark, *The Churching of America* (Piscataway, NJ: Rutgers University Press, 2005), 275.

and commitment are often less. Are growing numbers of Americans joining churches? Perhaps. But do those churches allow their members to persist in anonymity? Too often, yes.

My generation in particular—Gen-X—worships the god of options. Individuals reach their late twenties and even thirties uncertain of what they want to be "when they grow up," prompting at least a couple of writers to characterize the phenomenon as "delayed adolescence."[36] How many men (including me) have I counseled through the agonizing decision of whether or not to pursue this or that woman? After all, another woman could come along next month that's even "better." The consumeristic mind-set, the multiplicity of options, and the worry of buyer's remorse hinders the ability to make commitments in everything from jobs, to spouses, to restaurants, to houses. Commitments bind us, and in a culture where the maximization of short-term pleasure has a premium, binding commitments are threatening. Binding commitments, by their nature, are made in order to prevent individuals from living by caprice and fancy. They are freedom curtailing. They are pleasure postponing.

COMMITMENT PHOBIA AND LOVE

What does a fear of commitment do to love? It reconfigures love so that the binding or breaking of commitments becomes less relevant. Loyalty and fidelity are removed from love's ingredients. The brand of romantic love that Giddens described as characterizing the late eighteenth and nineteenth century wasn't static; it evolved. It served "to carve open the way" to something he calls the *pure relationship*. The pure relationship is the social relation that is entered "for what can be derived by each person from a sustained association with another; and which is continued only in so far as it is thought by both parties to deliver enough satisfactions for each individual to stay within it."[37] It is pure or uncontaminated by any moral obligation, any sense of duty or responsibility, any long-term commitment, any call to serve or care for the other. It exists *purely* for the sake of present utility, and it's constrained by nothing other than personal preference.

A culture characterized by such "pure relationships" is one where friendships, working partnerships, sexual partners, and church memberships are purely a function of what's immediately advantageous to one's own well-being and last only as long as that remains the case. Whenever a relationship becomes inconvenient or demands too much, it's left behind. Christians should ask themselves,

---

[36]I have heard R. Albert Mohler use this phrase in multiple speeches and articles. It can be found at www.almohler.com; see also, Diana West, *The Death of the Grown-Up: How America's Arrested Development Is Bringing Down Western Civilization* (New York: St. Martin's Press, 2007).
[37]Giddens, *Transforming Intimacy*, 58.

therefore, "Do I spend time only with people who are easy to spend time with? Do I avoid the person who is needy or difficult to relate to? Do I abandon a church when the going gets tough?"

COMMITMENT-LESS LOVE IN CHURCHES

When the idea of a binding commitment is removed from the definition of love, churches become places where personal sacrifices are seldom made, so the gospel is seldom pictured. (Fulfilling covenants with sinners always requires a self-sacrifice.) Instead, individuals will come and go—"church hop"—with little care. They join churches lightly and they exit lightly, since doing so does not violate their sense of love and its obligations. They don't stop to weigh the consequences of their departure on others. They don't feel the weight of their responsibility to others. They don't discuss the reasons for leaving with the pastors. They just go. They take their purchase back to the checkout counter. It's nothing personal. All in all, they ask little of others and give little in return.

What's tragic is that Christians who come and go from churches are merely mimicking so many pastors. A man comes for several years, hears of another opportunity, leaves, and thinks nothing of it. His understanding of love is devoid of any sense of long-term obligation to a flock.

In all of this, the connection between doctrine and practice attenuates. Christians profess belief in the gospel. Their symbolic burial and resurrection from the waters of baptism indicate that they mean to take up their crosses and follow their Lord, but the very ethic of their commitment-less love does not provide them with the opportunity to fulfill these professions with their actions. These sheep are so poorly taught and so imbued by the secular culture's commitment-less conceptions of love that a man's conscience is barely triggered (if at all) when he turns to his wife and says, "Honey, I'm tired of this church. Let's look elsewhere." As she quickly agrees and they lightly depart, they fail to recognize their breach of the new commandment Christ gave to his church— "love one another as I have loved you"—even though they may affirm this commandment in their minds. The world at large then looks to the Christian church and *hears* about "Christ's love," but it *sees* nothing different from what it's already known, because our commitments to one another are cheap and easy. So why would the non-Christian bother (unless he's entertained)?

Increasingly, Christians are not joining churches in the first place. The "experience provided by their church," says famous evangelical pollster George Barna, "seems flat. They are seeking a faith experience that is more robust and awe inspiring" than what the old local church can give them.[38] Barna himself is elated. Whether a Christian is "immersed in, minimally involved in, or completely

---

[38] George Barna, *Revolution* (Carol Stream, IL: Tyndale, 2005), 14.

disassociated from a local church is irrelevant to me (and, within boundaries, to God). What matters is not whom you associate with (i.e., a local church), but who you are."[39] Remember, love is all about self-realization and connecting, and apparently churches aren't helping these individuals along. Barna cites a number of statistics to make his point, such as the fact that eight out of ten believers "do not feel they have entered the presence of God, or experienced a connection with Him, during the worship service."[40] This is the case, in part, because churches haven't read the statistics like Barna has and discovered that "how Americans experience and express their faith" has been dramatically shifting.[41] That means local churches are actually getting in the way of the "dedicated" Christians who "are serious about their faith."[42] The solution, for some Christians, is to get local churches out of the way. Take control of your own spiritual journey. For others, the solution is to find one of the new "boutique churches" that offer the "customized experiences" Americans are looking for.[43] Either way, Christians can grow in maturity without all the hassles, bureaucracies, and redundancies of life in the traditional local church. The bottom line for Barna? You can take or leave church depending on what's good for you. You are your own spiritual portfolio manager, your own captain, your own shepherd.

Pastor and megachurch trendsetter Bill Hybels discovered his own church's over-dependence on consumeristic programs. The solution? His church, Willow Creek, intends to develop a "customized growth or 'workout' plan." If you go to a health club, he says, you get a personal trainer who tells you what you need. We need the same thing in our churches in order to produce self feeders.[44]

So how about a book on church membership and discipline? Hello! Is anyone there?

Step 5: Skepticism removes all judgment from love, causing us to expect unconditional acceptance from churches. Pragmatism also results.

Skepticism

Accompanying consumerism and commitment-phobia as an outgrowth of individualism in our culture today is a skepticism toward all forms of doctrine or dogma. To embrace any dogma as absolutely true—or in Francis Schaeffer's

---

[39]Ibid., 29.
[40]Ibid., 31.
[41]Ibid., 49.
[42]Ibid., 8.
[43]Ibid., 62–63.
[44]Hybels describes this at http://revealnow.com/story.asp?storyid=49. The quote is taken from Greg L. Hawkins and Cally Parkinson, *Reveal: Where Are You?* (Barrington, IL: Willow Creek Association, 2007), 65–66.

phrase, as "truly true"—is ridiculed as dogmatism. Dogma becomes equated with dogmatism.

In order for the individual to remain free to forge Westward, upward, outward into new domains of space and possibility, all the doctrines and mores of the old world must be held with a loose grip: perhaps what Mother taught me is true; perhaps not. I'll have to see if it works for me. If Grandfather's religion proves advantageous to my circumstances, I'll keep it. If it proves burdensome to the fulfillment of my own *telos* and my "manifest destiny," then it should be discarded, or at least watered down. Clearly, a pragmatic approach to life is often the outgrowth of skepticism toward truth.[45]

In our day and age, amazingly, skepticism has become the very foundation, the very bedrock, upon which all of our personal and political freedom rests—or at least what we perceive as our freedom.[46] This was the starting point for Descartes' search for truth. Yet skepticism assumed a new level of adamancy in the twentieth century. Responding to the devastation wrought by two world wars, a holocaust, and the totalitarian ideologies behind them, Karl Popper's open society sought freedom in the renunciation of all truth-claims. Similarly, Isaiah Berlin eschewed all forms of freedom that rested on some type of truth principle, opting to define freedom instead as thinly as "freedom from restraint" and nothing more. True freedom (what he calls "negative freedom") is not the result of living in accordance with the truth, even if it's self-determined truth. Rather, freedom is simply not being prevented from doing whatever I want to do. That's the one truth we can all agree on—"Stay out of my way."

More recent proposals present more of the same. Everything from John Rawls's "veil of ignorance" to Richard Rorty's "liberal ironist" requires the individual to treat every commitment, every doctrine, every conception of justice or freedom acquired elsewhere with *skepticism*—every commitment, that is, except the commitment to philosophical liberalism.[47] We don't have to agree with all the political and philosophical commitments of Allan Bloom in order to agree with how he characterized the change in our culture's cult of openness:

> Openness used to be virtue that permitted us to seek the good by using reason. It now means accepting everything and denying reason's power. The unrestrained and thoughtless pursuit of openness, without recognizing the inherent political, social, or cultural problem of openness as the goal of nature, has rendered openness meaningless. . . . Openness to closedness is what we teach. [48]

---

[45] Just think of Jeremy Bentham and John Stuart Mill in Britain or John Dewey and Richard Rorty in the United States.

[46] Colin Gunton describes how modern conceptions of freedom are a sham in *The One, The Three, and the Many: God, Creation, and the Culture of Modernity* (Cambridge, UK: Cambridge, 1993), 13, 33–37.

[47] Michael Sandel, *Liberalism and the Limits of Justice* (New York: Cambridge University Press, 1982), 179; Charles Taylor, *Sources of the Self* (Cambridge, MA: Harvard University Press, 1989), 27.

[48] Allan Bloom, *The Closing of the American Mind* (New York: Touchstone, 1987), 38–39.

SKEPTICISM AND LOVE

It's not difficult to see what happens to a culture's understanding of love when skepticism toward all truth becomes the one moral absolute: love becomes fluid, protean, malleable. Love becomes "anything goes," or at least "whatever works for you." Love becomes unconditional acceptance. If you love me with conditions, you don't love me.

The opposite of love, according to our thinking today, is judgmentalism, intolerance, or exclusivism, like racists, homophobes, and boundary-drawing churches. On the other hand, I know that you love me if you accept me as I am, and tolerate whatever I say or think without condemning it. In fact, loving me means more than just accepting me; it means accepting and affirming my lifestyle decisions as legitimate and good.

UNCONDITIONAL ACCEPTANCE IN CHURCHES

What's absolutely astonishing is that whole movements of evangelical and post-evangelical churches now call for Christians to deemphasize orthodoxy (right belief) for the sake of orthopraxy (right practice), thinking that this call will somehow free Christians to love truly and authentically. Mid-twentieth-century pastor D. Martyn Lloyd-Jones's indictment of the church in his generation is surely even more relevant today:

> There have been periods in history when the preservation of the very life of the Church depended upon the capacity and readiness of certain great leaders to differentiate truth from error and boldly to hold fast to the good and to reject the false. But our generation does not like anything of the kind. It is against any clear and precise demarcation of truth and error.[49]

As evangelical and post-evangelical leaders call the church to realign its emphases, tragically, they are calling for the church to capitulate to the worst perversions and prostitutions of love devised by the secular West over the last several centuries: love as self-expression, love as consumer satisfaction, love as "size matters," love as commitment-lessness, love as whatever works for you. Earlier I asked what happens when humans use idols to justify their actions and relationships. The answer is that they choose their own lifestyle, call it "loving," and then place God's stamp of approval upon it. Furthermore, any Christian institution that seeks to enforce its boundaries and policies becomes the target of criticism.

When conservative evangelicals trace out their theological ancestry, they are quick to say that someone like Friedrich Schleiermacher represents the

---

[49]From D. Martyn Lloyd-Jones, *Maintaining the Evangelical Faith Today* (Nottingham, UK: Inter-Varsity, 1952), 4–5.

place in the genealogy tree where theological liberalism sprouted a branch, and should not be confused with their own line. Schleiermacher, who was planted and cultivated in the nursery of Romanticism, asked not to be counted among those propositional theologians who "believe the salvation of the world and the light of wisdom are to be found in a new vesture of formulas, or a new arrangement of immediate proofs."[50] Rather, true religion, he said, "is to have life and know life in immediate feeling"; so he tells his reader "to fix your regard on the inward emotions and dispositions."[51]

Now, Schleiermacher's idea of "feeling" is a bit more complicated than the conscious sensations we describe in English as "feelings." Still, it's not hard to see how his approach to encountering God on some pre-reflective, intuitive plain mirrors the average conservative churchgoer who walks into the worship service on Sunday morning hoping to encounter a therapeutic experience of God's love through closing her eyes and expressing *her* love for God in the cycling chants of praise choruses. Schleiermacher may have been barred from the front door, but he snuck in the back, a door unlocked by an entire culture that has been duped into believing that love is primarily a matter of self-expression and self-fulfillment. "Emotivism," which is the view that all truth claims are simply expressions of our emotional attitudes, "has become embodied in our culture," says philosopher Alasdair MacIntyre. Hence, Christians today, like everyone else in our culture, will "talk and act *as if* emotivism were true, no matter what their avowed theoretical standpoint may be."[52] Evangelicals might claim to care about doctrine, but too often their religion is conducted on a purely emotional plane: "What's God saying to you?"; "The Lord is calling me to another church"; "What would Jesus do?"

The post-evangelicals then claim to have moved beyond the liberal-conservative theological divides and wag their fingers at the evangelicals, arguing that the evangelical's method of doctrinal formulation is merely a vestige of Enlightenment rationalism. That conversation is over, the post-evangelicals say. In so doing, ironically, they merely rehash Schleiermacher himself and completely fail to recognize that their very life and breath as post-evangelicals depends on the fact that their evangelical parents birthed and raised them in Schleiermacher's house, even if they said it was someone else's house.

THE INEVITABILITY OF PRAGMATISM

Whenever truth, dogma, and boundary lines are swept to the side in churches, pragmatism almost always follows, just as it does in philosophical circles. "Will

---

[50] Friedrich Schleiermacher, *On Religion: Speeches to Its Cultured Despisers,* trans. John Oman (New York: Harper and Row, 1958), 17.
[51] Ibid., 36, 18.
[52] Alasdair MacIntyre, *After Virtue: A Study in Moral Theory,* 2nd ed. (London: Duckworth, 1985), 22.

it work?" becomes the main question church leaders ask when considering their gatherings, ministries, and programs. It shouldn't surprise us, therefore, that pragmatism reigns supreme in churches in the postmodern West, whether the churches are revivalistic, liberal mainline, seeker-sensitive, emerging, or simply led by individuals who are really nice and do all they can to avoid the disagreements sometimes provoked by doctrine. Many explicitly orthodox revivalistic churches of the World War II generation, many supposedly orthodox seeker churches of the babyboomer generation, and many nonorthodox emerging churches of the Gen-Xers have handed the reins over to "what works." Each generation has simply discovered that something different works for its time and place.

In and of itself, thinking pragmatically is not a bad thing. The problem comes when pragmatism fills the vacuum left by the rejection of biblical principles, such that pragmatism becomes the only principle. Pragmatism, by its very nature, requires us to base our decisions on visible, even quantifiable, results. But surely the utility of statistics in a Christian church is limited at best, deceiving at worst. Does a large church mean that the preaching has been sound or entertaining? It's hard to say. How can we quantify the movement of the supernatural? How accurately can we evaluate those things that the Bible assures us can be seen only with eyes of faith? How well can we discern what's in the mind of God?

In other words, the very things that give life and breath to the church cannot be seen or measured. A hundred Boy Scouts can meet in a room, as can a hundred Masons, as can a hundred Muslims, as can a hundred people calling themselves "Christian." What's the difference between these groups? Statistically, nothing. What's the difference between them spiritually? Hopefully, everything. But spiritual differences can be seen only with spiritual eyes. They cannot be surveyed with the kinds of questions human beings are capable of answering by checking a box, at least until ministers and churches become able to discern which conversions are genuine and which ones aren't, and whether numerical growth in the church is a sign of God's decision in eternity past to bless a church with fruitfulness or merely the effectiveness of catchy programs.

Statistics may have their uses for churches, but the most important things about a church cannot be measured—the differences between fake and real, between flesh and spirit, between the minds of men and the mind of God. Only as we stand before God on the day of judgment will the real measurement of things be revealed. Sadly, too many pastors and churches attempt to measure their ministry by what is seen rather than what is unseen.

On just this point about the unseen, ironically, the demise of doctrine doesn't lead only to pragmatism; it can also lead to a new emphasis on the leading of the

Holy Spirit.[53] It's almost as if the loss of doctrinal, boundary-making thinking allows churches to veer toward numbers-counting or Spirit-chasing (or both). This latter option leaves evangelicals appealing more and more to what the Spirit might be telling us, or to how God might be at work right here, right now. "Let's get on board with what God's doing!" The theologically conservative Henry Blackaby talks this way; so does the emerging-ish Rob Bell. And doesn't this contradict my point about evangelicals capitulating to what can be seen and measured? Surrendering to the Spirit's movement is a sign of humility, right?

I certainly would not propose that Christians *shouldn't* submit their plans to the Spirit. He does wonderfully incline the hearts of believers in various directions. I'm simply observing that some churches that talk much about humbly submitting to what the Spirit *might* be saying simultaneously fail to scrupulously submit to what the Spirit *has* spoken in Scripture. I don't mean to conflate Scripture with the doctrines formulated by men, but I do assume that if Scripture is to have any value for human beings, we must be able to make concrete statements about what it's saying—i.e., doctrinal statements. If then neither Scripture nor doctrine guides how our churches gather, organize, and accomplish their Great Commission mandate, could it be that we are invoking the Spirit's name simply to justify our own fancies? In an era skeptical toward all dogma, won't this at least be a greater temptation?

Connecting the Dots

It isn't difficult to connect the dots between our culture's individualism, consumerism, reluctance to commit, and skepticism toward all forms of dogma to the reluctance of Christians to join churches, or at least to conceive of their Christianity as deeply dependent on their church membership. Any institutional house rules that bind or loose individuals and place them into hierarchical structures will inevitably be unpopular.

In a culture where the historical heroes have names like Franklin, Douglass, or Earhart, and where the fictional heroes have names like Jason Bourne or Indiana Jones; in a culture where the physical surroundings of our lives—from houses to clothes to dinner plates—are all the product of our choices, where divorce is up and job permanence is down, where all truth is held with a loose grip, and where people are enamored with statistics—in this kind of culture, we will grow up comparatively convinced of our ability to make wise choices about our spiritual

---

[53]For instance, Mark Noll writes, "The new charismatic movement blurred the barriers of Protestant-Catholic demarcation as participants together followed the wind of the Spirit." *Is the Reformation Over?* (Grand Rapids, Baker, 2005), 65. Though Noll does not present this as a negative example of doctrinal deterioration—insofar as his book attempts to further collapse the wall between Protestants and Roman Catholics—it does serve for our purposes as one example of the inverse relationship in contemporary churches between attention given to doctrinal distinctives and that given to movements of the Holy Spirit.

condition.[54] We'll think that we can manage our spiritual lives quite well. Compared to people in other times and places, therefore, we will probably be more likely to view a commitment and submission to one local church with either indifference or suspicion; and we'll justify doing so by redefining the word *love*.

I'm often leery of sociological blanket statements because, in the final analysis, they are unavoidably speculative. Who but God knows why people—much less whole societies—do what they do? Still, if the reader will permit some degree of speculation, I believe it's fairly reasonable to conjecture that Christians living in an individualistic society are more likely to find the doctrines of church membership and discipline a stumbling block, at least compared to Christians living in a culture less inclined to define individuals as isolated units.

Step 6: But what is individualism really? It's a hatred of authority. And behind the hatred of authority is a diminished God.

The Root Problem

But the drama of the Individual is more complicated than can be conveyed by this blanket statement. Many of the writers and church leaders explicitly calling for the de-institutionalization of the church aren't strident individualists but committed communitarians. They argue that the impersonal structures of membership classes, membership packets, members-only ministries, leadership hierarchies, traditional forms of service, extensive statements of faith, acts of discipline, and so forth stand in the way of broken and hurting human beings learning to love one another, to care for the outsider, and to bring healing to the larger community. The critics of a rigorous orthodoxy are committed not to free agency but to a relational conception of the human being. They believe that human peace, meaningfulness, and joy can be found only in community.

So here I am, arguing that many Christians in the West are anti-institutional and reluctant to join anything due to their underlying individualistic assumptions. But some of the most explicitly anti-institutional leaders and writers are also explicitly anti-individualistic! Am I missing the point?

---

[54]Sure enough, a 2007 press release entitled, "American Individualism Shines Through in People's Self-Image," from the polling organization of George Barna, observes, "Based on interviews with a nationally representative sample of more than 4000 adults, the self-image of American adults came through loud and clear. Most Americans think of themselves as leaders (71%) and believe they are well-informed about current events (81%). They almost unanimously view themselves as independent thinkers (95%), and as loyal and reliable people (98%). They also say they are able to easily adapt to changes and a whopping four out of five people believe they are making a positive difference in the world. Two out of three adults noted that they like to be in control of situations. And while most Americans contend that they are free thinkers who are "very open" to alternative moral views (75%), a huge majority support traditional family values (92%), resulting in a large majority who claim to be concerned about the moral state of the nation (86%). Interestingly, though, only one out of four adults is concerned enough to try to convince other people to change their views on such issues" (July 23, 2007; http://www.barna.org/FlexPage.aspx? Page=BarnaUpdate&BarnaUpdateID=275; accessed January 23, 2008).

COMMUNITARIANISM

It's worth observing that one prominent aspect of the so-called postmodern worldview over and against the modern view is the prominence given to the community over and against the individual. It does this descriptively, asserting that our very sense of self is necessarily determined by the overlapping linguistic, ethnic, economic, and gender groups we occupy. Sometimes it does this normatively, asserting that we as individuals *should* seek to live our lives with greater group or community mindedness since none of us are, after all, islands.

I appreciate and agree with certain elements of the communitarian literature, whether in its approaches to political philosophy or to the life of the local church community. It often provides a more sophisticated and realistic anthropology than most of what has preceded it. Yet insofar as much of it allows (even insists upon) its anthropology to form and determine its theology, we must handle it with care. The various social, ethnic, or national groups you and I occupy will no doubt shape how we understand God's revelation of himself in the Scriptures, as I suggested earlier, but that does not mean we cannot apprehend by his Spirit a right and true understanding of his Scriptures.

Not only that, but the postmodern and communitarian reaction against modernistic individualism remains derivative of that individualism, just as the counter-Enlightenment Romantics derived significant aspects of their worldview from the Enlightenment. The postmodern self may be socially constituted and delimited—no "I" exists in the more radical formulations—but within his limitations no authority exists to stay his hand or say to him, "What have you done?" He can come and go as he pleases, invoking this or that group membership according to whim.

ANTI-AUTHORITY-ISM

I do not believe that the communitarian proposal provides any true antidote to individualism and its corollaries such as consumerism. They argue that community is the antidote to individualism. It's not, which brings us to one of the central themes of this book: the real problem is anti-authority-ism. At the risk of sounding like the late modernist Friedrich Nietzsche or the radical postmodernist Michel Foucault, it's all about power. At the risk of sounding like a fundamentalist Sunday school teacher, it's all about disobedience. Some contemporary writers get this; others don't. It's not quite enough to say that the problem of modernity was individualism, because the term is too vague. The problem bequeathed by Descartes and everyone of his ilk is more accurately described as *autonomous* individualism—auto-nomos meaning "self law"—where we're letting the adjective, not the noun, do the real work of making our point. The solution to individualism is not community. The solution—one fears to say it without pages of qualifications—is to reintroduce a conception of submission to God's revealed will as it's located in the local church.

The campaign that Western culture has been waging for several centuries *for* the individual has been a campaign waged *against* all forms of authority. From elementary school through graduate school, Western educators have taught us to question authority: the authority of the church because of what it did to Galileo; the authority of the king because of his usurpations; the authority of the majority because of its tyrannies; the authority of males because of their exercise of brute strength and acts of oppression; the authority of the Bible because of its alleged contradictions; the authority of science because of its paradigm shifts; the authority of philosophy because of its language games; the authority of language because it has been deconstructed; the authority of parents because they're not cool; the authority of the market because of its extravagant inequalities; the authority of the police because of their fire hoses and night sticks; the authority of religious leaders because they'll make us drink the Kool-Aid; the authority of the media because of its biases; the authority of superpowers because of their imperialism. Are there any authorities left to question? When it comes to what we should believe and how we should live, a ubiquitous suspicion of authority lurks in the minds of most Westerners today, in part because we're familiar with authority's savage history of abuses.

From the very start, the Enlightenment's story of individualism has really been a story about the battle against authority, which is why Descartes' philosophical method begins with complete skepticism toward every external epistemological authority. From there, he constructed a worldview entirely on internal resources with his famous *cogito ergo sum*—"I think, therefore I am." One communitarian philosopher has characterized Descartes' project as yielding a "disengaged self."[55] But it's more than that. The self isn't simply unconnected or disengaged; it's defiant. Where Yahweh, the maker of heaven and earth, described himself to Moses as the self-defining, predicate-less "I AM" (*ego sum* in the Vulgate), Descartes grounded his knowledge of his own existence and, from there, his knowledge of all things including God in the predicate of his own rationality: "I know that I exist because *I am a thinking thing.*" With this famous turn to the subject, the individual became the adjudicator of all reality. Yahweh was dismissed. No longer was the individual to rely on the church, the parent, the king, or the teacher to dictate true and false, right and wrong; the individual was to judge reality for himself.

The Romantics of the counter-Enlightenment, as much as they rejected the ordered structures and doctrinaire propositions of their rationalistic predeces-

---

[55] Charles Taylor, *Sources of the Self*, chap. 8, esp. 155–58.

sors, shared in this same rejection of all external authority. In that sense, the Romantic and the Classicist were two children of the same parents, even if they looked different externally.

In my mind, the opening scene of Ayn Rand's 1943 *Fountainhead* captures the logical culmination of Descartes' turn to the subject and presents one of the most God-toppling, man-exalting moments in Western literature. It's worth observing how Rand's primeval imagery evokes the feel of the Bible's opening two chapters. Her hero is simultaneously Adam *and* God:

> Howard Roark laughed. He stood naked at the edge of a cliff. . . . The lake below was only a thin steel ring that cut the rocks in half. The rocks went on into the depth, unchanged. They began and ended in the sky. So that the world seemed suspended in space, an island floating on nothing, anchored to the feet of the man on the cliff. His body leaned back against the sky. It was a body of long straight lines and angles, each curve broken into planes. He stood, rigid, his hands hanging at his sides, palms out. He felt his shoulder blades drawn tight together, the curve of his neck, and the weight of the blood in his hands. . . . His face was like a law of nature—a thing one could not question, alter or implore. It had high cheekbones over gaunt, hollow cheeks; gray eyes, cold and steady; a contemptuous mouth, shut tight, the mouth of an executioner or a saint. He looked at the granite. To be cut, he thought, and made into walls. He looked at a tree. To be split and made into rafters. He looked at a streak of rust on the stone and thought of iron ore under the ground. To be melted and to emerge as girders against the sky. These rocks, he thought, are here for me; waiting for the drill, the dynamite and my voice; waiting to be split, ripped, pounded, reborn; waiting for the shape my hands will give them.[56]

From our standpoint, the problem with this fictional Howard Roark is not simply that he has an under-realized conception of his social embeddedness and need for community, though that's true. The problem is the idolatry of self. The problem is that he thinks he's God, and the philosophies of both modernism and postmodernism legitimate this ambition.[57]

If one objects that Ayn Rand's *Fountainhead* is an obscure piece of twentieth-century literature that most Christians probably haven't read, they're missing the point. Even if we cannot trace a direct line of genealogical causality between a particular book and the worldviews embraced within a culture, we need only remember the reasonable communitarian presupposition that an author like Rand, her many readers, and those writers who came before and after her all

---

[56] Ayn Rand, *The Fountainhead* (1943; repr. New York: Signet, 1993), 15–16.
[57] Should someone contest that postmodernism, in fact, abhors such grandiose ambitions and does all it can to deconstruct such claims, we need only ask the postmodernist why he thinks he has the authority to deconstruct. The truth is that the deconstructing postmodern individual remains just as autonomous—self-ruling—as the modern individual, even if he posits authority merely in his ability to declare all truth null and void. In that sense, deconstructionism deconstructs itself.

grew out of the same soil—the soil we still live in today. Isn't Howard Roark just one more American Adam? From the standpoint of how Christians define leadership, don't many churches look for visionary pastors like Roark—men who create whole new empires with a plan, a book, some personal dynamism, and, oh yes, the prayers of the church? Roark's braggadocio is an all too familiar picture of the successful leader, entrepreneur, and self-made man of today, secular and sacred.[58] And such a figure knows no authority but the limits of his or her imagination.

Now, it's probably an overstatement to say that Westerners today believe that all authority is always bad. Most people recognize its temporary utility in the organization of day-to-day life. Someone has to make laws. Someone has to teach the class. Someone has to run the office. That said, authority is something with which we "contract," to use the language of the early democratic theorists. It's something to which we, the governed, must give our consent. The final and absolute authority for what to believe and how to live remains the individual. The individual may temporarily cede his or her authority to another for the sake of a strategic advantage. So a man may agree to yield some of his own authority to a constitution. A woman may agree to yield some of her authority to a job contract. A couple may agree to yield some of their authority to one another in a wedding vow. But all such arrangements are finally temporary because they are contractual and rely upon the consent of free and equal parties.

In short, no true conception of authority exists, which is the point that nineteenth-century Danish philosopher and theologian Søren Kierkegaard makes in his essay "Of the Difference between a Genius and an Apostle" when he writes, "To honor one's father because he is intelligent is impiety."[59] What does Kierkegaard mean? We follow geniuses when what they say accords with our own sense of what is rational or right. No true acknowledgment of their authority occurs. In that sense, it's impious to transpose the language of the fifth commandment into such a domain; the child who honors his father because he is intelligent is not truly *honoring* his father. The difference between a genius and an apostle, then, is that, unlike a genius, an apostle speaks with divinely granted authority, and whether his words sound wise or foolish (cf. 1 Cor. 1:18ff.), he is to be obeyed.

---

[58] As it happens with Ayn Rand, however, it's not too difficult to speculate about possible lines of causality when we consider the immensity of the impact someone such as former Federal Reserve Chairman Alan Greenspan, who often boasted of his love for Rand's work, had on the entire U.S. economy and America's way of life in the last decades of the twentieth century. Is it unreasonable to think that the economic conceptions of growth and vitality that garner so much of our conscious attention when reading the morning newspaper, considering which candidate to vote for, or determining whether interest rates are conducive to refinancing our home mortgages, do not also deeply impact our expectations of growth and vitality at church? In her book *Greed: The Seven Deadly Sins* (New York: Oxford University Press, 2006), Phyllis A. Tickle argues that "the trajectory from Adam Smith to Ayn Rand to Arthur Andersen has been irreversibly plotted"; 40.

[59] Cited in Gilbert Meilaender, "Conscience and Authority," *First Things* (November 2007): 33.

AUTHORITY IN CHURCHES

Is authority a popular idea in churches? Everything from the debates over the role of women in the church and home to the debates over God's authority over the future and salvation suggests otherwise. Evangelicals speak and think in the language of authority about as often as they practice church discipline, which is to say almost not at all. What's striking is how these debates about authority among Christians are often played out in the language of love. To bar women from becoming pastors or sharing an equality of leadership in the home is regarded as a failure to respect, honor, and love women. To exclude an individual from the fellowship of the church for unrepentant sin is called unloving. To hold that God is sovereign over salvation and the future is regarded as a failure to recognize God's love. "But God is loving! He wouldn't do that," many are quick to say.

In the minds of many Western Christians, the ideas of love and authority remain almost wholly at odds. Perhaps the most significant sign of this fact is the scarcity of biblical or expositional preaching. A church that embraces sound, expositional preaching is a church that has at least begun to recognize God's intention to employ authoritative pronouncements through human mediators in our life and growth as Christians. A church that embraces sound, expositional preaching has at least begun to recognize that Christ enters the Christian's life with the authority of a king who commands repentance and obedience. So this church gathers to hear what the king has authoritatively said in his Word. Sadly, too few churches embrace such preaching as the center of their lives together. Preachers instead choose their therapeutic topics according to what they perceive the congregation needs. They want to scratch where the congregation itches. Again, a church that doesn't embrace expositional preaching is a church that has probably pitted love against authority.

Perhaps more than any other cultural theme we have discussed, the question of authority is relevant to the discussion of local church membership and discipline, because membership and discipline involve a life of submission. Church membership *is*, among other things, submission to the discipline of a particular congregation. In one sense, I believe that that act of submission is contractual and temporal in that no local church is ultimate. In another sense, I believe that that act of submission is *not* contractual in that it's predicated on ultimate realities accomplished by Jesus Christ's work of death and resurrection and his claim on Christian lives as king and lord.

If the DNA of our fallen natures and our cultural mind-sets are inherently suspicious of all authority, the practices of church membership and discipline, to put it bluntly, will make for a tougher sell. Different Christians and different churches will view authority with more or less suspicion. And no doubt, one of the very real difficulties we have to work through in this discussion is knowing what it means to submit in a fallen world where authority—including church authority—is so often abused. What do we do with the Jim Jones's cults of the world, where authority is used to induce mass suicide? How do we understand authority and its uses when Nazi officers like Adolph Eichmann use precisely this argument—"We were just following orders"—to justify massacring millions of people? In other words, this discussion will eventually have to give consideration to the question of how we balance conceptions of church authority with the authority of the individual conscience before God, lest we simply reduplicate the mistakes and terrors of history that both modernism and postmodernism are rightly set against.

Along these lines, it may be worthwhile at this point to offer a reader advisory. Part of me is sincerely worried about speaking favorably of authority in what follows and throughout this book in light of the number of Christian leaders who continue to abuse authority, whether in the church or the home. How many hurting Christians have known little other than selfishness from the hands of pastors, husbands, parents, or churches in the name of God or authority. Part of me is therefore inclined to tell any reader who already affirms the role of authority in the church to continue no further, for fear of affirming him in his abusive ways. My argument is, in one sense, intended principally for the opposite crowd—churches and leaders who cannot conceive of any role for authority. That said, I hope that a more careful biblical examination of the concept will demonstrate that godly authority is not something that steals life but authors life. It is something, I trust, that both the abusers and the eschewers of authority need to hear.

Wherever we're coming from, one crucial component of a Christian investigation into membership and discipline must include the question of whether our suspicions and affirmations concerning authority match the Bible's suspicions and affirmations.

Secularizing the Idea of Disobedience

Though the idea of individualism is helpful, we need to be aware of the fact that it can secularize the problem of Western culture. Let me illustrate with another example. We can talk about "insecurities" or we can talk about the "fear of man." The latter is about our relationship with other people in respect to God. The former is exclusively about our relationship with other people. It's secularized. Here's another example: We can talk about "consumerism" or we can talk about "greed." The two ideas get at the same thing, but the first idea is shorn of any supernatural awkwardness. "Consumerism" sounds like the civil words of a sociologist, while "greed" sounds like a pulpit-pounding fundamentalist preacher's word. But that's what consumerism is. It's plain old greed.[60] Greed is acted out among other human beings, yes, but greed is fundamentally a measurement of where we stand in relation to God. It's a form of idolatry (Col. 3:5; Eph. 5:5).

Sociologists' words such as *consumerism* and psychologists' words such as *insecurity* are helpful to a point because they enable us to separate one guise of sin from another. But when we go to actually address problems such as insecurity or consumerism, we won't get very far if we don't pull off these secular masks and call them by their old-fashioned, Sunday-school sounding names: fear of man and greed. For instance, we shouldn't address insecurity by pointing to its opposite—self-confidence; we should talk about the fear of God. We shouldn't address consumerism by reading sociological treatises but talk about the fact that *things* have supplanted God as an object of worship.

I'm lingering on this point because so much secular *and* Christian literature attempts to address individualism by giving three cheers for its opposite—community. The language and literature about individualism can help us to see and describe some of the symptoms of the problem: people are reluctant to make commitments to others and to be held accountable. People dismiss any sort of boundaries beyond their own preferences and foolishly think they can define themselves in a good and right way outside their connections to other people. But when we treat "individualism" as the root problem, we have prepared the way for what I believe is, if not a misdiagnosis, at least an insufficient diagnosis, because our analysis either excludes God or involves only a greatly diminished God.

Here's one example of an insufficient diagnosis. One academic writes, "My contention is that the distinctive failures of our era derive from its failures of due relatedness to God."[61] Our problems, he says, are a matter of "due relatedness." Well, that's sort of right. But is this how the apostle Paul or the prophet Jeremiah put it: "Thus says the Lord, 'I have observed a failure of due relatedness, O Israel'"? In one sense, yes, Israel failed to relate to God, but it's how they failed to relate to him that counts. They failed to obey him. They failed to listen to his commands. God is interested in a relationship with human beings, but he's interested in a relationship that is structured in a particular way. He's interested in an authoritatively asymmetrical relationship—that is, he's the king to be worshiped; we are not. Perhaps this author meant all these things to be packed into his thin adjective "due." But his emphasis—the noun—was clearly on this idea of relatedness. Even in speaking about a relationship with God, ironically, the relationship can be secularized when we pull God down to our

---

[60]See Phyllis A. Tickle, *Greed*, 38, 40.
[61]Colin E. Gunton, *The One, the Three and the Many*, 38.

level and deprive him of the things that make him God. With this theologian and with a number of others, relationality replaces lordship.[62]

When we pull off the somewhat secularized mask of individualism, what we find behind it is a fear of, nay, a hatred of, authority. It's not relationships that people are so afraid of; people long for relationships, as the entire Romantic movement attests to. Rather, it's a particular kind of relationship that people despise. The real problem then is not finally individualism; it's anti-authority-ism. Loneliness is not the problem. A refusal to live life on anyone else's terms is.

A Diminished God

Let me try to explain this in one other way. This emphasis on relationship, as I suggested earlier, has become very common in theological literature today, with more and more writers insisting on the fact that we as individuals do not precede our relationships; rather, it's our relationships that constitute us as individuals. "I" am not who "I" am until my mother and father, sisters and brothers, friends and enemies, culture and church interact with me and participate in the creation of my identity. Wolfhart Pannenberg refers to the "exocentricity" of human nature, meaning that God created us not to be egocentric but outwardly connected and constituted.[63] John Zizioulas argues that since the being of God consists of a community of persons, humanity in its rightful state likewise exists, not as individuals, but as persons in community.[64] Among these types of writers, sin is then characterized as a breaking of relationship or a despoiling of relational shalom between man and God, man and man, and man and cosmos. Salvation is regarded as a reconciling of broken relationships.

I can affirm all of this, and I hesitate to offer a critique because I believe the church can benefit from these kinds of insights. But I do fear there may be a deep hole right in the heart of this communitarian project—a greatly diminished God. In making such a claim, I don't pretend to account for every sentence in every book among writers of this ilk. For that reason, let us just assume that I'm only addressing a tendency that I've observed, one that, I hope, doesn't finally do justice to anyone. Still, addressing the matter in this fashion will allow us to see what *is* needed.

Here's how one recent writer characterizes sin: "The wages of sin is death, because, if our life has its basis in our relationship to God and to other people

---

[62]This is how Stanley Grenz characterizes Moltmann in *Rediscovering the Triune God: The Trinity in Contemporary Theology* (Minneapolis, Fortress, 2004), 84, citing Moltmann's *Trinity and the Kingdom* and *God in Creation*, trans. Margaret Kohl (Minneapolis: Fortress, 1993), 221.
[63]Wolfhart Pannenberg, *Anthropology in Theological Perspective* (Philadelphia: Westminster Press, 1985).
[64]John D. Zizioulas, *Being as Communion: Studies in Personhood and the Church* (Crestwood, NY: St. Vladimir's Seminary Press, 1985), 16–19; 36–65.

and if these relationships are corrupted, our very life is threatened to its core."[65] Again, that's true, but it doesn't go far enough. The wages of sin is death not just because our sin breaks our relationship with God, who is the source of life; the wages of sin is death because it offends against his glorious, beautiful, holy, resplendent majesty! The wages of sin is death because God's glory is weighty and infinite, and we have fallen short of it. The wages of sin is death because God is worthy of all honor, worship, and praise, and we have brushed him off. When his glory is not appropriately honored and valued, that is, when we fall short of his glory through sin, we become judicially guilty, and a payment is required. To say that no payment is required is to say that his glory really holds no value. Break something that's cheap and no one will care. Break something exquisite and precious, however, and its value is demonstrated—in part—in the fact that a payment is required. God, who is jealous for his glory and name, would have demonstrated that he's weightless and worthless should he have chosen to save sinful humanity without demanding a just payment for transgressions against his glorious person and character.

As such, sin is more than a broken relationship, and salvation is more than a restored relationship. Sin is *an offending against majesty*, and salvation is *a restoration to the adoration of majesty*—"having no other gods," in Moses' words; "loving God with heart, mind, soul, and strength," in Jesus' words.[66] This is why one Puritan prayer reads, "Let me never forget that the heinousness of sin lies not so much in the nature of the sin committed, as in the greatness of the Person sinned against."[67] What individualistic humans need are not just relationships, even relationships of mutual love and concern. Rather, humans need relationships that move them toward the worship and honor and prizing of God and his glory.[68] The communitarian solution, I fear, shows how individualistic our individualism has become—we value ourselves so much that we have difficulty conceiving how offensive our sin is against his glorious person.

The Bible's call to obedience and submission before God's authority is rooted in his glory and majesty. The despising of authority, therefore, is finally a despising of his glory. In other words, identifying the real problem as anti-

---

[65]Tom Smail, *Like Father, Like Son: The Trinity Imagined in Our Humanity* (Grand Rapids: Eerdmans, 2005), 238.

[66]Cf. John Calvin, *Institutes of the Christian Religion*, vol. 1., ed. John T. McNeill (Philadelphia: Westminster, 1960), 39.

[67]From the prayer entitled, "Humiliation," in *The Valley of Vision*, ed. Arthur Bennet (Edinburgh: Banner of Truth, 2002), 143.

[68]One other writer of a communitarian bent, Miroslav Volf, amazingly, *seems* to place a light, man-centered God right into the heart of his description of God's glory when he defines God's glory as "God's love" for "the good of the creation," in *Free of Charge: Giving and Forgiving in a Culture Stripped of Grace* (Grand Rapids: Zondervan, 2005), 62; also 39. I say "seems" because his statements are brief and could use further elaboration.

authority-ism and not just individualism doesn't even push us far enough. The real problem, finally, is a hatred of God's majesty and worth.

Step 7: Church membership, then, begins with repentance.

Repentance

If the root problem in our culture and in our churches is anti-authority-ism and the despising of God's glory, then the solution is not simply joining community and making relationships; the solution is repentance. It's a changing of heart and direction. This repentance includes joining a community and making relationships, but it's joining a particular kind of community where self is no longer sovereign and where one is called to obedience to others as an expression of obedience to God. It's the joining of a community where the worship of God is supreme in everything.

In the coming chapters, we will see that entering into biblical church membership means submitting oneself to a body of relationships with implicit authoritative structures, a body in which different members assume different roles even though together they constitute one body. It requires us to repent of self-rule. Most Christians don't think of themselves as repenting or, analogously, submitting when they join a church. Maybe they feel lonely and join the church for fellowship. Maybe they have considered the biblical arguments for church membership and become persuaded that it's the right thing to do. Maybe they've never thought about it at all and have just done what all the Christians they know do. But whatever their conscious experience, joining a church is fundamentally a matter of repentance and obedience. It's certainly not a matter of joining some club with various membership privileges, as when one joins a country club. Insofar as the word *member* carries that connotation in Western minds, it's an unfortunate word to use. Still, it's a good word to use, because submitting to a local church and becoming a member is an external enactment of what it means to submit to Christ and become a member of his body. It's keeping the imperative of what Christ has accomplished in the indicative. Submitting to a local church on earth, in the language of Christian ethics, is *a becoming of what we are* in heaven.

Conclusion

Here's the take-away from this chapter: among Christians today, the topics of church membership and discipline have been explicitly critiqued by some and quietly rejected by many. This is so, I have argued, because in our individualistic, skeptical, anti-authority, God-despising age, we are instinctively repulsed by the idea of *being bound* by anything. So we have redefined God and the expectations of his love in such a way that we are not required to do so. We have erected an idol and called it "love." And this idol called love has two great commands: "Know that God loves you by not permanently binding you to anything (especially if you *really* don't want to be)" and, following from it, "Know that your neighbor loves you best by letting you express yourself entirely and without judgment."

My hope is that identifying these problems will aid us as we turn, in the remainder of the book, to consider how belonging to a local church and submitting to its discipline should comprise the basic shape of the Christian life.

PART 2

LOVE REDEFINED

CHAPTER TWO

THE NATURE OF LOVE

"Bring me that higher love."
—*Steve Winwood*

Main Questions: What is God's love like and why does it offend us? What's the connection between our understanding of God's love and church membership?

Main Answers: God's love creates and affirms us, but it does so for the purposes of winning praise to himself. The holiness or God-centeredness of God's love offends us because it brings both salvation and judgment. Church membership and discipline therefore offend us because they picture both salvation and judgment, and draw a line between them.

Step 1: In ways we don't expect, God's love both attracts and repels us, which means God's gospel and God's church also attract and repel us.

The word *inquisition* refers to any judicial inquiry, but it is most famously used to refer to the ecclesiastical tribunals established by the Roman Catholic Church between the twelfth and nineteenth centuries for prosecuting deviations in doctrine and deed.

The Puritans may have a bad name for their excesses in matters of church membership and discipline, as we saw with Nathaniel Hawthorne's *Scarlet Letter*, but the Roman Catholic Inquisitions surely have an even worse reputation, and deservedly so. The individuals accused of heresy were tried in private. They were not always told what charges had been brought against them. They could not call witnesses to speak in their defense. Lawyers were often reluctant to defend the accused for fear of being charged with abetting heresy.[1] It's hardly surprising that, in the Spanish Inquisition, for instance, 40 percent of the accused were executed.

Fyodor Dostoyevsky sets the story "The Grand Inquisitor," from his novel *The Brothers Karamazov*, in sixteenth-century Seville, Spain, in what he describes as "the most dreadful period of the Inquisition, when bonfires glowed through-

---

[1] "Inquisition," in *The Oxford Dictionary of the Christian Church*, 3rd ed. F. L. Cross and E. A. Livingstone, (New York: Oxford University Press, 1997), 836–37.,

out the land every day to the glory of God." It's a strange tale. It begins with Jesus quietly appearing on the streets of the city, not as his second coming but only "to visit his children for an instant."

Everyone immediately recognizes Jesus and surrounds him with adoration, to which he responds with "infinite compassion." His "heart burns with love" for the people. He resumes the healing activity that marked his original ministry on earth. The people weep and kiss the ground on which he walks. The children throw flowers and cry, "Hosanna!" At one point, Jesus stops a funeral procession carrying the open coffin of a dead girl. He softly pronounces, "*Talitha cumi,*" and the girl rises with smiling and astonished eyes. The crowd sobs with wonder.

Meanwhile, an aged observer stands back and assesses the scene. Seeing only ballyhoo, the observer, the cardinal grand inquisitor himself, an individual whose authority would have come directly from the pope, eventually intervenes and arrests Jesus. He then steps into Jesus' prison cell and challenges him without a trace of intimidation:

> Is it you? You? . . . No, do not reply, keep silent. And in any case, what could you possibly say? I know only too well what you would say. And you have no right to add anything to what was said by you in former times. Why have you come to get in our way? For you have come to get in our way, and you yourself know it. But do you know what will happen tomorrow? . . . I shall find you guilty and burn you at the stake as the most wicked of heretics, and those same people who today kissed your feet will tomorrow at one wave of my hand rush to rake up the embers on your bonfire, do you know that? Yes, I dare say you do.

Along the way, the grand inquisitor reminds Jesus that he himself had given the church the authority to unite or exclude to itself whomever it pleased: "You gave your promises, you sealed it with your word, you gave us the right to bind and loose, and so of course you cannot even dream of taking that right from us now."[2]

Don't confuse Jesus for the institutionalized church. That seems to be the moral of this story. Is it? Perhaps it was one of Dostoyevsky's points.

A Love That Attracts and Repels

Dostoyevsky was no fan of the Roman Catholic Church and on more than one occasion pitted its cold authority against the warm light of Christ's love, though in his story he does seem to use the inquisitor to represent skepticism more broadly. This particular story famously ends with Christ responding to the inquisitor's incisive arguments—arguments which Dostoyevsky conceded

---

[2]*The Brothers Karamazov*, trans. David McDuff (New York: Penguin Books, 2003), 325–26, 328.

in personal letters that he found compelling—with only a kiss on the mouth. The kiss burns in the old man's heart, and love mysteriously prevails against rational skepticism.

With a little postmodern presumption (never mind authorial intent), I'd like to offer a different moral for the story. Dostoyevsky might have pitched the inquisitor as the bad guy, but I would propose that Jesus is really the bad guy.

We claim to find comfort in the fact that *God is love*, as the apostle John put it. We pine after him. We talk of him incessantly. We spend centuries waiting for him. We prepare for his coming by building grand religious edifices. But when this God who is love comes, we, like the grand inquisitor, imprison, interrogate, and then kill him. That's why Christ's compassionate acts could draw great crowds that in the next moment would turn and lunge at him with bared fangs, like a startled dog or provoked bear (Matt. 21:9; 27:20ff.; cf. Prov. 17:12). Every one of us does this, including the author of "The Grand Inquisitor."[3] The story is powerful because it points to something deep in all of our hearts—a hatred not just for God but for his love!

What people fail to realize is that true love—God's love—simultaneously attracts and repels *all* of us. It's a thing of beauty and a thing of gross offense to the fallen heart. That's why Jesus is the bad guy, at least in our minds. Gaze upon the love of God from one angle, and it will appear as the most resplendent thing in all the universe. But walk a few yards and look up again, and you will find that your lip snarls, your fists clench, and your heart becomes morally offended. It's the same thing you're looking at—God's love. You're just seeing it from a different angle.

Christ was crucified not just by the religious authorities of his day, as Dostoyevsky and so many Christian writers today would picture it. He was crucified by Everyman. He was crucified by you and me. Don't finally blame the Inquisition on Roman Catholic institutionalism. Blame it on your idolatrous heart and mine. The painter Rembrandt got it right when he painted himself into Christ's crucifixion scene as one of the crucifiers.

It's not ultimately the institutionalization of Christianity that so gravely offends our sensibilities, whether in Dostoyevsky or in current conversations about church institutionalism. Yes, legalistic structures are offensive, but the real offense goes far deeper. It roots in the nature of Christ's love itself. Christ's love, though beautiful to the natural man by common grace, also offends him (see 1 Cor. 2:14). We like all the talk of compassion and caring for the downtrodden.

---

[3]Kevin Vanhoozer gets it exactly right, I think, when he writes, "The love of God, as perhaps no other theological topic, is particularly vulnerable to Feuerbach's suspicion that doctrines are projections of human ideals," in his introduction to *Nothing Greater, Nothing Better: Theological Essays on the Love of God*, ed. Kevin J. Vanhoozer (Grand Rapids: Eerdmans, 2001), p. 2 n. 1.

Our eyes sometimes weep over acts of self-sacrifice by a mother, a brother, a friend, or a lover. Still, there's something deeper about God's love that offends our natural, unregenerate eyes.

As with God's love, so with his gospel and his church. His gospel and church simultaneously attract and repel. Within the space of a few verses, the Gospel of Matthew attests that the world will both persecute God's sons for their righteousness as well as give God praise for the sons' righteous deeds (Matt. 5:10, 16). Talk about double-mindedness. Yet don't we as church leaders and Christians secretly hope to build churches that elicit one reaction and not the other? Isn't that what the church growth writers promise? Later in the Gospel, Jesus sends his disciples out to heal and then warns them they will be persecuted (Matt. 10:1–25). How strange! People typically favor those who bring them healing. Not so in the Scriptures. The natural man at once commends and condemns God, his gospel, and his people.

So what is God's love, and how could we possibly hate it? Those are the first two questions that this chapter will attempt to answer, and after we answer them we'll understand further why church membership and discipline are so offensive to us. In chapter 1 we considered the false and idolatrous conceptions of love extant in our culture and our churches. In this chapter we want to consider love as the Bible defines it. Remember, our doctrine of the church is only as good as our doctrine of God. That's the case, in part, because Jesus asked the Father to help the church share *the same love* that he shares with the Father (John 17:26), and he said that we are to love one another *as* he has loved us (John 13:34). So if we can answer the question of what God's love is like, then we'll have gone a long way toward understanding the love that holds the church together and distinguishes it from the world.

Here's the short answer of what we'll find. God's love is often conceived these days as something universal, undiscriminating, and unconditional. And behind this conception, often, is man-centeredness. Yet in Scripture we actually find that God's love is utterly God-centered, which means it's more complicated than common conception would have it. It combines salvation *and* judgment. It's gracious *and* discriminating. It moves outward *and* inward. Church membership is a picture of all these things—of salvation and judgment, grace and discrimination, inward and outward care—and therefore defines God's love for the world.

Step 2: The doctrine of God's love is more complicated biblically and theologically than people realize. Theologians before Luther centered God's love upon God.

A Difficult Doctrine

D. A. Carson opens his slim but profound volume *The Difficult Doctrine of the Love of God* with the observation that the doctrine of God's love is, like the book's title suggests, more difficult than people realize. Many people cite their favorite proof-text and think themselves done with the conversation:

- "For God so loved the world that he gave his only Son" (John 3:16);
- "In this is love, not that we have loved God but that he loved us and sent his Son to be the propitiation for our sins" (1 John 4:10);
- And, of course, "God is love" (1 John 4:8).

There it is. God loves us. More than anything. That's his nature. End of discussion. Right? Not quite.

WHY THE DOCTRINE IS COMPLICATED BIBLICALLY

Carson's book traces out five different ways that the Bible speaks of God's love.[4] It speaks of:

- The peculiar love shared between the divine Father and Son: "The Father loves the Son and has given all things into his hand" (John 3:35); "I do as the Father has commanded me, so that the world may know that I love the Father" (John 14:31).

- God's providential love over creation: the word *love* is not used here, but he pronounces everything he has made as "good," and promises to send rain on the just and unjust alike.

- God's salvific love toward the fallen world: "For God so loved the world, that he gave his only Son, that whoever believes in him should not perish but have eternal life" (John 3:16).

- God's particular and elective love toward a chosen people: "It was not because you were more in number than any other people that the LORD set his love on you and chose you, for you were the fewest of all peoples, but it is because the LORD loves you and is keeping the oath that he swore to your fathers, that the LORD has brought you out with a mighty hand and redeemed you from the house of slavery, from the hand of Pharaoh king of Egypt" (Deut. 7:7–8). "As it is written, 'Jacob I loved, but Esau I hated'" (Rom. 9:13).

---

[4]D. A. Carson, *The Difficult Doctrine of the Love of God* (Wheaton, IL: Crossway, 2000), 16–21.

- God's conditional love toward his people based on obedience: "Keep your-selves in the love of God" (Jude 21). "If you keep my commandments, you will abide in my love" (John 15:10).

The basic insight here is that the Bible refers to God's love in different ways. And we should not absolutize any one category of his love, as if to say all his love is providential love or salvific love or something else.[5]

It's a commonsensical observation when you think about it. The human experience of love is very similar. The manner in which I love the trees in my neighborhood is different from the way I love the people in my neighborhood, which is different again from how I love my wife and children.

Still, for some reason we expect relative uniformity from God, even though he too is a person. All that to say, the doctrine of God's love is difficult, first of all, because of the various strands of biblical data.

WHY THE DOCTRINE IS COMPLICATED THEOLOGICALLY

The doctrine of God's love is also difficult because of the theological questions that arise from the biblical data. After all, we expect some type of consistency between these different strands of God's love, but it's hard to know how to put it all together. It's easy to understand why I would love my own children more than the other children in the neighborhood, but why would God love differ-ent objects differently, if indeed he does? Is there some underlying principle that informs how and why God might love differently from one situation to another?

Philosophers and theologians have struggled to come to terms with what exactly love is, much less what God's love is. Plato's conception of love starts with the idea of desiring or thirsting for the good and beautiful (*eros*). Love is a longing for what we lack. Hence, love has a uniting function. Our souls are divided from one another; and love "bridges the gulf." But consider what this definition, as intuitive as it seems, means for deity. If love is a longing for what one lacks, and if the gods lack nothing, which Plato says is the case, then the gods must not love. That, anyhow, is Plato's conclusion.[6]

Like Plato, Augustine's understanding of love begins with desire or a "motion" of soul toward some good.[7] He uses the word synonymously with "mighty affections."[8] And like Plato, Augustine believed that God lacks nothing. But

[5]Ibid., 21.
[6]Plato, "Symposium," in *The Collected Dialogues of Plato*, ed. Edith Hamilton and Huntington Cairns (Princeton: Princeton University Press, 1961), 533, 544, 553, 555 (or secs. 178, 191, 200, 202).
[7]For two very helpful discussions of Augustine on love, see the chapter on Augustine in Bernard V. Brady, *Christian Love* (Washington, DC: Georgetown University Press, 2003), 77–124; and Lewis Ayres, "Augustine, Christology, and God as Love: An Introduction to the Homilies on 1 John," in *Nothing Greater, Nothing Better*, 67–93.
[8]Augustine, *Confessions*, I.ix (15).

unlike Plato, Augustine knew that "God is love" based on the Scriptures. How did Augustine put all this together? His ultimate understanding of love included aspects of love as desire (*eros*) and love as gift (*agape*) for which he often used the Latin word *caritas* (charity).[9] Now, just to be clear, there is "love as desire" or attraction, which is usually prompted by some quality in the beloved, as in "I love you *because you are* beautiful" or "good" or "righteous" or whatever. This brand of love is typically referred to as *eros*. And there is "love as a gift," which is usually prompted by the quality of benevolence in the lover, as in "I love you *because I want* to do you good." This is what's referred to as *agape*. Where Plato opted for the first of these two definitions, Augustine combined them. God's love is shown in his gift of himself, which he gives in the motions or affections of his Spirit. So the Father ultimately gives himself to the Son with the affections of the Spirit, and derivatively he gives himself to us. True love is the affectionate gift of God in the Spirit. He writes, "Love therefore is God from God."[10]

God's love for us in the Spirit then leads us to love and adore God passionately in return: "So it is God the Holy Spirit proceeding from God who fires man to the love of God and neighbor when he has been given to him, and he himself is love. Man has no capacity to love God except from God."[11] For Augustine, in other words, love is a kind of boomerang, coming from God and returning to God, catching us up in the arc of its path.

I'm not aware of any place in which Augustine says that God most loves God in the way that Jonathan Edwards eventually would say it, but that's certainly the implication. He does explicitly say that human love, even love for other people and creation, should be given "with reference" to God. In a sermon, Augustine writes:

> You ought to love [your children and your wives] with reference to Christ, and take thought for them in reference to God, and in them love nothing but Christ, and hate it in your nearest and dearest if they don't want to have anything to do with Christ. Such, you see, is that divine sort of charity.[12]

We should love God for God's sake, and we should love our neighbors for God's sake. I should not love you for your own sake; I should love you because

---

[9]Augustine did not read Greek and so did not write in terms of *eros* and *agape*. Generally, he used the Latin word *caritas* (from which we get charity) as his word for love, but he would also use *amor*, a word more often associated with passionate love. Since his concept of love combined aspects of each, he denied their differences and said they could be used interchangeably. See Augustine, "The City of God against the Pagans," in *Cambridge Texts in the History of Political Thought*, ed. and trans. R. W. Dyson (Cambridge: Cambridge University Press, 1998), bk. 14, chap. 7.

[10]Augustine, *The Trinity*, 15.31; cf. 32. Even if Augustine's formulation of the Trinity does depersonalize the Holy Spirit by reducing him to the love exchanged between divine Father and Son, as some argue, I believe we can at least affirm what Augustine says here; i.e., we may need to add to what Augustine says about the Spirit, but we don't need to take away.

[11]Ibid.

[12]In Brady, *Christian Love*, 117.

you are created in *God's* image, because you belong to *him*, because *he* has commanded me to, and so forth. Love centered on anything other than God is the opposite of love: "If we love them for another reason, we hate them more than love them."[13] Summing all this up, Augustine writes:

> I call "charity" the motion of the soul toward the enjoyment of God for His own sake, and the enjoyment of one's self and of one's neighbor for the sake of God; but "cupidity" is a motion of the soul toward the enjoyment of one's self, one's neighbor, or any other corporal thing for the sake of something other than God.[14]

For Augustine, there are two basic kinds of love: a love centered on God and a love centered on anything else. One is from God and to God; the other is not. And there's a bright line in between these two kinds of love. Furthermore, truly loving another person means, quite simply, pointing him or her to God. Augustine writes, "Whoever, therefore, justly loves his neighbor should so act toward him that he also love God with his whole heart, and his whole soul, and with his whole mind."[15]

Bernard of Clairvaux, who is referred to as a mystic, laid a greater emphasis on the experience of loving God than Augustine did. He is well known for using the imagery of romantic love and intoxication from the Song of Solomon to describe our experience of loving God.[16] Yet Bernard's general thrust is similar to Augustine's. God loves us by enabling us to love him: "He loves for no other purpose than to be loved, knowing that those who love him are blessed by their very love."[17] For Bernard, love is its own reward. It's both give and take. We're united to him *for* him, but in the uniting we receive everything we could want.

Thomas Aquinas, like Augustine and Bernard, also conceived of love as coming from God and returning to God—like a boomerang. He too began with a conception of love as passion or desire and then combined it with a conception of love as gift, or desire for another's good. Love attracts one person to another and unites lover and beloved, but not only does it unite, it moves outward as well. Love is like a furnace, Aquinas said, which radiates outward bringing heat throughout a house. Hence, it's no good to say, "I love God but not my

---

[13]Ibid., 105.
[14]Augustine, *On Christian Doctrine*, 3.10.16.
[15]Ibid., 1.23. And elsewhere: "'Thou shalt love thy neighbor as thyself.' Now you love yourself suitably when you love God better than yourself. What, then, you aim at in yourself you must aim at in your neighbor, namely, that he may love God with a perfect affection. For you do not love him as yourself, unless you try to draw him to that good which you are yourself pursuing. For this is the one good which has room for all to pursue it along with thee. From this precept proceed the duties of human society" (*On the Morals of the Catholic Church*, trans. Richard Stothart, in *St. Augustine: The Writings Against the Manicheans and Against the Donatists: Nicene and Post-Nicene Fathers of the Christian Church*, vol. 4, ed. Philip Schaff [Whitefish, MT: Kessinger, n.d.], chap. 26, p. 55).
[16]Brady, *Christian Love*, 125–40.
[17]Ibid., 129.

neighbor." Just as God's love burns outward for the world to bring people to the love and worship of him, so our love of God burns outward for sinners to bring them to God's love.[18]

A TENTATIVE DEFINITION; A COMPLEX POSTURE

Let me offer a tentative definition of love at this point that pulls together these first three thinkers. What is love? Love is an affection for another's good. Something in you attracts me to want your good. Furthermore, the good that I want for you has a fixed and certain content to it—God. God is the good that God lovingly wants for others, and he's the good that we should lovingly want for others. We love our parents, friends, spouses, and enemies best when we desire for them to know the glory of God, a desire predicated on an even more ultimate desire to see his glory displayed. Again, I don't know whether any of these three thinkers explicitly said that God most loves God, but that's the general thrust of their thinking. God's love is God-centered; ours should be as well.

There's much more that needs to be said here. For the moment, let's consider what a God-centered love means for God's (and a Christian's) posture toward sinners. In short, it requires a complex posture. On the one hand, it's a posture of universal and undiscriminating affection for the good of every man and woman. It's the delight of giving to all because all are created in God's image. You can catch a glimpse of such love when an old Congregationalist minister in Marilynne Robinson's novel *Gilead*, waxing nostalgic, writes to his son, "You see how it is godlike to love the *being* of someone. Your *existence* is a delight to us."[19] To love one's child is to taste God's love for his son Adam and all his children by creation. (We're dealing in Carson's second category of love here, as defined above.) God created us. Our existence delights him, so he continues to provide even for his enemies (Matt. 5:45). "It's good," God says of our alive-ness. "Indeed, it's very good" (see Gen. 1:31). He loves us generally as his creatures, and he loves us particularly as individuals, each individual distinct from another (cf. Ps. 139:13–16).

Does God love humanity because of something intrinsically valuable or lovable in us? Logically, that would be impossible. He *created* us, and in his omniscience and sovereignty he wrote down every day of our lives before one of them came to be (Ps. 139:16). He is the source of everything we have, including every good gift that's been given since creation (James 1:17). As such, there is literally nothing that God could behold with affection in us that he did not give us in the first place (cf. 1 Cor. 4:7). (Can we create anything that our omniscient God did not think of first?) God loves everyone because God beholds *his own*

---

[18]Ibid., 164–79, esp. 165–66, 171.
[19]Italics original; Marilynne Robinson, *Gilead* (New York: Farrar, Straus and Giroux, 2004), 136.

handiwork, image, and glory in everyone. God's love is God-centered. When we as humans then love in a God-centered way, we love—as Augustine said—with respect to him, or for his sake. That means we burn to see his character and glory expressed everywhere—in ourselves, in our friends and family, in our enemies, in creation, in everything. From the vantage point of creation, God-centered love bears no judgment and draws no boundaries. It knows only pleasure and delights in the gift of itself.

On the other hand, God's God-centered love bears a posture that opposes everything that opposes God, just as you and I will oppose anyone who opposes the human objects of our love such as a friend or spouse. I love my daughters, so I have an affection for their good. How then can I not oppose anyone or anything that intends for their ultimate ill? So it is with God's love for God, and so it is for any true love of God that we have. Loving him means having affection for his glory and honor. A complex posture is therefore required. God loves all sinners insofar as they reflect his glory; he opposes them insofar as they don't. What that means is that a God-centered love must discriminate; it must have preferences; it must make judgments, and it must do so in light of sin and the fall. It is *not* universal, because it does not love anything that opposes God. God-centered love does *not* love sin. What is sin? Sin is anything that opposes God and intends God's ultimate ill. Therefore, God's God-centered love will discriminate between that which is sin and that which is not; between those who belong to sin and those who do not; between those who love him and seek his glory and those who do not.

For these reasons, the truly loving heart will combine aspects of love and hate.[20] It hates any perversions of his image or anything that might detract from his love, but this very hatred is premised on a love of the good. Aquinas put it like this: "Hatred of a person's evil is equivalent to love of his good."[21] He was therefore willing to speak in terms of "preferential love." Just as we should love those who are closer to us (I should love my children more than the other children in my neighborhood), we should also love those who are more like God in their character and virtue, because it's the very character and virtue of God for which our hearts should burn like furnaces; it's his beauty to which we should be drawn.

Augustine, too, clearly saw that such God-centered love requires a complex posture, sometimes calling for the admonishment and discipline of the very ones we love. In a passage very pertinent to church discipline and pastoral care he writes:

---

[20]See D. A. Carson, *Love in Hard Places* (Wheaton, IL: Crossway, 2002), 42, 182.
[21]In Brady, *Christian Love*, 174.

> We should never undertake the task of chiding another's sin unless, cross-examining our own conscience, we can assure ourselves, before God, that we are acting from love. If reproaches or threats or injuries, voiced by the one you are calling to account, have wounded your spirit, then, for that person to be healed by you, you must not speak till you are healed yourself, lest you act from worldly motives, to hurt, and make your tongue a sinful weapon of evil, returning wrong for wrong, curse for curse. Whatever you speak out of a wounded spirit is the wrath of an avenger, not the love of an instructor. . . . And if, as often happens, you begin some course of action from love, and are proceeding with it in love, but a different feeling insinuates itself because you are resisted, deflecting you from reproach of a man's sin and making you attack the man itself—it were best, while watering the dust with your tears, to remember that we have no right to crow over another's sin, since we sin in the very reproach of sin if anger at sin is better at making us sinners than mercy is at making us kind.[22]

The mere fact that we might discipline someone in love means that love is not undiscriminating. Certainly this is a biblical insight: "For the Lord disciplines the one he loves, and chastises every son whom he receives" (Heb. 12:6).

The larger point, again, is that a God-centered conception of love requires a complex posture, requiring both love and judgment. From the standpoint of creation, it's universal and indiscriminate. From the vantage point of the fall, it's not. It makes judgments and separates itself from that which does not love God.

Step 3: Many theologians since Luther have opted for a reductionistic understanding of God's love—love merely as unconditional gift. This common evangelical understanding of love today fundamentally changes the purpose of the church and the shape of church membership.

A Reductionistic Definition of Love

It's important for us to pick up the historical timeline with what comes after Aquinas, because the doctrine of Christian love continued to evolve through the work of several notable Protestants, and the evolution has not been altogether helpful. In fact, we find here one more matter which could have been added to chapter 1's list of cultural factors that stand in the way of church membership and discipline. I focused there on the overly sentimentalized, consumeristic, and self-centered conceptions of romantic love that have increasingly captured the popular imagination in the last couple of centuries. What I didn't mention was

---

[22]From Augustine's *Commentary on Paul's Letter to the Galatians* (57), in Garry Wills, *Saint Augustine*, A Penguin Life series (New York: Viking, 1999), 111–12.

the evolving theological understanding of love in Christian churches beginning
with Martin Luther, but especially coming into its own more recently with
thinkers like Søren Kierkegaard, Anders Nygren, Karl Barth, and others. The
theological understanding of love promoted by such thinkers, I believe, is taken
for granted by most evangelicals. The problem is that it risks placing man at the
center of God's love and thereby removes the need for any kind of judgment.
Church membership and discipline are a kind of judgment. They are a way of
saying, "This person belongs on the inside of our circle; that person doesn't,"
which is an act of judgment. If, however, there is no room for judgment in love,
then church membership—and much more—needs to be jettisoned.

Martin Luther represents something of a turning point in the doctrine of
love.[23] Like the authors we've already considered, a larger conversation would
be required to consider Luther's different streams of thought on love, such as his
affirmation of the ordinary life or his thoughts on marital love, much less how
the different streams flow together. Yet what's significant here is his emphasis
on God's universal and gracious call to salvation.

Where the Roman Catholic Church had been emphasizing man's work in
achieving salvation, Luther responded with the doctrine of justification by faith
alone, by which God's justifying grace is freely promised to all who believe.
It's said that where Rome emphasized man's love for God, Luther's rigorous
doctrine of sin led him to emphasize God's gracious and unconditional love for
man. Even while Luther's view on marital love included elements of love and
passion, his soteriology emphasized God's love as a selfless gift. This, anyhow,
is how Luther has been read through a number of thinkers who see themselves
as following in his path.[24]

The post-Luther conversation is pitched as a battle between *agape* and *eros*,
between a so-called Christian conception and a platonic one. Beginning with
Luther, it's said, the doctrinal definition of love increasingly leaned toward the
universal and undiscriminating side. Love is an agape gift, period. It shows
no concern for the worthiness or unworthiness of its object. Whether or not
Luther indeed meant for this emphasis to ultimately define his conception of
love (I'm not convinced he does), it became a leading interpretation ascribed
to him. God's salvific love toward the fallen world—Carson's third category—
increasingly defined Christian love altogether.

For instance, Søren Kierkegaard makes a strong distinction between Christian love and romantic love. Romantic love, Kierkegaard said, focuses in on "the
favourite's name, the beloved, the friend, who is loved in distinction from the
rest of the world"; Christian love never plays favorites but loves all mankind.

---

[23]Anders Nygren calls it a "Copernican Revolution" in the doctrine of love. *Agape and Eros,* trans. Philip S.
Watson (London: SPCK, 1982), 681.
[24]This particular argument can be found in Nygren, *Agape and Eros,* 681ff.

Romantic love "strains in the direction of the one and only beloved"; Christian love "press[es] in the opposite direction." Romantic love is "determined by its object." That is, it's drawn in by attraction. Christian love is simply "determined by love." It depends on self-renunciation. It's a gift. Romantic love can be changed to something else, like hate. Christian love "is never changed, it has integrity; it loves—and never hates."[25] In short, Christian love is always universal and unconditional, while anything that discriminates and has preferences is something else.

The twentieth-century Lutheran theologian Anders Nygren, in his famous book *Agape and Eros*, likewise wanted to separate Plato's idea of love as desire (*eros*) from a Christian idea of love as gift (*agape*). A good portion of the book is devoted to critiquing Augustine for combining the two and commending Luther for pointing the church back to *agape*. He compares the two kinds of love in a series of couplets:

> Eros is acquisitive desire and longing. Agape is sacrificial giving. . . .
> Eros is man's way to God. Agape is God's way to man.
> Eros is man's effort: it assumes that man's salvation is his own work.
>   Agape is God's grace: salvation is the work of Divine love. . . .
> Eros is the will to get and possess which depends on want and need.
>   Agape is freedom in giving, which depends on wealth and plenty.
> Eros is primarily man's love. . . . Agape is primarily God's love. . . .
> Eros is determined by the quality, the beauty and worth, of its object; it is not
>   spontaneous, but "evoked," "motivated." Agape is sovereign in rela-
>   tion to its object, and is directed to both "the evil and the good"; it
>   is spontaneous, "overflowing unmotivated."
> Eros recognizes value in its object—and loves it. Agape loves—and creates
>   value in its object.[26]

Notice that love is completely cut off from my attraction to an object. It's nothing but a self-sacrificing gift. It's an unconstrained, unaffected choice to give to the other person's good—more a result of will than heart. It's never conditional but always unconditional. There is no need for any act of judgment with such love because it is entirely a gift. It's for the unworthy as well as the worthy, the sinful as well as the righteous.

Karl Barth can also be placed within this tradition. God is the "one who loves in freedom," says Barth. He loves as "an end in itself." Others in the Augustinian and Reformed tradition might ask, "But doesn't God love for the sake of his glory?" Sort of, says Barth. He writes, "In loving us God wills his

---

[25]Søren Kierkegaard, *Works of Love*, trans. Howard Hong and Edna Hong (New York: Torchbooks, 1962), 36, 49, 63, 77.
[26]Nygren, *Agape and Eros*, 210.

own glory and our salvation. But he does not love us because he wills this. He wills it for the sake of his love. . . . God loves because he loves; because this act is His being, His essence and His nature. He loves without and before realizing these purposes."[27] In other words, he doesn't quite love for the sake of his glory. He loves us because he is loving; it's an end in itself (Barth points to Deut. 7:8 and Jer. 31:3 to support these assertions). But then, yes, he gets glory (and we get saved) because he's loving. God's love comes first; his glory and our salvation come second, as consequences of the fact that he loves. As with these last few authors, Barth views God's love entirely as a gift; it's not given because of anything he beholds in the object of his love.[28]

Today, some theologians have recaptured Luther's phrase "a theology of the cross" and explicitly set themselves against a "theology of glory" (as Luther did). Among other emphases, they too deny that God's love has anything like desire or attraction in it; it's all a free gift. For instance, Gerhard Forde writes, "This love of God that creates its object is contrasted absolutely with the love of humans. Human love is awakened by attraction to what pleases it. It must search to find its object and, one might add, will likely toss it aside when it tires of it."[29] Jürgen Moltmann's emphasis on God's suffering love relies on the same basic assumptions.

Once again, Marilynne Robinson's old Congregational minister provides a helpful illustration. He writes to his son, "Love is holy because it is like grace—the worthiness of its object is never really what matters."[30]

We have a wealth of riches in the insights of Luther and this particular vein of interpretation. When God's affection is set upon something, at that moment and only at that moment, it becomes something worthy, valuable, lovely. His love is not given to that which, prior to his loving it, was somehow intrinsically lovely. Rather, God's love *creates* that which is lovely and valuable. When he looks upon creation and says, "That is good," it really becomes good and lovely, because he has made it so.

This is precisely why God's gospel goes to the despised things, the lowly things, the things that are not. It's precisely there that God's love most obviously *creates* something lovely and lovable. He reaches out to thieves, murderers, to tax collectors, and prostitutes and then says to a self-righteous world that

[27]Karl Barth, *Church Dogmatics*, vol. 2.1, ed. G. W. Bromiley and T. F. Torrance (New York: T&T Clark, 2004), 28.2.3 (p. 279). See also Miroslav Volf, *Free of Charge* (Grand Rapids: Zondervan, 2005), 39. He explicitly builds on Barth and Luther on just these points.

[28]Barth writes, "God's loving is concerned with a seeking and creation of fellowship without any reference to an existing aptitude or worthiness on the part of the love. God's love is not merely not conditioned by any reciprocity of love. It is also not conditioned by any worthiness to be loved on the part of the loved, by any existing capacity for union or fellowship on his [the loved one's] side." *Church Dogmatics*, vol. 2.1, 28.2.2 (p. 278).

[29]Gerhard O. Forde, *On Being a Theologian of the Cross: Reflections on Luther's Heidelberg Disputation, 1518* (Grand Rapids: Eerdmans, 1997), 113.

[30]Robinson, *Gilead*, 209.

despises such as these, "Watch what I'm going to do. Watch how I'm going to love *them* and, by loving them, turn them into a people beautiful, resplendent, majestic; a people who will outshine the angels."

God's love is an *agape* gift given to the undeserving. Frederick Buechner, meditating on loving one's enemy, captures this idea sweetly: "And then there is the love for the enemy—love for the one who does not love you but mocks, threatens, and inflicts pain. The tortured's love for the torturer. This is God's love. It conquers the world."[31] Is such love not marvelous to behold? Earlier I said that God's love both repels and attracts us. What specifically attracts us? It's this remarkable gift of himself to the worthy and unworthy alike.

Ah, but there's the rub. It does attract us. How could it not? It's beautiful, and we *do* love him for such beauty, do we not? Paul even says that Christ's love "controls us" (2 Cor. 5:14). Now consider: aren't we to mimic God's love? How then should we love God? Are we to love God apart from his beauty? Are we to love him entirely as a benevolent gift and not as a response of worship? Also, what does it mean to bear "the affection of Christ Jesus" for a church, as Paul says he bears for the Philippians (1:8)?

The discussion of Christian love in theological circles has gone beyond this choice between *agape* and *eros*, turning lately to matters of "mutuality" and "reciprocal relation."[32] Yet I believe this basic distinction marks out an essential divide in many Christians' minds. We associate *agape* with grace and the idea of God's love being "unconditional," and we associate *eros* with works, righteousness, beauty, and the idea of "conditional" love. The problem is that this very true and wonderful emphasis on the free gift of God's love is reductionistic. It pictures only part of the biblical data about God, a part of the gospel, and a part of what the church is called to be. In fact, this *agape*-driven definition (love only as gift) overlooks at least two things at the heart of love in the Bible. First, it overlooks the divine Father's love for the perfect Son. Where does that fit into the definition of "love"? There is no suffering or self-sacrifice in the Father's love for the Son. It's pure pleasure, and the pleasure is based on the Son's moral beauty and perfection.[33] Second, it overlooks the question of *why* Christ had to die in order to save sinners. Why couldn't he just speak salvation into being like he spoke creation into being?

I fear that defining love only as an *agape* gift in fact substitutes something man-centered in place of Augustine's God-centered conception of love.[34] Con-

---

[31]Frederick Buechner, *The Magnificent Defeat* (New York: HarperCollins, 1985), 105.

[32]See the chapter, "Self Regard, Other Regard, and Mutuality," in Brady's *Christian Love*, 240–64; also, see Kevin Vanhoozer, "Introduction—The Love of God—Its Place, Meaning, and Function in Systematic Theology," in *Nothing Greater, Nothing Better*, 1–29, esp. 18–19.

[33]See Nygren, *Agape and Eros*, 678–80.

[34]Proponents of the *agape* definition explicitly argue that their definition is God-centered and that what came before was man-centered, e.g., Nygren, *Agape and Eros*, 681–84. I would agree, if we're talking about Rome's entire soteriological system versus Luther's. What concerns me is how love itself gets defined.

sider the matter this way: *why* does God love sinners unto salvation? The *agape* answer is, "Because he loves them! Period. He loves and he gives. That's what he does." There is no further incentive for God. His love for them is its own final end. He loves sinners for their sake and nothing more. Remember, Jesus died for us. He gave it all!

Yes, he did die for us, but did he really surrender *all*? Did he surrender his holiness? His mission? Did he surrender his commitment to obey the Father? Did he set aside his ambition to glorify the Father, and does he expect nothing in return from those he saves? Is he happy for them, once saved, to live however they please? Christ was crucified in the flesh, yes, but he did this for a particular end that was *larger* than saving people. He is saving a people so that they might be holy, loving, and united. He is saving a people that they might be consecrated to the worship of God.[35] He is saving a people not for their glory but for God's.[36] As soon as you say that Christ expects something of those whom he saves, like obedience, you've just conceded that God is after something. He has some goal in mind that *attracts* him. Yet notice what happens when you truly follow the *agape* line of thinking to its logical conclusion: if God's love is purely sacrificial giving and nothing more—I mean, really, an utterly pure sacrifice—then God surrenders his Godness, doesn't he? He must give up his holiness, his righteousness, everything. If I give up *everything* for you, it's because I love you more than I love myself. An *agape* conception of love, which I take to be fairly mainstream among evangelicals, implicitly assumes that God lives and loves ultimately for us. We are his highest love. He loves us more than anything, even his own glory. He idolizes us.

As such, God's law bends around us, and all judgment is ultimately vanquished. What after all is God's law? It's the requirements of his nature. And if his nature is set first and foremost on loving humanity, then it cannot be a sin for us to most love ourselves and to be proud. Aren't we to love what God loves and value what he values? Aren't we to call good and evil what he calls good and evil? If he most loves us, we should most love ourselves. God's righteousness becomes whatever's good for me. There's not some other brand of righteousness "out there" which would require him to judge us for hating him and most loving ourselves. All judgment can be set to the side.[37] If people

---

[35] As one would expect, proponents of pure *agape* love want a transformed people in their theological system, as well. Nygren attempts to avoid cheap grace, for instance, by saying that God's love "demands unlimited devotion" (*Agape and Eros*, 104). But this sounds like an internal contradiction in Nygren. It would seem there is something that attracts God's love after all—the prospect of unlimited devotion!

[36] This is where I fundamentally disagree with Miroslav Volf's statement, "God is an infinitely rich and most generous giver who receives nothing in return" (*Free of Charge*, 37). Nothing in return? So why does he command us to worship him?

[37] Theologians who adopt a pure *agape* conception of love will sometimes have other mechanisms in their theological systems for preserving God's judgment. But one can expect to find some measure of inconsistency in their theological system. Nygren, for instance, attempts to address the very argument here by demonstrating that his idea of love does, in fact, allow for judgment because (1) God requires us to accept his love, and (2) his

don't choose God, fine. Give them "not God." But we don't need to judge them. There's no reason. Send them on an infinite vacation of bliss on the other side of the universe.

WHY THIS IS SIGNIFICANT FOR CHURCH MEMBERSHIP AND DISCIPLINE

Why am I going into abstractions in a book about church membership? Consider what church membership and discipline are. They are anticipatory acts of judgment by a local congregation that foreshadow the even greater judgment or assize to come. They are a declaration on earth of who will belong to God's people in heaven (Matt. 16:19). They are an assessment of who *belongs* and who doesn't. If God most loves God, then God may freely choose to judge those who do not love him. Indeed, he must judge. If that's the case, then the anticipatory judgments of church membership and discipline can be seen as merciful and kind. These practices become a gracious warning of an even greater judgment to come.[38] If, however, God loves man the most, then God is nothing but inconsistent to judge anyone. In fact, his nature would constrain him *not* to judge. Hence, the so-called anticipatory judgments of church membership and discipline would be not only cruel and hateful but also flat lies.

In short, if we define love as nothing more than "unconditional giving" or "God's free gift of salvation"—as many evangelicals do—then we might have a theological system that will tend toward man-centeredness and, therefore, universalism. Every man-centered theological system eventually goes the way of universalism and has ever since the Serpent promised Eve, "You will not surely die," for making herself "like God" (Gen. 3:4–5). A system may inconsistently maintain a role for God's judgment and church membership for a while, but eventually the tensions in the theological system will make themselves felt. The doctrine of judgment will move into the background and then quietly vanish altogether. As this happens, the practices of church membership and discipline will do the same, unless they are reconfigured to meet a market demand. "Membership has its privileges," says the credit card commercial. "Come for the authentic community," say the postmodern clergy.

We'll come back to these matters shortly, but first we need to consider some of the biblical data for God's love for God and for man. Then we'll be in

---

love requires unlimited devotion. Otherwise, he says, we will be judged (*Agape and Eros*, 102–4). The problem is that these two provisos contradict his conception of *agape* by smuggling in an Augustinian God who desires God-centered worshipers.

[38]Calvin writes, "But the church binds whom it excommunicates—not that it casts him into everlasting ruin and despair, but because it condemns his life and morals, and already warns him of his condemnation unless he should repent." *Institutes*, trans. Ford Lewis Battles, 1214.

a better position to define God's love and God's gospel and ask whether there is room for any judgment in love—and in church membership!

Step 4: The Scriptures show that God's love is holy—it centers on himself.

God's Love for God

"You are my beloved Son; with you I am well pleased," says the divine Father to Jesus at Jesus' baptism (Luke 3:22). This is not Genesis 1:1, but it could be. The Father's love for the Son is the beginning of everything (see John 17:5, 24). (We are dealing now with Carson's first category, as described above.)

Why is the Father well pleased with the Son, a pronouncement repeated seven times in the New Testament?[39] The context of these words in the Gospel of Luke helps us with the answer. Immediately following the baptism, Luke presents a genealogy stretching back to Adam, who is actually referred to as "the son of God" (Luke 3:23–38, esp. 38). Jesus, this son of Adam, must be the one toward whom all history has been pointing, a last Adam, as it were (cf. 1 Cor. 15:45). Then, right after retracing all human history in the genealogy, Luke presents this son of Adam being led by God's Spirit into the wilderness where he would meet Adam's old nemesis Satan. The stage is set for a reenactment of the temptation of Eden, only now it's not a lush garden; it's a barren wilderness, and Jesus has been fasting for forty days and nights. Indeed, not only does this scene reenact Eden, another reenactment is overlaid upon it—Israel's forty years in the wilderness.

Yet in response to these challenges, the Son does what neither Adam nor Israel could do. He refuses a false provision but relies entirely upon God's words (Luke 4:4; Deut. 8:3). He refuses to grasp at a false offer of authority and glory but worships God alone (Luke 4:6, 8; Deut. 6:13; cf. Gen. 3:5-6). He refuses a false claim to entitlement but trusts God's dominion wholly (Luke 4:12; Deut. 8:16; Ex. 17:2-7).

The Son's perfect obedience to the Father is the testimony of John's Gospel as well. The Son's food is "to do the will" of the Father and "to accomplish his work" (John 4:34; 6:38; cf. Matt. 4:4). He does "nothing of his own accord, but only what he sees the Father doing" (John 5:19, 30; 17:2). He speaks and teaches just as the Father taught him (7:17; 8:28; 12:49–50). He has come in the Father's name and authority, not his own (5:27, 43; 7:17; 8:28). "For I have not spoken on my own authority, but the Father who sent

---

[39]Matt. 3:17; 17:5; Mark 1:11; 9:7; Luke 3:22; 9:25; 2 Pet. 1:17.

me has himself given me a commandment—what to say and what to speak" (12:49; cf. 14:10).

A CONDITIONAL LOVE?

Is the Father's love for the Son "conditional" on the Son's obedience? Does the Father burn with love for the Son because the Son obeys? It sounds that way when the Son says, "If you keep my commandments, you will abide in my love, just as I have kept my Father's commandments and abide in his love" (John 15:10). The parallelism here is striking. We'll abide in Christ's love through obedience, just as the Son abides in the Father's love through obedience.[40]

There's a larger biblical backstory worth noticing here as well. When God made a covenant with David, he promised David that he would punish his son when he committed iniquity (2 Sam. 7:14). Yet when that covenant is repeated in the post-exilic Chronicles, that particular threat is omitted (see 1 Chron. 17:13). Could that be because David's only son of consequence following the exile is Christ? If we turn then to the Psalms, we find a Davidic figure who is in fact rewarded for his righteousness. This is most clear in Psalm 45, which reads, "You have loved righteousness and hated wickedness. Therefore God, your God, has anointed you with the oil of gladness beyond your companions" (Ps. 45:7). God has anointed this king *because* he loved righteousness and hated wickedness (see also Ps. 21:5–7), which the book of Hebrews affirms of Christ (Heb. 1:9). Again and again this messianic Davidic figure says, "The LORD dealt with me according to my righteousness" (Ps. 18:20; cf. Ps. 7:8; 26:1; 35:24). Jesus was anointed as messiah and king not simply because he was the Son of God. He won the anointing through his righteousness (cf. Ps. 2:7)!

This particular stream of texts is only one of the streams that flows into the broad and deep ocean of Christology and should not be read in separation from the other streams that affirm the Father's eternal and assured love for the Son. Still, Jesus is the one who "learned obedience" through what he suffered (Heb. 5:8). Jesus is the one who would say to his disciples, "If you keep my commandments, you will abide in my love, just as I have kept my Father's commandments and abide in his love" (John 15:10). Jesus is the one of whom the Father said he was well pleased, a pleasure grounded, at least in part, in the moral perfection of the Son. Indeed, the Father's declaration of pleasure in his Son occurred at Jesus' baptism, a baptism that was performed "to fulfill all righteousness" (Matt. 3:15).

In the mystery of the incarnation, it appears that Jesus of Nazareth, the God-man, was the recipient of what we might call God's "conditional" love. In his sinlessness, of course, Jesus the God-man kept the law perfectly, and the

---

[40]See Carson, *The Difficult Doctrine*, 40.

judgment pronounced upon him was "righteous." As the eternal Son, of course, the Father's love for the Son is infinite and assured. Still, there is at least one textual stream that runs through the course of redemptive history that suggests that the Father presented the incarnate Son with a kind of conditional love, or a love that was grounded upon Christ's obedience.[41] The good news for us is that Jesus met the conditions![42]

There is a vital lesson here. It demonstrates that the Father loves the Son *because of* the Son's perfection. He described himself as attracted to certain qualities in his Son, qualities with which he was "well pleased." It was true in the incarnation, and we have every reason to think it was true in eternity past and will be in the future as well. The Son reflects the Father's own character and glory to him, and the Father loves him for that reason. The Father's love for the Son is not indiscriminate and arbitrary. There is a reason for it. We can even say that there is a condition for the Father's eternal love. What if the Son did *not* perfectly submit to the Father's will and so did *not* perfectly reflect the Father's image—would the Father not love him just as much? Well, that's hypothetical, and we don't know. What we do know for certain is what the psalmist sang and the author of Hebrews attributes to the Father regarding the Son: "You have loved righteousness and hated wickedness. Therefore God, your God, has anointed you with the oil of gladness beyond your companions" (Ps. 45:7; Heb. 1:9). God's love, even for the Son, is bound up with his righteousness. God does not love even himself apart from his own law. His love is intrinsically conditioned by all his other attributes. In short, Jesus the beloved Son pleases the Father because he fulfilled the command given to Israel, "You shall love the LORD your God with all your heart and with all your soul and with all your might" (Deut. 6:5; cf. 6:6).

Love as attraction and *love as gift* are not separated in the Father's love for the Son. The Father is attracted to the Son, and he freely gives the Son all that he has. He communicates himself to the Son entirely. The apostle Paul explains that in Christ "all the fullness of God was pleased to dwell" (Col. 1:19). Jesus himself testified that "the Father loves the Son and has given all things into his hand" (John 3:35; see also Matt. 11:27); and "the Father loves the Son and shows him all that he himself is doing" (John 5:20); and "For as the Father has life in himself, so he has granted the Son to have life in himself" (John 5:26). So complete is the self-communication of the Father to the Son that Jesus could

---

[41] These are the kinds of texts that have led some theologians in the past toward either an adoptionist Christology or a functional Christology.

[42] The point being made here is analogous to the question of whether Jesus the God-man could have sinned. Was Christ *able to not sin* or *not able to sin*? In one sense, Christ could have sinned because the temptations set before Jesus the man were real. In another sense, no, he could not have sinned because he perfectly desired to do his Father's will. In this I'm following G. C. Berkouwer's approach to the sinlessness of Christ in *The Person of Christ* (Grand Rapids: Eerdmans, 1954), 251-67, esp. 262–63.

say to his disciple Philip, "Whoever has seen me has seen the Father" (John 14:9). Paul could also say, "He is the image of the invisible God" (Col. 1:15), and the author of Hebrews wrote, "He is the radiance of the glory of God and the exact imprint of his nature" (Heb. 1:3).

Incidentally, I recently heard a preacher expound on the Father's love for the Son as expressed at Jesus' baptism. The preacher went on about how the Father could love the Son unreservedly because there was no sin in the Son to hinder his love. The Son was perfect and without flaw, and so the Father could love him without restraint or reservation. Imagine such perfect and sweetly flowing love—the love of infinite perfection for infinite perfection![43] As he preached, however, I felt a growing and oppressive weight on me. "I will never be so perfect," I thought. "God will never be able to love me so unreservedly." The weight mounted until, remarkably, the preacher turned to saying that *this exact same love* was given to every Christian on the grounds of . . . well, that's getting ahead in our story. In the meantime, I simply offer this observation. God's love and God's law are not so far apart as we evangelicals tend to think. In fact, they are bound together.

DEMONSTRATING LOVE THROUGH OBEDIENCE?

If the Father's love for the Son consists in communicating all his glory to the Son (cf. John 17:5) and receiving due pleasure in return, the Son's first love and greatest pleasure consists in receiving the Father's glory, which he does through obeying the Father. Zeal for the Father's house, name, and reputation consumes the Son (John 2:17), for the reproaches that fall upon the Father he takes personally; yet he bears them all for the Father's sake (Ps. 69:7, 9). Jesus says that all he does is to please the Father (John 8:29), so he points to his obedience as a sign of his love for the Father: "I do as the Father has commanded me, so that the world may know that I love the Father" (John 14:31).

Nothing is more valuable to the Son than the Father, so his greatest pleasure is found in communicating the Father's glory to all the universe (cf. John 17:4). He does this by conforming his life to the Father's will entirely. He essentially says, "God the Father is so precious and valuable that I'm going to put him on display with all my life and actions. So, if you see me, you will have seen the Father." This is perfect love shown through perfect obedience.

A SELF-LOVE?

Is God's love for God a self-love? No and yes. No, because in the Father's love for the Son he loves another person, the one eternally begotten from himself.

---

[43]See also John Piper's chapter, "The Pleasure of God in His Son," in *The Pleasures of God* (Sisters, OR: Multnomah, 2000), 25–45.

Yes, because in the Father's love for the Son he loves his own being—the exact imprint of his nature—God from God, light from light, true God from true God. He beholds his own marvelous image in the Son.

In God's love for God, giving and receiving, it appears, merge. Glory is given. Glory is received. Glory is reflected. Glory's gift is redoubled and shared. Yes, there remains an asymmetry between Father and Son. The Father sends, while the Son goes. The Father commands, while the Son obeys. The Father initiates, while the Son responds. Never once on the pages of the New Testament is the order reversed.[44] Still, there are no losers amidst these different roles or vocations. The relationship of authority and obedience is no threat to pleasure, glory, and love. Both Father and Son "win" and share in the glory of redemptive victory. Authority and obedience are made the very vehicle through which love is demonstrated.

All this is surprising in our present Western context, where we decry all forms of hierarchy and authority as inimical to love. Love is construed as vulnerable and self-giving, while authority is regarded as exploitative, and submission is regarded as demeaning. In order to promote relationships and communities of love, therefore, we're told to level all such hierarchies in our churches and homes and replace them with egalitarian structures or non-structures. (Ironically, this proposal itself relies on a kind of power structure to produce love.)

Certainly any selfish use of power, whether exercised through a formal hierarchy or not, is itself the antithesis of love—it's the assertion of force by one person over another for selfish gain. It's not surprising that humans in a fallen world would conclude that love and power or love and authority are therefore antithetical and that all permanent (noncontractual) hierarchies should be leveled. What's even more surprising is the fact that the Bible places the unfallen love of the Father and Son into this type of authoritative structure. Not only that, it uses the horribly corrupted abuses of power by Herod and Pilate, in which an innocent man is made to suffer, to provide the greatest demonstration of the Son's love for the Father and for humanity.

How then should we understand the relationship between love, authority, and obedience? The answer no doubt affects how we understand love in the local church, as well as the love the church should have for the world. Does love ever take an authoritative stand toward members of the church or the world? Does love ever require obedience in the church?

---

[44]Carson writes, "Not once is there any hint that the Son commissions the Father, who obeys. Not once is there a hint that the Father submits to the Son or is dependent upon him for his own words and deeds" (*The Difficult Doctrine*, 40).

LOVE AND HOLINESS

While gazing upward at the perfect love between Father and Son, there is one more thing we need to consider, and that's the relationship between God's love and God's holiness. After all, the relationship between love and holiness in the history of the church, as with the relationship between love and authority, is checkered, to say the least.

In retelling this history, it's tempting to characterize churches since the time of Christ as veering into the ditch on one side of the road or the other. Either they have veered too far toward holiness and separation, thereby forsaking love, or they have veered too far toward love and assimilation, thereby forsaking holiness. The Puritans and the Fundamentalists provide common stereotypes for the former overemphasis. Romantics, Liberals, and—maybe lately—Emergents provide common stereotypes for the latter. It is tempting to narrate history in this fashion, yet I think it would be better to say that some churches have veered too far toward what *they think* is holiness, while other churches have veered too far toward what *they think* is love. If a church has abandoned holiness, it has abandoned love, and if it has abandoned love, it has abandoned holiness. Holiness and love are mutually implicating and work in concert, not in opposition.

In describing the relationship between God's holiness and love, Jonathan Edwards argues that God's holiness is his perfect and pure devotion to the pleasure he has in himself and his glory—the Father devoted to the Son and the Son to the Father. His holiness *is* his love of himself. Edwards writes, "The holiness of God consist[s] in his love, especially in the perfect and intimate union and love there is between the Father and Son."[45] Or elsewhere, "God's holiness is his having a due, meet and proper regard to everything, and therefore consists mainly and summarily in his infinite regard or love to himself, he being the greatest and most excellent Being."[46]

I'm not sure if Edwards meant to sum up God's holiness entirely as a property of God's affections, as if to say, "God is holy because he has holy affections." Certainly we should emphasize that God's holiness is not simply a property of his affections but of his being.[47] God's very being is holy! Still, insofar as we are speaking of God's love or affections, I believe that Edwards is absolutely right to say that God's holiness consists in his infinite love to himself.

People often define *holiness* as the fact that God is "set apart." But the fact that he is "set apart" doesn't tell us what he is set apart *to*.[48] If God hates sin,

---

[45]Jonathan Edwards, "Treatise on Grace," in *Works*, 21:186.
[46]Jonathan Edwards, "Miscellanies" No. 1077 in *Works*, 20:460.
[47]Thanks to Steve Wellum for this clarification.
[48]Peter Gentry, drawing on the work of French evangelical scholar Claude-Bernard Costecalde, argues that the word *holiness* in the biblical literature is less well defined as "separated" and better defined as "consecrated to"

it's because sin opposes something that God loves, and what does God most love? He most loves his glory (e.g., Isa. 48:8–11). Theologian Wayne Grudem captures this in his definition of God's holiness: "God's holiness means that he is separated from sin and devoted to seeking his own honor."[49] That helps to explain the strange juxtaposition of transcendence and immanence in the song of praise sung by the seraphim in Isaiah's vision: "Holy, holy, holy is the LORD of hosts; the whole earth is full of his glory!" (Isa. 6:3). The holiness of God does not separate his presence out from the earth, but just the opposite; it fills the earth with his presence so that he might display his unique and exclusive glory.[50] Holiness, it seems, requires not just a *not of* but also an *in*—so that God may be glorified.[51] So David sings, "Ascribe to the LORD the glory due his name; worship the LORD in the splendor of holiness" (Ps. 29:2). To make manifest his holiness is to make manifest his glory (Ezek. 28:22; see also Ex. 15:11).

Edwards rightly helps us to see, then, that God's holiness and God's love appear to be two perspectives on the same reality.[52] Looking at God's triune being from the "inside," we see love. Looking at his three persons from the "outside," we see holiness. In other words, consider the relationships inside the Godhead itself, between the Father, Son, and Spirit. From that angle, we see these perfect cords of divine love—three persons bearing a perfect affection for one another's good and glory. However, when we step outside of that relationship and look at the same thing in relation to everything else in the universe, we see what the Bible calls "holiness"—the fact that he is purely and undistractedly devoted to loving his own glory.

What exactly then is the relationship between holiness and love? Holiness is the measure of love's devotion to God, or, more specifically, the purity of love's devotion to God. How purely does God love God? That's how holy God is. How purely does a man love God? That's how holy a man is. Or another way to say it would be that God's love is directed by God's holiness. It always and only moves toward holy ends. In that sense, God's love is constrained by God's holiness, like water is constrained by the pipe through which it flows. Of course, that means that God's holiness ultimately serves the purposes of his love, as the pipe does water.

It's this holy affection or holy love that divides the universe in two. And there's a bright and clear boundary line in between the two sides, one as clear as the boundary between the inside of the garden of Eden and the outside, the

or "devoted to"; see Peter J. Gentry, "The Covenant at Sinai," in *The Southern Baptist Journal of Theology*, vol. 12 (Fall 2008): 48.
[49]Wayne Grudem, *Systematic Theology* (Grand Rapids: Zondervan, 1994), 201.
[50]Cf. J. Alec Motyer, *The Prophecy of Isaiah: An Introduction and Commentary* (Downers Grove, IL: InterVarsity, 1993), 77.
[51]Michael J. Gorman, "You Shall Be Cruciform for I Am Cruciform," in *Holiness and Ecclesiology in the New Testament,* ed. Kent E. Brower and Andy Johnson (Grand Rapids: Eerdmans, 2007), 153.
[52]Caldwell, *Communion in the Spirit*, 50, 54.

inside of Noah's Ark and the outside, the inside of a house covered by a smear of blood on the night of the Passover and the outside, the inside of the Israelite camp in the wilderness and the outside, the inside of the Promised Land and the outside. It's a boundary as clear as the Jordan River. On one side of the line is *the holy*; on the other side is *the unholy*. On one side are to be those who bear a God-centered love; on the other side are those who love idols. On one side are those who listen to God's Word and God's law; on the other side are those who listen to other voices (see Gen. 3:17).

When Paul refers to God's chosen people as "holy and beloved" (Col. 3:12), he's not talking about two unrelated things. The local church that chooses to emphasize God's love but not God's holiness is a church that doesn't actually understand what God's love is, because God's love is wholly fixed upon God and his glorious character in all its aspects. Such a church has probably substituted an idol in place of God's love. As such, the church that hesitates to draw sharp membership borders or to practice church discipline because these things don't seem loving needs to know that it's been duped into a man-centered caricature of love. It's been co-opted by the culture. It may well be worshiping an idol.

On the other hand, the church that, for one reason or another, seems to emphasize God's holiness and yet fails to do so in service to love is a church that misunderstands God's holiness. God's holiness means to fill the earth with God's glory, including the radically distinct way that God sent his Son to call not the righteous but sinners to repentance. Sure enough, the one whom the demons recognized as the "Holy One of God" was the very one who would reach out to touch the man with the unclean spirit in a way that the "holy" people of Israel would not (Mark 1:24). A holy church is a church that abstains from sin and that dwells among sinners, both of these activities being a property of holiness. It's in but not of the world, both of these postures, again, being a property of holiness. Missions and evangelism are not merely the result of God's love but of his holiness. He is so utterly consecrated to his own glory that he wants everyone to be consecrated to his glory! Again, a church that thinks it's holy but does not pour itself out in evangelism and acts of service is not a holy church. Those who belong to God's "frozen chosen," beware.

Notice, then, that both love and holiness have an inward and an outward impulse. They are inward in that they conspire to draw people to the love of God; they are outward in that they want more and more people to know this very love. God's holiness and love in the hearts of God's people is a purifying furnace that burns brighter and brighter with love for the lost—that they might know God and that he might be magnified in their lives.

Consider again why it is that God's love simultaneously attracts and offends us. It attracts us because it moves outward to embrace. It attracts us because it's a gift that is mercifully *inclusive*—it aims to include more and more people in spite of their unworthiness. It's a gift given to those who are immanently unworthy of such love. Yet it offends us because it's all about God, and our proud and idolatrous hearts don't like that fact. It offends us because people are included not for the honor of their name; they are included for the honor and praise of his name. They are included not for what they can bring, but for what they will be asked to give—worship. The God-centeredness of worship, of holy lives, and of holy ambitions offends us. It's judgmentally *exclusive*—it excludes the worship of all other things besides God. It excludes the worship of *me*.

Step 5: The Scriptures show that God's purposes in redemption are also holy, centering on himself.

God's Love for Sinners

If the Father's love for the Son is characterized by the Father's giving himself to the Son *and* his utter attraction to the Son, what about God's love for sinners? Didn't we just say that his love for sinners is characterized by pure agape? A pure gift? Yes and no.

From our standpoint, yes, God's gift of salvation through Christ is a pure gift of love to undeserving sinners.

- For God so loved the world, that he *gave* his only Son. (John 3:16a)

- For all have sinned and fall short of the glory of God, and are justified by his grace as a *gift*, through the redemption that is in Christ Jesus. (Rom. 3:23–24; also 5:15–17, 6:23)

- For by grace you have been saved through faith. And this is not your own doing; it is the *gift* of God. (Eph. 2:8)

We do not deserve God's redemptive love. We cannot earn it. He must give it to us not only apart from any qualities in us, but in shocking contradiction to what we are.

From God's standpoint, however, no, God's gift of salvation is given *in response* to the person and work of Christ. Christ won our salvation. He earned it. God loves us because he loves his beautiful Son and wants his Son's righteous beauty spread and proclaimed by transferring that righteous beauty to his Son's bride.

- Father, the hour has come; glorify your Son that the Son may glorify you, since you have given him authority over all flesh, *to give eternal life to all whom you have given him.* (John 17:1–2)

- But now the righteousness of God has been manifested apart from the law, although the Law and the Prophets bear witness to it—the righteousness of God through faith in Jesus Christ for all who believe. (Rom. 3:21–22)

- It was fitting that he, for whom and by whom all things exist, in bringing many sons to glory, should make the founder of their salvation perfect through suffering. For he who sanctifies and those who are sanctified all have one source. That is why he is not ashamed to call them brothers. (Heb. 2:10–11)

- Although he was a son, he learned obedience through what he suffered. And being made perfect, he became the source of eternal salvation to all who obey him. (Heb. 5:8–10)

The love of the Father for the Son is given to unworthy recipients *based on the worthiness of Christ.* (Here we find the fourth strand of love described by Carson, God's special love for his people.)

In fact, there's even a sense in which I want to qualify my statement, that he gives the gift of salvation as a pure gift "from our standpoint." We must keep in mind that the gift has a purpose that transcends us: God gives the gift of his grace to unworthy recipients so that they too would look like the ultimate object of his love—Christ:

- Christ loved the church and gave himself up for her, that he might sanctify her, having cleansed her by the washing of water with the word, so that he might present the church to himself in splendor, without spot or wrinkle or any such thing, that she might be holy and without blemish. (Eph. 5:25–27)

- And we all, with unveiled face, beholding the glory of the Lord, are being transformed into the same image from one degree of glory to another. (2 Cor. 3:18a)

The conflagration of the Father's affection for the Son is so great that he wants hundreds of millions of faces to look just like Jesus' face. It's finally about Jesus.

Kierkegaard distinguished Christian love from romantic love, saying that the latter focused on "the favourite's name . . . in distinction from the rest of the world" and that it "strains in the direction of the one and only beloved."[53] But

---

[53]Kierkegaard, *Works of Love*, 36.

that's Christian love! The favorite's name toward which the Father and Christian alike strain is Christ's, while Christ in turn strains toward the Father's name and calls his people to do the same (see John 16:26–27; 1 Cor. 15:28).

God's love for anything other than the glory of the Son is conditional on that first love. This is my brief and imprecise way of saying what Jonathan Edwards takes approximately a dozen pages to say in *The End for Which God Created the World* as he distinguishes "ultimate ends" from "subordinate," "chief," "highest," or "last ultimate" ends.[54] All other activities of God are contingent upon this one highest end—the proclamation of his glory. Edwards writes:

> All God's love may be resolved into his love to himself and delight in himself. . . . His love to the creature is only his inclination to glorify himself and communicate him[self], and his delight in himself glorified and in himself communicated.[55]

God's love for humanity at creation is bound up with the display of his image. His love for humanity in redemption is bound up with the display of his Son's image. He gives to us because he is attracted to the display of glory. His love for us is always conditional upon that.

Can love be given conditionally? The answer must be "yes" if we assume a person is capable of loving some things *more* and other things *less*. I love my job, yet I love my wife more than my job. If circumstances were such that I had to choose between my wife and my job, the job would be sacrificed. Does the conditional nature of my love for my job mean that I don't really love it? Not at all. I genuinely take pleasure in it, and hopefully for God-glorifying reasons. Still, my love for my wife is greater, which means, under certain circumstances, my love for my job could become conditional upon my love for my wife.

By this token, we might say that if there is anything in life that I love unconditionally, it must be whatever I love *most*—whatever it is I would keep after sacrificing everything else. Everything else in life that I love, then, I love upon the condition that it does not threaten that which I most love.

If God is uppermost in his own affections, then all other loves must finally be conditional upon that first love. The judgments of God's first love could then be rendered upon other things that God does love truly, albeit conditionally. This point may be buried deep into this chapter, but note how radically it flies in the face of one of our culture's principle assumptions about love, namely, that all things worthy of the name love must be "unconditional." Love can be conditional, and indeed God's love for mankind is *always* conditional. At cre-

---

[54]In the version reprinted in Piper's *God's Passion for His Glory* (Wheaton, IL: Crossway, 1998), 125–36.

[55]Bruce W. Davidson, "The Four Faces of Self-Love in the Theology of Edwards," *Journal of the Evangelical Theological Society*, vol. 51 (March 2008): 89; orig. found in *The Works of Jonathan Edwards*, vol. 18: *The "Miscellanies"* 501–832, ed. Ava Chamberlain (New Haven: Yale University Press, 2000), 239.

ation, it was conditional upon man's keeping of the law (Gen. 2:15–16). Upon redemption, it's conditional upon the righteousness of Christ and the ability to display Christ's glory.

The good news of Christianity is *not* that God has decided to love a people unconditionally. It's that he has decided to grant his "conditional love" fully and assuredly to a people contrary to what they deserve because Christ satisfied his conditions. David Powlison has the perfect phrase for this: God doesn't love his chosen people unconditionally; he loves them "contra-conditionally."[56] He loves his people contrary to what they deserve and then changes them into what they should be. He gives them his Spirit by which they can live according to his righteous standards or conditions, thereby displaying his image once more. His people are then free to fulfill his purposes for them in creation. As the Old Testament prophets promised, God both forgives his people's iniquity and places his law within them, so that they will walk in his statues and be careful to obey his rules.

All the riches of the Father's love for his beloved Son are extended to these adopted sons and fellow heirs. All the affections of the Father's love for his beloved Son are extended to the Son's bride. We the church, remarkably, are incorporated into the "vast, unmeasured, boundless, free" love of the Father for the Son.

New Testament scholar Richard Bauckham has observed that the key attributes of the relationship between the divine Father and Son in John 10 become the basis of Jesus' prayer for his disciples in chapter 17:

- In John 10 Jesus describes himself and the Father as *one* (v. 30). In chapter 17 he asks the Father to make his disciples one in the same fashion (vv. 11, 21, 22, 23).

- In chapter 10 Jesus says he has been *consecrated* by the Father (v. 36). In chapter 17 he asks the Father to consecrate his disciples (v. 17).

- In chapter 10 Jesus says the Father *sent* him into the world (v. 36). In chapter 17 he asks the Father to send them into the world (vv. 18, 21, 23).

- In chapter 10 Jesus says that the Father is *in him* and that he is in the Father (v. 38). In chapter 17, speaking again of his disciples, he says to his Father, "That they also may be in us. . . . I in them and you in me . . . so that the world may know that you sent me and loved them even as you loved me" (vv. 21, 23, 26).[57]

---

[56]See David Powlison's chapter, "God's Love: Better than Unconditional," in his book *Seeing with New Eyes* (Phillipsburg, NJ: P&R, 2003), 163–70.
[57]Richard Bauckham, "The Holiness of Jesus and His Disciples in the Gospel of John," in *Holiness and Ecclesiology in the New Testament,* ed. Kent E. Brower and Andy Johnson, 109; cf. A. J. Köstenberger, *The Missions of Jesus and the Disciples according to the Fourth Gospel* (Grand Rapids: Eerdmans, 1998), 186–97.

In the boomerang of God's love, the disciples are incorporated into all the affections, entitlements, and purposes the Father gives to the Son.

Natural man may take offense at the God-centeredness of God's love. If only his eyes would be opened, first, to how great this love is and, second, to what God promises man in the gospel. How great is God's love for God! The fires of God's love must burn over something. In God's love for God, his love burns for nothing other than the most exquisite beauty; for nothing other than matchless moral rectitude; for nothing other than universe creating and sustaining power; for nothing other than a perfectly careful justice; for nothing other than his all-encompassing wisdom of his Son, a Son who images back to him his own self. When the Father beholds the Son, the fires of his love burn for all this—with infinite delight and pleasure in the good of this perfect Son. That is how great this love is.

What is fallen man then given in the gospel? This same love! Think back to my story of hearing the preacher preach on Jesus' baptism. The Father's love for the Son should be oppressive to us, because we are not worthy of it. I dare say that we are like the homely girl who flips through the pages of a fashion magazine and feels despondent because she doesn't look like the artificially implanted, airbrushed models on the pages before her. Therefore she fears she will never be loved and adored for her beauty, as she wants to be. It's in this vein that we should behold the love of the Father for the Son. We will *never* look like Jesus, and the Father's love for the Son indeed rushes forward like mighty waters on account of his beauty. Ah, but here is the good news of the gospel: such love will be given to you and me, ugly sinners—the rush of the mighty waters of the Father's love upon us. Upon you. If only we repent and believe.

Such love has a transformative effect on the sinner because, as Augustine put it, such "love is God from God." It "is God the Holy Spirit proceeding from God who fires man to the love of God and neighbor." He loves us to the point of loving him in return with the same love and obedience demonstrated by Jesus for the Father. Consider these astounding promises from Jesus:

- Whoever has my commandments and keeps them, he it is who loves me. And he who loves me will be loved by my Father, and I will love him and manifest myself to him. (John 14:21)

- If anyone loves me, he will keep my word, and my Father will love him, and we will come to him and make our home with him. (John 14:23)

- In that day you will ask in my name, and I do not say to you that I will ask the Father on your behalf; for the Father himself loves you, because you have loved me and have believed that I came from God. (John 16:26–27)

Then, praying to the Father, Jesus says, "I made known to them your name, and I will continue to make it known, that the love with which you have loved me may be in them, and I in them" (John 17:26). (Here we find Carson's fifth strand of biblical love, what he calls "conditional love.")

God's love is given to sinners on account of Christ, but this love is not shorn of its holiness. It is holy and it creates holiness. It creates the holy obedience of love.

Step 6: Therefore, we can define love as "the lover's affirmation of and affection for the beloved and the beloved's good in the Holy."

What Is Love?

So what is love? Can we systematize the various strands of biblical data? I think we can, and with a little help from Jesuit Jules Toner and feminist Margaret Farley we will find ourselves right back with Augustine and Edwards. Ultimately, we'll find that love is a boomerang—God's boomerang.

LOVE'S THREE COMPONENTS

In his book *The Experience of Love*, Jules Toner attempts to simply observe what happens in the act of love. How do we experience love? His answer revolves around several ideas: response, union, and affirmation. To begin with, love is a *response* to some quality that we perceive in the beloved. The quality provokes or affects us to want to *unite* with the beloved on account of that quality, but we don't want to unite with the beloved in such a way that destroys the integrity of who the beloved is. Rather, love *affirms* the beloved in his very being "for himself and in himself." The lover gives himself to the beloved to the point of identifying himself with the beloved.[58]

Toner makes a wonderful distinction between *giving oneself* and *giving of oneself*. When I *give of myself* to you, I give you something that I possess such as wisdom, joy, my goods, or strengths. Of course, I don't really risk losing anything in the process, because I gain praise for such giving. Indeed, I can give all that I have, even my body to the flames, and have not love. When I *give myself*, however, I don't just give something that I have, but I give my whole self. I identify my *self* and all that I am with you. What strengths I have become yours, and what sorrows you have become mine. Any glory that I might have becomes yours, and all the glory that you have is the glory that I most enjoy. It's mine, too. There is a kind of interpenetration between my identity and yours,

---

[58] In Brady, *Christian Love*, 242–46.

one that does not violate the integrity of either identity but joins them together. Toner summarizes, "I love you because you are you. And I would be you by love without ceasing to be myself because I must be I in order that you may be you in the way that I alone can make you be you."[59]

Like Toner, feminist Margaret Farley defines love as an "affective affirmation which is responsive and unitive," but she also notices that it can be used to describe foolish and destructive loves. Such a love must truthfully and justly affirm the beloved. There must be a just affirmation of the beloved, which in turn depends on a just affirmation of the self (hence, "Love your neighbor as yourself").[60]

I don't think either Toner or Farley gets us the whole distance of where we want to go, and their definitions even risk blurring the Creator/creature distinction. But their insights are helpful and provide language for my mostly Augustinian-Edwardsian definition of love here. True godly love, I believe, consists of three things: (1) the lover's affirmation of and affection for the beloved and (2) the beloved's good (3) in the Holy.

1) *The lover's affirmation of and affection for the beloved . . .* Love always begins here. The pure essence of this can be seen in the Father's pleasure in the beloved Son, as well as in his affirmation of creation as "good." It can also be seen in God's salvific desire for sinners. In spite of the fact that we have rebelled against him, he continues to affirm our existence as a good thing in the call to salvation: "For God so loved the world . . ." (John 3:16) and "The Lord is . . . not wishing that any should perish" (2 Pet. 3:19).

Yet this aspect of love is hardly exclusive to God. It characterizes all love, whether we're talking about loving morally or immorally; loving in an erotic, platonic, or divine way; loving a person or food. To love something is to be glad it exists because of some quality in it. It's to affirm it. It's to have an affection for it. In Toner's language, this is the responsive aspect of love, and even the responsive desire to unite. In the language of the historical conversation, it's eros.

Indeed, it's probably easiest to see this aspect of love in the romantic or erotic domain. Consider the Song of Solomon, where two lovers are enveloped with affection and pleasure in and through one another. Each declares to the other that the other's love is better than wine (1:2; 4:10). Friends tell them to be drunk with love (5:1). The lover never stops exulting in the beloved's beauty. The beloved confesses to being sick with love (2:5; 5:8) and twice abjures other women not to awaken love at the wrong time (2:7; 8:4). Why such abjuring? Because "many waters cannot quench love, neither can floods drown it" (8:7a).

---

[59]Ibid., 245–46.
[60]Ibid., 256.

The pleasures or affections of love are powerful, controlling, and life-directing, like wine or fire. Though a man might be despised for doing so, he still might "offer for love all the wealth of his house" (8:7b). Song of Solomon's emphasis clearly falls on the experience and sensations of love—on the pleasure of it.

2) *. . . and the beloved's good . . .* Toner is right to talk about not violating the integrity of the one we love, and Farley is right to say that such love must be in accordance with truth and justice. We all know, for instance, that romantic love can become exploitative and invasive. What keeps such affection from becoming self-serving? True love takes pleasure in the other person's good or benefit. To love another person truly is to love his or her good or benefit, however we might define that good.[61] Maybe I'm taking pleasure in seeing you prosper financially, recover emotionally, grow in grace, or win the race. The point is that my claim to love you is validated by my pleasure in your genuine good.

Once again, my desire for your good presumes that, in Toner's language, I affirm you as created in God's image and worthy of all my respect. I affirm that you, in some God-derived sense, are worth loving, and I affirm my desire to see even more good come to you. It means I don't want to just *give of myself* to you, but I want to *give myself* to you. I want to treat your sorrows as my own and to let you treat my strengths as yours. I want to give you any glory that belongs to me, and any glory that belongs to you I will count as a cause for my own celebration. In other words, there's a sharing of identities and all that's entailed by those identities. I begin to represent your identity because I want your good; and you, if you love me, begin to represent mine.

We see this in the Scriptures between fathers and sons, where the shared identity between fathers and sons is to be a vehicle for love and doing one another good. Fathers and sons can even be said to share one another's guilt and blessing (e.g., Ex. 20:5–6). We see it in the institution of marriage, where the woman takes the man's name and they share a one-flesh union. Man and wife are to do one another good, not just giving of themselves but giving themselves. So close is this union and interpenetration that Adam calls his wife "bone of my bones and flesh of my flesh" (Gen. 2:23–24), while Paul tells husbands to "love their wives as their own bodies" (Eph. 5:28). We see it in the citizens of Israel, who shared an identity and the command to do one another good. The king, especially, would take on the nation's name and was to give himself entirely for the nation's good. And we see it in the church.

In other words, God built certain institutions into the very fabric of humanity and redemptive history where the elements of love were to be transacted. Both natural relationships (father/son) and covenanted relationships (husband/

---

[61]This is where I think Charles Taylor's argument for defining morality, identity, or (for our purposes) love according to some conception of the good is very helpful; see Charles Taylor, *Sources of the Self* (Cambridge, MA: Harvard University Press, 1989), esp. 78–90.

wife) were designed to be vehicles for affective affirmations of response and unity. In fact, the covenant becomes in the course of redemptive history the primary location for mutual identification and love, as well as shared guilt or blessing.[62] As we will consider more carefully in chapters 4 and 5, a covenant does not create relationship, it affirms one. Moreover, a covenant is more than a commitment to that relationship; it's a bending and bowing of one's entire identity around another person.

In one sense, we might say that love can involve self-sacrifice, but it's never entirely selfless. To love truly is always to experience some kind of pleasure, even if it's only a few seconds of pleasure before the heart stops and the breath ceases in a last act of loving self-sacrifice. A person will sacrifice himself for his friend when the pleasure he takes in his friend's life surpasses the pleasure he takes in his own. The pleasures of giving love are every bit as strong as the pleasures of the selfish person, if not greater, for it's better to give than to receive (Acts 20:35).

This is the very thing that is so beautiful and selfless about love—the finding of genuine pleasure in the good of someone else. In the final analysis, love involves both giving and receiving. A person may give himself, but, if he's giving in love, he always receives pleasure in doing so.

3) . . . *in the Holy*. To become truly biblical in our understanding of love, a third component is required. The good that the lover desires for the beloved is not just any so-called good; the good must be the personal God of the Bible—Father, Son, and Holy Spirit. More than that, it's the good of submitting and conforming oneself to God, just as Christ submitted himself entirely to the Father as a sign of his love. Loving another means wanting that person to know, experience, receive, enjoy, and adore the God who is all satisfying and worship worthy—to know him fully even as we are fully known. Loving another means taking pleasure in that person's movement toward conforming to and enjoying this greatest of goods, God.

---

[62]Theologians and exegetes often discuss the Protestant idea of the imputation of Christ's righteousness in the terms of the law court, since the *dikaios* word group is a legal/judicial one. Yet the law-court metaphor is just that—a metaphor that can help with certain aspects of imputation but does not explain the theological concept entirely. N. T. Wright's oft-quoted critique of imputation falls short precisely because he treats the metaphor, as it were, univocally. He writes, "Righteousness is not an object, a substance or a gas which can be passed across the courtroom"; in *What Saint Paul Really Said* (Oxford: Lion Book, 1997), 98. Well, sure, that's very clever-sounding, but he's not really critiquing imputation here. Imputation is a judicial idea, yes, but also a covenantal one. Entering into certain kinds of covenants involves my identity and all that I am, such that all that's mine becomes yours and all that's yours becomes mine. When I married my wife, for instance, my student loan debt actually became hers, and her Honda Civic actually became mine. Neither the Honda nor the debt floated across the courtroom. Still, there really was this "sweet exchange," at least from my perspective. So it is with the sweet exchange of Christ's righteousness and my sin. By *giving himself* to his people in the new covenant, what he possesses becomes ours, and what's ours becomes his. In that sense, Wright is correct to point to the covenantal aspects of God's righteousness in Christ. I even appreciate his point in the same chapter of this critique that the book of Romans, most fundamentally, presents us not with the realities of the law court but with a "theology of love" (p. 110). Yet somehow he misses the fact that the shared identity of biblical covenants involves exchanging not just obligations but debts and blessings. Somehow he misses the fact that the exchange of sin and righteousness between Christ and sinner—these legal or judicial realities—is also a covenantal reality, and a nuptial one, at that.

This is what Augustine meant by saying that we should love others "with respect" to Christ or "for the sake of" Christ, and it is precisely the point that Toner misses when he says that we should love another human "for himself and in himself." Love is an affective affirmation that is responsive and unitive and for the other's good, but it's an affective affirmation in the Holy—always and only. To love another human is to love him in creation (by virtue of God's work) and for redemption (by virtue of God's work).

This is also the point missed by the interpreters of Luther such as Kierkegaard, Nygren, and Barth. The issue is not finally a matter of love as desire (eros) versus love as gift (agape). It's whether the desire is for the Holy One and the gift is the Holy One. Insofar as theologians miss this last point, as I said, they have a theological system that will bend toward man-centeredness, even if other elements in their system help to prevent it from doing so.

To be fair, the Augustinian tradition has its weaknesses as well. Specifically, it can underemphasize the fact that God's love does affirm humanity. This tradition, in some of its formulations, is so adamant about ensuring that love remains centered on God that it tends to overlook the fact that God did affirm creation as good, and that he does affirm sinners in his desire not to see any perish. John Piper, building on Edwards, likes to say that God doesn't love us by making much of us but by enabling us to make much of him. He illustrates the point by placing us before the Grand Canyon, gazing at its splendor. We don't look at the Grand Canyon to feel good about ourselves but simply to look on in awe.

In a sense, Piper's description here of God's love might sound like the boomerang I've been describing, and it certainly makes for a nice sermonic sound bite, but I think his formulation is a little too severe. Maybe I'm pressing his illustration further than he intended it to go, but it's worth observing that the Grand Canyon does nothing to interact with its viewers, much less to affirm the existence of those looking at it. The existence of the viewers is of absolutely no consequence—one might as well be replaced by another. Not so with God's love for us. According to Genesis 1, he affirms our existence. He doesn't need to, but he does. What's more, he does make much of us. He makes more of himself, and everything he makes of us gets redirected to him, but there is an affirmation.

Perhaps what I'm getting at comes down to the difference between affirming and enabling. He doesn't just enable us to make much of him. He enables us to make much of him, in part, by affirming us in our existence and redemption. A recent personal encounter with forgiveness reminded me of how precious these truths are. Only several weeks ago I shaded the truth with a fellow elder in response to a question he asked me about my prayer life. I wanted him to think that I prayed more than I do. Right after giving my answer, I felt deep shame for having lied, but I was too proud to quickly correct the error. By God's grace, I had difficulty sleeping that night, and in the morning I confessed my lie to him. Immediately and graciously he forgave me. Tears came to my eyes with his forgiveness. In spite of my sin, I was affirmed—remarkably, graciously, wonderfully affirmed. There was no glory to me in that; in fact, there was just the opposite—glory to him who forgave me.

Piper's Grand Canyon illustration of the beatific vision is wonderful, but is there some way to tweak the illustration by getting the beautiful sight to somehow reach out and embrace sinners?[63] Notice that many illustrations of heaven in the Bible are feasts! This is no minor point for the purposes of this book's argument. As we'll see in chapter 4, both baptism and church membership are a New Testament reenactment of "God saw that it was good." They are the church's affirmation and embrace of God's new creation in individual lives.

Still, Pipers's and Edwards's and Augustine's general thrust is exactly right. Love is inherently God-centered. Love concerns the praise and worship and glory of God. Love is the enjoying of God and the enjoying of him anywhere and everywhere he chooses to make himself manifest. So a mortal may scarcely pray a better prayer for another mortal than Paul does by asking the Father to enable the Ephesians "to know the love of Christ that surpasses knowledge, that you may be filled with all the fullness of God" (Eph. 3:19).

This third aspect of love presents us with the line that divides the world's understanding of love and a biblical understanding. The world can understand the first two aspects of love—love as an affirmation of and affection for the beloved and the beloved's good. But ever since Adam and Eve's fall in the garden, the world has been constitutionally opposed to this third element of love—love as affection for another's good in or through God. After all, the world wants to be God (Gen. 3:5). We have swallowed Satan's lie that our greatest pleasure would never be found in conforming our existence to him and the law of his character. So we define love to exclude him deliberately, the very source and being of love. One of the greatest ironies of the postmodern West might be this: that great symbol of pleasure in our culture for which it (consciously or not) most emphatically rejects God—sex—is the very thing God has given humanity so that it might have an analogy, a category, a lan-

---

[63]What Piper's illustration misses is wonderfully captured by Edwards's more biblical illustration: "The creation of the world seems to have been especially for this end, that the eternal Son of God might obtain a spouse toward whom he might fully exercise the infinite benevolence of his nature, and to whom he might, as it were, open and pour forth all that immense fountain of condescension, love, and grace, that was in his heart, and that in this way God might be glorified." From Jonathan Edwards's sermon, "Church's Marriage to Her Sons, and to Her God," *Sermons and Discourses 1743–1758*, vol. 25, ed. Wilson H. Kimmach (New Haven, CT: Yale University Press, 2006), 187.

guage for knowing what the unadulterated enjoyment of him will be like in glory (see Eph. 5:22–33). In other words, we reject God for sex, but sex is exactly what he's given us in order to faintly grasp the experience of a perfect union with him.[64]

Idolatry, after all, is nothing other than substituting some other great good, some other "first love," into God's place in defiance of the first, second, and greatest commandments (Deut. 5:7–8; 6:5; Mark 12:28ff.). By this token, we find that sinful human love can contain the first two elements of love—an affection for the beloved's good. But because the sinner constitutionally cannot conceive of God as being the true and greatest good, he will act out his "love" for the beloved by giving the beloved whatever idol he has substituted for God. Sadly, such idolatrous love inevitably warps toward destruction. Consider the workaholic father, who truly desires, in some sense, the genuine good of the children that he never spends time with. The most significant tokens of his love toward them are toys, exotic trips, or tuition payments, the very things that he most values, nay, worships. He genuinely identifies himself with these children, sharing his strengths, taking on their weaknesses, but there is no knowledge of the Holy. The entire exercise will prove futile.

Consider the legalistic, rule-driven mother who oppresses the children, whom she genuinely loves, with her endless demands. She worships her own image, and therefore strives to demonstrate to the whole universe that she is capable, that she measures up, that she is righteous and worthy. The burdensome rules she imposes on her children are, ironically, expressions of her love for them. She identifies herself with them and wants their good. She wants, with all the love she is capable of, for them to "measure up" just as she desperately wants to measure up. But again, there is no knowledge of the Holy.

Consider, finally, the church that bears a true affection for the good of its community but does so with a man-centered love. That church's primary desire will be to draw people into its community by whatever means possible. Technological gimmickry, entertainment, and sloganeering seem to work best in our present-day context, just like appealing to people's fears and superstitions seemed to work well in a medieval context. Yet to whatever extent this church's love is indeed man-centered, it will never grow in holiness and a true love for God. The numbers may increase but worship will not.

---

[64]So D. A. Carson writes, "It is as if the only pleasure and intimacy in this life that comes close to anticipating the pleasure of the church and her Lord being perfectly united on the last day is the sexual union of a good marriage." *Love in Hard Places*, 191. Likewise, John Piper writes, "God created us with sexual passion so that there would be language to describe what it means to cleave to him in love and what it means to turn away from him to others," in *Sex and the Supremacy of Christ*, ed. John Piper and Justin Taylor (Wheaton: IL: Crossway, 2005), 28; and again, "God made us powerfully sexual so that he would be more deeply knowable. We were given the power to know each other sexually so that we might have some hint of what it will be like to know Christ supremely," 30.

The implicit principle in all three examples is that the Bible presents us with only two possible greatest goods: God or something else. Every greatest good besides God is an idol, which is precisely why we discovered in chapter 1 that idolatry is at the heart of this world's ideas about love. It's nothing short of tragic, then, when God's people mimic love as the world defines and practices it. After all, only God's regenerate, new-creation people have been freed from the dominion of sin in order to love Father, Son, and Spirit truly, or to see that God is the ultimate good for the beloved.

All three elements of love can be found in what's probably the most well-known description of love in the Bible—1 Corinthians 13. In the chapter's first three verses, Paul distinguishes love from angelic acts of speech, understanding, faith, and even altruistic self-sacrifice. Apparently love is not love without some type of affective element.[65] Yet love requires not just any affirmation and affection but affection for the beloved's good. Verses 4 through 7 therefore present a list of actions, or, at least, dispositions of heart, that demonstrate an utter devotion to the beloved's good. Patience, kindness, a lack of envy, not insisting on one's own way, persevering in hope—all are actions or attitudes that presuppose a fundamental care for the beloved over and above oneself and one's liberties.

The final culmination or fulfillment of this love is the moment when the perfect comes and the partial passes away; the moment when we see him face-to-face and know him fully, even as we are fully known (1 Cor. 13:10, 12). Ironically, it's not uncommon for non-Christian couples to ask for 1 Corinthians 13 to be read at their weddings, probably because these first two sections present the first two aspects of love with an elegance rarely matched in all literature. More significantly, the chapter's final five verses are vague enough to avoid what would offend them if they understood all that was at stake—to behold "the perfect," to "know fully" God and God's perfect love.

Step 7: God's love, God's gospel, and God's church offend us because they all center on him.

The Heart of the Offense: It's Not Our Party

Earlier I claimed that God's love repels us. How could it be that God's love offends us?

THE OFFENSIVENESS OF GOD'S LOVE FOR GOD

God's love offends us because the greatest object of God's love is God, not us. "For from him and through him and to him are all things. To him be glory

---

[65]D. A. Carson, *Love in Hard Places*, 21–22.

forever" (Rom. 11:36), the apostle Paul says, after spending eleven chapters explaining the nature of redemption. If "all things" includes love, which surely it does, then all true love is *from* God, *through* God, and *to* God. Love, as I say, is like a boomerang, going out from God and drawing love back in return.

The boomerang of God's love is thrown outward in God's call for all humanity to worship him, not ourselves. The boomerang returns in the praise and glory he receives in both salvation and judgment. "How unsearchable are his judgments and how inscrutable his ways! . . . To him be glory forever" (Rom. 11:33, 36). Since God's love is centered on God, humans will be judged, which would not be the case if his love centered on us.

Hence, we can also say that God's love is offensive to us because it renders judgment against us. And we would be his judge.

Since God is the greatest object of God's love, God's *gospel,* in spite of the things that the world might like about it, ultimately offends us. After all, God's gospel involves applying God's own righteousness through faith to the sinner, leaving the sinner with nothing to boast in. All glory goes to God with God's gospel (Rom. 3:21–27), not to us. Also, his gospel calls us to a life of righteousness. It even claims that love is shown through obedience. That's a tough sell in a culture that equates love with absolute freedom.

Since God is the greatest object of God's love, God's *church,* in spite of the things that the world might like about it, ultimately offends us. After all, the church is the very outpost of people who have capitulated to this offensively self-glorying God. These traitors have been duped into promoting this megalomaniac. They are supporting his regime. What about our ways and our glory?

The borders of membership and discipline offend us because they remind us of God's judgment, which we despise. "What? He thinks he can exclude me?" Indeed, it's the very borders, boundaries, or walls around the church that remind unregenerate eyes that this outpost is what it is—conquered territory in *our* country. Ask any occupied nation how it feels about its occupiers. The response will be immediate—indignation and outrage. How do nations treat their own when their own take sides with the enemy? They are despised. They are called traitors. They are charged with criminal activity. Often, they are hanged.

That these militaristic metaphors may sound unloving and aggressive is something I concede entirely. These metaphors of walls and forts *are* unloving, precisely because "love," in the domain of the natural man, is defined as "I'm the center, not God." To say that "God is the center" is, by definition, an unloving thing to say. The metaphors *are* aggressive precisely because God's love, in fact, aims to destroy the unloving by making them loving. He aims to redefine the natural man's love so that God himself, not the man, becomes its ultimate object. The act of creating the new man is the act of destroying—killing—the old.

Death, then resurrection. Not only that, but he aims to do all this through the offensive act of evangelism and the foolish act of preaching. The audacity!

The boundaries of the church are the boundaries between two domains—one where God is at the center and one where we are at the center. There is no middle ground between these two domains. This doesn't mean it's always clear who belongs to which domain, but we do well to remember, as Jesus said, that none of us can serve two masters. Either we will hate the one and love the other, or we will be devoted to one and despise the other. Or as the apostle John said, we cannot love both God and the world. If anyone loves the world, the love of God is not in him. Or, again, as Jesus said, whoever is not with God is against him, and whoever does not gather with him scatters. We are either inside the fort, or outside.[66]

God's love, God's gospel, and God's church offend us because we are *glory thieves*, to borrow Paul David Tripp's phrase. God created us to enjoy and display his glory, but sin has twisted our hearts, so that now we try to steal what rightfully belongs to him. Tripp illustrates the point with the simple story of a young boy at a little girl's five-year-old birthday party. He looks down at his own small bag of party favors and then over at her mountainous pile of gifts. Bothered by the comparison, he crosses his arms, juts out his lower lip, and utters an audible *humph!* In fact, he repeats the *humphing* over and over to ensure that everyone hears it. Finally, one of the mothers at the party leans down, draws his face toward her own, and says something profound: "Johnny, it's not your party!"[67]

What's true of five-year-olds is true of all of us: we treat life as if it's *our* party. We want the mountain of gifts and the kudos to belong to us, not to someone else. Not even to God. Our lives are spent conspiring toward this end. God responds to our conspiring not with a gospel of "unconditional love," but with a gospel of "contra-conditional love." The idea of unconditional love suggests that he is content to love us exactly as he finds us, but that's not quite right. He loves us when he finds us, but he loves us by changing us into what we should be.

If life were our party, as we and little Johnny wish, boundary lines would not make sense. There's a universe of difference between a God who most loves God and a God who most loves man. One is holy; one is not. Any theological system that makes humanity the primary focus of God's love is a system that (ultimately) loses its need for borders or boundaries, holiness or righteousness, justice or mercy. Mercy becomes meaningless and entitlement everything. The membership lines between church and world will eventually vanish, or at least

---

[66]Matt. 6:24; 12:30; 1 John 2:15.
[67]Paul David Tripp, *Instruments in the Redeemer's Hands: People in Need of Change Helping People in Need of Change* (Phillipsburg, NJ: P&R, 2002), 34.

take on a vacuous and oxymoronic function more suited to business marketing—"Join as you are; *everyone* is special here!" Yet the vanished line between church and world would be the least of our problems. An indiscriminate God bound to pacifying most every human whim and hankering would be the real danger.

On the other hand, bowing down to God's love for God—submitting to his glory—means being incorporated into it, sharing in it, and enjoying the most beautiful of beauties forever.

Step 8: God's love and God's judgment work in concert, not in opposition. This also is offensive.

The Offensiveness of Judgment

Speaking of things that offend contemporary Western sensibilities, there's one more matter that stems from God's primary love for God that we need to consider, and that's the relationship between God's love and God's judgment. The Bible teaches very clearly that judgment is God's (Deut. 1:17). It teaches that judgment is his own activity—no one taught him (Isa. 40:14). In fact, it teaches that he loves judgment (Isa. 62:8) and that he is a God of judgment (Isa. 30:18; Mal. 2:17). Only a moment's thought is needed to consider how the Bible is strewn with acts of God's judgment: the fall, the flood, Babel, Sodom and Gomorrah, Pharaoh and the Red Sea, the death of the first generation of Israelites in the wilderness, the Passover Lamb, the death of Christ on the cross, the eternal lake of burning fire.

This is particularly relevant to the practices of church membership and discipline, since these practices are, as I said earlier, forms of judgment. It's not an ultimate or final judgment, but it is an anticipatory one, which is why Jesus would commission his disciples with language as strong as, "If you forgive the sins of any, they are forgiven them, if you withhold forgiveness from any, it is withheld" (John 20:23). What then should we make of the relationship between love and judgment?

The first point to establish here is that love and judgment are not ultimately opposed. Rather, they work in concert, as we saw with love and holiness. The key here is to consider the relationship between love and law, since I am treating *judgment* as a verdict rendered according to the law—a pronouncement of what the law requires.[68] In a fallen world, real life often presents us with

---

[68] See T. D. Alexander's excellent discussion of love and law in his chapter on Deuteronomy entitled, "Love and Loyalty," in T. D. Alexander, *From Paradise to Promised Land: An Introduction to the Main Themes of the Pentateuch* (Grand Rapids: Baker, 1995), 162. Is Deuteronomy, a book filled with so many laws, really a book about love and loyalty? "At the heart of this covenant," says Alexander referring to the burden of Deuteronomy, "is a commitment by both parties to love the other wholeheartedly and faithfully."

situations in which love and law are in conflict. Our affections seem to dictate one thing while the law seems to dictate something else, whether we're talking about man's law or God's. Systematic theologians will sometimes reinforce this notion that love and law are in tension, even within God himself.[69]

The challenge for us, I believe, is to step back and recognize that no tension ultimately exists in God's eternal plan between love and law.[70] Law is the very thing that protects what is most loved and cherished. I don't mean to say that "protecting something precious" is the very essence of what the law is or does; philosophers can argue about that. But I do think it's fairly easy to see that one of the primary reasons we institute laws and render judgments by them is to protect something precious. It's against the law to murder, because life is precious. It's against the law to steal, because property is precious. It's against God's moral law to lie, because truth is precious. Every five-year-old who values his toys and every king who values his gold understands this much about law. That's why both kids and kings will declare, "Don't touch these things, or else!" In that sense, one might say that laws function like fences or security systems. People erect fences and install alarm systems when they want to guard something precious.

This is why breaking a law results in a penalty or act of judgment. An act of judgment speaks to—or better, declares—the value or worthiness of the thing being protected. If no penalty or judgment follows the transgression of a law, we learn that whatever the so-called law is guarding must not be worth much. If the penalty for transgression is severe, we learn that it is precious. Judgments teach. I discovered at a young age, for instance, that lying to my parents yielded a stronger penalty than squabbling with my brother over a toy. The lesson I learned from these different penalties is that truth is more precious than toys. The very idea of a penalty may be repugnant to human beings, but a penalty is what gives meaning to the law as a guardian of worth (or schoolmaster or tutor; cf. Gal. 3:24). If the law is the sentry guarding that which is precious, the penalty or judgment is the sentry's pointy bayonet. It gives the law its prick, substance, and meaning.

---

[69]For instance, Donald G. Bloesch writes, "Biblical faith portrays God as having two sides: holiness and love. These are the perfections that shape the interaction of God with his people. They are integrally related, and yet they coexist in a certain tension, one that highlights their paradoxical unity rather than resolves it. God's holiness is his majestic purity that cannot tolerate moral evil. God's love is his outgoing, tenderhearted embrace of the sinner. God's holiness is his separateness from what is unclean and profane. God's love is his willingness to identify with those who are unclean in order to help them. God's holiness transcends the passing world of death and decay. God's love incarnates itself in this world corrupted by sin." *God the Almighty: Power, Wisdom, Holiness, Love* (Carlisle, UK: Paternoster, 1995), 139–40.

[70]The tension that we experience in this present age between God's love and God's law results from at least one of three places. First, we might have a man-centered conception of his love that is colliding with the almost necessarily God-centered nature of his law. I think this is a fairly common mistake evangelicals make. Second, there does seem to be real tension between God's ultimate love for his glory and his conditional love for sinners (e.g., 2 Pet. 3:9). Ultimately, I think we must say that this tension will dissolve, but since it's a tension that Scripture presents as a reality in this present age we should expect to feel it as well. Third, it does seem like a man-centered God would experience tension between love and law as humans choose things that he, in his infinite wisdom, knows are not good for them.

God says to Noah, "Whoever sheds the blood of man, by man shall his blood be shed" (Gen. 9:6a). The severity is because human life is precious. Taking life must therefore result in the severest of earthly punishments. Letting a murderer go free is to say, "The life which he took wasn't worth much anyway."

In sum, law is love's sentry, and judgment is the sentry's bayonet. Law and judgment protect whatever love most loves. They fight injustice, oppression, exploitation. Biblical scholar Leon Morris draws out this point by comparing the biblical mindset with our own:

> With us legalism has acquired the notion of a soulless, rigid application of the letter of the law to the detriment of human values. Not so did the Hebrews understand judgment. For them law was the bulwark against oppression. The poor and the weak looked to law to save them from the might of the rich and the powerful. "Save me, O God, by thy name, and judge me in thy might," said the Psalmist (Ps. 44.1), and such pleas are common. We may put a distinction between kindness and legal processes but we should be clear that the Hebrews did not.[71]

Love and law—or love and law's judgments—work in concert, not in opposition.

To apply this first principle to God, then, we maintain that, insofar as God's affections uphold something as most precious, he will evaluate or judge all things by whether they, too, ascribe proper value and worth to that thing. He intends for us to call "good" what he calls "good" and to call "evil" what he calls "evil" (Mal. 2:17). If, therefore, God loves his glory more than anything, upholding it as most precious, everything in the world that redounds to his glory would be called "good." Anything opposed to his glory would be called "evil," the *law of God* would be that which upholds the standards of his glory, and the *judgment of God* would be rendered according to these glory-promoting laws. On the other hand, if God loves us more than anything—if his greatest affections are bent toward our glory—God's law and judgments would bend in precisely the same direction. His law would ultimately uphold your glory and mine, and his judgment would do the same, even if that meant judgment would have to fall sometimes upon God himself—"God, how dare you."

If love and judgment work in concert, a number of application questions for the local church spring to mind: could it be that the exclusivistic nature of church membership, when rightly practiced, is, in fact, loving? Also, though church discipline can no doubt be motivated by things other than love, could it be that the members of a local church who love one another and the world in a godly fashion will sometimes be required to pursue the course of excommunication?

---

[71]Leon Morris, *The Biblical Doctrine of Judgment* (1960; repr. Eugene, OR: Wipf & Stock, n.d.), 22.

A second principle concerning God's love and judgment is that all God's judgments serve the God-centeredness of his love. His love evaluates and assesses in accordance with his God-centeredness. His love expects, it demands, and it enacts penalties in accordance with his God-centeredness.

What's interesting to notice in the Genesis 9 passage cited above is why human life is described as "precious": "Whoever sheds the blood of man, by man shall his blood be shed, for God made man in his own image" (v. 6). The preciousness of human life, it seems, is found entirely in the fact that humans image God. Our worth is derivative. It's derived from the one we image. Killing a human is wrong *not* because God loves us more than anything, but because he loves his own glory more than anything.

That is why King David knew that his murder and adultery were ultimately sins against God (Ps. 51:4). A law of protection had been placed around life and marital fidelity, two things made precious because of their relatedness to God. To kill is to destroy one made in the image of God. To cheat, at the very least, is to speak lies about God's fidelity to his people. To do either one as an image bearer is to present a blasphemous portrait of what God himself is like. David's sin, though enacted against Uriah and Bathsheba and his own body, was finally against God and God alone. He broke God's law. He fell short of God's glory. He exalted the idols of his lusts over and above God. He treated the glory and worth of God with utter contempt.

God's law is the infinitely high fence that protects his infinite worthiness and glory. It's the guardian (and declarer) of his glory. To contravene his law is to disregard his infinite worthiness. To put this in less abstract terms, saying no to God is saying, "What you think doesn't mean much to me, because you don't mean much to me."

The very structure of the Ten Commandments confirms the priorities of God's love. The prohibitions in the second table of the law, which forbid harming other human beings (through the dishonor of parents, murder, adultery, theft, false witness, and coveting), are grounded in the first table, particularly the two injunctions against other gods and idols. His glory and fame are the uppermost purpose of his law and his judgments, from the flood in Genesis to the fiery lake in Revelation.

Why do humans despise God's judgments? It's not just threat of pain or loss. People will accept pain and loss for the things they love. No, our heartfelt repugnance toward God's penalties and acts of judgment roots principally in the fact that God most values and cherishes something different from what we most value and cherish. He loves his glory most. We love ours most, which is precisely why Adam and Eve jumped on the Serpent's offer to be the evaluators of "good and evil" for themselves (Gen. 3:5).

One implication of this second principle is that a theological system that presents a God who loves his creatures more than anything is a system that will probably tend over time toward universalism and the eradication of divine judgment, as well as a radical reprioritization of ethics. A man-centered system will still draw boundaries and enact judgments, but since the human self has become the most valuable thing in the universe, the law will be restructured to offer protection in accordance with this new mandate. The sentries will be recommissioned, almost like the U.S. Secret Service transitioning from one presidential administration to the next. In a man-centered system, the two tables of the law will be flipped, as it were, so that any laws pertaining to "God" become grounded in the laws pertaining to man. With God's love flowing principally toward humanity, the concept of holiness will eventually empty of any meaning, like pipes that dry up. Also, any doctrine of eternal judgment or damnation will dry up. Man-centered systems might inconsistently keep such a doctrine for a time because the doctrine can easily be found on the pages of Scripture, but the inevitable logic of the system will eventually determine that, if humanity is most precious and if God loves man more than himself, there is no higher law that constrains God to do anything other than grant all humanity eternal bliss.

Even the so-called law of "respecting human choice," popular in some theological traditions, surely would not require damnation or hell. If God loved man more than anything, why not, as I asked earlier, send those who reject him to the other side of the universe for an eternal vacation of bliss, blinding them to the fact that he sustains and gives them joy even there? Some form of universalism is inevitable, whether it's articulated or not. A God-centered God can choose to save all or none. A man-centered God, it seems, is required to save all by the mandate of his own first affections.

By the same token, a church that worships a man-centered God will begin to downplay and eventually erase the Bible's boundaries, such as the boundaries between heaven and hell, the church and the world, or this world and the next. Probably, ethical boundaries will dissolve as well, such as the boundaries between male and female leadership or homosexual and heterosexual lifestyles. New ethical boundaries will emerge in their place, boundaries more than likely to accord with the ethical boundaries of political and popular culture. Eventually, the church will look just like the world, and the reason for this should be plain: man-centeredness is the cardinal moral principle of the kingdom of this world. It's the very thing that constitutes fallen humanity as fallen humanity.

Step 9: A loving church is a church that seeks out the Holy to affirm and separate it from the unholy.

Conclusion: What Is a Loving Church?

God's love is a boomerang that natural man loves and despises. We love the embrace of the boomerang as it flies outward; we despise the demand of the boomerang as it calls us back to loving him with all our heart, mind, soul, and strength. We also despise the suggestion that his love will cause him to judge. He says, "You shall have no other gods before me. For from me and through me and to me are all things." We say, "That's offensive. I will burn you at the stake for that. I don't care if you're walking around healing people. You want me to bow before you? How dare you!"

God's gospel is a boomerang that natural man loves and despises. We love the announcement of forgiveness and love through no merit of our own; we despise the call to repent, forsake everything, and follow Jesus. We despise the exclusiveness of this call.

God's church is a boomerang that natural man loves and despises. We love the idea of a warm fellowship that will embrace us; we despise the fellowship's requirement that we abandon the familiar blandishments of family and friends and submit to its oversight and discipline. What's worse, belonging to the church means going back to those families and friends and sharing a foolish gospel with them. It means saying to those who gave birth to us, "I'm still with you, but I'm not of you." We know how they'll respond: "That's exclusivistic! That's arrogant! That's not love!" But like Bunyan's Christian pleading with his townspeople to repent before destruction comes, it's our very love for them that wants them to see the eternity of difference between what we were and what we are. The line between these two domains must be sharp and bright—for their eternal good.

HOLINESS AND LOVE

Holiness and love are not what people expect. People expect that love calls the church to mission, while holiness calls the church to worship. Both are true, but it's also true that holiness sends us on mission, while love calls us to worship. Holy love or loving holiness has both an outward and an inward, or better, an upward, impulse—again, like a boomerang. There's a time and season for everything—a time for inclusion and time for exclusion, a time for going forth and a time for drawing back, a time for building up and a time for breaking down, a time for affection and a time for rejection.

Consider Jesus' high priestly prayer. He does not ask the Father to take the church out of the world, but he does ask the Father to keep them. "I do not ask that you take them out of the world, but that you keep them from the evil one" (John 17:15). He has guarded them from the forces of evil, and he wants the Father to do the same (17:12). More specifically, he asks the Father to keep them in his name (17:11). These are a people marked off by and for the name of God himself. They are to be separate and distinct, even though they will be hated for this, just as Jesus was hated (17:14). Jesus is also adamant in his prayer about those in the church being *in* and *with* the world. Therefore he asks the Father to consecrate them to his ministry: "Sanctify [consecrate] them in the truth; your word is truth. As you sent me into the world, so I have sent them into the world" (17:17–18).[72] Why does he send them? Christ intends for the church to fill with the knowledge of God's glory as the water covers the sea (Hab. 2:14; Isa. 6:3). As New Testament scholar Richard Bauckham puts it, "God makes them holy, dedicated to him, not in order to remove them from the world, but in order to send them into the world to make God known."[73]

Yet, it's by this holiness, this simultaneous going forth and drawing back, that the church defines love for the world. In other words, the church is to go *into* the world, but it is to go as a united and distinct people, a people who are marked off by God's name. Jesus says to the Father, "The glory that you have given me I have given to them, that they may be one even as we are one, I in them and you in me, that *they may become perfectly one*, so that the world may know that you sent me *and loved them even as you loved me*" (John 17:22–23). Notice what Jesus didn't say here. He didn't say that the world will perceive the Father's love when the church acts just like the world, or when the church embraces non-Christians into its community, or when the church scatters as individuals anywhere and everywhere. Rather, he says the world will know the Father's love through the church's united life. Surely this is why Jesus had told his disciples earlier to love one another as he had loved them—so that the world would know they belonged to him (John 13:34–35).

Is the church "missional," as so many today contend?[74] Yes, insofar as the boomerang of God's love is hurled outward in the gospel-carrying

---

[72]Richard Bauckham convincingly argues that the Gospel of John makes a distinction between the "purification" of sins, which the disciples have already received (13:10; 15:3), and their sanctification or consecration to the work of Christ's ministry. Consecration, he argues, is a better translation of *hagiazine* in verse 17 since the word "sanctify" suggests that Jesus has in mind the idea of being made ethically holy here. The context of verse 18, however, suggests that he has the idea of his disciples' being set apart to his work. Richard Bauckham, "The Holiness of Jesus and His Disciples in the Gospel of John," 111.

[73]Ibid., 113.

[74]At a conference of the International Missionary Council in 1952, Wilhelm Anderson, building on the work of Karl Barth, proposed that both church and mission should be taken up into the *missio Dei*—the mission of God. Missions is not just a function of the church, and the church is not just the outcome of missions. Rather, both are grounded in a triune God on mission. The church has a missionary—we now say "missional"—nature. Johannes Blauw captured the basic premise in the title of his 1962 book, *The Missionary Nature of the Church*. Ecumenicals embraced this way of speaking more fully with the merger of the IMC and the World Council of Churches in 1961, followed by Roman Catholics' and Vatican II's pronouncement that "the Church on earth is by its very nature missionary since, according to the plan of the Father, it has its origin in the mission of the Son and the Holy Spirit." "Decree on the Church's Missionary Activity," *Ad Gentes Divinitus*, in *Vatican Council II: vol. 1, The Conciliar & Post Conciliar Documents*. rev. ed., ed. Austin Flannery (Costello, 1987), 813. Signaling this shift in thinking among many, the World Council of Churches in 1969 dropped the *s* from its journal *International Review of Missions* to become *International Review of Mission*. This history is recounted in Craig Van Gelder, *The Essence of the Church: A Community Created by the Spirit* (Baker, 2000), 32–36; also, David Bosch, *Transforming Mission: Paradigm Shifts in Theology*

church. Yet the missional emphasis becomes man-centered or unholy as soon as it sets this emphasis over against the boomerang's returning arch—against God's gathered people; against God's own glory. The purpose of God's love for sinners, like the purpose of his affirmation of creation, is that he might be glorified and worshiped. This glory and worship is best seen on earth in his gathered people, which is why the believer's heart should so prize such gatherings. A church that doesn't spend itself reaching out for lost sinners is not loving—or holy, but a church that doesn't spend itself in helping those lost sinners conform more and more to the glory and worship of God is not holy—or loving.

GLORY SEEKERS

Christians should not be glory thieves but glory seekers: "To those who by patience in well-doing seek for glory and honor and immortality, he will give eternal life" (Rom. 2:7). They should go into the world seeking God's glory wherever they can find it, affectionately affirming it and identifying themselves with it. They should do this at several levels, corresponding with God's providential love, his universal love, and his special love for his people.

Since God's glory is evident in creation (e.g., Ps. 19:1–5), God's people should seek it out and affirm it there.

Since God's glory is evident in the pinnacle of his creation, humankind, God's people should seek it out and affirm it there as well. Even if his image has become warped and hazy, like a charred but unburnt photograph pulled from the ashes of a fire, a Christian's heart should be warmed by the memory of what once was and could be again. Mother Teresa has written:

> God has identified himself with the hungry, the sick, the naked, the homeless; hunger, not only for bread, but for love, for care, to be somebody to someone; nakedness, not of clothing only, but nakedness of that compassion that very few people give to the unknown; homelessness, not only just for a shelter made of stone, but that homelessness that comes from having no one to call your own.[75]

God has identified himself with all sinners everywhere by placing the stamp of his image upon them. He says in essence, "Every child of Adam is mine, and they all reflect something of me." That is, he loves them. Christians should

---

of Mission (Orbis, 1991), 362–68. Darrell Guder claims credit for the proliferation of the term missional church based on his edited book by that title in Darrell Guder, "The Church as Missional Community," The Community of the Word: Toward an Evangelical Ecclesiology, ed. Mark Husbands and Daniel J. Treier (Downers Grove, IL: InterVarsity, 2005), 114.

[75]Originally quoted in Life in the Spirit: Reflections, Meditations, Prayers, Mother Teresa of Calcutta, ed. Kathryn Spink (San Francisco: Harper & Row, 1983), 24–25.

therefore seek out God's glory in the bars, alleyways, and abortion clinics; the law firm, market floor, and football field.

More than either of these things, a Christian is someone with eyes particularly alert for the holy, like the beloved searching for her lover, straining to hear his name spoken, to catch a whiff of his garment. The charred photograph is not enough. She wants to reach out and touch him and to know his live embrace.

In this world the Christian finds Christ's live and holy embrace in the local church, as the church reaches out to affectionately affirm, unite, and identify itself with the Christian. "Yes, you belong to Christ. You are his. He's not back yet, but we are standing in his place until he does. If you suffer, we will suffer with you. If you rejoice, we will rejoice with you, because he has promised that his glory shall be ours and ours shall be his."

A church that loves with the love of Christ is a church that burns to affirm any gospel-created divine loveliness it sees in the lives of others:

- For its own sake, the church desires to unite to the presence of that divine loveliness in the life of individual Christians, because every Christian increasingly displays both the universally shared characteristics of God, such as compassion and mercy, as well as whatever unique perspective on God's glory that God has given to each member of the body. The church burns to identify itself with and to share in each one's divinely given beauty. Members "yearn" for one another "with the affection of Christ Jesus" (Phil. 1:8). Body members don't just give of themselves to one another; they give themselves to one another. Hence, "if one member suffers, all suffer together; if one member is honored, all rejoice together" (1 Cor. 12:26).

- For the individual's sake, the church burns for each member to be protected from the attacks of the world, the flesh, and the Devil and to be guided into all righteousness and greater loveliness, just as a mother desires such things for her children. As church members yearn for one another with the affection of Christ Jesus, they pray that one another's "love may abound more and more, with knowledge and all discernment," so that each will "approve what is excellent, and so be pure and blameless for the day of Christ, filled with the fruit of righteousness that comes through Jesus Christ, to the glory and praise of God" (Phil. 1:9–11). The church desires the individual's good, the good which is God.

- For the world's sake, the church burns for each believer to be marked off and held up as a hope-giving example, a love-inspiring model, a life-giving light. The church wants to distinguish the individual from the world, so that the world might see that there is another, better way, so that it, too, might give glory to the Father in heaven and follow him (Matt. 5:13–16; 1 Pet. 2:12).

- For Christ's sake, the church wants to unite and to keep each Christian to itself in preparation for the bridegroom's coming, washing him or her with the water of the Word so that the individual might be holy, radiant, without wrinkle or blemish upon the bridegroom's arrival (2 Cor. 11:2; Eph. 5:27; Phil. 1:11).

- For God's sake, the church wants to hold up each individual before the entire world and proclaim, "Look, here is God's glory, his wisdom, holiness, and love" (see Eph. 3:10).

Churches are to be seekers of glory, holiness, and love.

Upon the grounds of such holy love Jesus intends for the church to exercise the authority of *affirming* faith, *binding and keeping* faith, and *giving oversight* to that faith. He doesn't burden the church with his love and then leave it with no ability to act on that love. Rather, he gives the church an authority that he does not give to the individual Christian. Specifically, he hands a pen to the church and says, "Write the names of all those who profess and follow me. Include them, and tell the world they are one of us now. You might even call the papers and wake the neighbors and tell them to rejoice. My children have made it home."

It's the topic of love and authority that we turn to now.

CHAPTER THREE

THE RULE OF LOVE

"We got to let love rule."
—*Lenny Kravitz*

Main Questions: What is authority? How does it relate to love? And what role does it play in the church?

Main Answers: Authority, grounded in holy love, creates life. It creates a whole new reality that is both marked off and shaped.

Step 1: The idea of authority frightens us, for understandable reasons. Love and authority—do they really belong together?

Dystopia

Recently I finally got around to reading George Orwell's dystopian novel *Nineteen Eighty-Four*. Writing in the 1940s, Orwell takes aim in the book at the totalitarianism of Stalinist Soviet Union, but this literary rifle, like a shotgun, sprays its ammunition far more widely. It challenges the concept of authority generally and tempts one to think that ushering love into the presence of authority will leave love battered and thrashed every time, like placing a person into a cage with an ill-tempered gorilla.

The particular culprit in Orwell's novel is the authoritarian party of Big Brother. "Big Brother is watching you!" say posters and video screens throughout the city. The party treats as a threat every loyalty apart from loyalty to itself. It methodically cuts all social ties—parent from child, friend from friend, lover from beloved. It defines justice on its own terms. It surgically extracts every hope and honest affection from the lives of those it rules, and it rules not only their words and thoughts but also their hearts. Its goal is nothing less than conversion. Says a representative for Big Brother concerning political dissidents (and every citizen, by extension):

> We convert him, we capture his inner mind, we reshape him. We burn all evil and all illusion out of him; we bring him over to our side, not in appearance, but genuinely, heart and soul. We make him one of ourselves before we kill him. It is intolerable to

us that an erroneous thought should exist anywhere in the world, however secret and powerless it may be.[1]

The methods that the Stalinesque party uses for the exclusive end of preserving its power are threats, propaganda, mass starvation, torture, and execution. And even more sickening—it conducts these activities through the governmental agencies of the Ministry of Truth (which propagates lies), the Ministry of Peace (which wages war), the Ministry of Plenty (which plans mass starvation), and, best of all, the Ministry of Love (which tortures and kills).

The party succeeds. The lead character, Winston, spends most of the story resisting Big Brother. But, beaten and brainwashed at the story's end, he gazes up with tears in his eyes at a picture of his demigod dictator. He scolds himself for exiling himself for so long from "the loving breast" of this tyrant. The novel closes with the outrageous words, "He loved Big Brother." Winston was fully converted.

While reading *Nineteen Eighty-Four*, my head and heart were tempted in two directions. My head continued to affirm the biblical idea of authority while my heart wanted to suspect it. There's a moment in the novel, for instance, when the reader looks through Winston's eyes into the faces of his mother and baby sister as they sink to their deaths, sacrificing themselves so that Winston may live. The reader sees their faces and feels anguish, but so oppressed is Winston's life by fear, hatred, and pain in this totalitarian world that he struggles mentally to register the moment as a tragic one. His heart is simultaneously hard toward them but in conflict with itself over that fact.

The villain responsible for this soulless, fear-haunted, and hateful world—and for Winston's emotional dissonance—is authority. Authority enervates, vitiates, and finally immolates life. It saps and steals the truly human from the human. In the face of these realities, any blithe and chirpy affirmation that "authority is good" in a book on theology might seem at least naïve if not callous and stupid. Surely this world has known too much suffering at the hands of authority already. Surely the democratic impulses for freedom, equality, and even some kind of autonomy are correct. Of course, this line of reasoning doesn't stop with political systems. It extends heavenward. Surely, God doesn't mean to rule us and so stifle whatever life, love, and creativity he might have given us, does he?

Consider again what was proposed in the last chapter: God's love centers on God; his love exercises authority; it even executes judgment. It calls us to conform to his character. Love and authority apparently work hand-in-hand. What may prove even more unsettling is what we'll consider toward the end of

---

[1] George Orwell, *Nineteen Eighty-Four*, centennial ed. (New York: Plume Harcourt Brace, 2003), 263.

this chapter and in the next: Christ hands his authority to the church and calls it to rule. He even calls the churches we attend to rule—over us!

Can this be right? Can this be biblical? Big Brother's party had a "Ministry of Love" for torturing people. What prevents the story of the love between God and his people as we have begun to describe it from culminating in one more dystopia? "God loves you, so convert or I will have to kill you." Isn't that what Charlemagne's paladins, swords in hand, said as they enforced Christian "conversion" on pagan Europe? Neither the politics nor the theology of authority is simple. Any attempt to consider the authority of the church in the world must reckon with the reality of its abuse. Easy assertions and proof-texts won't do.

So drastic and dangerous is this idea that we need to spend time seeking to understand authority. For the bulk of this chapter we will seek to understand what authority is and whether God means for his people to exercise it. It may seem that I'm spending a lot of time on preliminaries, but uniting to a local church is not just a matter of "joining" something like a civic society, a country club, or a chess team. It's not about contracting as a self-sovereign with some organization, paying dues and receiving the due benefits in turn. No, such ideas completely miss the connectedness implied in the biblical metaphors for the church such as family, citizenship, temple, vine, or body. Furthermore, as we noted earlier, joining a church is not about *giving of yourself* as you might do with another organization; it's about *giving yourself*, which is an act of submission. It's about identifying your name with all those who belong to the church. It's about being united in heart, mind, and mission. It is, in sum, to submit your discipleship to Christ to a geographically bound, numerically concrete group. It is to submit, it is to be ruled, and it is to rule.

Step 2: Therefore, many church leaders and pastors today present us with a vision of the loving community of relationships that downplays the idea of authority.

Another Path: Community

Of course, there is another path we could take. We don't *have* to talk about authority. As we saw in chapter 1, many theologians and church leaders are presenting an alternative vision that attempts to tie individuals to the church without recourse to a hierarchical concept of authority. Their rallying cry is "Relationships!" or "Community!" Whether these Christians and leaders realize it or not, their cry echoes what so many "communitarian" philosophers, political theorists, sociologists, and theologians have been saying for decades, and for understandable reasons: everyone is looking around at the busyness of modern urban life, the detachment that people feel, and the shallow nature of relationships and are asking the same question: "What social glue will hold us together?"

Commuters travel fifty miles to and from work. Business partners on opposite sides of the globe have more face-to-face time than next-door neighbors. Friendships open and close with the flip of a cell phone. Parents pressed by busy schedules let video games babysit their children. Megachurch superstar pastors squint their eyes through the glare of stage lights to see the onlooking faces.

Amidst the hustle and bustle, all are scratching their heads and wondering how to keep so many disconnected lives from straying into further estrangement. This, many would say, is one of the great challenges of life in the democratic, capitalistic, globalizing, and secular cultures of the West.[2] What holds people together? Nobody wants to answer that question by bringing back the hobgoblin of pre-modernity—authority.

In fact, this is where we will begin, not with a discussion of authority and how it gives structure to a local church and its members but by glancing at the alternative, this popular idea of relationships and community.

THE RELATIONAL TURN

In the social sciences, the communitarian conversation stems from what is sometimes called the "relational turn," according to which the formerly peripheral matter of relationships comes into the substantive center of human existence (ontology).[3] We *are* our relationships and cannot divorce ourselves from them without an identity crisis.[4]

In theology, the significance of relationships (the dialectic of I and Thou) reorients every category of systematic.[5] It has been observed that:

- God's very being is defined not by the substantive Greek categories of static being, but by the fact that he is three persons in community;
- human persons bear a "relational analogy" to God's Trinitarian community;
- love is a matter of "mutuality";
- sin is the breaking of community;
- Christ reconciles us to himself and restores us to a relationship with God;
- Christ also restores us to a relationship with his body, the church community;

---

[2]Thanks to Os Guinness, who suggested to me that any argument for church membership would have to account for the peculiar conditions of modern urban life. I return to this matter more practically in chapters 6 and 7.

[3]For a brief overview of this turn, see F. LeRon Shults, *Reforming Theological Anthropology: After the Philosophical Turn to Relationality* (Grand Rapids: Eerdmans, 2003), 11–36.

[4]Michael Sandel, *Liberalism and the Limits of Justice* (New York: Cambridge University Press, 1982), 179; Charles Taylor, *Sources of the Self* (Cambridge, MA: Harvard University Press, 1989), 27.

[5]See esp. F. LeRon Shults, *Reforming Theological Anthropology*; and *Reforming the Doctrine of God* (Grand Rapids: Eerdmans, 2005).

- and the eschaton will sum up all things in our participation in the divine community.[6]

We touched on several of these matters in chapter 1, and behind them is the question of what holds people together in our individualistic culture. The answer—relationships—seems like a tidy and attractive way to do that without recourse to pre-modernity's hobgoblin. Everybody likes relationships. Sign up me and my church for this solution, please.

PROGRAMMATIC RECOMMENDATIONS

Predictably, several programmatic lessons for churches follow. For starters, we must (we're told) recover an understanding of the church as a community of people rather than as an impersonal institution.[7] If relationships are what constitute the church's essence, any structures that exist should be organic, liquid, or natural. The church is a "spiritual organism that has an organic expression."[8] Just consider the titles of several recent books written for church leaders: *Natural Church Development* (1996); *Liquid Church* (2002); *Organic Church* (2005); *Seeds for the Future: Growing Organic Leaders for Living Churches* (2005); *Organic Community* (2007); and *Reimagining the Church: Pursuing the Dream of Organic Christianity* (2008). Then browse through the delectable choices on the menu of church models (as one author excitedly lists them): seeker-oriented church, purpose-driven church, cell church, G12 cell church, café church, café-style church, clusters, workplace church, pub church, club-culture church, enterprise church, cyber church, network church, culture-specific church, midweek church, project church, seven-day-a-week church, post-Alpha church, table church, household church, menu church, multicultural church, dispersed church, and more.[9] To borrow from Shakespeare, we might exclaim, "O brave new world, that hath such churches in it!"

We're also told that preaching should not be monological but dialogical. Our congregations should speak and learn from a multiplicity of viewpoints.[10] No one individual or groups of individuals has the authority to say what God thinks.

---

[6]The titles of a number of key books making these arguments tell the story themselves: *The Trinity and the Kingdom* (1981 in English); *Being as Communion* (1985); *After Our Likeness: The Church as the Image of the Trinity* (1998); *The Social God and the Relational Self* (2001); *Like Father, Like Son: The Trinity Imaged in Our Humanity* (2005); *Trinity in Human Community: Exploring Congregational Life in the Image of the Social Trinity* (2006).
[7]See the discussion on this topic in chapter 1.
[8]Frank Viola, "Why I Left the Institutional Church," http://www.theooze.com/articles/article.cfm?id=2075.
[9]Stuart Murray, *Church After Christendom* (Milton Keynes, UK: Paternoster, 2004), 67–98.
[10]See O. Wesley Allen Jr., *The Homiletic of All Believers: A Conversational Approach* (Louisville: Westminster, 2005); Doug Pagitt, *Preaching Re-imagined: The Role of the Sermon in Communities of Faith* (Grand Rapids: Zondervan, 2005).

We're told that conversion should not be treated as a one-time event because faith often comes gradually and grows gradually. Better to speak of conversion as a journey, a process, a conversation, or at least a "continuing conversion," which, like a conversation, implies a continual openness to new perspectives.[11] Individuals experience change differently and so do cultures. In the history of Christian missions, furthermore, the whole idea of a "decisive-moment" conversion has often led the church toward oppressive practices. As one author warns:

> Sensitive Christians shy away from this terminology [of conversion], aware that it connotes pressure to conform to particular beliefs and behavior, and implies submission to the superior wisdom and righteousness of those already "converted." Conversion historically has often meant an imperialistic (and sometimes coercive) demand for obedience to the institutions, creed and ethical norms of a dominant church.[12]

Our goal as Christians should not be to require outsiders to conform to our beliefs and behaviors in an instant, both because relationships take time and because relationships involve listening as much as they involve speaking.[13]

Christian mission and evangelism are relational activities. They are relational in their process—we pursue Christ's mission by cultivating relationships—and they are relational in their end, serving the purpose of communion. "Ultimately," says theologian Simon Chan, "all things are to be brought back into communion with the triune God. Communion is the ultimate end, not mission."[14]

In all of this the concept of authority, even God's own authority, gets set to the side, or at least relativized.[15]

---

[11]See George R. Hunsberger, "Evangelical Conversion toward a Missional Ecclesiology," in John Stackhouse, ed., *Evangelical Ecclesiology* (Grand Rapids: Baker, 2003), 123–26; Darrell L. Guder, *The Continuing Conversion of the Church* (Grand Rapids: Eerdmans, 2000). Stuart Murray exclaims with wonder, "A key discovery of the [Anglican and ecumenical] Decade of Evangelism in the 1990s was that many people journey to faith gradually rather than suddenly"; in *Church After Christendom*, 11. Did anyone really ever say otherwise?

[12]Murray, *Church After Christendom*, 31–32. The larger, more well-known argument along these lines is presented by David Bosch in his critique of what he describes as the Enlightenment missionary paradigm, especially his critique of militaristic metaphors and what he perceives as the Western missionary movement's overlap with colonialism and ideas of manifest destiny, *Transforming Mission* (Maryknoll, NY: Orbis, 1991), 284–345. See also Brad Wheeler, "One of the Dirtiest Words Today: C--------n," http://www.9marks.org, "Conversion."

[13]See Bosch, *Transforming Mission*, 427, 453; Tite Tienou, "Christian Theology in an Era of World Christianity," in *Globalizing Theology: Belief and Practice in an Era of World Christianity*, ed. Craig Ott and Harold A. Netland (Grand Rapids: Baker, 2006), 45–51.

[14]Interview with Simon Chan by Andy Crouch, "The Mission in Trinity," in *Christianity Today*, June 2007, 48 (http://www.christianvisionproject.com/2007/06/the_mission_of_the_trinity.html).

[15]E.g., Theologian Jürgen Moltmann exclaims Christ's lordship, but then he presents a picture of God as Lord giving way to the picture of God as Father, which then gives way to the picture of God as Friend, in *Church in the Power of the Spirit* (Minneapolis: Fortress, 1993), 114–21, esp. 118.

IMPLICATIONS FOR CHURCH MEMBERSHIP

Given the reinvigorated emphasis on relationships and on the *process* as opposed to the *event* of conversion, it's not too hard to predict the sort of advice that will follow when the topic comes to church membership and discipline. In a word, never mind! We are not interested in division, but in connection.

A popular phrase bandied about by some church leaders is "belonging before believing."[16] Churches want outsiders to feel the invitation and embrace of a loving community.[17] Boundaries make outsiders feel measured and judged, so let the unchurched, the pre-churched, the semi-churched, and the de-churched feel like they belong even before they believe. And don't make any demands on the post-churched and the anti-churched, because the demands will push them even further away.[18]

In Dan Kimball's book about reaching the unchurched, *They Like Jesus but Not the Church*, he advocates doing whatever we can to lower the wall in order to draw non-Christians inside:

> Our goal should not be to get people to "go to church." We should be inviting people to participate in the life of the church community and to participate in the activity of God, not merely inviting them to attend our worship services. . . . We need to understand that in most cases in our emerging culture, belonging precedes believing. In today's culture, people don't come to have trust and understanding until they feel like they belong. Then the Spirit moves in them, bringing them to a point of belief.

Kimball wants to be sensitive to culture, and culture says, "Let me belong to the people of God; then I'll believe." Does that mean culture is determining who the people of God on earth are?

A slightly more careful way of talking about belonging before believing is to say that churches should adopt a "centered-set," not a "bounded-set," approach to their lives together. Bounded-set churches create boundaries around what they consider right behavior and right belief, and then they patrol those boundaries. Centered-set churches focus on bringing people into a relationship with the person at the center, Christ. The first model is said to be static and institutional. The second model is said to be dynamic and loving. The first emphasizes organizational purity. The second emphasizes inviting, embracing, and growing people. The first requires people to reach a certain standard just to join the club. The second reaches out to everyone, no matter how different

---

[16]See Murray, *Church After Christendom*, 10–23, for a surprisingly elaborate discussion on this topic.
[17]See Dan Kimball's story in this regard, in *They Like Jesus but Not the Church: Insights from Emerging Generations* (Grand Rapids: Zondervan, 2007), 160–61.
[18]These categories can be found in Murray, *Church After Christendom*, 25.

or broken they happen to be.[19] When the matter is put like this, who wouldn't choose the centered-set model?

Advocates of the centered-set church admit that these churches might be a little messier, their borders a little fuzzier. But that makes sense. Sinners are messy, even forgiven ones, and relationships in this world are dynamic, mercurial, and seldom in full view. We cannot see everything God sees. One explicit advocate of a centered-set approach writes:

> We, because of our finiteness, can only look at external criteria—what people say and do. Consequently, to us conversion often looks more like a process than a point, and the church more like a fuzzy body made up of people with different degrees of commitment to Christ. The problem here is not the true nature of spiritual realities, but the limits of our human perception. . . .
>
> This is a problem particularly for those of us from the West for whom institutional order and planning are so important. It is clear that we need to rearrange our priorities. We must make people more important than programs, give relationships priority over order and cleanliness.[20]

Surely the author is correct to point to the limitations of our ability to know who truly belongs to Christ and who does not, which is why Christians have distinguished the visible church (all those who profess Christ) from the invisible church (those who truly belong to God) at least since Augustine. Could it be, however, that the advocates of the centered-set church are presenting us with yet another either/or, when what we want is a both/and? Whether or not people are aware of the bounded-set/centered-set jargon, the basic ideas now permeate the everyday consciousness of many evangelicals.

A while ago I participated in a blog discussion on the topic of church membership. I made the point that church membership, among other things, affords assurance of salvation. One of the commenters responded as follows:

> I don't attend church for the membership, I attend for the fellowship. Frankly, I don't care if a church gives me assurances or not [sic]. My purpose in being Christian isn't affected by assurance from others. To me, fellowship is far more important—being connected with others that share my beliefs; being a part of their lives and having them be a part of my life. I don't need others [in order] to have faith or belief, or to be a Christian. But fellowship, not membership, does give me something I can't get otherwise and allows me to give it as well.

---

[19]Paul Hiebert, *Anthropological Reflections on Missiological Issues* (Grand Rapids: Baker, 1994), 110–36; Murray, *Church After Christendom*, 12–38; Michael Frost and Alan Hirsch, *The Shaping of Things to Come: Innovation and Mission for the 21st Century* (Peabody, MA: Hendrickson, 2003), 47–50; cf. Darrell Guder, et al., who more carefully call for a congregation that's part bounded-set, part centered-set, in *Missional Church: A Vision for the Sending of the Church in North America*, ed. Darrell L. Guder (Grand Rapids: Eerdmans, 1998), 205–12.
[20]Hiebert, *Anthropological Reflections*, 134.

That individual places a commendable emphasis on fellowship and rela-tionships. An individual's relationship to a local church should be characterized not nominally or consumeristically but relationally. That is, participation in a local church should be filled with the give-and-take of relationships, not just whether the church satisfies certain needs. The problem is that this individual seems to have an overrealized conception of his own salvation and ability to be self-deceived ("Frankly, I don't care if a church gives me assurances or not"). The church is not something to which the individual believes he should submit. He maintains all control. The unarticulated assumption working in the back-ground is that relationships and authority, like love and authority, are at odds. The centered-set idea of the church suffers from a similar reductionism.

WHAT'S RIGHT ABOUT THE RELATIONAL IMPULSE

I am no fan of artificial and inauthentic churches or authoritarian and judgmental churches. Both hinder the work of the gospel, because whatever is producing the inauthenticity, judgmentalism, or lifeless formality is directly opposed to the gospel.

In fact, I am fully on board with the impulse to "community" represented in so many recent "conversations," whether in books, on blogs, or between friends. In his book *Church Re-Imagined*, Emerging church leader Doug Pagitt writes:

> I truly believe that community is where real spiritual formation happens. Most people come to faith not by an isolated effort but through living day by day with people of faith such as their families or friends. . . . Community as a means of spiritual forma-tion serves to immerse people in the Christian way of living so that they learn how to be Christian in a life-long process of discovery and change. Christian community can and should be context for evangelism and discipleship, a place where faith is professed and lived.[21]

I couldn't agree more with these remarks. The church community should give shape to our Christian lives and be the context for our evangelism and discipleship. And, to be clear, such spiritual formation isn't simply about keep-ing individual Christians "on track," as if we were all just useful devices in one another's lives.[22] Rather, the church community presents a picture of our new communal identities in Christ and then gives further shape to those new identities. Authors Tim Chester and Steve Timmis are correct: "Our identity as human beings is found in community. Our identity as Christians is found

---

[21]Doug Pagitt, *Church Re-Imagined: The Spiritual Formation of People in Communities of Faith* (Grand Rapids: Zondervan, 2003), 27.
[22]Ibid.

in Christ's new community."[23] We don't attend family dinner simply because it's good to eat. We do so because of who we *are*—members of the family. In this vein, mainstream Protestant confessions and descriptions of the local church have been only partially right whenever they have limited the purpose of the local church to the edification of Christians. The church is also about worshiping God and reaching the world. The local church is the place where new individual identities and a new corporate identity are displayed, glorifying God and challenging the world.

Further, I oppose what many of these conversations are opposing—a program-driven, institutionalized conception of church. In his book *Reimagining Church*, Frank Viola describes an institutionalized conception of a local church and what he would like to see it replaced with:

> I readily admit that all churches (even organic churches) assume *some* institutions. But I'm using the phrase "institutional church" in a much narrower sense. Namely, I am referring to those churches that operate primarily as institutions that exist above, beyond, and independent of the members that populate them. These churches are constructed on programs and rituals more than relationships. They are highly structured, typically building-centered organizations regulated by set-apart professionals ("ministers" and "clergy") who are aided by volunteers (laity). They require staff, building, salaries, and administration. In the institutional church, congregants watch a religious performance once or twice a week led principally by one person (the pastor or minister), and then retreat home to live their individual lives.[24]

Viola, like more and more people today, wants something different:

> I have a dream that countless churches will be transformed from high-powered business organizations into spiritual families—authentic Christ-centered communities—where the members know one another intimately, love one another unconditionally, bleed for one another deeply, and rejoice with one another unfailingly.[25]

Picking on buildings, salaries, and church administration wholesale might miss the point, but insofar as those buildings and staff members and programs keep the church body as a whole from being equipped for works of ministry (Eph. 4:11ff.), he's exactly right. I propose that his dream, as it's articulated in the quote above, sounds like what the New Testament describes.

The concern about so many of these conversations is that they throw the baby out with the bathwater. A number of them are reacting to one imbalanced formulation only to adopt another. That's the worst-case scenario, anyhow. The

---

[23]Tim Chester and Steve Timmis, *Total Church* (Wheaton, IL: Crossway, 2008), 50.
[24]Frank Viola, *Reimagining Church* (Colorado Springs: David C. Cook, 2008), 17–18.
[25]Ibid., 28.

best-case scenario is that they will move toward a more biblical and *unimagina-tive* model of the church. The fact is that something's missing. Indeed, the very thing so many church leaders want to jettison (authority) is precisely what they should not jettison in order to get what they are after (live-giving relationships and community).

Step 3: Yet God is not a God of just relationships, he's a God of authority, and authority is what holds the church together.

Not Just Relationships but Authority

The question of what holds people together is a good and necessary question. We need to remember that the Bible is concerned with another question as well, namely, how God's people are to be marked off. Still, the Bible clearly demonstrates a concern with drawing and holding God's people together. Judgment in the Bible is often pictured as a divine dispersing or casting out. Redemption is pictured as a bringing back and holding together. At the Tower of Babel, we see humankind dispersed. At Pentecost, we witness the Holy Spirit going out and drawing people of many nations back together. In this regard, pastors and church leaders face the same questions faced by sociologists and political theorists confronted with the realities of autonomous individualism: how do we build community?

But, as we just said, the answer "relationships" or "community" does not provide a sufficient answer, at least in regard to churches, which is our concern here. It's like saying that self-confidence is the solution to insecurity. Self-confidence is the opposite of insecurity, so it kind of makes sense, but ultimately it cuts God out of the picture. Let me explain further biblically, theologically, and philosophically. If we were to do a biblical word search on "relationship" or "community" and another on "obey" or "keep" or "follow," we would find none of the former and much devoted to the latter. Yes, the word *fellowship* can be found, but this proves my point, insofar as a Christian fellowship is a Christian community with a Godward shape.

Word searches aside, where exactly does one find an emphasis on relationships, plain and simple, in the Bible? Does the Bible not emphasize the adjectives and nouns together: *loving* relationships, *holy* relationships, *obedient* relationships, *Spirit-filled* relationships? God did not create the planets to wander in whichever way they pleased, first in one relationship to the sun, then in another. No, he created them to move in an *orbiting* relationship to the sun. Hence, a new question arises: what force produces the adjectives? What gravitational pull compels two persons not just to relate, but to relate in a manner that's holy and loving? Some other force must give structure to those relationships and cause them to be loving, holy, and so forth. What is it?

Theologically, God is not interested merely in relationships, but in particular kinds of relationships. He created humanity to image and enjoy the pleasure of his glory. Therefore he calls humanity into a relationship of obedience or conformity to that image. God-to-human and human-to-human relationships should serve the particular end of imaging or worshiping God. This is what love wants. This is what love burns for. For instance, the divine Father burns for the divine Son to image and enjoy the pleasure of his glory, and so the Father communicates all his fullness to his Son. That is what the divine Father-Son relationship is like. They are not two randomly wandering planets, but two persons abiding in a relationship structured in a particular way.

Consider also a father and his children. The father expresses his love for his children not simply by virtue of the fact that he's "in relationship" with them. Rather, the Bible says that he expresses his love within that relationship by training, encouraging, exhorting, and disciplining those children. But what gives the father the right or license to train, encourage, exhort, and discipline his children? Why should they not discipline him?

Philosophically, these matters get a little more complicated, but let me address them very briefly because so many evangelical writers and speakers at the practitioner's level are jumping on the "community" bandwagon without realizing that the ideas in play have trickled down from academic conversations, conversations that just might throw out assumptions that the practitioners don't want to throw out.

Behind the bounded-set versus centered-set discussion is the more complex discussion of a "substance ontology" versus a "relational ontology" involving the essence of our triune God himself. Broadly speaking, relational ontologies argue that God and the universe, at the most fundamental level, are not just plain *being* or substance, as such, but person-in-relation. (The philosophical backdrop includes names like Hegel, Husserl, Whitehead, and others.) When theologians then absorb such ontologies into their theological works, they downplay or jettison the importance of God's nature and emphasize instead the primary role of his person or persons. It's said that God's love, for instance, should not be treated as a property of his nature, but as a property (or decision) of his person. For love to be love, it must be given freely and not constrained by "ontological necessity,"[26] which is a fancy way of saying it cannot merely be constrained by a person's nature (as in "he loves because he's loving by nature.

---

[26] John Zizioulas, *Being as Communion: Studies in Personhood and the Church* (Crestwood, NY: St. Vladimir's Seminary Press, 1985), 44, 46.

He can't help it"). Since a person's nature ontologically constrains him, we're told to do away with *nature* as constitutive of being and to make *relationship* constitutive of being. In other words, we *are not* our nature; we *are* our relationships. That preserves God's—and ultimately our—freedom.

There are at least three problems with this. First, it seems to make freedom and love god. We no longer worship God for his nature; we worship him for the choice he made to love, which means we really worship love and the idea of love and the feeling of being loved, which means we really worship ourselves.

Second, there's something different about my relationship with my wife and my relationship with a carrot. Those differences have much to do with what I, my wife, and the carrot substantively *are*. I'm not saying that my relationship with my wife or the carrot doesn't inform what all three of us are. Surely it does. Until I married her, she was not a wife. Until I pick up a carrot with the determination to eat it, it is not food. But at no point will I marry a carrot or use my wife as a salad garnish. Likewise, God's being is not merely defined by the fact that he is three persons in relationship. As we considered in the last chapter, the fact that God is holy, love, and one is wonderfully fixed, static, and certain. These are properties of his nature. This brings us to the third point.

Our triune God is a person-in-relation, but putting it that way is reductionistic. God's three persons are not merely in a relationship with one another; they are in a holy relationship. That is, it's a relationship determined and fixed by his holy nature. It's a relationships with a direction, a focus, a point, a *telos*. The Father is utterly fixed up loving the Son in all his perfection, and the Son the Father, and both the Spirit, and the Spirit both. God is holy because his affections are utterly set apart from sin and set upon loving his own glory above all. The loving relationships within the three persons of the Godhead are *utterly constrained* by God's holy nature. Instead of speaking of God as persons-in-relation, we would be more biblical to say that God is a persons-in-holy-nature. The idea of persons-in-relation is also reductionistic because distinguishing between God's persons and nature, though helpful for some purposes, is finally an intellectual abstraction. There is really no such thing as a "person" without some kind of "nature" to give direction, motion, energy, and substance to that person.[27] Try to imagine it, if you can.

Since God has a holy nature, thankfully, his commitments are not dynamic, no matter how dynamic the course of our relationship with him may be (from the human side). He is a God who keeps his promises, because he is a God

---

[27]Contemporary conversations about the Trinity often give primacy to God's three persons rather than to his one nature. For the reasons I just explained, I can't help but follow Robert Letham, who quotes Gregory of Nazianzus to make the case for giving equal primacy to both. Gregory writes, "No sooner do I conceive of the one than I am illumined by the splendor of the three; no sooner do I distinguish them than I am carried back to the one." In Robert Letham, *Holy Trinity* (Phillipsburg, NJ: P&R, 2004), 463.

who *is* holy and faithful. If we take all this talk about relationships and community outside of God's nature, character, and holy purposes for creation, we ultimately end up with relativism. Throw out God's nature and we throw out his character and commitments. Some theologians euphemize this as "pantheism" or "panentheism," but relativism is the logical outcome of a God without a fixed nature, one defined primarily by "relationality." If he is nothing other than a persons-in-relation, what's to keep him from becoming despotic, or obsessive-compulsive, or happy-clappy, or anything else?

Thankfully, our lives have a purpose, namely, to attain to the pleasure of imaging him who is perfect in holiness, justice, righteousness, and love. Therefore, it's not just restored relationships that are needed; it's a restored rule—a new kingdom. God's authority is the force that gives structure to our relationships. It is to human beings what the gravitational pull of the sun is to the planets. In order to answer the question of what holds the church together, therefore, we need to return to the topics of authority and holy love.

Step 4: What is authority and how does it relate to love? Authority is the authorization we have from God to create and give order to life.

Love's Rule

ADAM AS KING

The issue of authority goes right to the heart of our existence. We were created to rule. The idea is there in Genesis 1. God created Adam and Eve in his image, and then he gave them dominion over all the earth. He even tells them to "subdue" it (Gen. 1:28). Humanity images God, at least in part, by exercising authority.

In Genesis 2 God brought all the animals before Adam so that he could examine and then name them. By naming something, it's often remarked, one defines it and sets its course. One exercises authority over it. God also told Adam "to work" the garden and "keep it." The garden was Adam's domain, and Adam was to be the first conqueror on behalf of God's holy love.

In other words, God gave Adam authority over a plot of land—the right to do things or to demand that things be done.[28] Authority is not just power. It's the legitimacy to exercise power. It's authorization to accomplish a particular task, to act in a particular capacity, to seek a particular end.[29] Every human being has

---

[28]See R. S. Downie, "Authority," in *The Oxford Companion to Philosophy*, ed. Ted Honderich (New York: Oxford University Press, 1995), 68–69.

[29]My understanding of authority here has been aided by Christopher J. H. Wright (who acknowledges indebtedness to Oliver O'Donovan) who has given me the word "authorization," from *The Mission of God: Unlocking the Bible's Grand Narrative* (Downers Grove, IL: InterVarsity, 2006), 53. However, I want to fill out this idea a little differently than Wright does, who then defines this "authorization" as a "legitimating permission" or

been created and authorized to exercise authority, to exercise divinely sanctioned rule. In a very real sense, then, we could say that authority, as God intended it in the garden, is nothing more than the God-given entitlement we have as human beings to make decisions and act in a God-imaging and God-sanctioned sort of way, no matter how significant or insignificant the decision may seem. One man's eating and drinking for God's glory is no less an exercise of authority, qualitatively, than another man's commanding armies to build vineyards, houses, gardens, and parks, if he commands those armies in the fear of the Lord (see Eccles. 2:4–5; 11:13; 1 Cor. 10:31). The two men's domains may vary dramatically in size, but both men equally fulfill Adam's mandate to exercise loving dominion.

To be human, according to Genesis 1, is to rule something, even if it's just the thoughts inside your head. This is why Adam and every one of his sons and daughters are understood to be a kind of king.

Did the fact that God granted Adam and Eve dominion lay the groundwork for all political imperialism? Economic exploitation? Environmental degradation? Business monopolization? Social degradation? The question pushes us ahead in the Bible's storyline and requires us to account for the fact that, beginning in Genesis 3, Adam and Eve sought an "alternative legitimation" for their decision-making power, as the sociologists might put it.[30] Ever since the fall of humankind, humanity has sought to legitimate or justify its decisions and actions through something other than God's word and will. What has resulted is a broken and cursed world wherein, first, humanity's exercise of authority is not necessarily effectual. Man gains his food only by the sweat of his face (Gen. 3:17–19). Second, post-fall humanity's exercise of authority is, in one sense, never legitimate.[31] It's uniformly sinful because man uses his decision-making power to seek something other than God's glory. Third, post-fall humanity's exercise of authority involves a rejection of God's authority and whatever mediators God might send to speak on his behalf (e.g., Pss. 2; 124:1–2). For instance, parents have a God-given authority over their children, but children, operating with their own sense of moral legitimacy, reject their parents' authority until required or incentivized to do otherwise.[32] Adopting

---

"freedom to act within boundaries." I think it's better to say that God's authorization of our activity is his *legitimating commission*. After all, a person who has been given authority—such as presbyter or a prime minister—is given that authority to accomplish some task or fulfill some purpose. That means, yes, they have the freedom of action in the relevant domain. But the point of that authority is not the *freedom* to do whatever one pleases (even within bounds) but the *purpose* one has to fulfill the task for which he or she has been given authority (perhaps Wright acknowledges as much elsewhere). Cf. Oliver O'Donovan, *Resurrection and Moral Order: An Outline for Evangelical Ethics*, 2nd ed. (Grand Rapids: Eerdmans, 1994), esp. 121–24. I think O'Donovan captures this difference I'm getting at by referring to freedom as "purposive action" (p. 122) and reality as teleological.

[30]See Peter L. Berger and Thomas Luckmann, *The Social Construction of Reality: A Treatise in the Sociology of Knowledge* (New York: Anchor Books, 1966), 92ff., 157; cf. O'Donovan, *Resurrection and Moral Order*, 104.

[31]We retain a kind of *de facto* authority but not a *de jure*, morally legitimate authority.

[32]It's right here that the sociological approach to understanding authority becomes inadequate for theological purposes, which I mention in response to the biblical exegetes who adopt a sociological definition wholesale. Ever since Max Weber's foundational work in the sociology of authority, the concept of authority is often under-

an alternative authority structure necessarily means dismantling and destroying the old one.[33] A man will not serve two masters (Matt. 6:24). So in one sense, unquestionably yes, God's command to Adam and Eve to rule and to subdue laid the groundwork for every abuse of authority in history, but, in another sense, absolutely not.

ADAM CROWNED WITH GLORY

Adam and Eve misused and abused the authority they had been given by relying upon someone else's authorization, namely, the Serpent's (Gen. 3:1–6). If we consider the idea of authority as God intended it, however, we find an altogether different thing from what humanity has corrupted and abused. Psalm 8, an inspired commentary on Genesis 1:28, raptures with wonder at God's decision to give Adam and Eve authority.

The first and last verses of Psalm 8 tell us that the psalm is principally about God's majesty: "O LORD, our Lord, how majestic is your name in all the earth! You have set your glory above the heavens. . . . O LORD, our Lord, how majestic is your name in all the earth!" (Ps. 8:1, 9). What then does the psalmist see the majesty of God in?

> When I look at your heavens, the work of your fingers,
>   the moon and the stars, which you have set in place,
> what is man that you are mindful of him,
>   and the son of man that you care for him?
> Yet you have made him a little lower than the heavenly beings
>   and crowned him with glory and honor.
> You have given him dominion over the works of your hands;
>   you have put all things under his feet,
> all sheep and oxen,
>   and also the beasts of the field,

---

stood to include not only the authority figure's right or legitimacy to rule, but also the actual compliance and subjective acceptance of this rule by those who are ruled. Weber himself defined authority as "the probability that a command with a specific given content will be obeyed by a given group of persons," a definition which measures "authority" by that probability. *The Theory of Social and Economic Organization* (New York: Free Press, 1947; repr. 1964), 152. From an entirely materialistic standpoint, which excludes a conception of divine authority and which presupposes that all authority is socially constructed, this definition makes sense. In that sense, it suits sociology's descriptive purposes. It is unfortunate, however, when Christian scholars simplistically adopt the secular academy's definitions wholesale. For instance, Bengt Holmberg, writing on ecclesial authority in the Pauline epistles, seeks to understand authority in the church through the lens of Weber and his successors. So he writes, "The 'invisible' and specific characteristic of an authority relation is that the ruler and the subordinate both consider it the duty of the latter to obey. . . . This means that the authority-holder's claim to be entitled to give orders is justified by reference to a legitimation that is valid to the one who submits to authority," in *Paul and Power: The Structure of Authority in the Primitive Church as Reflected in the Pauline Epistles* (Eugene, OR: Wipf & Stock, 1978), 127. But from a Christian worldview, that's patently not true. As with the illustration of the child who rejects his parents' authority, God's authority and the authority he gives to human mediators may or may not be recognized, due, as we have already seen, to competing legitimating structures. Some secular theorists understand this quite well, e.g., Joseph Raz, *The Authority of Law* (New York: Oxford University Press, 1983), 8; R. S. Downie, "Authority," in *The Oxford Companion to Philosophy*, 69.
[33]Berger and Luckmann, *The Social Construction of Reality*, 157.

the birds of the heavens, and the fish of the sea,
whatever passes along the paths of the seas. (vv. 3–8)

The psalmist considers the magnificence of God's created universe; he considers the comparatively diminutive stature of the human being; he considers the fact that God has made every son and daughter of Adam ruler over this universe; and he is astounded. He cannot help but shout of God's majesty. Even more surprising, perhaps, is the language he uses to describe God's gift of authority to humanity: God has crowned Adam, Eve, and all their children with glory and honor—God's own glory and honor, shared with us. Every human we have ever known or passed on the street—crowned, by creation, with God's glory and honor.

How remarkable. God is all powerful, all knowing, infinite in every way, but he hands the rule of creation over to finite us. Earth, Mars—whatever we can fill and subdue (questions of scarcity of resources aside, for the moment). Could it be that he's like a father saying to his son, "Build this tree house with me," or like a mother saying to her daughter, "Bake this cake with me," even though the parent knows the child will not do it nearly as well?[34] God's rule of Adam is nothing if not generous. Caring, glory sharing, honor bestowing—he uses his authority to authorize. He bends down, scoops us up, and says, "Here, rule on my behalf. I'll give you everything you need. I'll guide you, because I want you to share in the pleasure of my work and in my glory." God wants us to share in his glory because as we share in it, we image or display it for all to see.

In short, we can see God's majesty as we reflect upon his authority and how he has used it generously to create life and bless it with his own glory and honor. O Lord, our Lord, how majestic is your name in all the earth.

Adam and Eve's rule was not, therefore, to be an abusive, life-stealing rule. God did not commission them to inaugurate all great acts of colonialism, imperialism, or authoritarianism that would follow. Just the opposite. Adam and Eve's rule was to be a fruit-bearing, cultivating, empowering, equipping, authoring-life-in-others rule. The common Latin root of the words *author* and *authority* provide an indication of the purpose behind human authority—to author life. God granted man authority, the right to rule, in order to author life, just like God's rule authors life. Rulership, we can say, is the right of a creator to create. It's taking something (or nothing, in God's case) and giving order, shape, or function to it with some purpose in mind—an order, shape, or function that did not previously exist. It's the teacher teaching, the coach coaching, the mother mothering. To have authority is to have the right and power to create, just as the teacher, coach, and mother have license to perform their respective functions. The one who creates is typically the one with the right of

---

[34] I received these examples from Bruce Ware.

rule. The author has authority. This is why God the creator has all authority in creation (and why Christ the re-creator has all rule in the new creation). Another and perhaps marginally better king than Adam, King David, captured the life-authoring, life-creating essence of godly authority in his final words:

> When one rules justly over men, ruling in the fear of God, he dawns on them like the morning light, like the sun shining forth on a cloudless morning, like rain that makes grass to sprout from the earth. (2 Sam. 23:3–4)

Authority justly used in the fear of God is like the sun nourishing the grass and causing it to grow. It creates life. It authors growth.

It should be obvious, then, why Paul would say that "there is no authority except from God" (Rom. 13:1). God, by virtue of the fact that he is creator of the universe, is its ultimate authority (consider his final words to Job). As the only I AM, authority is intrinsic to him alone. All other authorities in this universe, therefore, have derived their authority from him. We are only stewards, tenants, landlords, undershepherds, and sons, and all our authority is accountable to him.

SUMMARIZING LOVE'S RULE

How then can we summarize love's rule, at least as God intended it in creation? Love is an affection for the beauty of God in all his perfection. It's a response to that beauty; it's a desire to unite with that beauty and be identified with it; it's a desire for that beauty to continue to shine and be enjoyed by all the universe. Rule is the activity of creating order, shape, or function for some purpose. Godly authority or rule, quite simply, is the *operation of love*. It's what the furnace of godly affections *does*, as those affections reach out to give order, shape, or ability to people's individual or corporate lives so that they might know the supreme good that is God. It's the teacher teaching, because he wants his students to know the beauty of God's world. It's the coach coaching, because he wants his players to know the joy of glorifying God with their skill and determination. It's the mother mothering, because she wants her children to love the Lord with their hearts, souls, and minds. The furnace in the heart of the godly teacher, coach, and mother burns for the glory of God; it burns with love for those made in his image; it burns with hate for the sin that kills those same ones; it burns for those under their charge to know the joy, freedom, and pleasure of being with God in his holiness.

From one angle we can say that holy love is the ground for every godly and good use of authority; it provides authority's purpose and framework.[35] From

---

[35] I'm taking the language of "ground" from Oliver O'Donovan.

another angle we can say that the nature of holy love itself—its DNA—requires a *commissioning*, an *authorization,* an *authoritative action.* Holy love never sits idle. It necessarily acts to create or, if need be, recreate for the purposes of God's glory, and that act of creating is its commissioning or authoritative action.

What a hellish lie has made humans despise the idea of authority! Divine authority grounded in holy love does not sap and steal the truly human from the human—just the opposite. It creates the human, and it authorizes the human to participate in, or mimic, that which is most satisfying—the divine life. The call to obedience is nothing more than a call into the pleasure of consciously imaging a perfect God. The rule of God's love, his call to obedience, is a commissioning—a great commissioning. God equips us with all the tools of consciousness and creativity that we need to image him; he hands us the planet and then he authorizes us to go about living, loving, building, singing, conquering, investigating, caring, and speaking in such a way that his glory is manifested and displayed.

Human authority should be grounded in holy love in order to be and do likewise. Any authority we've been given, whether the authority of a father or a vice president of finance, should be used to create life and authorize rule in others. The rule others receive from us should in turn be used to create life and authorize rule in still others. And all our authority should use whatever license it has been given to point others toward this greatest of goods, God. When we point them to God wherever he has revealed himself, we author life in them.

To jump ahead in the storyline, preaching is therefore an exercise of loving authority because it points people to God's revelation. Discipleship is an exercise of loving authority because it seeks to see people conformed to the image of God. Evangelism is an exercise of loving authority because it points people to salvation and the rule of the ultimate king. Evangelism is the only way for others to become true rulers. We are commissioned to preach, to make disciples, and to evangelize; yet preaching, discipling, and evangelizing are themselves a kind of commissioning. If people are offended by God and his authority, should we be surprised when they take offense at preaching, discipleship, or evangelism?

Step 5: What is submission and how does it relate to love? Submission is love for God and giving oneself to the pursuit of his glory.

Love's Submission

We have defined authority as it was intended at creation. It is the license to create order, shape, and function according to the mandates of holy love. How then shall we define submission or obedience as it was intended at creation?

ADAM AS PRIEST

The issue of submission goes right to the heart of our existence. We were created to submit. The idea is there in Genesis 1. God created Adam and Eve in his image, and then he called them to display his image, not their own. Humanity images God by exercising authority, but doing so in such a way that shows the world what *he* is like. In order for a human being to exercise perfect authority, he must perfectly submit to God. Submission precedes authority, or, we might say, the godly individual does them simultaneously. The Roman centurion, a man under authority with authority, understood this perfectly well (Matt. 8:9).

Adam was not the great king; he was a vice-king, ruling on behalf of the great king. To use another metaphor, well developed in redemptive history, Adam was a priest. He was not king so that he could do whatever he pleased. He was king so that he could mediate God's holy love, life-giving rule, and glory. He was a priest called to image God's likeness to others—to the cosmos.

Submission, then, is the image's decision to conform itself to the image maker. If I have been created to display the righteous and loving character of God, I will submit my life to that purpose as I go about the tasks for which God created me. Godly submission involves obeying commandments and laws, but it's more than just that. It is, more totally, loving God, embracing his glory, and so giving myself and all my resources to the cause of his glory. Like authority, submission is an operation of love. It begins with love for God and all that he is. It begins with an affirmation of his beauty and goodness and a burning to unite with him and his goodness. Out of these affections, then, the lover of God then conforms or submits himself to God's way, God's truth, and God's life.

So Jesus, who perfectly loved the Father, submitted himself to the very utmost for the Father. Likewise Adam should have submitted himself to God out of love for God, and Eve should have submitted herself to helping Adam because Eve should have loved not just Adam, but Adam's God (see Ruth 1:16).

SUBMITTING TO OTHER HUMANS

Speaking in terms of submitting to other human beings, then, we can say that submission is accepting as a requirement of love the license of the one in authority to govern. If you have authority over me in some particular context, I accept the prerogative you have been given by God to lead the way in that domain. I submit to acting in accordance with your charge. I submit myself and my resources to pursuing your purposes. I submit to being corrected when I am acting out of accord with your charge. I do all of this because I love God and believe that he has given you license to administrate the requirements of his holy love in this particular context.

However, since godly submission is an operation of holy love, godly submission in this world should never, ultimately, be to just another person, which would be idolatry. When we submit to others, we do so within their capacity as kings, yes, but these kings are not the ultimate kings. They are priestly kings, meaning their authority is merely mediating another's. Godly submission to a human being is really submission to God, at least if God has put that authority in place. God does give some, not all, the license to rule over others, and we should submit to them. But we should do so only in obedience to God and never beyond where God's law would permit us to go. Ultimately, we will give an account to him, not to his human mediators.

LIFE CREATING OR LIFE THREATENING?

In a fallen world, the language of submitting to another's purposes, even God's, can sound frightful. After all, it means surrendering our plans and purposes, which seems to extinguish our unique and creative potentiality. Hasn't God made each of us unique? Doesn't submission merely squander that? Surely God means for us to develop our individuality and employ our unique gifts, right?

That's exactly right, but we develop our individuality and employ our gifts by submitting them to his purposes. Our gifts should be used in accordance with his character. It's precisely because our individuality and unique gifting need to be developed in a holy direction that we submit them as raw material to him and to those he has placed over us. A student submits to a teacher and an athlete to a coach because the raw material needs to be developed. Or, like Adam in the garden, knowing that petunias need to be cultivated in one way and roses another, godly authority, typically, governs by asking people to act in accordance with their creation design. It helps the runner to run fast, the thinker to think sharply, and the dancer to dance elegantly. I say "typically" because, in a fallen world, sometimes a godly authority will ask us to do things we are not very good at and never will be. Still, God's governance of our lives fundamentally calls us to do what we were corporately created to do—worship him in all of our uniquely gifted diversity.

Godly submission, like godly rule, is about creation. We submit ourselves and our resources to another for the sake of the new creation to come. Eve, as helper to Adam, was to picture this posture more concretely. Her entire resumé of gifts, talents, and perspectives were to be employed in Adam's administration as they both sought to push the borders of Eden and God's glory to the furthest reaches of the globe. But, finally, both Adam's rule and Eve's submission were to picture the two postures all humans were to assume at all times in an infinite variety of ways, moving from one context to another.

Standing at the head of the Psalter, Psalm 1 provides the basic orientation of the entire Psalter and the fundamental disposition all humanity should bear toward God. It seems to reach back to the garden of Eden and grab the fecund symbol of a fruitful tree in order to picture the creative powers unleashed through humanity's submission to God and his word:

> Blessed is the man
>> who walks not in the counsel of the wicked,
> nor stands in the way of sinners,
>> nor sits in the seat of scoffers;
> but his delight is in the law of the LORD,
>> and on his law he meditates day and night.
>
> He is like a tree
>> planted by streams of water
> that yields its fruit in its season,
>> and its leaf does not wither.
> In all that he does, he prospers. (Ps. 1:1–3)

Submission to God's law, remarkably, doesn't extinguish this man's life or unique and creative potentiality. It multiplies it. He is blessed, and from him come the fruits of blessing in the lives of others. Unless a seed goes into the ground and dies, Jesus said before his own death, it will not bear fruit (John 12:24). For the man, it all begins with his delight, his affections, his love. He loves God and his Word.

SUMMARIZING LOVE'S SUBMISSION

Both authority and submission are operations of God's holy love. They are what his holy love does when it puts on hands and feet and gets to work. Authority says, "Let's build a kingdom for God's glory." Submission says, "I'll help."

Both give and both receive but perhaps in the opposite order. Authority gives a commission and then receives the pleasure of a new creation unfolding: "That is good. That is very good." Submission receives the commission and then gives itself to the pleasure of creating what was commissioned. It is pleasure giving to the receiver because perfect authority asks it to create only that which it's been designed to create: "Yes, that is good, because I was made to do it." It's the pleasure a musician feels as he composes and a writer feels when he writes.

Does authority receive more glory than submission because it's leading the charge? The very question misses the point of where glory comes from and to whom it belongs. Paul knew: "For from him and through him and to him are all things. To him be glory forever" (Rom. 11:36).

Step 6: At the same time, we rightly mistrust authority because sin, in its very essence, is the abuse of the authority God has given his creatures.

Our Fallen Rule

When we stop to consider the fact that all human decision making can be understood as submitting to God by assuming his delegated authority, we stumble upon five perhaps surprising lessons concerning sin and what happened to authority after the fall.

SIN IS AUTHORITY ABUSED

First, sin is disobedience, but sin can also be defined as misuse of our delegated authority. Sin is the misappropriation of the rule that God gave to Adam. Every action or decision a human makes "in the flesh" and not "in the Spirit," to borrow Paul's language, is an abuse of authority. Sin is authority wrongly exercised or wrongly legitimated. It is ruling for one's own sake rather than for God's, for worldly love rather than for holy love. Whether we're talking about a five-year-old snatching his sister's toy or a king snatching another kingdom and enslaving its subjects, the action is qualitatively the same—authority has been abused; the child and the king both have rejected God's ultimate rule and violated their respective stewardships.

Moreover, it shouldn't be too difficult now to see why our hatred of authority and submission to God and his glory are so tightly bound together. God's authority and God's glory, though essential attributes of his very nature, are also the prerogatives due him by virtue of creation. The heart of our sin is the complaint we file against this prerogative, since we want to be god (Gen. 3:5). We don't want to submit ourselves and our raw material to his lordship. We would prefer to create ourselves, our righteousness, our meaning and worth, our own rules and our own rule, for then, it seems, glory would be ours.

AUTONOMY AND TYRANNY ARE MADE OF THE SAME STUFF

Second, the isolation and autonomy of the Western individual is made of the same stuff as the tyrant's abuse of the masses. Both individuals have rejected God's authority and decided to rule on their terms. Fortunately, the catastrophic effects of the autonomous individual's rejection of God's authority are better contained than the tyrant's, which is precisely why I believe Christians can affirm certain strains of philosophical liberalism, as I do, in regard to the public square. Philosophical liberalism, at its best, is a defensive mechanism for throwing the rascals out—an intermittent veto power.[36] Still, it's important to see that autonomous individualism and tyranny are most fundamentally differences of degree, not kind.[37] As important as this defensive posture is for citizens of the state, the citizens of God's kingdom must have a different, more complex view of authority.

Incidentally, it's ironic that so many writers today seem to blame autonomous individualism and the breakdown of community on the Enlightenment or on contractualist thinking, as if these things were a peculiar problem to modernity. Autonomous individualism didn't begin with the Enlightenment or philosophical liberalism. It began with the human response to God's covenant of works. Specifically, Adam and Eve swallowed the Serpent's lie and determined to be like God, knowing good from evil, on their terms (Gen. 3:5). What the shift from pre-modernity to modernity signified, really, was that this Satanic whisper gained a moral and philosophical credibility in the so-called Christian West (even if it had always been implicitly believed and practiced). The Enlightenment did not bring us radical free agency and atomism; Genesis 3 did. The Enlightenment, at most, gave it a temporary public legitimacy.

HUMANS WILL MISUSE AUTHORITY, AND GOD HATES IT

There's a third and fourth lesson we can learn from the fact that all human decision-making is an exercise in God's delegated authority and that sin is, by definition, an abuse of authority: God hates the abuse of authority, even more than George Orwell does. Not only that, but God is far more suspicious of human authority than I was when I read *Nineteen Eighty-Four* or than any philosophical liberal has ever been. God is, in fact, quite certain that humans *will* abuse whatever stewardships they have been given. Is there an elder or con-

---

[36]William H. Riker, *Liberalism against Populism: A Confrontation between the Theory of Democracy and the Theory of Social Choice* (Prospect Heights, IL: Waveland Press, 1982), 8–11, 244. Certainly these points are not uncontested, but I think he's right when he writes, "In the liberal view, the function of voting is to control officials, *and no more*," 9; emphasis original. See also the proceduralist approach of Brian Barry in *Democracy and Power: Essays in Political Theory 1* (Oxford: Oxford University Press, 1991), chap. 2.

[37]Compared to the ironically optimistic anthropologies of contemporary liberal theorists such as John Rawls, an earlier era of democratic theorists knew full well that popular governments would quickly slide toward their own kinds of tyrannies. In the famous Federalist 10, James Madison decries the "mischief of factions," whether constituted by a majority or minority of the whole, whose interests harm the interests of a nation, including the potential to oppress those who oppose them. This tendency to harm others is not the product of authority, says Madison, but freedom: "Liberty is to faction, what air is to fire, an aliment without which it instantly expires." After all, the root cause is in the nature of humankind: "The latent causes of faction are thus sown in the nature of man. . . . So strong is this propensity of mankind to fall into mutual animosities, that where no substantial occasion presents itself, the most frivolous and fanciful distinctions have been sufficient to kindle their unfriendly passions, and excite their most violent conflicts." Madison and the other defenders of the U.S. Constitution knew that this problem could not be solved by removing the causes of faction but only by "controling its effects" [*sic*]; hence, separation of powers, federalism, popular elections, judicial review, eventually a bill of rights, etc. Similar concerns are expressed in Federalist 51. Quotes taken from Alexander Hamilton, et al. (New York: Bantam Classics, 1982), 43–45.

gregation, congressman or president, parent or husband, who can rightly claim never to have misused those under his or her charge through sinful passivity or over-activity? If so, this person is self-deceived. Surely one of the first steps in overcoming the abuse of authority is for those in authority to acknowledge their propensity to selfish exploitation. Whether a society of relationships is established by kingly prerogative, the organic ties of family or friendship, or individual contract, humans will exploit whatever opportunity they have to subdue and take advantage of one another. Following Adam and Eve's expulsion from the garden, this must be the first lesson of the Bible, as Cain rises up against his brother Abel and kills him. Indeed, these are two of the most significant lessons of the Old Testament: humans *will* misuse authority, and God *hates* it.

Furthermore, one's potential to do harm increases as more power and authority is placed into his or her hands. The idolatrous kings of Egypt or Assyria attest to this fact (e.g., Ex. 1:8–22; Isa. 10:5–19), and so do the kings of Israel. From Saul in 1 Samuel to Zedekiah in 2 Kings, every king of Israel employs power for selfish gain, to the point of murder. God's prophets therefore excoriate Israel's kings and shepherds who "are like wolves tearing the prey, shedding blood, destroying lives to get dishonest gain" (Ezek. 22:27).[38]

But it's not just the injustices and abuses of the nation's leaders that concern God. Like James Madison's warning against factions or Alexis de Tocqueville's warning against the "tyranny of the majority," God decries the tyrannies that arise from majorities and minorities alike: "The people of the land have practiced extortion and committed robbery. They have oppressed the poor and needy, and have extorted from the sojourner without justice" (Ezek. 22:29).[39] God promises to judge all such abuses: "I have poured out my indignation upon them. I have consumed them with the fire of my wrath. I have returned their way upon their heads, declares the Lord GOD" (Ezek. 22:31).[40]

God is a God of justice, who despises exploitation in any form. As King David said, "The LORD is a stronghold for the oppressed" (Ps. 9:9), and King Jehoshaphat: "There is no injustice with the LORD our God, or partiality or taking bribes" (2 Chron. 19:7). Moses said, "He executes justice for the fatherless and the widow, and loves the sojourner, giving him food and clothing" (Deut. 10:18).

Interestingly, the closing argument for the Old Testament's case against the human use of authority ever since the fall is presented by Jesus. On one occasion in which Jesus was walking in the temple, his authority was challenged by

---

[38]Also, 2 Kings 21:16; Jer. 2:5–9; 10:21; 23:1–3; 50:6–7; Ezek. 22:6; 34:1–10; Zech. 11:17. For an excellent discussion of these passages, see Timothy S. Laniak, *Shepherds after My Own Heart: Pastoral Traditions and Leadership in the Bible* (Downers Grove, IL: InterVarsity, 2006), chaps. 7–8.
[39]Also, Isa. 61:8; Jer. 2:34; 19:4; Ezek. 22:7.
[40]Deut. 27:18–19; 2 Kings 23:26–27; 24:3–4.

Jerusalem's chief priests, scribes, and elders (Mark 11:28). He responded with a parable that encapsulated the basic error. He described them as tenants who were not satisfied with being tenants; they wanted to be owners. They were vice-kings determined to be kings, so they beat and killed the landowner's messengers, and then they killed the landowner's son and heir, thinking they would gain the land (Mark 12:1–12). These representatives of Israel, these proxies for the nation and, really, for humanity, were not content to steward God's rule. They wanted their own rule. They would even kill God's Son to get it. And so they did. The crucifixion of God's Son, the culminating act of ethnic Israel's history, is emblematic of humanity's hatred for God's rule, a point affirmed by Rome's complicity in the act. It's emblematic of the manner in which every son and daughter of Adam will pervert justice and abuse authority to gain his own way. It's emblematic of God's hatred for such perversions, as well as the strange, unexpected way he uses his Son's submission to the greatest injustice of history to accomplish salvation and glory.

For any Bible reader who considers himself "religious" or "righteous," and for any pastor, church leader, or seminarian reading this book, the parable of the tenants is a splash of cold water to the face. In the Gospels, the assault against God's reign and the essence of tyranny are distilled into their purest form and then given personifications—religious leaders, and it's these who receive Christ's greatest ire.

Power and authority in the hands of fallen human beings is a double-edged sword. Used for love's sake, it authors life and creates order. Used for any other purpose it destroys those made in the image of God (see Gen. 9:6). The entire Old Testament teaches this lesson. Christ's crucifixion teaches this lesson.

Neither rules, nor institutions, nor any forms of hierarchy in this fallen world will ultimately yield love or freedom. Any writer today who pits authority against love has the storyline of the entire Old Testament to back him up. In fact, we should probably say that the Old Testament's critique of the human situation is far more radical and thorough going than any master of suspicion or postmodern deconstructionist. There is no misty-eyed utopianism in the Bible. In fact, Israel's rejection of God and exile makes the story of Israel into its own kind of dystopia.

SUSPECT THOSE AT THE TOP . . . AND AT THE BOTTOM

Fifth, the Bible calls us to suspect both those in authority and those who refuse to submit to authority—both those at the top and those at the bottom. In one sense, it must be true that "power corrupts," as the adage goes. Greater power and authority lead to a greater opportunity to sin, which can lead to a harder heart (think of Pharaoh). At the same time, it must be true that a person who is given power and then abuses it is merely exposing the corruption that already lies dormant within every human heart, the corruption that hates and rejects God's authority. People refuse to submit to authority only partly because they fear injustice and being harmed. That was the canard Satan used with Adam and Eve. "For God knows that when you eat of it your eyes will be opened," the Serpent said, suggesting that God was trying to cheat them out of something that was rightly theirs. Really, it was their lust for self-rule that induced Adam and Eve to believe the lie.

Their experience is universal. "You will be harmed if you submit," Satan tells us, to which we gladly respond, "Not only that, but I won't be able to take and assert what's rightly mine." The apostle Paul's description of this interchange suggests that it's nothing other than a conspiracy (Eph. 2:1–3).

In short, a robust doctrine of sin not only recognizes that power corrupts, but it recognizes that it corrupts the already corrupted. The person is self-deceived who only suspects those at the top of the hierarchy and not those at the bottom. The Bible indicts both.

Step 7: Christ's life, death, and resurrection present the world with a picture of authority redeemed, an authority which he then hands to his people.

Love's Redeemed Rule

We have just considered the Bible's understanding of authority among fallen humanity. Usher love into the same room as authority and love will often find itself battered and thrashed, like a person in a cage with an ill-tempered gorilla. But what about the Bible's understanding of authority among redeemed humanity in the church?

CHRIST REDEEMS AUTHORITY

The Old Testament indeed teaches that all have sinned and fallen short of glorifying God with their dominion, but, remarkably, it teaches the opposite lesson as well. Prophetically and typologically, the Old Testament points to a time when God will write another son of Adam into the script of history who will rule precisely as the first Adam was supposed to rule—in "wisdom and understanding," in "counsel and might," in "knowledge and the fear of the LORD" (Isa. 11:2). In fact, this son of Adam will not just be written into history; his reign will author a new age that yields an order and harmony reminiscent of Eden—"the wolf shall dwell with the lamb, and the leopard shall lie down with the young goat" (Isa. 11:6)—while reckoning with the present evil age. This king, a miraculous shoot sprouting from the felled stump of King David's line, "shall not judge by what his eyes see, or decide disputes by what his ears hear, but with righteousness he shall judge the poor, and decide with equity for the meek of the earth" (Isa. 11:3–4). Perhaps most remarkably, this human king will come bearing the name, titles, and attributes, and therefore the authority of God himself:

> For to us a child is born,
>   to us a son is given;
> and the government shall be upon his shoulder,
>   and his name shall be called
> Wonderful Counselor, Mighty God,
>   Everlasting Father, Prince of Peace. (Isa. 9:6)

What's more, this coming king will execute a perfect rule because he will be in perfect submission to the Father. He will come as a priest seeking to mediate the glory of another. God will say to him, "You are my servant, Israel, in whom I will be glorified" (Isa. 49:3), and he, in perfect humility and submission, will say of God, "Morning by morning he awakens; he awakens my ear to hear as those who are taught" (Isa. 50:4).

So Christ came as king and priest. When Jesus Christ came, he explicitly invoked Isaiah when he announced, "The kingdom of heaven is at hand" (Matt. 4:15–17; 11:4–6, 9–10; Isa. 9:1–2; 40:1–5; 61:1ff.). In the life and ministry of Jesus Christ, God's authority was perfectly imaged and human authority was perfectly redeemed. Christ's authority didn't steal or squander life; it created, authored, empowered, and commissioned life, and it did so because it was perfectly grounded in a holy love for God and God's people. Where the psalmist praised God's majesty for bestowing authority, glory, and honor upon humanity by creation, the Christian can praise the majesty of Christ for bestowing his authority, glory, and honor upon the church by re-creation.[41] Once again, the author has authority, only it's the author of re-creation that has authority among the re-created; and he uses his authority to authorize life and rule in others for the Father's glory.

- Jesus exhibited his life-giving, restorative authority by "healing every disease and every affliction among the people" (Matt. 4:23–25; 9:35).

- Jesus refused Satan's temptation of "all the kingdoms of the world and their glory" since worship belongs to the Lord God alone (Matt. 4:8–10).

---

[41]I encourage readers toward G. E. Ladd's *Theology of the New Testament* for a classic treatment on the topic of Christ's in-breaking rule, and Thomas Schreiner's *New Testament Theology* for a more up-to-date presentation.

- Jesus astonished the crowds, "for he was teaching them as one who had authority" (Matt. 7:28–29).

- A Roman centurion, himself "a man under authority, with soldiers under" him, recognized Jesus' authority and knew he could use it to heal his servant (Matt. 8:5–9).

- The disciples observed that "even winds and sea obey him," which happened, saving the disciples (Matt. 8:27).

- The demons were subject to Jesus' command, and he claimed to have bound Satan (Matt. 8:29–32; 9:32–33; 12:28–29).

- Jesus claimed to have "authority on earth to forgive sins" and proved it by healing a cripple, causing a crowd to glorify God "who had given such authority to men" (Matt. 9:6–8).

- This "Son of David" and "Lord of the Sabbath" established a kind of new Israel: "He called to him his twelve disciples and gave them authority over unclean spirits, to cast them out, and to heal every disease and every affliction" (Matt. 9:17; 10:1; 12:18).

- Jesus claimed that he would erase the most fundamental alliances known to humanity and redraw all the alliances and boundaries *based entirely on who would and would not love him* and *who would and would not do his will* (Matt. 10:34–39; 12:50; also 8:22).

- Jesus pronounced judgment upon his enemies (Matt. 11:20–24).

- Jesus used his rule not to impose a heavy yoke but a light, rest-giving one, since he is gentle and lowly in heart (Matt. 11:29).

- Jesus specifically contrasted his rule with the rule of the "great ones [who] exercise authority" by "lording it over" others. He instead "came not to be served but to serve, and to give his life as a ransom for many" (Matt. 20:25, 26a, 28). His rule was a priestly rule. He pointed his followers not only back to Isaiah's promised king but to Isaiah's promised servant (cf. Matt. 12:15–21; Isa. 42:1–3; 53:3–6).

- Jesus claimed that "all authority in heaven and on earth has been given to me" (Matt. 28:18).

Jesus came to declare a kingdom, bind the Devil, demonstrate rule over creation, free the captives, heal the lame, raise the dead, call a people to himself, win salvation, and usher in a new creation and royal priesthood for that creation. Generally speaking, he came to claim the identity and prerogatives of God himself, including God's loving authority over all that he has created.[42] Yet Christ exercised his rule by submitting his life as a sacrifice. He stood up to lead and then he surrendered himself to the purposes of that leadership. The kingdom was won by a bloody act of ransom, and that ransom authored life—a new life and a new creation.

CHRISTIANS TO IMAGE CHRIST'S AUTHORITY

How should would-be converts and Christians respond to Christ's authority? They should obey it, plain and simple. Sometimes the New Testament uses the language of obedience, sometimes the language of leaving everything and following him, and sometimes the language of repentance, but these are all ways of saying the same thing—submit to Christ's in-breaking rule.

The point of the last chapter was to add another layer of meaning to these activities. Such activities of obedience, we argued, are in fact the activities of love. Love and obedience to Christ go together. Loving God and neighbor is what occupants of Christ's in-breaking kingdom do (cf. Rom. 13:8–10). We obey what we love. When our heart cherishes something, it acts automatically to fulfill its laws or requirements. All this can be summed up by saying that conversion involves the swapping of our heart's allegiances.

There is one more layer to add. To submit to Christ is to be authorized by Christ to act in his stead. His authority, through our obedience as believers, leads to our authority. Just as Adam should have exercised a God-glorifying dominion by equipping his children to exercise a God-glorifying dominion, so Christ does commission Christians to exercise a Christlike authority. He commissions them to create, to give order and ability, and to equip others to extend his dominion to the ends of the earth.

- Jesus commissions his disciples to act as salt and light to the world so that the world might "give glory to your Father who is in heaven" (Matt. 5:13–16)

- Jesus tells his disciples not to hate, sexually exploit, divorce, lie, and retaliate (Matt. 5:21–42). Indeed, they should love their enemies and do good to them exactly because their heavenly Father "sends rain on the just and on the unjust" (Matt. 5:43–48).

---

[42]For more on Jesus' claim to God's identity and prerogatives, see Richard Bauckham, *God Crucified: Monotheism and Christology in the New Testament* (Grand Rapids: Eerdmans, 1999) and Christopher J. H. Wright, *The Mission of God*, chap. 4.

- In fact, Jesus sums up all the Law and the Prophets by telling his followers to do to others what they would have others do to themselves (Matt. 7:12).

- Jesus calls people to leave everything and lose their lives by following him (Matt. 8:22; 10:39; 16:24–26).

- Jesus calls more laborers to the harvest (Matt. 9:37).

- Jesus gives his disciples the authority to bind demons, heal, raise the dead, and preach the good news of the kingdom (Matt. 10:1, 7–8).

- Jesus tells people to care for his children (Matt. 10:42).

- Jesus identifies himself with those who do the will of his Father in heaven (Matt. 12:50).

- Jesus gives the church authority to bind and loose (Matt. 16:15–20).

- Jesus gives the church authority to render judgment upon itself (Matt. 18:15–20).

- Jesus says he will divide humanity between those who care for the least of his brothers and those who don't (Matt. 25:31–46).

- Jesus authorizes his followers to make disciples and instruct them (Matt. 28:18–20).[43]

Jesus commissions his followers to exercise his authority. That means they are to heal, give life and not exploit it, preach, evangelize, cast out, bind and loose, teach, render judgment on imposters, care, and make disciples. They are to do these things in all the earth, just as Adam was supposed to. All this they are to do by taking up their crosses and giving themselves entirely to him. They will love him to the utmost by seeking to authorize others to live life within his kingdom. The Great Commission in Matthew 28 is not just the last episode of Matthew's Gospel. It is the Gospel's crescendo and natural culmination. It is the *summa* and highest point of disciples' commission. All the work that Christ commissions his people to do on earth comes to a point here, because nothing in this world is more life-authoring and loving toward others than ushering them into an obedient relationship with God and helping them to grow in their obedience. That's why evangelizing, preaching,

---

[43]I have restricted the quotations here primarily to Matthew. Several other passages to note along the lines of the church's authority include Luke 10:19; 24:46–48; John 14:26; 20:21–23; and Acts 1:8. References to the church's end-time authority can be found in 2 Tim. 2:12; Rev. 2:26–27; 5:10; 22:5.

discipling, and church planting are activities of love and of love exercising its Christ-commissioned authority. This is also why these activities constitute the church's primary focus.

To become a Christian is to submit oneself to the rule of Christ—in every area of one's life. Christians have moved from one kingdom to another. It's not one's body that has moved, like moving from one country to another. It's one's heart and allegiances. Whether Christians eat or drink, command armies to build vineyards and parks, or share the gospel, they are to do it by faith for the glory of God.

With such submission comes authority or authorization. When we submit to Christ, he authorizes us to go and do likewise. He commissions us to exercise the loving authority of calling others into his kingdom.

TWO COMPETING REALITIES

The move from one kingdom to another is all-encompassing. It's like moving from one field of energy to another, or from the gravitational pull of one body to the gravitational pull of another. Better than either of those analogies is the language used by theologian Oliver O'Donovan. He describes Christ's kingdom and man's kingdom as two different "realities." *Authority created/redeemed* and *authority fallen* are grounded in two different realities. Fallen man, O'Donovan says, refuses to recognize the true reality of the ultimate good, God. Instead, "the sin by which man has bound himself is the determination to live fantastically, in pursuit of unreality."[44] His life is based on a lie. The grounds on which he makes his decisions and actions, that is, his sense of being authorized to do as he pleases, is an illusion. But then God's rule comes crashing in, bringing reality with it: "The authority of redemption lies in its power to determine the present reality of the world with which we have to do."[45] It destroys the old and brings in the new:

> The term "authority" warns us that when redemption is presented to us it does not encounter a vacuum. It encounters an apparent structure of order which is presented within the world, criticizing it and transforming it. It brings true reality to bear upon the appearances of reality which our world . . . presents to us. The effect of this is twofold: our world is judged, and it is recreated.[46]

Here's what I think O'Donovan is saying. It's as if humanity, hired as a store manager, entered God's store called "Creation" and changed all his price tags, stamping on every item a price sticker that is completely out of sync

---

[44]O'Donovan, *Resurrection and Moral Order,* 109.
[45]Ibid.
[46]Ibid., 104.

with the value and price assigned by God at the store's opening. The cheap becomes costly and the costly becomes cheap. The authority of redemption is the license to return those price tags to their true value, an activity that will inevitably be fought by customers whose values now align with the false prices.

When a person becomes a Christian, the price tags on everything are restored to their original value. Before, a man would spend his entire life to buy this world. Now, he knows it profits a man nothing to gain the world but forfeit his soul. Before, he had to spend his days running around asking, "What shall we eat?" or "What shall we drink?" or "What shall we wear?" Now, he seeks first the kingdom of God and his righteousness. Before, he sought the praise of men. Now, he seeks the reward that comes from the Father in heaven. Before, worldly wealth. Now, poverty of spirit. Before, laughter, now mourning. Before, bravado. Now, meekness.

For three reasons that are relevant to church membership, I like the connection O'Donovan makes between authority and the language of "reality." First, it communicates the radical disjuncture between a fallen view of reality and authority and a redeemed view. It's as if the unbeliever dwells in a moral world of illusions and mirages while the believer, by comparison, abides between the brick walls and upon the concrete floors of God's truth.[47] That's quite a switch. Only one of these two can possibly have true moral authority or legitimacy for his or her actions. Second, this language communicates how all-encompassing this change is: we are faced with competing *realities*. A reality includes everything. Third, the change is directed and accomplished by God. The switch involves not just changing one interpretive grid for another, one legitimating structure for another, or one set of conversations for another, though, surely, the change will be mediated through such anthropological realities. Rather, "the Holy Spirit brings God's act in Christ into critical opposition to the falsely structured reality in which we live. At the same time and through the same act he calls into existence a new and truer structure for existence."[48] The invasion begins top down, not bottom up.

Authority redeemed, like *authority created*, is a wonderful, life-giving, rulership-bestowing thing to be embraced and rejoiced in by God's people; it's a radically different thing from what we have all encountered as *authority fallen*. This is why the born-again, Holy Spirit–indwelt Christian can turn to the headwaters of the entire Psalter, Psalm 1, and read about the blessed man whose "delight is in the law of the LORD" (v. 2). Delight in the law? Indeed, if

---

[47]Anyone who has seen any of the movies in *The Matrix* trilogy knows that they are premised on a similar analogy.
[48]O'Donovan, *Resurrection and Moral Order*, 104.

a person is united to Christ by the Spirit, he or she will increasingly savor every word that comes from the mouth of God.

Step 8: The local church is where Christians enact their submission to Christ and practice his loving rule toward others.

What Does This Have to Do with Church Membership?

In this chapter we've established that authority grounded in love creates life, that Christ represents God's authority, and that Christian love is shown in the exercise of Christ's authority. But what does all of this have to do with church membership and discipline? The answer is simple: if submitting to authority causes growth, then the Christian needs some place to enact submission to Christ and to practice a loving rule toward others. The Bible's solution is for Christians to submit to the membership and discipline of the local church.

Any charlatan can say, "I have submitted to Christ's rule." Yet submission is so anathema and counter-intuitive to our fallen natures that we can easily deceive ourselves into thinking we have submitted to him when we haven't. How easy it is to say the words, "Christ is my Lord," but to do them is a different matter altogether. The authoritative structures of the local church provide the professing Christian with the opportunity *to do* those words, "Christ is Lord."

A PERSONAL ILLUSTRATION

I'm not entirely sure when God converted me, but one of my best guesses is that it occurred through the circumstances of several church meetings during my mid-twenties. I was raised in churches by faithful parents and named Christ as my Savior at a young age, but I seldom attended church throughout college and graduate school, living entirely for myself and the ambitions of the world during those years.

By the conclusion of graduate school, the many regretful decisions of high school and college had left me in a state of spiritual malaise. I moved to Washington DC, and decided to join a Baptist church that had been recommended by a graduate school friend.

When asked in a membership interview to explain my understanding of the gospel, I used the words *substitutionary atonement*, which I had heard my friend use, although I wasn't entirely sure of what the words meant and hoped the pastor wouldn't press me on them.

God's Word was powerfully preached in this church, pointing to a big God and a merciful Christ. The embrace of its membership was sweet and warm. One older man named Dan invited me to join his family every Saturday morning for breakfast and a study of Isaiah, and I was frequently invited to dinner at members' homes. The preaching, meanwhile, was fearless. Little by little my head began to turn from one direction to another.

A crucial moment occurred a little over a year into membership. The church had just voted to change its constitution to a "plural elder led" model, which means that a church is led by a plurality of elders, but it remains "congregational" because the congregation retains final say in significant matters, such as the choosing of elders. The pastor—our single elder—then put five elder nominations before the congregation at a members' meeting. Remarkably, all five men failed to pass the constitutionally mandated 75 percent threshold. For my part, I voted for three and against two, basically for incidental reasons.

When the failed vote was announced, the church drew in its collective breath and wondered what the pastor would do next. A week later, we found out: he was nominating the same five men and asking the church to vote on them again. I was appalled. Didn't he say we were a congregational church? Hadn't he heard the church's voice in the last vote? Who was this pastor to think he could go against the church's "will"?! I determined to vote against all five this time as a protest vote.

One week before the second vote, the pastor held an informational meeting in order to discuss his decision to re-nominate the same five. He told us that, standing before God, he could not in good conscience nominate a different set of men. And, as the congregation's one formally recognized elder, he was asking us to trust him. He was very clear and forthright as he spoke, and obviously convinced of his position, but there was no anxiousness or forcefulness in his bearing, as if he *had* to get us to see things his way. No, he was simply asking us to follow him.

For the record, I have now known this man for thirteen years, and that is the only time I recall hearing him ask us to trust him in this manner. He doesn't play the "trust me" card often.

In retrospect, this was my rich-young-ruler moment. Jesus wasn't asking me to sell all my possessions in order to follow him; he was asking me instead to forfeit my sense of democratic propriety and my self-rule. The pastor's request could have seemed absurd, just like the request to sell everything. But by God's grace, it made sense. Something changed in my heart whereby I wanted to affirm this man's leadership. So I did. I thought to myself, "If I am incapable of submitting and deferring to him, a man who has proven faithful, will I be capable of submitting to anybody?"

In the year or two following this series of meetings, my life began to change. My desires to be with the people of God dramatically intensified. My hunger to put off sin grew. A new longing to see others discover Jesus and grow in the knowledge of him developed. Over the same time, the church began to trust me with more responsibility—the chance to teach Sunday school, the opportunity to lead a men's Bible study, the position as church deacon for member care. Through my act of submission, I became a kind of ruler once more—someone authorized to author life in others.

There are two ways someone might interpret what happened to me through this series of meetings and over the years that followed. A sociologist might point to Max Weber's conception of a charismatic leader and to the group dynamics of institutional loyalty necessary for all social organizations to operate. Another interpretation, one which doesn't need to disavow entirely the first but which also views the events with eyes of faith, would say that I may have been converted by God through the very decision to submit to this pastor's authority by voting for these five men.

REPENTANCE

Consider again Jesus' words to the rich young ruler, as well as every occasion in which he called for sinners to repent. Forsaking our self-rule and submitting to Christ's rule will almost always mean forsaking something on earth—some man-made idol that has occupied the role of God until that point. The rich young ruler's idol was money. Mine, fresh out of graduate school with a degree in political philosophy and democratic theory, was intellectual pride and personal autonomy. In both cases, God asked us to submit by doing something that, to the natural self, seemed outrageous. Yet it's the very act of submitting to God, often mediated through an earthly authority, which produces spiritual life.

It's nothing short of tragic, therefore, when a church or a pastor accepts a philosophy of evangelism, discipleship, and church life entirely premised on offering people incentives to come to Jesus. It's easy to do, because no authoritative stance is required. No command to repent or turn from sin is necessary. Just offer people what they already want, such as meaning, love, success, relationships, or purpose. Yet new life doesn't come when people are offered what they already want. Giving people what they want simply confirms the old life. People acquire a new life by being told that the old life has to die and new things must be desired. Unfortunately, that's an authoritative statement. It's a command, and we hate commands.

The Christian life begins when we repent and believe (Mark 1:14). It begins when we turn away from our own rule and submit ourselves to the rule of Christ. This means recognizing that the reality we once believed in is an illusion. We now live and breathe, work and play, believing in a new reality, a new rule. We recognize that the price tags on everything in the universe are different than we once thought. All our relationships and ambitions bend toward new purposes, as if a new and larger sun showed up in our solar system. Becoming a Christian means beginning to love, for the first time in our lives, as God truly intends us to love. It means that we experience the initial inklings of loving him with all our heart, soul, mind, and strength and our neighbor as ourselves. That love is not yet a conflagration, but the sparks of these affections are now lit within our souls.

Evangelicals often talk about becoming a Christian by "entering into a relationship with Christ." In one sense, that's true. Moreover, it's true that life and reality are relational at their most basic levels, just as God is a being in relation. But I believe it would be more biblical (in light of the command to repent) to say that, upon becoming a Christian, an individual enters into *a new kind of relationship* with Christ. After all, a non-Christian is in a relationship with Christ. It's merely a relationship typified by rejection, rebellion, and therefore God's wrath. The difference between a Christian and a non-Christian is not most fundamentally a question of relationship; it's a question of authority and love. It's a question of the heart's allegiances.

This means that the advocates of a centered-set church model are half right. Entering life in the church should mean more than just crossing some doctrinal boundary line. If that's how a church has been practicing member ship, it should repent because it's fomenting hypocrisy. Church membership, at least as Jesus intends it, is indeed about cultivating a relationship with Christ and moving continually toward Christ, like the centered-set church folk say. It should mean swapping one reality for another, one rule for another, one set of price tags for another. Nothing in one's life will remain unaffected. Belonging to a church is not just about moving toward Christ in some vague relational way. It's about far more. It's about conforming our lives more and more to his image. It's about obeying his commands as a lifestyle. It's about repenting and repenting again and repenting again, every time seeking greater conformity to his glorious image.

What's the earthly mechanism for mediating this continual repentance? Where do we find the authoritative structures that offer us the opportunity to enact our submission to Christ and to practice his loving rule through teaching, discipleship, and discipline? It's within the life of a local church's membership we both submit and rule.

I believe that evangelicals can regard church membership dismissively or even disdainfully because they assume that their personal discipleship with Christ and their church membership are utterly separable things. What I will contend in the next two chapters is that church membership is where and how our discipleship to Christ occurs. Church membership should give shape to our entire lives. This is the case because it's not just relationships that give substance to a Christian life; it is Christ's authority, mediated through other human beings.

When we enter the church, we enter a whole new reality, one with borders and a center. This new reality, if indeed it is new, will be marked off. Everything about us should be distinct. Our words, symbols, and even institutional rules, therefore, should indicate as much.

Step 9: The local church is a new reality, with marked-off borders and a center.

The Borders of the Church

Church membership begins, then, with the act of submitting to baptism. "Repent and be baptized," Peter told the crowds who asked what they had to do to be saved (Acts 2:38). Does that mean baptism saves us? No, it's what Christ commands a new Christian to do as the first step of obedience to him. It symbolizes one's submission to Christ and one's unity with him in death and resurrection, but it occurs through submitting oneself to the authority and oversight of human beings in a local church. Only after we submit to the church are we authorized to proclaim its gospel message to one another and to the world.

In other words, the local church should have very clear borders surrounding it. On the inside should be those who have repented and been baptized (and receive the Lord's Supper); on the outside should be those who have not, or who have been excluded. But this boundary line is the very thing that makes so many people today nervous, such as those who advocate a centered-set church over against a bounded-set church.

The problem with bounded-set churches, says anthropologist Paul Hiebert, is that they try to classify people according to what they *are*. There are at least two problems with doing this, he says. First, classifying people according to what they *are* relies on static conceptions of being inherited from the Greeks rather than from the Bible's relational view of human beings, as we've discussed. Second, it requires us to make our best guesses about people, since we cannot truly see them as God sees them. This leads the bounded-set church to continually ask, "Do this person's beliefs and behaviors conform to what *we think* makes somebody a Christian?" As a result, the church focuses all its attention on patrolling the boundaries, making sure the right people are on the inside and the wrong people are on the outside.[49]

The problem with these arguments is that Jesus says a person must be born again to enter the kingdom of God. Paul says a person must be a new creation. Churches should therefore be extremely interested in what people *are*. Are they born again? Are they new creations? Though churches certainly do not see what God sees in a professing believer, Jesus still commands the church to baptize his disciples (Matt. 28:19–20). Apparently, the epistemic limitations inherent

---

[49]Hiebert, *Anthropological Reflections*, 115–16.

in our finitude and falleness didn't worry him so much that he decided to with-hold this authority. Where advocates of a centered-set church want to create multiple classes of believers at various stages of the journey,[50] the Bible sees just two: believing or not believing; children of God or children of the Devil; baptized or not baptized. The church is called to draw a line—a boundary—right down the middle.

I am not suggesting that people cannot come to faith gradually, or even hand their allegiance over to Christ gradually. This is what we see with Jesus' disciples, as their eyes opened not instantaneously but gradually. Jesus seemed to illustrate their growing faith by healing one blind man in two stages (Mark 8:22–26). This is how I would characterize my own conversion. It felt like a process, a journey, a gradual shifting, with a couple of punctuated moments. It may be that my experience, like the disciples' and the blind man's, was gradual because God's gift of spiritual sight was given gradually (though I do believe justification and regeneration occur in one decisive moment).

Still, we must not lose sight of the fact that the church publicly represents an alternative reality to the world. We have to cross the border. We want to be on the inside, not the outside, of that new reality. God really does save people. The Spirit really does make them new creations. Christ really does bring them from death to life, and he has expressly authorized the church, as we'll consider in the next chapter, to publicly represent this alternative reality. Whether people's decision to swap allegiances comes gradually or quickly, a point comes when they *must* decide to change their jersey: "You've been playing for the red team. You've been thinking about switching to the blue team. What's it going to be—red or blue?" Conversion occurs at the moment the decision is made.

Baptism, then, is putting on the new jersey. It's when we publicly identify ourselves, by the church's representative authority, with his death and resur-rection. All the thinking and journeying come to a head right there. Through the church Jesus asks whether we will die to ourselves and our own rule, be buried with him, and trust that he will raise us up with him according to a new power and rule. Perhaps Jesus had universal human indecision in mind when he commissioned the church to baptize. Perhaps he had in mind especially the postmodern fear of commitment. Either way, what's clear is that contemporary churches, in their effort to contextualize and exercise compassion, can unintentionally and unlovingly undermine their Lord as they tell sinners that they do not need to make the decision for which the Lord is calling.

---

[50]Hiebert divides people into seekers, believers, baptized members, and elders; Guder divides them into the unchurched, the nominal, the seekers, the congregation, and the covenant community, *Missional Churches*, 210–11.

Step 10: Yet we must always keep in mind that authority in this fallen world is both complex and mixed.

The Complex Nature of Authority in the Here and Now

Ironically, the epistemological issue that Hiebert raises cuts both ways, and it helps to transition us to the next chapter. It's true that the church cannot see with the eyes of God into the hearts of professors. Then again, it's precisely because of that limitation that Jesus does not leave individuals in charge of determining who truly spoke for his kingdom. Instead, he established a church and expressly gave the church this authority. Does Hiebert assume that individuals can properly see God's opinion of themselves or their own hearts? I suppose the answer to that question comes down to whether one's doctrine of sin contains the possibility of self-deceit.

No doubt, reality in this age between Christ's ascension and return is difficult to discern. Authority redeemed, like authority created, might be a wonderful, life-giving force, but authority fallen remains a similarly potent force in this world. When God invaded the world in Christ, he did not simply supplant one reality with another. The two realities became simultaneous, like two film projectors casting their light upon the same screen. It's not always easy to discern where one image on the screen ends and another image begins, or which film projector is projecting which image.

The exercise of authority among God's people will therefore remain a complex matter until the Lord returns, both because our world continues to present us with simultaneous examples of authority redeemed and authority fallen and because still-sinful Christians are capable of both. Good and godly authority does exist in this world—it has entered into history once more—but it's not always easy to discern what godly authority looks like compared to worldly authority, much less to practice it. Just consider the church in Corinth. On the one hand, the Corinthian Christians suffered from an over-aggrandized sense of their victory and rule in Christ, as attested to by Paul's sarcastic and exasperated ejaculation, "Already you have all you want! Already you have become rich! Without us you have become kings! And would that you did reign, so that we might share the rule with you!" (1 Cor. 4:8).[51] On the other hand, Paul has to rebuke the church body for its failure to exercise precisely the kind of corporate authority it should have exercised in one man's life (5:4–5). The moral of this story is that it's all too easy for churches, in the name of godliness, to exercise

---

[51]This verse plays a prominent role in Anthony Thiselton's argument that one of the Corinthians' principle sins was an over-realized eschatology; see Anthony C. Thiselton, "Realized Eschatalogy at Corinth," in *New Testament Studies* 24 (1978): 510–26; see also Thiselton's qualifications of this thesis in *The First Epistle to the Corinthians*, The New International Greek Testament Commentary (Grand Rapids: Eerdmans, 2000), 40.

worldly authority while completely failing to exercise the godly authority to which they are called. In fact, any given exercise of authority can be simultaneously grounded in a love for God and a love for the world.

At a popular level, evangelicals talk often about "servant leadership," as if that's the magic phrase that strikes the balance and answers all the questions. But what typically follows that phrase is a description of what it means to serve, with little explanation given to what it means to truly lead or exercise authority. Is godly authority nothing other than service, synonyms with univocal meanings?

Among theologians, writers will sometimes make distinctions between different kinds of authority, such as the "authority of counsel" versus the "authority of command" or "political authority" versus "spiritual authority." Truly, there are different kinds of authority called for by different kinds of occasions. But jumping in too quickly with such distinctions misses the point that authority in any domain, in any capacity, can be exercised in a godly or worldly fashion. If you compare the actions of a godly authority and a worldly authority, they actually might look the same (within certain moral bounds). Jesus made commands, declared judgments, and asserted his prerogatives, just as every prince or prime minister does. But Jesus loved his subjects to the utmost for God's glory. His intent was different, even when some of his actions were similar, which is not to say that godly authority is entirely a matter of intent. Since worldly authority represents a perversion of godly authority, it will bear both similarities and differences, as every instance of perversion does. The difficulty lies with sorting out which is which.

With all that in mind, how precisely are churches to follow the example of Christ? Can the church make commands, declare judgments, and assert its prerogatives? Then again, what church can claim to follow in the way of Christ without sin?

These complexities are worth keeping in mind as we consider how Christ does in fact authorize—commission—the church to exercise his authority within his kingdom. On the one hand, churches and church leaders can be tempted by the over-realized eschatology of the Corinthians. On the other hand, they can be tempted to define authority or to structure the church in such a fashion that all the dangers of fallen authority are removed. As with James Madison and the other authors of the U.S. Constitution, there is an understandable impulse to ask how to structure a government in order to alleviate the threat of faction, tyranny, entrenched interests, and abuse, given the corruptible nature of humankind. The problem is that Christians and church leaders shouldn't go about organizing their churches according to what's safe, per se, but according to what's faithful to God's Word. Also, could the very nature of two overlapping realities suggest that God may just call churches to wield some tools that if used in the Spirit will bring good, but if used in the flesh will bring harm?

Conclusion

As college freshman Charlotte says at one point in Tom Wolfe's 2004 novel *I Am Charlotte Simmons,* college is a place where "nobody asked anybody out on a date unless they were already spending most nights in each other's beds, and even then the boy would word it along the lines of 'Whatcha doing tonight? Wanna chill?'"[52]

The culture these days likes to talk about relationships and community. With relationships like these, it's no wonder. When I studied political theory in graduate school, communitarianism was all the rage among many of my secular postmodern colleagues. You don't have to be a Christian to want community and relationship, especially if humans *were* created for relationships. The Bible uses a concept similar to "relationship," but it's a fuller concept. It's the idea of a holy obedience to God's loving and life-giving authority. To be holy is to grab hold of all one's relationships and change their bearing, their purpose. That's why, as we read through the Bible, we won't find references to "relationship"; we'll find references to obedience, holiness, and lordship.

When the theologian or pastor talks the talk of relationship and community rather than the talk of obedience and holiness, he just might be hawking a postmodern prosperity gospel. The poor man's prosperity gospel is: "Never mind all that stuff about obedience and holiness; Jesus wants to make you rich and happy!" But many of us today in the West are rich. We don't need the poor man's prosperity gospel. Rather, we suffer from ennui, angst, and media overload. The relationships we do have are shallow and unsatisfying, so the intellectual sophisticate offers a postmodern prosperity gospel instead: "Never mind all that stuff about obedience and holiness; Jesus will give you relationships, purpose, community."

---

[52]Tom Wolfe, *I Am Charlotte Simmons* (New York: Farrar, Straus, and Giroux, 2004), 362–63.

CHAPTER FOUR

THE CHARTER OF LOVE

"The power of love is a curious thing
make a one man weep,
make another man sing."
—*Huey Lewis*

Main Questions: What authority does Christ give the local church and why?

Main Answers: Christ authorizes the local church to proclaim and protect the gospel, to recognize or affirm those who belong to him, to unite them to itself, to oversee their discipleship, and to exclude any imposters. He gives the local church this authority in order to protect and display his gospel in a fallen world which continually misunderstands and misportrays his gospel love.

Step 1: In this fallen world, hypocrites and heretics confuse the world about the gospel and the nature of Christ's love. Therefore, Christ authorizes the church to mark off the people of God.

It's a caricature. It confirms the world's worst stereotypes about hypocritical churches and Christian leaders. It's offensive and grotesque. But William Faulkner's novel *As I Lay Dying* accurately portrays too many ministers and professing Christians, a portrayal that the world takes for the real thing.

Addie Bundren, wife and mother in rural Mississippi, is dying. Her children and husband take turns recounting their experiences of watching Mother expire, each coping differently with their loss. Then, midway through the story, for three brief pages, Faulkner introduces one more character—the whited sepulcher Reverend Whitfield. No background is provided. Faulkner simply drops the reader into a new subplot with the reverend's own words:

> When they told me she was dying, all that night I wrestled with Satan, and I emerged victorious. I woke to the enormity of my sin; I saw the true light at last, and I fell on my knees and confessed to God and asked His guidance and received it. "Rise," He said; "repair to that home in which you have put a living lie, among those people with whom you have outraged My Word; confess your sin aloud. It is for them, for that deceived husband, to forgive you: not I."

Like Hawthorne's Reverend Dimmesdale, Faulkner's Reverend Whitfield once had a secret affair with a member of his flock, Addie. He recalls that "she had sworn then that she would never tell it," but he realizes that "eternity is a fearsome thing to face." So he determines to beat her to the punch.

Traveling by horseback to the Bundren family home, Whitfield prays, "Praise to Thee, O Mighty Lord and King. By this token shall I cleanse my soul and gain again into the fold of Thy undying love." Ah, a true Christian, this Whitfield. The man has sinned and now seeks peace with God and peace with neighbor. He yearns once more for the Lord's love and forgiveness. After praying silently, he says:

> I knew then that forgiveness was mine. . . . It was already as though it were done. My soul felt freer, quieter than it had in years; already I seemed to dwell in abiding peace as I rode on. To either side I saw His hand; in my heart I could hear His voice: "Courage. I am with thee."

How fortunate that he felt God's forgiveness before reaching the Bundren home! She dies before he arrives. The need for a messy confession has passed; for God "is merciful; He will accept the will for the deed." Whitfield then enters the grief-stricken home, reflects on the deceased woman now facing "the awful and irrevocable judgment" for her sin, and pronounces magisterially, "God's grace upon this house."

Addie might lie in hell, her sin unconfessed, but Whitfield can rejoice for his own soul's sake: "Praise to Thee in Thy bounteous and omnipotent love; O praise."[1]

After the publication of *As I Lay Dying,* Faulkner was asked in an interview if Whitfield was a hypocrite. He answered, "No, I wouldn't say he was a hypocritical man. He had to live a hypocritical life. That is, he had to live in public the life which the ignorant fanatic people of the isolated and rural South demand of a man of God, when actually he was just a man like any of them."[2]

The caricature well embodies how the world views Christianity, the church, and our talk of love, righteousness, and forgiveness. And there's merit to the caricature. Blowhards and blackguards like Whitfield, a tawdry TV preacher before the age of television, do exist. It's not difficult to think of fallen leaders, fallen Christians, or fractured churches that confirm this very stereotype.

What's utterly tragic, therefore, is the fact that Whitfield seems to be no Christian. He is a counterfeit, and, like all counterfeits, he makes us cynical and steels us against the real thing. The irony that people often miss is that

---

[1] Quotes taken from William Faulkner, *As I Lay Dying* (New York: Vintage International, 1990), 177–79.
[2] Frederick L. Gwynn, et al., eds., *Faulkner in the University* (Charlottesville, VA: University of Virginia Press, 1959), 114.

counterfeits simultaneously hide and reveal something true. There is something true in Reverend Whitfield's religion that is beautiful and glorious, even though Faulkner's cartoon drawing contorts it beyond all recognition: there is an all-loving God who exercises his bounteous love in the very act of saving some and not others. There is an all-loving God who displays his omnipotent love in the very act of forgiving the worst of hypocrites and adulterers. And there is an all-loving God who beckons the praise of a marked-off, boundaried people as he pronounces his blessing upon them and calls them to pronounce that blessing among others: let the nations praise his generous and powerful love.

But who would believe it when hypocrites like Whitfield hit the headlines?

Instances of hypocrisy or heresy will always receive more publicity when it involves a church leader like Whitfield, but it's not really the headlines that should worry us. It's our own lives. It's the life of the average church member. For every act of hypocrisy that hits the press, are there not ten thousand instances of hypocrisy in our own lives, some small and some not so small? Our non-Christian neighbors, colleagues, and friends hear us profess the name of Christ with our mouths and with our church affiliations, yet they watch us and wonder, "If Jesus is all that you say he is, why does your life look like mine? Can the born-again gospel you talk about really be true?" More than the headline makers, it's the daily life of the average Christian that ultimately forms the world's perception of Christ and his gospel.

Let Him Be Removed

It's this kind of tragedy that the apostle Paul wrestles with in 1 Corinthians 5. A man in the Corinthian church was sleeping with his father's wife, and Paul seems to have placed himself in the shoes of the church's non-Christian neighbors when he exclaims, "It is actually reported that there is sexual immorality among you, and of a kind that is not tolerated even among pagans" (v. 1). It's as if Paul is saying, "The world doesn't even do this! What do you think they're going to think?" He was rightly concerned about the name and fame of Christ. He was concerned about the church, its witness, and its life of holiness. He was concerned about the man, that he was self-deceived and living in danger of damnation. In Paul's mind, the solution was straightforward: remove the man. He writes:

> Let him who has done this be removed from among you. For though absent in body, I am present in spirit; and as if present, I have already pronounced judgment on the one who did such a thing. When you are assembled in the name of the Lord Jesus and my spirit is present, with the power of our Lord Jesus, you are to deliver this

man to Satan for the destruction of the flesh, so that his spirit may be saved in the day of the Lord. (vv. 2b–5)

Paul is calling the church to exercise its Christ-given authority to exclude the man. This raises a number of questions. First, he tells the church to let the man "be removed," but removed from what exactly? Also, why does he assume the church has the authority to remove the man? The man is accountable to God, not to them, right? Who gives them the right to remove him? And then why does Paul talk of his spirit being "saved in the day of the Lord"? What's the connection between his belonging to this church and his salvation? Finally, Paul seems to have some other goal in mind besides holding people together. If his goal is not merely to hold the church together, what is it?

We will eventually get to these questions, but one thing should be clear to us: Paul calls for an authoritative, institutional act in order to defend the gospel's witness. Apparently, the gospel and the institutional elements of a church's life may not be as disconnected as we sometimes think.

An Institutional Charter

We do disconnect them, after all. One theologian, Kevin Vanhoozer, has written about his younger days as a professor in which he avoided teaching the doctrine of the church because it seemed to contain only the matters that have historically divided Christians like baptism, polity, the role of women in the ministry, and so on.[3] Besides, none of these things are essential for salvation. Now, Vanhoozer has recovered his interest in ecclesiology because he chooses not to focus on these divisive matters; rather, he writes about a "mere ecclesiology." A mere ecclesiology is one that focuses on the fact that the church is an implication of the gospel and is content to set aside the external matters of polity and practice.[4] The person and work of Christ has made us *a people*, so let's focus on affirming this, not the things that divide us.

Among theologically minded evangelicals, Vanhoozer's approach strikes me as fairly common. Conferences and books sound the call for affirming the center, establishing the essentials, and redefining the core doctrines for a new generation. Maybe that means defining the gospel in a way that better accords with the narrative of redemptive history. Maybe that means defining conversion less individualistically. Maybe that means defining the church's essence as "on mission." But no matter the approach, church polity seldom, if ever, enters the conversation. It's shoved to the side. What J. L. Reynolds said in 1846 sounds

---

[3] "Evangelicalism and the Church: The Company of the Gospel," in *The Futures of Evangelicalism: Issues and Prospects*, ed. Craig Bartholomew, Robin Parry, and Andrew West (Grand Rapids: Kregel, 2003), 46 n. 13.
[4] Ibid., 46–55.

like a joke: "Church polity has become the absorbing topic of the Christian world."[5]

Among pragmatically minded evangelicals these days, the future of the church is said to depend on getting our practices just right. The assumption is that church polity is infinitely flexible. Churches should do whatever works. Conferences and books sound the call for contextualization, multi-campuses, video feeds, cultivating the right in-house culture, better small-group ministries, sensitive evangelistic programs, and so much more.

In short, some evangelicals recommend affirming the doctrinal center; others recommend toying with the structures. What's ironic, however, is that these two impulses can work at cross purposes. Surely evangelical churches should affirm the doctrinal center, but what's overlooked by so many, theologians and practitioners alike, is the fact that Jesus grants the church authority for very specific structural purposes. In Matthew 16, 18, and 28, he, in effect, hands the apostles a rolled-up scroll sealed in wax with his own royal stamp. When the apostles open the scroll, they find a charter for something called the church, a word they have heard before but which he is now putting to a new, formal use. This charter formalizes the church's existence on earth, establishes its authority, outlines its basic rights and privileges, and describes the essentials of belonging. What does this charter say? That's what we will consider in this chapter.

What we'll find is that Jesus never envisioned a church shorn of all its authority, responsibility, and structure—the very things that entangle us in the issues that Vanhoozer says divide Christians, such as the proper administration of the ordinances and membership. It's this structured church that Jesus intends to use as the medium for conveying his gospel message—for protecting it, displaying it, holding it up and making it attractive, and putting it to work. The church is an implication of the gospel, as Vanhoozer argues. Yes, but the authoritative structures are a significant part of that implication. Form and content are tied together. What protects the church from year to year and generation to generation is the power to bind and loose. It's the actions of identification, the borders, the boundaries, the oversight, the ordinances, the actions of internal judgment, the teaching, and the rites of passage, all exercised on earth.

These are the types of matters that Paul has in mind in 1 Corinthians 5. He doesn't merely want to hold the church together—unity for unity's sake. He means to mark off the church from the world, and in so doing protect and display the gospel.

---

[5]J. L. Reynolds, "Church Polity or The Kingdom of Christ, In its Internal and External Development," in *Polity*, ed. Mark Dever (Washington DC: Center for Church Reform, 2001), 296.

It's also what Jesus appears to have in mind in the Gospel of Matthew. For the purposes of our discussion of church membership and discipline, Jesus commissions the church in Matthew to exercise loving authority in five ways:

1) He authorizes his church *to proclaim and protect* the good news of his in-breaking kingdom and salvation.
2) He authorizes his church *to affirm* with joy those whose lives and professions of faith indicate that they belong to him by uniting them to his body and his family.
3) He authorizes his church *to unite* believers to itself and its care-giving embrace.
4) He authorizes his church *to provide oversight* to these children, guiding, directing, and equipping them through his Word toward a closer union with him and all God's children.
5) He authorizes his church *to bar* and *to exclude* any imposters who would harm the members of the family, degrade his name, and so hinder the church's witness to the world.

Christ gives the church this authority precisely because of the complexities of authority and the ambiguities of truth and love in this present age. Precisely because God's love has broken into this world but has not yet declared its final victory, Christ intends for this love to be *defined*—"This is love. This is not." Precisely because two film projectors are casting their light upon the same screen, Christ hands this pen to the church and tells it to draw a border, as best it can, around the images that his projector is casting, which is exactly what we see in the Scriptures.

Step 2: In the Gospel of Matthew, Jesus demonstrates concern over who is identified with his name and who is not, because identifying with him is identifying with the heavenly Father.

The Context of Matthew

REPRESENTING HEAVEN ON EARTH

Who on earth speaks for heaven? Who represents its will? Perhaps we've known too many Reverend Whitfields to believe that anyone can. Yet the popular assumption these days that "no one can claim to represent heaven" is itself, ironically, the very act of speaking with heaven's authority.

Like today's anti-religion skeptic, the super-religious Pharisees and Sadducees assumed they spoke for heaven, and so they maligned all challengers. They sought to expose Jesus as a fraud by asking him for a "sign from heaven" when really they believed he was in league with the Devil (Matt. 16:1; 12:24). The chief priests and elders likewise challenged Jesus' authority (21:23). Behind such challenges, again, was the assumption that they were God's specially covenanted representatives: "We have Abraham as our father" (Matt. 3:9).

In Matthew's Gospel, Jesus responds to such assumptions. He argues throughout the book that he, in fact, speaks for heaven on earth, as do his followers.[6]

- Jesus claims that the kingdom of heaven is at hand in his ministry (3:2; 4:17).

- Jesus professes to know who will both receive the kingdom of heaven and inherit the earth (5:3, 5).

- Jesus teaches his disciples to pray that God's will would be done on earth as it is in heaven (6:10).

- Jesus tells them not to store up their treasures on earth, where moth and rust destroy, but to store up their treasure in heaven, where moth and rust don't (6:19–20).

- Jesus tells his disciples that the secrets of the kingdom of heaven have been given to them (13:11).

Lesson after lesson is devoted to who will receive the kingdom of heaven and who won't. The poor in spirit will (5:3). Little children will (11:25; 19:14). Those who are humble like little children will (18:4, 14). Those who do the will of his Father in heaven will (12:50). Those who bear fruit in keeping with repentance will (3:7–10; 7:15–23; 12:33–38). Those whom God chooses will (19:25–26; 20:14–16; 22:14).

In other words, Matthew's Gospel is preoccupied with the question of who on earth represents heaven and what their lives are like. What's more, it answers that question by pointing to a dramatic once-in-history change of regime. Under the old covenant, ethnic Israel spoke for heaven. Now Christ and his followers will. God can raise up children for Abraham from the stones, says John the Baptist (3:7–9), and Jesus promises that "many will come from east and west and recline at table with Abraham, Isaac, and Jacob in the kingdom of heaven, while the sons of the kingdom will be thrown into the outer darkness" (8:11–12).

---

[6]See Jonathan Pennington's work on the contrast between heaven and earth in *Heaven and Earth in the Gospel of Matthew* (Grand Rapids, Baker, 2009); a brief version of his argument can be found in "The Kingdom of Heaven in the Gospel of Matthew," in *Southern Baptist Journal of Theology*, vol. 12 (Spring 2008): 44–51.

Jesus even calls out a new twelve to be the new heads of a new nation, and then promises that they would sit on twelve thrones and judge Israel (10:1–4; 19:20). Political, cultic, and ethnic boundary markers would no longer set off the family of God. Rather, "whoever does the will of my Father in heaven is my brother and sister and mother" (12:50).

Who then on earth speaks for heaven? First, Jesus does. He was explicitly affirmed as the "beloved Son" by a "voice from heaven" at the beginning of his earthly ministry (3:17; cf. 17:5), and then he claims to have "all authority in heaven and on earth" at its end (28:18). Yet not only does Jesus represent heaven, but his people do as well: "All things have been handed over to me by my Father, and no one knows the Son except the Father, and no one knows the Father except the Son and anyone to whom the Son chooses to reveal him" (11:27).[7]

WHO REPRESENTS JESUS?

Who then are Jesus' people? The regime change from ethnic Israel to Jesus Christ and his people as God's representatives on earth brings another problem: how do we determine who truly represents Christ or belongs to his people? With ethnic Israel, you might say, the institutional connections were built in. A person represented Israel—and, therefore, God—if he was circumcised, kept the Sabbath, kept the food laws, belonged to the nation-state of Israel, and so forth. But how does the world know who credibly speaks for Christ?

Matthew's Gospel devotes more attention to this question than one might first notice. On the one hand, Matthew answers the question by characterizing the lives of these followers. They produce fruit in keeping with repentance (3:8; 7:15–20). Their lives are marked by a radical other-worldliness (5:3–12). They don't run around like pagans obsessed with earthly provision but seek first the kingdom (6:31–33). They hear Christ's words and put them into practice (7:24–27). Matthew's Gospel also repeatedly addresses the matter of hypocrisy.[8] Perhaps it was a significant problem among the churches for which Matthew wrote his book?[9]

On the other hand, Matthew's Gospel sometimes frames this discussion about who represents Jesus by talking about who does and does not credibly bear Jesus' name.[10]

---

[7]See also "sons" language in Matt. 5:9, 16, 45, 48; 6:1, 8–9, 26, 32; 7:11; 10:29.
[8]See Matt. 6:1, 2–3, 5–6, 16–17; 13:24–30, 36–43, 47–50; 22:1–14; 23:3, 8–10; 24:45–51; 25:1–13.
[9]Frank Thielman, *Theology of the New Testament* (Grand Rapids: Zondervan, 2005), 105–9.
[10]Commentator John Nolland describes Matthew's phrase "into the name" as an expression of solidarity with Jesus, in *The Gospel of Matthew*, The New International Greek Testament Commentary (Grand Rapids: Eerdmans, 2005), 1268.

- Jesus tells his disciples that receiving *in Jesus' name* those who are humble like children is receiving Jesus himself (18:5).

- Jesus promises to be present whenever two or three are gathered *in his name* (18:20), like Yahweh's presence with his Old Testament people.

- Jesus commands his disciples to travel to the ends of the earth, baptizing more disciples into *his name* as well as into the names of the Father and Spirit (28:19).

At the same time:

- Some will claim to have done great works of prophecy, exorcism, and mighty works *in Christ's name*, but Jesus promises to tell them to depart since they are workers of lawlessness, never doing the will of the Father in heaven (7:21–23).

- Others will come *in Christ's name* by claiming to be the Christ, but they will lead many astray (24:5).

In short, some will credibly profess his name; and some will wrongly profess it. "See that no one leads you astray," said Jesus, anticipating such false professors (24:4).

How then can the world know which professions are credible and which are not? Does anyone on earth have the authority to distinguish one type of profession from another? These questions are difficult but unavoidable, and they bring us to Matthew's ecclesiological texts in chapters 16, 18, and 28.[11]

Step 3: In Matthew 16, 18, and 28, Jesus gave the apostles and the apostolic church the power of the keys. This authorized the church to guard the gospel, to affirm credible professions, to unite such professors to itself, to oversee their discipleship, and to exclude hypocrites.

---

[11]By way of summing up this section, Jonathan Pennington is worth quoting at length: "Another clear function of Matthew's heaven and earth contrast theme is to provide a clear identity for the followers of Jesus. Matthew wants his hearers to understand that those who follow Christ are the true people of God and to encourage them with this reality. Jesus defines this new or true people not by ethnic pedigree, including having Abraham as one's father (3:9–10; 8:11–12; 23:9), nor by positions of honor (23:2–11), but as those who do the will of the Father who is in heaven (7:21; 12:50), as those whose lives bear the fruit of following God's commands from the heart (3:7–10; 7:15–23; 12:33–38). This theme creates a heaven-oriented *identity* for the disciples in the midst of a hostile earthly world. The world is depicted as bipartite—heaven and earth—and Jesus' disciples are the true people of God aligned with heaven, as opposed to the rulers (Roman and Jewish) on earth. In this way, Matthew's heaven and earth theme is an important part of his ecclesiology (see esp. 16:17–19; 18:14–20). "The Kingdom of Heaven in the Gospel of Matthew," 49.

Three Ecclesiological Texts

AUTHORITY GIVEN TO A NEW TWELVE (MATTHEW 16)

"Who do people say that the Son of Man is?" Jesus asked his twelve disciples. Some said that he was in accord with the prince of demons (Matt. 9:33). Others said he was a glutton and a drunkard (Matt. 11:18). Still others said he was John the Baptist, Elijah, or one of the prophets (Matt. 16:14).

It wasn't clear who this man was, with his strange sermons, strange claims to authority, and strange associations. As we noted earlier, the world does not immediately recognize the perfect incarnation of God's love and authority when it comes. Some things about God's love are unexpected to natural eyes. True love needs to be explained to fallen sinners when it shows up—"Here it is. This is it."

After hearing the disciples list several wrong answers, Jesus asks again, "But who do you say that I am?" Perhaps representing all of them, Peter replies, "You are the Christ, the Son of the living God" (v. 16). Jesus affirms Peter's answer, "Blessed are you, Simon Bar-Jonah! For flesh and blood has not revealed this to you, but my Father who is in heaven" (v. 17; cf. 11:27). Apparently, Peter's ability to see this alternative reality had nothing to do with dimmed lights, the right music, or Jesus' authenticity, but with the fact that the heavenly Father had opened his eyes. Not only that, but Jesus was clearly interested in what Peter believed, the content of Peter's confession.

Interestingly, Jesus doesn't stop at this point. He doesn't say to Peter and the others, "Great, now you know. You'll be just fine." No, Jesus wants more people to understand the truth of who he is, and he wants them gathered together upon this truth that Peter has confessed. He therefore continues, "You are Peter, and on this rock I will build my church, and the gates of hell shall not prevail against it" (v. 18). It's worth noticing the parallel grammar between Peter's "You are the Christ" and Jesus' "You are Peter." Peter had just defined Jesus' identity and role in redemptive history—he is the Messiah, the Son of the living God. Jesus defines Peter's identity and role in redemptive history—he is the rock or foundation on which the church will be built. Hence, there's a play on words between *petros* (Peter) and *petra* (rock). This church will be the true church, not some false church that hell can prevail against.

Following the Reformation, many Protestant commentators and theologians objected to the idea that Peter should be the rock, for fear of legitimating the Roman Catholic institution of the papacy.[12] Yet today many (most?) evangelical

---

[12]Rock as "Peter" and rock as "Peter's confession" are, perhaps, the two most common interpretations offered. Other interpretations have also been put forward, such as Jesus himself or Jesus' teaching (cf. Matt. 7:24), e.g., Robert H. Gundry, *Matthew*, 2nd ed. (Grand Rapids: Eerdmans, 1982, 1994), 333–34.

commentators acknowledge that the text reads fairly plainly as if Peter is in fact the rock.[13] The larger point, I think, is that Jesus builds the church on both Peter and his confession. As commentator Craig Keener puts it, "Jesus does not simply assign this role arbitrarily to Peter, however; Peter is the 'rock' *because* he is the one who confessed Jesus as the Christ in this context."[14] Theologian Edmund Clowney says it this way: "The confession cannot be separated from Peter, neither can Peter be separated from his confession."[15]

Sure enough: if we read into the book of Acts, we discover that Christ begins building his church on the rightly confessing Peter, not just on Peter and Peter's confession. The ambassador doesn't travel without the king's edict, and the edict doesn't travel without the king's ambassador. Throughout the New Testament, furthermore, Christ builds his new people upon all the apostles as they traveled about proclaiming the truth of Peter's confession (Eph. 2:20; Rev. 21:14). Even if Christ addresses Peter uniquely in Matthew 16:17–19, they all seem to be involved by verse 20.[16] These are facts of history. God could have used other men. They were not the *ultimate* or *essential* foundation of the church, but they were its *historical* or *instrumental* foundation—the ambassadors that Christ used to first proclaim his gospel. Peter is singled out here, perhaps as first among equals, because he is the first to rightly confess the king's edict: "Behold, Jesus is the Messiah."

How does Jesus then build upon this confessing Peter, or, rather, what does Peter *do* in his capacity as the foundation?[17] We find that Jesus answers that question in the next verse: "I will give you the keys of the kingdom of heaven, and whatever you bind on earth shall be bound in heaven, and whatever you loose on earth shall be loosed in heaven" (v. 19). Like the previous verses, this verse abounds with questions on which commentators differ.[18] But everyone seems to agree that he is giving Peter authority by giving him the keys of the

---

[13]For instance, D. A. Carson writes, "If it were not for Protestant reactions against extremes of Roman Catholic interpretation, it is doubtful whether many would have taken 'rock' to be anything or anyone other than Peter." "Matthew," in *The Expositor's Bible Commentary*, vol. 8 (Grand Rapids: Zondervan, 1984), 368. See also Craig Blomberg, *Matthew*, New American Commentary (Nashville: Broadman, 1992), 251–53; Leon Morris, *The Gospel According to Matthew* (Grand Rapids: Eerdmans, 1992), 422–24; Donald A. Hagner, *Matthew 14–28*, Word Biblical Commentary, vol. 33b (Dallas: Word, 1995), 470; Craig S. Keener, *A Commentary on the Gospel of Matthew* (Grand Rapids: Eerdmans, 1999), 427; R. T. France, *The Gospel of Matthew*, The New International Commentary on the New Testament (Grand Rapids: Eerdmans, 2007), 620–23; David L. Turner, *Matthew*, Baker Exegetical Commentary on the New Testament (Grand Rapids: Baker, 2008), 404–5, 406–7.

[14]Keener, *Commentary on the Gospel of Matthew*, 427; original emphasis. Similar suggestions are made in Morris, *Gospel According to Matthew*, 423; and Nolland, *The Gospel of Matthew*, 669.

[15]In *The Church*, Contours of Theology, ed. Gerald Bray (Downers Grove, IL: InterVarsity, 1995), 40; see also Kevin Giles in *What on Earth Is the Church? An Exploration in New Testament Theology* (1995; repr. Eugene, OR: Wipf & Stock, 2005), 54.

[16]For helpful discussions on Peter as "typical" versus Peter as "unique," see Carson, "Matthew," 364, or Ulrich Luz, *Matthew 8–20*, trans. James E. Crouch, Hermeneia (Minneapolis, MN: Fortress, 2001), 366–68.

[17]Commentator Ulrich Luz concisely connects verses 18 and 19, saying, "What v. 18a expressed 'architectonically,' v. 19 says functionally. Now Peter's function as a rock is stated"; i.e., this is what Peter *does* as the foundation. In *Matthew 8–20*, 364.

[18]What are the keys? Are the keys given exclusively to Peter or to all the apostles? What's the relationship between the authority of the keys and the authority to bind and loose? What's the object—the "whatever"—of

kingdom. Further, I think we can say, somewhat uncontroversially, that the connection between verses 18 and 19 means that "the church is the agency of kingdom authority on earth."[19] In other words, if Peter is the foundation of the church, and if Jesus gives him the keys of the kingdom in order to act in his capacity as the foundation, then it would seem that Christ's kingdom will be extended *through* the church. Perhaps more controversially, I would argue that the kingdom will be extended through the church *alone*, since no other organization or individual on earth has been given the keys of the kingdom— not philanthropic organizations, social agencies, governments, political parties, or even well-meaning individuals.

It's not immediately clear in Matthew 16 *what* Peter and, by extension, the apostles are given authority to bind and loose on earth, the *object* of binding and loosing. What should be clear, I hope, is that this passage is where we just might find an answer to the question posed above—does anyone on earth have the authority to distinguish one type of profession of Jesus' name from another? Christ clearly has that authority. Christ affirms that Peter's profession credibly comes from the Father. But then, astoundingly, he gives Peter (and the apostles) an authority to declare that certain things on earth represent the realities of heaven. This act of authorizing the apostles follows immediately on the heels of Jesus' telling the disciples to beware of the leaven—or teaching—of the Pharisees and Sadducees (16:5–12). The Pharisees and Sadducees do not have the authority to represent heaven, even if they think they do. A regime change is transpiring.[20]

EXTENDING THIS AUTHORITY TO THE WHOLE CHURCH (MATTHEW 18)

In Matthew 18 the same phrase concerning binding and loosing is again used, only this time the keys of the kingdom are not explicitly mentioned, and the "you" is plural: "Truly, I say to you, whatever you bind on earth shall be bound in heaven, and whatever you loose on earth shall be loosed in heaven" (v. 18). Whether or not Jesus is giving the keys only to Peter in chapter 16, which I don't think he is,[21] most agree that the authority of the keys is extended to all the disciples and, ultimately, to the local church in chapter 18. In other

---

the binding and loosing? Should the perfect passive participles be translated? What's the relationship between Peter's actions on earth and decisions made in heaven?

[19]Turner, *Matthew*, 405.

[20]Craig Blomberg, "Matthew," in *Commentary on the New Testament Use of the Old Testament,* ed. G. K. Beale and D. A. Carson (Grand Rapids: Baker, 2007), 35; W. D. Davies and Dale C. Allison Jr., *Matthew*, vol. 2, The International Critical Commentary, ed. J. A. Emerton, et al. (Edinburgh: T&T Clark, 1991), 603.

[21](1) Jesus asked all the disciples the question; (2) Peter probably answered on behalf of all of them; (3) Jesus tells all of them to keep quiet about Peter's answer. Also, as Clowney points out, "Peter is not the rock in contrast to the eleven, but in contrast to those who claim to carry the key of knowledge (Lk. 11:52), to sit in Moses' seat (Mt. 23:1-2), and to be Abraham's seed (Jn. 8:33)." Edmund Clowney, "The Church as a Heavenly and Eschatological Entity," in *The Church in the Bible and the World,* ed. D. A. Carson (1987; repr. Eugene, OR: Wipf & Stock, 2002), 40.

words, this astounding authority given to Peter (and the apostles) in chapter 16 appears to be handed to the local church in chapter 18 in the context of church discipline. So whether the authority belonged to Peter or all twelve apostles, that authority is handed to every church, which is what I mean when I refer to the apostolic church.[22]

Here's the context: Jesus speaks about confronting a Christian brother when he "sins against you" in order to gain him back (18:15). If the offender doesn't listen, the offended should take one or two others along (v. 16). If he still doesn't listen, the offended should "tell it to the church," and if he still doesn't listen to the church, he should be treated as an outsider (v. 17).

At this point Jesus explains the church's license to act in this disciplinary capacity by repeating in Matthew 18:18 the commission of chapter 16. This authority or power of the keys from chapter 16 is put to actual use by a local church for the purposes of excommunication.[23]

In the next verse, Jesus seems to respond to anyone who might question whether the local church could really be said to have such authority. Again, astoundingly, he ties the church's decisions to heaven: "Again I say to you, if two of you agree on earth about anything they ask, it will be done for them by my Father in heaven" (v. 19).

The authority that the church exercises is God's authority. The church represents him as an ambassador (cf. 2 Cor. 5:20; Eph. 6:20). People listening to an ambassador speak know that the king stands behind him. So it was with ancient Israel: the whole world was supposed to know that Israel belonged to Yahweh because they bore his name and he dwelt in their midst. So it is with the local church: it bears his name and he dwells in their midst. So Jesus concludes the point by promising, "For where two or three are gathered in my name, there am I among them" (v. 20). Those who do not profess his name credibly should be cast out.

These two passages present the only places in the Gospels where Jesus uses the term *ecclesia* (church). These passages elicit disagreements, but no one, from what I can tell, contests the fact that Jesus is handing his authority to Peter, the apostles, and ultimately the church. A key is clearly a symbol of authority in the Scriptures (Isa. 22:15, 22; Luke 11:52; Rev. 3:7; cf. Rev. 1:18; 9:1; 20:1). Whatever it finally means for the apostolic church to bind and loose on earth, this community of two or three gathered in his name seems to have an authority that even the individual Christian does not have (cf. Matt. 18:15). When one

---

[22]More specifically, the church is "apostolic" because (1) it is built on the foundation of the apostles (Eph. 2:20; Rev. 21:14); and (2) it guards and proclaims the apostles' teaching (2 Tim. 1:13–14). The Roman Catholic Church adds a third element, namely, apostolic succession through the supposedly papal office of Peter.

[23]Carson helpfully describes 18:18 as a "special application" of the authority of the keys in 16:19; in "Matthew," 374.

Christian sins against another, for example, the offended one does not have an authority that the gathered church has to formally remove the offender.

ACTING ON THIS AUTHORITY TO THE ENDS OF THE EARTH (MATTHEW 28)

Jesus' Great Commission in Matthew 28 says nothing explicit about the disciples' authority of the keys, but as Jesus does in Matthew 16 and 18, he invokes his own authority and then authorizes them, once more, to make declarations on behalf of heaven:

> All authority in heaven and on earth has been given to me. Go therefore and make disciples of all nations, baptizing them in the name of the Father and of the Son and of the Holy Spirit, teaching them to observe all that I have commanded you. And behold, I am with you always, to the end of the age. (Matt. 28:18–20)

Jesus claims to have the authority of heaven, and on that basis he authorizes his disciples to make more disciples, not just by sharing the gospel but by baptizing and teaching. Notice that Jesus doesn't tell his disciples to simply hold up a megaphone or turn on the radio transmitter and holler out the gospel, letting people receive the message as God wills so that they can begin to call themselves Christians but carry on with their lives, detached from the message's source or from one another. No, there's more to do. Making a disciple involves baptizing people and then teaching them everything Christ commanded.

Why the extra steps? Based on the larger concerns of Matthew, we might suppose that Jesus cares about who publicly bears his name (as well as the Father's and the Spirit's). We must remember that the issue of hypocrisy shows up throughout the book. Jesus commissions his followers not just to preach but to undertake the "institutional" work of affirming credible professions of faith through baptism, to publicly vouch, "This one wears Christ's name and represents heaven on earth." He wants those who are so affirmed to learn everything he has commanded.

Ultimately, I believe we'll find that the Great Commission is not just about evangelizing; it's about church planting and church building. Notice that Jesus promises to "be with" his disciples to the end of the age, just as he promised in the ecclesial context of Matthew 18 to be present whenever two or three are gathered in his name.

Does someone who has not passed through the waters of baptism have the right to speak for Jesus and the heavenly Father? Does Jesus simply leave it up to the conscience of every man or woman to declare before the world, "I speak for Jesus and the Father in heaven, so heed me"? Jesus promised that imposters will do this (7:21–23; 24:5), but is it okay to do in principle? I suppose the answer depends on how we understand the church's authority here in Matthew 28 and in chapters 16 and 18. My tentative answer is no, because I believe that Jesus has given Peter and the local church the power of the keys precisely so that God's people on earth have an institutional mechanism, as it were, to mark off who credibly speaks for him, to hold them together, to teach them, and to oversee their lives together. I believe that Christians must therefore be united to a church. That's the argument that still needs to be made.

What Is This Authority?

What exactly is this authority of the keys, what does it mean to bind and loose, and what do these passages in chapters 16 and 18 have to do with the Great Commission in chapter 28? When these three chapters are held up against the rest of Matthew's Gospel, it's hard to escape the sense that something *institutional* is going on.[24] Elsewhere, Jesus talks about the connection between heaven and earth in terms of praying, seeking, and receiving, all of which at least speak to relational matters, but in these chapters he uses language that authorizes and commissions. He talks about keys, binding and loosing, and the ordinance of baptism. It sounds as if he's preparing for his departure by leaving certain structures in place. After all, the entire conversation begins with Jesus' promise to "build his church" (16:18). The authority in question here has to do with his work, through Peter and others, of building some type of assembly.

I don't claim to offer the final or even best analysis of these passages in what follows, but I will do the best I can by offering a six-step argument.

1) The difficulty of Matthew 16:18–19 springs, at least in part, from the mixed metaphors. Several matters, such as the verb tenses in verse 19, make interpreting Matthew 16:18–19 difficult. But what's most difficult, for me at least, is that Jesus mixes up half a dozen metaphors. He begins in verse 18 with a building and foundation metaphor (cf. Matt. 7:24). Yet he talks about building not a structure but an assembly of people. He jumps to a gate metaphor, but this is at least a little confusing because he speaks of the gate "prevailing," which is a word that sounds offensive, when gates are designed to be defensive. Then, in verse 19, he uses what sounds like another gate or door metaphor, but the emphasis is on the keys, which are used to open or

---

[24]Contra Carson, who says that the use of *ecclesia* in chaps. 16 and 18 have "no emphasis on institution, organization, form of worship, or separate synagogue" ("Matthew," 369). Carson's point in context is that Jesus' use of the word *build* (16:18) doesn't necessarily point to something institutional, since the idea of "building" a people springs from the Old Testament (he points to Ruth 4:11; 2 Sam. 7:13–14; 1 Chron. 17:12–13; Ps. 28:5; 118:22; Jer. 1:10; 24:6; 31:4; 33:7; Amos 9:11). Perhaps he means something different from what I mean by "institution," but I would use the word "institution" to describe elements of Old Testament Israel's life together, elements represented in some of these very passages (e.g., structures of authority; membership boundaries; laws that are applicable only to members). If that's the case, then it seems that what I've been calling a regime change almost mandates replacing one set of institutional structures for another. In short, it's not enough to say that involving people means there's no "institution," as I will be assuming in my argument throughout this section.

close gates. He is not talking about keys to a gate but keys to a kingdom, by which he means a saving rule or reign. Can you have keys to a rule? Finally, he doesn't say the keys should be used to open or close something, but to bind and loose something. Typically, things are bound not with keys but with rope, glue, gravity, or laws.

To over-literalize, it's as if Jesus is saying, "I will build my assembly of people upon you and your confession, Peter. You're the poured cement that will be protected from any gates that attack you. I will then give you, the poured cement of the assembly, keys for locking and unlocking my saving reign. Anything you tie up with rope on earth will be tied up in heaven. Anything tied up on earth that you cut loose will be cut loose in heaven." One metaphor follows another, and the connection between each is not immediately obvious. Still, it is essential to recognize each metaphor in the process of interpretation.

2) We should let each metaphor both have its say and condition the other metaphors. I've noticed in some discussions of this passage the tendency to smother one metaphor with another. For instance, an author might sum up the meaning of 16:19 by emphasizing the fact that keys are for opening and closing to argue that Peter and the apostles will open and close the kingdom for people by preaching the gospel. This makes it sound as if, to use an earlier illustration, the keys of the kingdom are given to Peter and the church to do nothing more than turn on the megaphone or radio transmitter and declare the gospel. But what about the adhesive element in the words *binding* and *loosing*? And what about the idea of *assembly* bound up in the word *church*, which Jesus says he is building? Does Jesus give Peter the keys just to license a bunch of free agents? This particular tendency—to overgeneralize—seems common to Protestant, and especially evangelical, commentators. Perhaps we evangelicals are reluctant to be bound or loosed by anything on earth.

Or an author might decide that Jesus means for the keys to bind and loose, which means we can then altogether forget the fact that keys are used for opening and closing doors. Keys are simply the *authority* to do whatever it means to bind and loose. Critical scholars seem to favor this tactic, since it means introducing fascinating historical data about demon possession or the rabbinical interpretation of Jewish law (*halakha*).

Or since binding and loosing are clearly used in the context of church discipline in chapter 18, then the keys of the kingdom must be all about church discipline. Never mind the fact that Jesus kicks off this conversation in 16:18 by talking about building his church. Smothering chapter 16 with chapter 18 is the tendency of at least some of the older confessions and explanations.[25]

---

[25]E.g., see chap. 30, "Of Church Censures," Westminster Confession; or Question 83 in the Heidelberg Catechism.

Now, surely it's true that there are times when speakers or writers follow a word or phrase with another simply to illustrate or explain the first, as in "he is the head of the body, the church" (Col. 1:18). The word *church* further explains or specifies what the author, Paul, means by *the body*. Likewise, some have argued that the authority of the keys is nothing other than the authority to bind and loose.[26] I think I agree, but there's still a reason why Paul, in the first example, uses the word *body* and the word *church*, else he wouldn't waste his ink. They are two different words that rely on two different associations of meanings, each of which lends itself slightly differently to our understanding of whatever Paul is getting at. The same is true with *keys* and *binding* and *loosing*, even if the latter is explicating the former.

As we move through Matthew 16:18–19 from the building metaphor to the church metaphor to the keys metaphor to the kingdom metaphor to the binding and loosing metaphor, we need to let each metaphor properly stand up and have its say. At the same time, of course, context is king, which means that we need to let each metaphor condition or help interpret the adjacent metaphors. We know that Paul, in Colossians 1:18, is not talking about Christ's physical body, because the adjacent metaphor tells us so; he's talking about the church. Yet there's something about the church that resembles or bears an affinity to a physical body, which is why he uses the word *body*. One of our goals in thinking about mixed metaphors of building, church or assembly, keys, and binding and loosing, I believe, is to consider how we might put together the ideas of "opening and closing" with "sticking and unsticking" in the context of building a people.[27] Let's consider several of these metaphors in Matthew 16.

Building and rock. Christ promises to build a people upon the rock or foundation of the rightly confessing Peter. Some commentators wonder whether there are references here to the church as a new temple or to Peter as a kind of rock like Abraham (Isa. 51:1–2).[28] Whatever you might decide in answer to these types of background questions, Christ's words "upon this rock I will build" suggest the idea of building something that didn't already exist, something that holds together as a unit, as when one builds a building.

Church. Christ is building a church, an end-time assembly of people. This makes sense in light of the regime change we've been discussing. Ethnic Israel was a unified people, built by God.[29] Now, Christ is establishing a new community and rejecting corporate Israel.[30] So he is building something, as we

---

[26]E.g., Davies and Allison write, "In our estimation, it is most natural to think of v. 19a as being explicated by what follows: to have the keys is to have the power to bind and loose"; in *Matthew,* 254.
[27]The very challenge of doing this is what seems to send those within the critical tradition fleeing for answers in either source or redaction criticism; see, e.g., Davies and Allison, *Matthew,* 640–41.
[28]E.g., Luz, *Matthew 8–20,* 362–63; Nolland, *The Gospel of Matthew,* 670-72.
[29]See note 24 above.
[30]Davies and Allison, *Matthew,* 603.

said, but it's an assembly of *people*. These people, like a physical building, are meant to be held together upon one foundation. In other words, this is not the department of motor vehicles handing out driver's licenses to people who have no real attachment to one another except that they are all drivers. Rather, a corporate entity is being built.

Keys. Commentators debate the relevance to Matthew 16 of the passages cited above about keys (Isa. 22:15, 22; Luke 11:52; Rev. 3:7; cf. Matt. 23:13). The fact that Jesus does not proceed to talk about opening and shutting, as he does, say, in Revelation 3, but about binding and loosing, makes interpretation a little more difficult. Still, even with these difficulties, think for a moment about what a key is. It's something that opens or shuts a door, allowing or preventing a person from entering into a new space or domain. Whether we are talking literally about keys to a house or figuratively about keys of knowledge or keys to someone's heart, the basic idea is that the person with keys can *move into* some new domain, such as the domain of knowledge or a domain of intimacy. The basic idea of the metaphor is both entry and exclusion.

Kingdom. The keys aren't the keys of the church, per se, but the keys of the kingdom, and Christ's kingdom in the New Testament, as so many have said, is not a geographic domain but a rule or reign. We do occasionally find Christ speaking about his kingdom in spatial terms, as when he says to the teachers of the Law and Pharisees, "You shut the kingdom of heaven in men's faces. You yourselves do not enter, nor will you let those enter who are trying to" (Matt. 23:13 NIV; cf. 7:21; 18:3; 19:23). But to let this metaphor stand up and speak, we must note that we are talking about Christ's rule. We are talking about entering into a domain where certain principles, beliefs, laws, a way of living, salvation, and other blessings apply.

Binding and loosing. The fact that we are talking about entering not a realm but a rule becomes relevant when we get to the metaphor of binding and loosing. Multiple explanations for these words are given.[31] What is perhaps the most common discussion revolves around whether Jesus is using the terms binding and loosing in a technical rabbinic fashion to refer to the interpretation of Jewish law or whether something is prohibited or allowed,[32] as suggested by the Good News Bible's translation of Matt. 16:19b: "What you prohibit on earth will be prohibited in heaven, and what you permit on earth will be permitted in heaven." The thought here is that Jesus has just told the disciples to beware of the teaching of the Pharisees, and now he is declaring Peter a kind of new chief

---

[31]Davies and Allison present thirteen possibilities, ibid., 630–32.

[32]Consider, e.g., that the word variously translated "relaxes," "breaks," or "annuls" in Matthew 5:19 ("whoever relaxes one of the least of these commandments") is the same word for "loosed" (*lyō*), which is clearly referring to a commandment. Discussions of this can be found in most commentaries or in standard Greek theological dictionaries such as Gerhard Kittel's *Theological Dictionary of the New Testament* or Colin Brown's *Dictionary of New Testament Theology* under the entries for *deō* and *lyō*. See also BDAG.

rabbi because he confessed rightly.[33] Other writers want to emphasize not just interpreting law, in a teacher-like fashion, but also pronouncing or withholding forgiveness based upon law, in a judge-like fashion.[34] Still other writers argue that it's not laws that are bound or loosed but people,[35] just as Paul will speak of being bound in or loosed from a marriage (e.g., 1 Cor. 7:27, 39).[36]

So how do we navigate through these and other possibilities? Let me offer three guidelines for how we should go about interpreting the binding and loosing metaphor: (1) We shouldn't simply import an external technical definition into this verse by assuming, for instance, that whatever the rabbis meant by the terms *must* be what Jesus means right here.[37] (2) We shouldn't smother it with an adjacent metaphor, such as the keys, but let it speak for itself. Binding something, if it means anything, means making something stick, or tied up, or caught in a gravitational pull, or effectually imposed upon, whether we're talking about constellations of stars (Job 38:31), donkeys (Matt. 21:2), laws (Matt. 5:19), or people (Matt. 12:29). It's a metaphor that has to do with ropes, or glue, or principles that constrain. Loosing, of course, is just the opposite. So whether you want to mix your metaphors, or not, you must place these words into a sentence, and you need to squirt into the sentence's meaning at least a little glue or glue remover. (3) We should also let the adjacent metaphors moderate or condition how we interpret the binding and loosing metaphor. Here, that means we should recall that the discussion is about building *a people* and that Peter has been given keys to extend a rule, which includes extending law.

3) *The metaphors of binding and loosing refer to both people and principles.* To synthesize these various points, I argue that Peter's (and the church's) authority to bind and loose grants him the responsibility to bind both people and principles. I'd say that the "whatever" in verse 19 in fact means *whatever*—

---

[33] E.g., Davies and Allison, *Matthew*, 638–39; France, *The Gospel of Matthew*, 625–26.

[34] E.g., Luz, *Matthew 8–20*, 365; Nolland, *The Gospel of Matthew*, 677–82.

[35] E.g., Carson, "Matthew," 372; Blomberg, *Matthew*, 254; Keener, *Commentary on the Gospel of Matthew*, 430; Turner, *Matthew*, 408. This also seems to have been the position of at least some Baptists historically. In 1697 Baptist Benjamin Keach wrote, "The Power of the Keys, or to receive in and shut out of the Congregation, is committed unto the Church" ("The Glory of a True Church and Its Discipline Display'd," in Dever, *Polity*, 71). Baptist minister Benjamin Griffith in 1743 similarly wrote, "The keys are the power of Christ, which he hath given to every particular congregation, to open and shut itself by. . . . By virtue of the charter and the power aforesaid…they are enabled to receive members in, and to exclude unworthy members as occasion may require." In "A Short Treatise Concerning a True and Orderly Gospel Church," republished in Dever, *Polity*, 99.

[36] The root words for binding and loosing (*deō* and *lyō*) are often used in the New Testament to refer to people. Matthew uses the word for *binding* to refer to people in 12:29, 14:3, 22:13, and 27:2. He doesn't use the word for *loosing* in this context, but in 21:2 he uses binding and loosing together to refer to tying or untying a donkey. The root word for *loose* is often used in the New Testament to refer to laws or commandments (e.g., Matt. 5:19), but the root word for *bind*, which is used forty times, is in fact *only* used to refer to animals or people (apart from our verses in question), with one exception. The one exception is in the context of marriage and has fairly direct application to a person: "a married woman is bound by law to her husband while he lives" (Rom. 7:2).

[37] Carson warns against this word-study fallacy: "In this fallacy, an interpreter falsely assumes that a words always or nearly always has a certain technical meaning—a meaning usually derived either from a subset of the evidence or from the interpreter's personal systematic theology." *Exegetical Fallacies*, 2nd ed. (Grand Rapids: Baker Academic, 1996), 45.

both people and principles. Just as "a married woman is bound by law to her husband" (Rom. 7:2), so Peter's authority of binding and loosing involves both people and law, or principles. Remember, Jesus established Peter as the church's foundation *because* of his right confession. It all began with the person and his confession. Likewise, Peter must now ensure that the right people belong to the church according to a right confession.[38] At times this will mean evaluating people; at times it will mean evaluating how a doctrine has been articulated or extends into implications. The point is that the church extends God's kingdom rule with the right people believing and obeying the right doctrines, and now Peter (and the apostolic church) has the authority to make that call. Rule, or *governance*, always involves both people and laws.

To those who argue that the object of binding and loosing is *things*, such as Jesus' commandments, I want to ask, *don't Jesus' commandments in turn bind and loose people?* (e.g., Matt. 18:15–18). To those who argue that the object of binding and loosing is *people,* I want to ask, what exactly would you say does the binding or loosing? It's other people, yes, but isn't it other people as they *apply* things such as Jesus' commandments? In short, it's hard to imagine how one might talk about binding and loosing people without principles or about binding and loosing principles with no regard for people. For that reason, I think a broad interpretation of "whatever" in "whatever you bind and loose" makes the most sense.

Further, I think we can say that the power to bind and loose involves binding and loosing people because my interpretation is at least partly controlled by the metaphor of a key. Now, honestly, I'm not entirely sure how I would characterize the relationship between the keys and binding and loosing. Is the power of the keys simply the power of binding and loosing?[39] Are binding and loosing a subset of the power of the keys?[40] My opinion is that they refer to the same basic authority and that the keys are exercised *by* binding and loosing. (Henceforth, I will refer to both simply as the power of the keys.) But both sets of metaphors are needed to explain what this authority is. However we relate them, Peter is given the keys for the sake of building a church, for the sake of building an assembly of people. Whatever is being bound or loosed, then, presumably pertains to people and the growth of the church.

4) The metaphor of keys isn't just about making a way available but for uniting people to the church on earth. If the key metaphor conditions the bind-

---

[38] Admittedly, there are different ways of getting to this same conclusion. For instance, Ulrich Luz insists that binding and loosing has to do with the interpretation of law, but then draws (I assume) from the metaphor of the keys to say something similar to what I just said: "One may conclude from the text that it is Peter's task to open the kingdom of heaven for *people*, and to do it by means of his binding interpretation of the *law*" (*Matthew 8–20*, 365, emphasis mine).

[39] Davies and Allison, *Matthew*, 635; Luz, *Matthew 8–20*, 364.

[40] Nolland, *The Gospel of Matthew*, 681.

ing and loosing metaphor, the opposite is true as well: the latter conditions the former. Keys, I have said, are for admitting (or excluding) people into a new domain, yet I propose that Jesus means for the party with the keys not just to admit people, as it were, through a door into an undefined space; he means to admit them into something to which they will stick—into a society to which they will *belong*. In other words, he doesn't just mean to admit them; he means to unite them to the body of Christ in heaven through uniting them to the body of Christ on earth, however we might end up defining the church on earth. The adhesive element of the binding and loosing metaphor recommends this interpretation, and the preceding verse recommends it: Jesus is building not a group of unassociated individuals but a church, a gathering. The first-century, ancient Near Eastern cultural backdrop also recommends it; people did not think in the same kinds of individualistic categories that we do today. The storyline of Matthew recommends it, given that Jesus is replacing one corporate people with another. The subtheme we have observed of guarding against hypocrisy by watching out for deceivers and by properly professing Jesus' name recommends it, too. Once again, Jesus doesn't mean for Peter to simply hand out licenses to free agents. He means to build a single people together upon a single foundation with a single profession so that the world might know who rightly speaks for him.

Jesus is granting Peter an institutional charter. By using the word *institutional* I don't mean something static or inert. I simply mean that Jesus is authorizing Peter to establish a society of people on earth that has definite boundaries, a common source of identity, a shared set of beliefs and rules, and so forth. Like all societies, this society is to be built with *people* who all have certain *things* or *principles* in common, like a bird watchers' society or a libertarians' league or the Boy Scouts. But it's not birds or politics that unite the people of this society; it's their submission to Christ's rule. The church on earth, then, is the society of people who share Peter's profession that Jesus is the messiah king, the Davidic son. It's the society where Christ's kingdom is represented, presented, put into effect, displayed, and extended.

But aren't Christians united by the blood of Christ's covenant? Yes, and we'll get to that in the next chapter. My point here is one that I think evangelicals often miss; namely, that we're also united through our shared allegiance to his kingly, messianic authority. If, furthermore, the one with messianic authority delegates some of his authority to a proxy on earth—in this case, Peter and the apostolic church—then our unity through Christ's rule will necessarily translate into being united to this proxy, to the apostolic church on earth.[41] We are united

---

[41] I will distinguish between a Roman Catholic and a Protestant conception of the church as an earthly proxy later.

federally by Christ's work on the cross, yes, but we're also united politically, as it were, by our shared obedience to this messianic ruler and to his proxy with the power of the keys.

By the same token, anyone who claims "Jesus is the Christ" and attempts to bear his name publicly must belong to this society on earth, the church. There is one rock on which the true church is built and against which the gates of hell will not prevail, and there is one set of keys, which now belongs to the church. No one else has them. A person who claims "Jesus is the Christ" but refuses to submit to the king's key-bearing agent on earth hasn't really submitted to the king. His profession is false. If we are united through our submission to Christ's rule, and if he gave the keys of rulership to Peter and the apostolic church, then everyone who professes his name must submit to the apostolic church.

5) The power of the keys (binding and loosing) speaks to both entering into the new community and maintaining its life. Are the keys of the kingdom used in ushering people into the new community of the church, or for maintaining the life of the community? Some are adamant that it's one or the other.[42] In light of the foregoing conversation, I think it makes the most sense to say that the keys of the kingdom give Peter and ultimately the church authority over both the entryway into the new community and the maintaining of its life together. I don't mean to say that these verses give us license to jump in with polity specifics of *how* this is actually done, but simply that the authority for both uniting and maintaining the life of the church on earth starts here.

When Jesus characterizes Peter as the foundation on which the church would be built, it's hard to think Jesus is not talking about the church's entryway. Yet it's hard to see how the idea of binding and loosing does not involve both the entryway *and* the maintaining of the church's life, particularly if binding and loosing does involve law, doctrine, or believing the right things. To put it crassly, one must believe the right things to get in, and one must believe the right things to stay in. The same is true of Jesus' reference to binding and loosing in Matthew 18 in the context of church discipline—church discipline begins as an act of maintaining the church's life, but it culminates at the church's exit door.

Theologically, this makes sense insofar as the church is built and the kingdom is extended according to the same principles by which the church and kingdom are maintained: repentance and faith. Without repentance or faith, there is no church because there is no kingdom rule. Ultimately, I basically agree with Leon Morris on Matthew 16:18–19: "Good reasons may be brought forward

---

[42]Compare, e.g., Luz, *Matthew 8–20*, 364, and France, *The Gospel of Matthew*, 625, with Nolland, *The Gospel of Matthew*, 676, 681.

for holding that Jesus meant that the new community would exercise divinely given authority both in regulating its internal affairs and in deciding who would be admitted to and who excluded from its membership."[43]

6) The Great Commission represents a culmination of the commissioning work begun in Matthew 16 and 18. I have already noted a couple of the subtle textual ties between chapters 16, 18, and 28: Jesus implicitly or explicitly invokes his authority in all three, as well as his relationship with the heavenly Father. He authorizes the disciples to act on his behalf in all three. And he promises to be with disciples identified together by his name in chapters 18 and 28. As to whether we can make a connection between chapter 28 and the prior two chapters exegetically or only theologically, it does appear that the authority originally granted in chapter 16 and applied in one particular capacity in chapter 18 comes to a culmination and a new kind of expression in 28:16–20.

Some of the commentators who argue that binding and loosing pertain only to interpreting law make this link.[44] The way that Jesus' command to teach everything he commanded traces back to the teaching authority granted in chapter 16. Yet if my reading of the keys and binding and loosing is correct, we might want to broaden that link. Not only might the command in chapter 28 to teach trace back to chapter 16, so may the command to baptize new disciples. To baptize someone, after all, is to publicly identify him or her with the death and resurrection of Christ Jesus. It's to say they bear the name of Christ. It's to identify them with Christ's people, the church. It's to mark them off as entering the kingdom and the church. In a sense, the Great Commission, at least theologically if not exegetically, seems to give expression to the power of the keys in action. That is, the church exercises its authoritative keys by baptizing people into the church and teaching them everything that Christ commanded. Though the connections in Matthew would be more tenuous, I believe the case can be made from the passages on the Lord's Supper in the Gospels and 1 Corinthians that the keys are exercised through the Lord's Supper as well, particularly as it pertains to the maintenance of the church's life together.[45]

---

[43] Morris, *The Gospel According to Matthew*, 427. Craig Keener says something similar: "In both functions—evaluating entrants and those already within the church—God's people must evaluate on the authority of the heavenly court. . . . Peter must thus accept in the church only those who share Peter's confession of Jesus' true identity" (*Commentary on the Gospel of Matthew*, 430); cf. John 20:22–23. See also Turner, *Matthew*, 408.

[44] Luz, *Matthew 8–20*, 368; Nolland, *The Gospel of Matthew*, 672; Davies and Allison, *Matthew*, 639.

[45] Michael Horton tidily sums up the power of the keys this way: "Through preaching, baptism, and admission (or refusal of admission) to the Communion, the keys of the kingdom are exercised." *People and Place* (Louisville: Westminster, 2008), 243. Further, tying the ordinance to the exercise of the keys has a respectable place in the history of interpretation. E.g., the Augsburg Confession reads, "The power of keys or of bishops is used and exercised only by teaching and preaching the Word of God and by administering the sacraments. . . . In this way are imparted not bodily but eternal things and gifts, namely, eternal righteousness, the Holy Spirit and eternal life. These gifts cannot be obtained except through the office of preaching and of administering the holy sacraments." Article 28, "Power of the Bishops," *Creeds of the Churches,* 3rd ed., ed. John H. Leith (Louisville: Westminster, 1982), 98.

Who then should we say has the authority to baptize and affirm professions of faith? Who is charged with protecting the name of Christ and separating legitimate professors from the charlatans? Who is charged with maintaining the life of the community and overseeing the discipleship of Christ's people? It's only the apostolic church on earth, because only the apostolic church has the authoritative keys of the kingdom and the prerogatives of binding and loosing.

FIVE ASPECTS OF A CHURCH'S AUTHORITY

So what does Christ authorize the church to do in Matthew 16, 18, and 28? Christ authorizes the church to act in at least five respects as pertains to membership and discipline, which can be illustrated from the New Testament more broadly.

First, Jesus authorized the apostolic church *to be the proclaimer and guardian* of the good news of Jesus Christ. Remember, the entire conversation began with Jesus asking the disciples who he was. Peter's confession, along with Peter the apostle, is the rock on which the church is built, and he was given the keys of the kingdom to bind and loose (among other things) applications of the truth. We see this aspect of the keys in motion, for instance, when Paul rebukes the Galatian churches for listening to a false gospel. He chastises them for not protecting this gospel as they should have done (Gal. 1:6–9), and he concedes that even his own authority as an apostle depends upon his keeping to this message (1:8; also 2:11ff.).

Second, Jesus authorized his church *to affirm* any individual who credibly professes the gospel, just as Jesus affirmed Peter for his profession of faith. First comes a confession of faith, then comes an affirmation of both the confession and the individual who makes it. This, too, seems to be one aspect of exercising the keys of the kingdom for binding and loosing, because an affirmation is done formally through baptism. The early church therefore baptized "those who received his word" (Acts 2:41), those who had "received the Holy Spirit" (Acts 10:47), and those who "believed" (Acts 8:13; 18:8). It baptized people into the "name of Jesus" (Acts 2:38; 8:16; 10:48; 19:5; 22:16; Rom. 6:3), no doubt because they professed Jesus as Lord (Rom. 10:9). By contrast, Jesus did not authorize the church to affirm a profession of faith in Paul, Apollos, or Cephas (1 Cor. 1:13–16). He did not authorize it to affirm the faith of "anonymous Christians" or those who never confess Christ with their mouths (cf. Rom. 10:9). He authorized it to make a public declaration of the fact that so-and-so belongs to him when his or her profession is credible.

It's probably worth pointing out that I'm making a distinction here between *to affirm* and *to acknowledge*. Yes, anyone, even a non-Christian, can acknowledge that so-and-so "is a Christian." What I mean is that the church has the power of formal, public affirmation, in the way a White House press secretary formally affirms the president's words. I might personally acknowledge what the president of the United States said, but I would not presume to stand in front of the Washington press corps and formally affirm what he said. The president has not given me such authority. Within the church, that formal recognition occurs through the act of baptism and the distribution of the Lord's Supper. At no place in the New Testament do we find individuals baptizing themselves or feeding themselves the Lord's Supper. Nor do we see anyone besides the church exercising that authority, including the greatest of prophets, the pre-apostolic John the Baptist. Not even he had the authority to baptize, to formally affirm an individual as belonging to Christ's body (e.g., Acts 11:16; 19:3–4). In the New Testament we see apostles, the apostolic church, or someone representing the apostolic church conducting baptisms and distributing the Lord's Supper.

Third, Christ authorizes his apostolic church on earth *to unite* such professors in its care-giving embrace. I treat this at least as an implication of what happens when a church affirms an individual's profession of faith, but more likely it's another example of what it means to bind or loose on earth. We first see the apostolic church exercise this authority to unite new believers to itself in Acts 2: "Those who received his word were baptized, and there were *added* that day about three thousand souls" (v. 41; cf. 2:47; 4:4).

By using the language of "uniting" I don't mean to suggest that the church has some type of power to unite believers to the mystical body of Christ, as one will find in some Roman Catholic or Orthodox formulations. Rather, I mean that submitting to Christ the king requires us to submit to his rule as it's represented on earth, which in turn requires us to unite with that apostolic society which holds the keys of the kingdom, the church. Perhaps a better word than *uniting* is *receiving* (cf. Matt. 10:14, 40). Protestants sometimes speak of "receiving a person into membership." The passive sense of the word *receiving* implies that God is doing the giving. If the apostolic church perceives that a profession of faith is credible, it has no choice in whether to unite an individual to itself through baptism. As Peter declared, "Can anyone withhold water for baptizing these people, who have received the Holy Spirit just as we have?" (Acts 10:47). The implicit answer is no. No one has the right to withhold from a Christian what Christ has already given. He is Lord. On the human side of things, however, the act of baptism occurs only when authorized by an apostle, the apostolic church, or a representative of the apostolic church where there is no church (e.g., Acts 8:26, 36). Hence, we read that Peter "commanded them to be baptized in the name of Jesus Christ" (v. 48).

Fourth, Jesus authorizes his church *to bar* and *to exclude* any imposters who would harm the members of the family, degrade his name, and so hinder the church's witness to the world. We have already seen Jesus refer to this aspect of the church's authority in Matthew 18 (cf. Matt. 7:15–23). Peter appears to wield this authority when disciplining Ananias and Sapphira for lying to the Holy Spirit (Acts 5:1–9), and then again when he appears to exclude Simon the magician from fellowship saying, "Your heart is not right before God" (Acts 8:21). Many other such examples could be listed from the New Testament (e.g., 1 Cor. 5:5; 2 Thess. 3:14; Titus 3:10; 2 John 10–11).

Fifth, Christ authorizes his church *to provide oversight* to any professors, guiding, directing, and equipping them through his Word toward a closer union with him and all God's children. This is implied by points three and four above, and it becomes explicit in Matthew 28 when Jesus tells the apostles to teach those whom they baptize. Uniting an individual to the body requires some level of knowledge; disciplining an individual, if the church is to do so with any integrity, also requires the church to continue in its oversight. Also, the apostles clearly assume that Jesus' words imply that, at the very least, the church leadership must exercise oversight on behalf of the congregation. So Paul tells the elders in Ephesus, "Pay careful attention to yourselves and to all the flock, in which the Holy Spirit has made you overseers, to care for the church of God, which he obtained with his own blood" (Acts 20:28; also, 1 Pet. 5:2; Heb. 13:17). Yet the church's work of oversight is also a clear implication of all the "one another" commands throughout the New Testament. Jesus tells the Father that he has guarded and kept all the children the Father had given him except one (John 17:12; also, 12:28–29; 18:9). Members of churches, likewise, should strive to keep one another in the love of God, having mercy on those who doubt, snatching some from the fire, showing mercy mixed with fear to still others (Jude 21–23).

To summarize, Jesus grants the apostolic church authority to guard and protect the gospel, to affirm credible gospel professions, to unite such professors to itself, to bar or exclude non-credible professors, and to oversee the discipleship of believers. It has the authority to draw a line in the sand around those who give a credible profession of faith.

What the Charter Says

A few moments ago, I said that it's hard to escape the sense that something *institutional* is going on when looking at chapters 16, 18, and 28 of Matthew's Gospel. In fact, I think that is what's happening. Jesus effectively hands his disciples an institutional charter. What does the charter say? Drawing from Matthew 16, 18, 28, and other places in the New Testament, I propose that it says this:

> I hereby grant my apostolic church, the one eschatological and heavenly gathering, the authority to act as the custodians and witnesses of my kingdom on earth. I authorize this royal and priestly body, wherever it's manifest among two or three witnesses

formally gathered in my name, to publicly affirm and identify themselves with me and with all individuals who credibly profess my name and follow me as Lord; to oversee the discipleship of these by teaching them everything that I have commanded; to exclude all false and disobedient professors; and to make more disciples, identifying these new believers with the Father, Son, and Holy Spirit through baptism.

Jesus is king, and in these chapters he is granting the nobles a charter that authorizes them to build on his land.

One begins to see how extraordinarily foolish it is for so many evangelicals to presume that they retain this authority for themselves, which they do whenever they say that their Christian faith belongs to them and that they don't need a church to affirm it. Would we presume to recruit someone for a professional football team and offer him a contract or offer someone a position in the British prime minister's cabinet? Of course not. Likewise, we would not try to join the army by asking the army to join us. We know that we don't have the authority. Who then has the authority to formally affirm and unite someone to the body of Christ? Christ does, certainly. Beyond that, these three passages in Matthew tell us he gave this authority to the apostles, who were uniquely commissioned with the apostolic message to establish the foundation of the church. But once that foundation was established and the apostles died, that authority did not pass along to every individual on the planet. That authority was passed on to the church. Only the apostolic church has the authority to baptize.

Precisely because we live in between the kingdom's inauguration and its consummation, precisely because authority remains a complex matter in this era, precisely because Christians are simultaneously justified and sinful, precisely because we are so prone to self-deceit, precisely because the two radically opposed but overlapping images of love are cast upon the same screen, and precisely because the world needs someone to distinguish true love from worldly love, Christ has authorized no individual, but rather the apostolic church, to mark off a people for himself and to hold them together.

Step 4: Even with all its imperfections, the church represents Jesus on earth. It gives witness to his coming salvation and judgment.

An Earthly Charter

How then should we understand the relationship between the apostolic church's binding and loosing on earth and what transpires in heaven? Interpreters tend to focus on whether the verbal phrases in Matthew 16:19 and 18:18 should be translated in the simple future ("shall be bound/shall be loosed" KJV, NIV, NRSV,

ESV) or in the past perfect ("shall have been bound/shall have been loosed" NASB). Both are technically legitimate translations, but they seem to lead to different theological conclusions, Protestants often opting for the latter and Roman Catholics for the former.

I'm not convinced that it matters how you translate it, because the point is that Jesus is using the charge to establish the church as his representative on earth;[46] and when one party exercises authority on behalf of another, that new party's representative authority is, in a sense, timeless. If anything, it has a present and future bearing. Think of a babysitter or nanny who represents a parent's authority. Parents put babysitters in charge until the parents' return, at which time any promises or warnings the babysitter made will be vindicated. Likewise, Jesus' charge to the church to act as his representative could have been given in past, present, or future terms. Let me illustrate this with another analogy.

Jesus is like the owner of an apartment building telling the landlord, "Tell the tenants that your decisions are my decisions." That is a present reference. Here is a past reference: "If you like the tenants, then I already like them." Here is a future reference: "If you have a problem with them, they're going to have a problem with me."[47] Does this mean a building owner expects the landlord to have a perfect read on his mind, or that he thinks he will agree with every decision the landlord ever makes, or even that he forbids the tenants from appealing directly to him in instances of disagreement with the landlord? Not at all. The owner is simply establishing that, as a matter of principle, the landlord speaks on his behalf. Jesus made a similar point only a few chapters earlier: "Whoever receives you receives me, and whoever receives me receives him who sent me" (Matt. 10:40).

The real question that divides Protestants and Catholics is what kind of representative the church is, which can be illustrated with the differences between two analogies I have already used—a landlord and an ambassador. A landlord as representative can both declare and enact. He not only declares who may rent an apartment, but he has the power of attorney to rent the apartment. An ambassador, on the other hand, can only make declarations on behalf of his king. He can tell his king's foreign opponent, "My king will act decisively if you don't remove your forces," or even "My king hereby declares war upon you."

---

[46]If anything, in fact, translating them as simple futures—"shall be bound/loosed"—strikes me as more appropriate given the verse that follows 18:18: "Again I say to you, if two of you agree on earth about anything they ask, *it will be done* for them by my Father in heaven" (v. 19). First, the indicative phrase "it will be" in v. 19 occurs in the same tense and aspect (future middle) as the indicatives ("shall be") preceding the participles in v. 18. Second, the verse affirms that decisions on earth *will be done* by the Father in heaven. This accords with Jesus' promise in chap. 16 that the gates of hell will not prevail against this church—he's talking about the true church, not any false churches that hell *will* prevail against.

[47]In fact, notice that the past reference is the most strained, which is probably because, again, a representative's authority, though timeless in one sense, does have a present and future bearing. Its vindication occurs when the ultimate authority *shows up*.

While the Roman Catholic Church essentially teaches that the church is more like a landlord (with the power to enact),[48] it is better to liken the church to an ambassador (with the authority to declare). Nothing in this passage compels us to answer that question one way or another, including whether the phrase in question is referring to something in the past or the future. We need the rest of Scripture to answer it.

What is important for us to recognize here is that Jesus has charged the church with speaking for him on earth, and he wants all the world to know it. A church member living in unrepentant sin needs to know that the church speaks for Jesus. Jesus will come to vindicate the church's warnings against unrepentant sin. A non-Christian who rejects the church's gospel needs to know that the church speaks for Jesus. Jesus will come to vindicate the church's call to repentance. The point is not whether the church can omnisciently or divinely discern every individual's ultimate state at any given moment.[49] The point is that the world should heed the church's promises and warnings because Jesus has given the church authority to speak on his behalf, as an ambassador, and he will come and vindicate its words.

The church will get it wrong sometimes. On occasion it will wrongly bar or exclude people who are truly Christians, and sometimes it will wrongly embrace people who are not Christians. But that doesn't mean the church's authority has vanished. Any promises or warnings given by a babysitter might turn out to be wrong as well, but that doesn't diminish the babysitter's authority to command as long as the parents are absent. The fact that the church can make mistakes is no excuse for the world to ignore its warnings and promises, any more than a child can say to a babysitter, "It's possible you are wrong about when I'm supposed to go to bed. Therefore, I can legitimately ignore you and stay up and watch television." If I learned that my daughter said that to a babysitter when I arrived home, I would discipline her for rejecting the authority I had given the babysitter.[50] I would explain to her that this act of rebellion was a rejection of *my* authority.

The earthly church, it's important to remember, is an eschatological representative. Its life and declarations point to an end-time reality. It points to what *will be*. Yet just as my own Christian life imperfectly points to what will be,

---

[48]At least since Cyprian, the Roman Catholic Church has tended to use the metaphor of church as mother: "You cannot have God for your Father if you have not the Church for your mother" (Cyprian, *The Unity of the Catholic Church*, Ancient Christian Writers, trans. Maurice Bévenot (New York: The Newman Press, 1956), 48 (sec. 6). Clearly, the "metaphor" is an even stronger version of a representative role than a landlord. The *Catechism of the Catholic Church*, which bears Joseph Ratzinger's *Imprimi Potest*, defines binding and loosing this way: "The words *bind* and *loose* mean: whomever you exclude from your communion, will be excluded from communion with God; whomever you receive anew into your communion, God will welcome back into his. "Reconciliation with the Church is inseparable from reconciliation with God" (italics original); *Catechism of the Catholic Church* (New York: Doubleday, 1995), 403.

[49]Critics of regenerate church membership will sometimes charge its advocates of making this claim; e.g., see James Bannerman's comments in note 51.

[50]I consider the question of dissenting from the church's authority in chap. 7.

so does the church on earth. The church on earth does not perfectly represent God's end-time people, but it should do the best it can.[51] That is its job. Christ gave the church authority to bind and loose—to make public affirmation of inclusion or exclusion based on a person's adherence to the gospel. He meant to make a clear and real representative connection between the Father's authority in heaven and the church's declarative authority on earth.[52] The good news is that he's not bound to vindicate the church's mistakes, any more than I'm bound to vindicate a babysitter's mistakes. The Second Helvetic Creed describes the church's representative, declarative authority this way:

> For we see that a master does give unto the steward of his house authority and power over his house, and for that cause delivers him the keys, that he may admit or exclude such as his master will have admitted or excluded…the Lord does ratify and confirm that which he does, and will have the deeds of his ministers to be acknowledged and esteemed by his own deeds.[53]

The phrase we need to notice here is, "The Lord . . . will have the deeds of his ministers to be acknowledged and esteemed by his own deeds." In other words, Jesus will have the world know that the church speaks for him. A phrase from Luther also captures this representative connection: "It is as a judgment of Christ himself." Again, the church speaks for Jesus. The church has authority not because it's omniscient but because Christ has commissioned it to stand and speak—or better, to go and speak—in his place.

Step 5: The church, therefore, is Christ's proxy on earth.

Christ's Proxy and Conversion

The loving rule of Christ creates and holds a people together. It creates a whole new reality from scratch. It creates the church—a society with center and bound-

---

[51]Right here is where the Presbyterian critique of regenerate church membership strikes me as misguided. See, e.g., the Presbyterian James Bannerman's *The Church of Christ*, vol. 1 (Edinburgh: Banner of Truth, 1991), 73–80. The point of regenerate church membership is merely that the visible church *aspires* to represent the invisible church as closely as it can, not because a church can give "witness to the secret work of God done on the soul of a brother" (79), but because churches should do exactly what Bannerman prescribes—attempt to assess "intelligent professions of belief" (74). The "Donatist tendency" for which he and others critique regenerate church membership seems to miss the distinction between the *exertion* toward a wholly regenerate church and the *expectation* of a wholly regenerate church.

[52]What's always been slightly surprising to me is that Calvin picked up Cyprian's metaphor of church as mother. Speaking of the visible church, Calvin says, "For there is no other way to enter into life unless this mother conceive us in her womb, give us birth, nourish us at her breast" (*Institutes*, 1016). I recognize that Calvin meant slightly different things than the Roman Catholic Church means, and I do want to affirm the church's instrumental role in our salvation; yet the language of *birthing* simply gives the church too much credit. The Holy Spirit causes us to be born again (John 3:1–8). The church's instrumental role is better described ambassadorially and declaratively.

[53]John H. Leith, *Creeds of the Churches*, 156–57.

aries, purpose and definition. Given contemporary culture's idolatry of love and pronounced disdain of authority, this all seems a bit ironic. The church is pulled and held together by authority, and that authority is what's used to define love. That authority is grounded in his love, to be sure, but his love commissions his rule to declare a people as his own, who in turn define love. As we saw in chapter 2, this is why love and obedience move so closely together throughout the Gospel of John.

Christ then hands this loving rule to the church, as I said above, to act as his proxy. The church, likewise grounded in his love, then executes his rule (to declare like an ambassador, not to enact like an apartment building landlord) by uniting individuals to itself and by overseeing their discipleship. It does this by proclaiming his gospel, calling people into his new creation, and then marking off the ones who come, with baptism and the Lord's Supper.

What does this mean from the perspective of the individual? Well, let's return to the topic of conversion. Conversion, as we have said, is typically defined by systematic theologians as repentance and belief, at least on the human side of the equation. From the beginning of Jesus' ministry he proclaimed, "The kingdom of God is at hand; repent and believe in the gospel" (Mark 1:15). To repent is to relinquish one's own rule and to yield to God's rule. Entering the kingdom of God means submitting oneself and all of one's resources to the rule of God and trusting his provision of salvation. If Christ then hands aspects of his rule over to the church to function as his proxy, this means that, for the believer, the converted one is immediately ushered under the authority of the church. It's like a football team owner hiring a player and then telling the player that, if he wants to play, he has to listen to the team coach. In order to submit to the owner, a player must submit to his coach. The owner hires, but the coach schedules the practices, picks the lineup, and calls the plays. Christians submit to Christ by submitting to the apostolic church in whatever areas of authority Christ has given the church authority.

This is precisely why Peter responds to the Jews who were crying out with conviction for the crucifixion of Jesus, "Repent and be baptized every one of you in the name of Jesus Christ for the forgiveness of your sins, and you will receive the gift of the Holy Spirit" (Acts 2:38). He doesn't just tell them to repent. He also tells them to be baptized. This doesn't mean that baptism is regenerative or that it transfuses grace. Peter is simply saying, "Tell the owner that you're done trying to be your own boss and that you want to play for him now, and then prove it by reporting immediately to his coach." Repentance is publicly demonstrated in baptism; it's demonstrated in submitting to the church's authority. Submit to Christ, Peter is saying, by submitting to the church. Baptism doesn't mean only this, but it means at least this.

Conversion is not merely about crossing a boundary. It's about changing allegiances and submitting to a whole new reality. It's orbiting a new sun. If repentance is conducted through the church and if repentance is more than a one-time event but submission to a new rule, then the life of repentance is a life lived out within the context of the church. The church gives shape to the Christian life.

Step 6: The fact that the church is Christ's proxy on earth means that the Christian must submit to the church on earth, which means submitting to the local church.

Submitting to a Universal or Local Proxy?

Must a Christian join—or submit to—a *local* church? Can't Christians simply submit to the universal, apostolic church? "Being in a right relationship with God and His people is what matters," says George Barna; "the core issue isn't whether or not one is involved in a local church, but whether or not one is connected to the body of believers in the pursuit of godliness and worship." The bottom line: "You see, it's not about *church*. It's about *the Church*—that is, the people who actively participate in the intentional advancement of God's Kingdom in partnership with the Holy Spirit and other believers."[54] So why not get baptized at youth camp or a men's crusade? Why not follow a few super apostles from conference to conference like Grateful Dead groupies, at least in the summer months? Why not attend one church for the music, another for its sermons, and another for its small groups? Just make sure you are personally "in the Word" and have a few "accountability relationships." Complement your regimen of daily Bible reading with a list of questions you ask your Christian buddy at your weekly Sunday morning tee-off times.

Surely we must say that membership in the universal church is constituent of being a Christian, while membership in the local church is not. On the last day, the repentant thief on the cross, we assume, will be found belonging to the universal church even though he never joined a local church. Writing to the Corinthians, Paul refers to them as "the church of God that is in Corinth" and then describes them as "called to be saints *together with all those who in every place* call upon the name of our Lord Jesus Christ, both their Lord and ours" (1 Cor. 1:2). As long as two Christians call upon the name of Christ, therefore, what does it matter if they belong to separate local churches, or any local church at all?

The short answer is that the local church is where the church on earth *is*. Not only that, it's where the church in heaven *is*. Notice that Paul refers to the

---

[54]George Barna, *Revolution* (Carol Stream, IL: Tyndale, 2005), 37–38.

church in Corinth as *"the* church of God that is in Corinth."* He doesn't say *a* church. Christ's eschatological (end-time) heavenly assembly is represented *there,* among *those* people. The assembled Christians in Corinth are, in Ed Clowney's phrase, a colony of heaven. If you have ever stood inside the embassy for your own nation in a foreign country, your fellow citizens working behind the desk will tell you, "You are standing on the soil of our nation." But the homeland of God's people is nowhere on this planet. There are only ambassadors and embassies. The church on earth is those embassies of ambassadors gathered together in the name of Christ. What that means is that an individual cannot meaningfully, truly, or authentically submit one's life and discipleship to both Christ and his earthly proxy in something other than the local church. If submitting to Christ means submitting to the authority of inclusion, the authority of oversight, and the authority of discipline of his apostolic representative on earth, then how can getting baptized at youth camp accomplish this? How can the conference circuit discipline its groupies, or how can Christian golf buddies help to protect the apostolic gospel from generation to generation?

WHERE IS THE CHURCH ON EARTH?

Jesus gave the apostles the authority to bind and loose on earth. If we agree that Christians need to submit to the apostolic church on earth, the inevitable question is, *where does the Bible say the church on earth is?* Do Christians who gather for a one-time concert constitute a church? I know of one Australian Anglican who thinks so. A church is a gathering; a Christian concert is a gathering; so a Christian concert is a church, right? What about three Christian moms who regularly meet at the local park and perhaps talk about the Bible while their children play? Do they constitute a church? What about two Christians bumping into each other in the cereal aisle at the grocery store?

One way to determine the location of the church on earth is to examine all the instances of the word *church* (*ekklesia*) in the New Testament and simply ask where the New Testament authors locate it. In the New Testament, we find references to the eschatological universal church (Matt. 16:18) and local churches (Matt. 18:17). There are some disputes at the margins about whether house churches can be distinguished from city churches (e.g., 1 Cor. 16:9; Col. 4:15–16), or whether Luke refers to "the church" as a regional designation (e.g., Acts 9:31). But generally we find that all the references to churches, aside from references to the universal church, devolve to local churches, even if they are referred to as the church of a particular region.[55] There is no reference to a

---

[55] Again, Acts 9:31 is the only instance I know of this occurring. However, F. F. Bruce describes this as a reference to the church of Jerusalem, now scattered in chap. 9, which would make sense in light of the fact that the last reference to "the church" is the church in Jerusalem being persecuted by Saul and scattering. This seems

couple of Christians spending time together or even doing good works. There's
no reference to a multinational administrative structure. Not even the apostle
Paul and his traveling band refer to themselves as the church. In the New Testament, the church on earth, at least gauged by where the word *church* shows
up, looks like the local church and nothing else. This is helpful to a point, but
significantly sized epistles such as 1 John or 1 Peter never mention the word
church. Peter's first letter is written to the "elect exiles of the dispersion" (1 Pet.
1:1). Are those Christians scattered off by themselves or in smaller groups—some
at camp, some attending conferences, some golfing, some attending multiple
gatherings but submitting to none?

Throughout church history, churchmen and theologians have given different answers to the question of where the church on earth is. Both the Roman
Catholic and Greek Orthodox traditions say that the church exists wherever
the Eucharist is properly dispensed by a bishop properly connected to Peter
and the larger structures of their respective communions. Yet both traditions
also ultimately require the presence of the congregation.[56] The great difficulty
with that era of Christendom, West or East, was that it blurred the line between
church and nation, between church membership and citizenship.

Only partially moving beyond that error, the Magisterial Protestant Reformers said that the church on earth exists wherever the right preaching of the
Word and a disciplined administration of the ordinances occur. The problem
was that even a non-regenerative doctrine of infant baptism allowed them to
continue blurring the line between membership and citizenship (not to dispute
infant baptism here, per se). Free-church confessions have generally agreed with
the Reformers concerning preaching and the ordinances, but they have placed
a little more emphasis on the congregation and the subjective faith of their
congregants. One of the rising critiques these days against all these traditions
is that such definitions turn church into a weekly event or a set of activities or
even a place. For instance, British authors Chester and Timmis write, "Church
is not a meeting you attend or a place you enter. It is an identity that is ours
in Christ. It is an identity that shapes the whole of life so that life and mission
become 'total church.'"[57] These kinds of critiques reflect both the missional and
the "communion ecclesiology" impulses I mentioned in the Introduction.

What's remarkable about even the historical examples is that they all, in
one form or another, and in more and less convincing ways, involve the congregation. They all involve groups of gathered Christians, and individuals are
expected to submit to one such group. My point here is not to debate whether

---

reasonable when one compares Acts 8:3 and Acts 9:31. *The Book of Acts*, New International Commentary on
the New Testament (Grand Rapids: Eerdmans, 1988), 196.
[56]See Miroslav Volf, *After Our Likeness* (Grand Rapids: Eerdmans, 1998), 130–31.
[57]Tim Chester and Steve Timmis, *Total Church* (Wheaton, IL: Crossway, 2008), 18.

a superstructure does or should exist atop those local gatherings (I don't think it should). Nor is my point to debate whether those superstructures or anything in the local gatherings themselves have contributed to a kind of institutionalization that has wrongfully overwhelmed the congregations (I think they have). My point is simply that, as best we can tell, Christian life in the New Testament and throughout church history has always been placed within a local congregation, at least by intent. The only exception occurs when an individual or a group seeks to plant a church where none exists, as with Philip and the Ethiopian eunuch (e.g., Acts 8:26–39; notice also that the Lord commissions Philip). Only in the consumeristic West over the last few decades has this basic idea been questioned.

Certainly the congregational context of the Christian life is assumed everywhere in the New Testament, even when the word *church* is not used. John didn't use it in his first epistle, but he writes of individuals who were not part of them: "They went out from us, but they were not of us; for if they had been of us, they would have continued with us. But they went out, that it might become plain that they all are not of us" (1 John 2:19). His first epistle is as clear on the love and obedience to be exercised toward believers as any book of the Bible. By the time we get to John's second and third epistles, it's hardly surprising to find him more explicit about not extending the hand of fellowship to some (2 John 10) while extending it to others (3 John 5–10).

Peter may not use the word *church* once in his epistles either, but he describes his readers with clear corporate metaphors in his first epistle (2:5, 9). He mentions their baptism (3:21). He tells them to be of one mind and to show hospitality to one another without grumbling (3:8; 4:9). He encourages them to use whatever gifts they have been given to serve one another (4:10). He warns them that judgment begins with the "household of God" (4:17). Finally, he commands them to "be subject to the elders" (5:5). Who was supposed to be subject to the elders, and what were the elders overseeing? Peter's readers, scattered over a broad region, were no doubt living in bounded, clearly delineated churches.

Submitting to the local church is how we submit to Christ's lordship. It's the fruit of repentance. It's obedience to the one whom we profess as "the Christ, the Son of the living God." It's *where* the believer submits. It's *the place* on earth that this happens.[58] Those with missional and *communio* impulses are correct to affirm the church as a people, but both groups seem to have lost the ability to distinguish between the church and a collection of Christians; between the church of God in Corinth and three Christian mothers meeting at the park or working in a homeless shelter. From one angle, a local church is represented in the lives and activities of its members, just like Christ is represented in the

---

[58]Notice the apt title of Michael Horton's theology of the church, *People and Place: A Covenant Ecclesiology.*

lives and activities of churches and Christians both. This is why Paul is so concerned about the private immoralities of an individual church member in Corinth (1 Corinthians 5). There is a federal identity between the Christian and the church, such that each can representatively "speak" or "act" for the other, a matter which we'll consider further in the next chapter.

From another angle, however, we must maintain the distinction between a local church and a group of Christians. The difference lies precisely in the fact that Christ has handed a charter of authority to the church, not to Christians generically. One might say that the whole (the local church) is more than the sum of its parts (the individual members) because of this charter. As such, I do not personally have the authority to baptize my friends or my children simply because I am a Christian. I have not been authorized to affirm before the world on behalf of Christ that they will belong to his end-time heavenly people. As an elder of my local church (or even as just a member) and together with my church I have that authority, but it's not really *my* authority. It's the church's. I simply exercise it.

Is the distinction between a church and a group of Christians vague and academic? I don't think so. Every employee of an organization who has access to a company credit card understands that a difference exists between using company money for business and for personal pleasure. One use is ethical while the other is not. Admittedly, the line between business use and personal use is not always clear. My own "business lunches" are often with personal friends, and the conversations will touch on personal matters. Can I charge the company? This question is best answered on a case-by-case basis. When it comes to comparing churches and Christians, it's not a question of money but of authority. And, frankly, it may not always be clear whether some activity or gathering is a function of the local church proper or simply a group of Christians. It's important to realize, however, that the further a church or individual Christian moves beyond the explicit organizational responsibilities handed to it by Jesus (to preach the gospel, to protect the gospel, to unite credible professors to itself, to exclude false professors), the more unclear this line will become. But the difference between a church and a bunch of Christians at camp, at the park, or in a stadium remains.

The local church is the place where a gathering of Christians can responsibly and meaningfully carry out the charter given in Matthew 16, especially as it's further clarified in chapters 18 and 28, and in 26 in the episode of the Lord's Supper. As a concession to my non-free church friends, I'll say that it's *at least* this. We can illustrate the difference between a church and a collection of Christians in this way: I can easily imagine a summer camp counselor watching a seventeen-year-old boy undergo conversion over the course of a summer, which is followed by a seemingly credible profession of faith. Should the camp counselor then baptize the boy? He can, if he can baptize him according to the authority of the charter Jesus handed the apostles in Matthew 16. Has this counselor, together with several others, determined to continue indefinitely in overseeing the boy and one another; to regularly proclaim the Lord's death through the Lord's Supper; to discipline the boy or one another should they revert to following in the ways of the world; to teach one another everything that Christ has commanded; to guard, protect, and proclaim the gospel; and to make more disciples among not just other teenagers but among all comers who do not yet know Christ? If so, yes, he can baptize that boy on behalf of the church. If that counselor cannot commit to all this, that is, if there is no church to speak of, he does not have the authority to baptize the boy. The camp counselor's desire to protect the gospel in the boy's life and in the eyes of the broader public should impel him to send the boy to a church saying, "Join it! Be guarded. Be watched over. Be cared for. Be protected. Be loved."

Missional and *communio* authors understandably react against institutionalism in churches. Yet their critique of church as a place, an event, or a set of activities misses the distinction between a church and a group of Christians. They miss the fact that Christ established an organization, and its members don't have the authority to use the company credit card whenever and however they please. Christians can use it whenever they have formally gathered together in Christ's name and the Spirit of Christ is present through Word and ordinance (cf. Acts 4:31; 6:2; 14:27; 15:30; 20:7). After all, it's this gathering of Christians to exercise the power of the keys that constitutes the local church on earth. This is what both Jesus and Paul say.

Jesus:

> If he refuses to listen to them, tell it to the church. And if he refuses to listen even to the church, let him be to you as a Gentile and a tax collector. Truly, I say to you, whatever you bind on earth shall be bound in heaven, and whatever you loose on earth shall be loosed in heaven. Again I say to you, if two of you agree on earth about anything they ask, it will be done for them by my Father in heaven. For where two or three are *gathered in my name, there am I among them.* (Matt. 18:17–20)

> Go therefore and make disciples of all nations, baptizing them in the name of the Father and of the Son and of the Holy Spirit, teaching them to observe all that I have commanded you. And behold, *I am with you always*, to the end of the age. (Matt. 28:19–20)

Paul:

> When you are *assembled in the name of the Lord Jesus and my spirit* [perhaps meaning, his spirit as an authority-conferring apostle] *is present, with the power*

of our Lord Jesus, you are to deliver this man to Satan for the destruction of the flesh, so that his spirit may be saved in the day of the Lord. (1 Cor. 5:4–5)

For, in the first place, *when you come together as a church*, I hear that there are divisions among you. And I believe it in part, for there must be factions among you in order that those who are genuine among you may be recognized. (1 Cor. 11:18–19)

Christians do comprise "the church," but Paul and Jesus both speak as if it's the gathering that constitutes us as a church, just like a basketball team must gather in order to be considered a "team." This formal gathering has an existence and an authority that none of us has separately. The whole is greater than the sum of its parts, because Christ has given the whole an organizational charter. Nineteenth-century Congregational pastor John Angell James put it like this: "A church member is something more than a Christian, just as a citizen is something more than a man. Each has duties arising from the relationship—to state or to church."[59]

The church on earth is located in the local church. If Christ calls us to submit to him by submitting to the apostolic church, he intends for us to do this through the local church. To refuse his lordship by refusing to submit to a true local church, if one exists where one geographically abides, calls into question whether we have truly been converted. It's true that we must choose to join, and it's true—in some places in this world—that we have to choose *which* church to join. But not joining, if a local church exists, is not really an option. Membership in the local church is voluntary, and it's not voluntary.

Apparently, some in the early church failed to recognize this fact, which is why the author to the Hebrews warned his readers about "neglecting to meet together, as is the habit of some" (Heb. 10:25). Such sinful neglect, he said, leads to "a fearful expectation of judgment, and a fury of fire that will consume the adversaries" (Heb. 10:27).

In order to systematize the above discussion and give it a little more precision, I think we can say that joining a local church is required by at least six factors: the nature of what the universal church is, the nature of authority, our biblical obligations to the "body," the biblical commands to submit to the elders or overseers, the nature of our salvation, and the nature of our new identity in Christ.

1) The nature of the universal church requires it. It's not about belonging to a church; it's about belonging to *the* church, say some. Is that right? Let's con-

---

[59]John Angell James, *Christian Fellowship or The Church Member's Guide*, ed. and abr. Gordon T. Booth, from the 10th edition of vol. 11 of the *Works of John Angell James*, 1861 (Shropshire, England: Quinta Press, 1997), 7.

sider who Jesus wants Christians to belong to. Jesus said that he would "build his church," referring to the universal church, the gathering of Christians from all times and all places. But has that church ever gathered? In one sense, yes, it has begun to gather in heaven (Heb. 12:22–23; Eph. 2:4–6; Col. 3:1, 3). But in another sense, no, it's not yet fully gathered. The universal church is a heavenly and eschatological body.[60] When Jesus says he will build his church, he surely has this final society ultimately in mind (Matt. 16:18). Make no mistake, when an individual becomes a Christian, he belongs to the universal church—Christ's body. It *is* about belonging to the church.

Yet Jesus also tells his disciples to bind and loose this heavenly and eschatological gathering on earth. The love, holiness, and beauty of that end-time body needs to be demonstrated now. The forgiving and merciful and righteous *togetherness* of the church needs to be embodied now. Christ and his person need to be displayed now. Christians cannot display the life of this final society, this end-time gathering, this heavenly city, this Christ, all by themselves. They need other Christians. We can't forgive, forbear, and love sitting all by ourselves on an island, nor can we receive forgiveness and forbearance. It's as the citizens of this end-time society love one another that the world knows what it means to be Christ's disciples (John 13:34–35).

The universal church is a heavenly body because it has begun to gather in heaven, but it's also an eschatological body because the complete gathering of the end times has already begun on earth.[61] The homeland has sent out ambassadors and built up embassies here and now, which is why Paul refers to "the church of God in Corinth" (1 Cor. 1:2; 2 Cor. 2:1).[62] Those gathered believers in Corinth are an outpost, a foretaste, a colony, a representation of the final gathering. It's all about belonging to *the* church, but, here and now, it's all about belonging to *a* church because that is where we put flesh upon our proclamation and our faith.

In short, the nature of the universal church requires professing Christians to submit to the local church.

2) The nature of authority and submission requires it. The idea of belonging to a local church—indeed the very concept of a local church—is superfluous if our idea of relating to Christ and other Christians is premised wholly on some vague conception of relationship between mutual sovereigns that is bereft of all authority and moral necessity. If Christ commanded us only to cultivate a relationship with him and other believers, it's hard to see why we would join a church, much less why local churches existed in the first place. Why not simply interact with other believers as it fits our schedules, personal needs, social prefer-

---

[60] Clowney, "The Church as a Heavenly and Eschatological Entity."
[61] See ibid., 93–98.
[62] See also 1 Cor. 10:32; 11:22; 15:9; 2 Cor. 2:1; Gal. 1:13; Phil. 3:6; 1 Tim. 3:15.

ences, self image, and, oh, okay, the needs of the few people we happen to care about? In fact, the very idea of "gathering" would seem superfluous.[63] Why talk about the church at all except in the most abstract terms? Incidentally, this points us to the problem with any conception of community and relationship that is bereft of authority. Such a community is, finally, nothing more than an amalgamation of individuals who may or may not share a sentimental regard for one another. Really, everyone remains autonomous, because the only true antidote to autonomy is not just relationship but submission.

If we try to conduct our discipleship with Christ by casually nibbling and grazing wherever we please, moving back and forth between one field and another, it's difficult to see how we will ever truly submit to the church of God. We may give of ourselves to this or that Christian or church, but we will never truly give ourselves. Submitting to the church on earth means walking up to a group of people and saying, "I believe what you believe. Now put me to work supporting our mutual cause however you need me. You can count on me."

In short, the nature of authority and submission require professing Christians to submit to the local church. It requires commitment.

3) Our biblical obligations to the "body" require it. In 1 Corinthians 12 Paul describes a church body with a variety of gifts, but the same Spirit; varieties of service, but the same Lord; and varieties of activities, but the same God empowering them all in everyone for the sake of the whole: "To each is given the manifestation of the Spirit for the common good" (1 Cor. 12:4–7). Paul then describes the interdependence of this body:

> For just as the body is one and has many members, and all the members of the body, though many, are one body, so it is with Christ. For in one Spirit we were all baptized into one body—Jews or Greeks, slaves or free—and all were made to drink of one Spirit. For the body does not consist of one member but of many. If the foot should say, "Because I am not a hand, I do not belong to the body," that would not make it any less a part of the body. And if the ear should say, "Because I am not an eye, I do not belong to the body," that would not make it any less a part of the body. If the whole body were an eye, where would be the sense of hearing? If the whole body were an ear, where would be the sense of smell? But as it is, God arranged the members in the body, each one of them, as he chose. If all were a single member, where would the body be? As it is, there are many parts, yet one body. (1 Cor. 12:12–20)

---

[63]For an example of someone who opts for an authority-less conception of the Trinity and the church, which, strikingly, ultimately yields a conception of *ekklesia* which somehow manages to have any concept of an actual "gathering" choked out of it, see Kevin Giles, *What on Earth Is the Church?* He writes, "Most of the uses of the word *ekklesia* in Paul are used of Christians generally, with no thought that they all met face to face at least sometimes. This means, then, that the meaning 'assembly' in these instances has completely disappeared" (121). No assembly? Doesn't that mean my Christian life becomes all about me calling the shots? I fear that theologians who, for understandable reasons, aim for egalitarianism, ironically, always end up with atomism—a kind of a "priesthood of all believers" *reductio ad absurdum*.

Clearly, Paul is using the words *member* and *body* in this context as biological metaphors, comparing the church with a human body. He doesn't mean that the church is actually a human body or that the members who comprise it are actually arms and ears. He is very concretely saying that every individual in the church is incomplete without the others, just as Adam was incomplete without Eve. Their identities and experiences are to be interconnected and mutually dependent. So Paul writes, "If one member suffers, all suffer together; if one member is honored, all rejoice together" (1 Cor. 12:26).

When I first considered how 1 Corinthians 12 applied to church membership, I wanted to nail down whether Paul was referring to the local body in Corinth or to the body of Christ universally by using the language of one body or member. Consider the sentence, "Now you are the body of Christ and individually members of it" (1 Cor. 12:27). Does he mean here that the Corinthians comprise their own body, distinguishable from the body of the Galatians or the body of the Romans, and that they are members of this body? If so, it would seem strange that he would include himself in that body, as he does when he says, "For in one Spirit we were all baptized into one body" (v. 13). Paul, who is not a member of the church in Corinth, seems to assume that he has been baptized by the same Spirit into the same body as the Corinthians. So does he mean the local body or the universal body?

The issue is not so difficult when we remember that the local body is an expression or an embassy for the eschatological universal body. In any one use of the word, Paul might lean toward one emphasis or another. When he writes, "The parts of the body that seem to be weaker are indispensable" (1 Cor. 12:22), he is leaning into an emphasis on the local body, based on contextual factors. Yet when he writes, "For in one Spirit we were all baptized into one body" (v. 13), he is leaning into a universal emphasis and reminding us that the local is a manifestation of the universal. Language is art as much as it's science, and I'm suspicious of the New Testament commentator who says it must be one instead of the other, but Paul tends to use the image of Christ's body in order to allow for both meanings to resonate (see also Rom. 12:5; Eph. 4:12; Col. 2:19), since the universal is present in the local.

If that's correct, 1 Corinthians 12 is a wonderful illustration of how the local church today should begin to embody the final eschatological gathering of God's people through the submission of God's people to one another. God arranged the members in the body, each one of them, as he chose, so that each part might contribute uniquely to the whole. The foot and hand both should submit all their "footness" and "handness" to the body, not to extinguish their uniqueness but to put them to good use for the sake of the whole body. The body needs every member to be complete. Each diverse member submits his or her gift to the common good: "To each is given the manifestation of the Spirit for the common good" (1 Cor. 12:7). The entirety of 1 Corinthians 14, in fact, presses home the point of striving after gifts that build up the church (vv. 3–4, 12, 17, 19).

The gifts of the Spirit are eschatological gifts. They signify a new age and a new authority, but they are submitted for use in a particular place now. Unity and love should be pictured now—even imperfectly (1 Cor. 13:9)—as a witness to the unity and love of glory. "Let all things be done for building up" (14:26).

Christians these days have a hard time submitting to the body, not just because we resent the idea of authority, but because our minds can't help but respond like consumers. A consumer has authority. A consumer thinks he is the head, and the rest of the body exists to serve him and fulfill his personal narrative. Not only that, but he gets a little nervous when others are different from him. Jews *and* Greeks? Slaves *and* free? No, thank you, I'll stick with the free Greeks. The consumer is always looking for the right fit. He's looking for something with enough rooms, a well-designed kitchen, a good-sized backyard for the kids, and nothing too old that might take a lot of work. Sure, how about something with a little curb appeal?

Paul responds, "On the contrary, the parts of the body that seem to be weaker are indispensable, and on those parts of the body that we think less honorable we bestow the greater honor, and our unpresentable parts are treated with greater modesty" (1 Cor. 12:22–23). The consumer mind-set and the mind-set of submission to the whole body are diametrically opposed to one another. One employs the church and all its resources for its own pleasure. The other gives itself and all its resources over to the church for God's pleasure. Submitting to the entire body doesn't only mean submitting to its authority; it means submitting to its livelihood and good. "Let all things be done for building up" (14:26).

It's in this context that Paul grabs back the pretty lyrics of 1 Corinthians 13 from the wedding party and reads it to the local church. Do you want to exercise, practice, enact, embody, and define the glorious love of heaven, he asks us? Then do it in a local church, a church where factions are pitted against one another (1 Cor. 1:12–13), where people have big heads (4:8), where members are sleeping with their fathers' wives (5:2), where members are suing and defrauding one another (6:1–8), where members are getting drunk on the communion wine and not leaving enough for others (11:21–22), where spiritual gift one-upmanship is rife (chaps. 12, 14), where the meetings arc threatened by disorder (14:40), and where some are saying there is no resurrection of the dead (15:12). Bind and submit yourself and your gifts to *these* kinds of people. Love them with patience and kindness, without envy or boasting, without arrogance or rudeness, not insisting on our own way, not irritably or resentfully, not rejoicing at wrongdoing but rejoicing at the truth.

People often complain about the sinners they find in the local church, and with good reason. It's filled with sinners, which is why Paul calls Christians to love one another by bearing all things, believing all things, hoping all things, enduring all things. If you won't love such backstabbers and defrauders like this, don't talk about your spiritual gifts, your vast biblical knowledge, or all the things you do for the poor. You are just a noisy gong. Don't talk about your love for all Christians everywhere; you are just a clanging cymbal. But if you do practice loving a specific, concrete people, all of whose names you don't get to choose, then you will participate in defining love for the world, the love which will characterize the church on the last day perfectly because it images the self-sacrificing and merciful love of Christ perfectly.

In short, our obligations to the body require us to submit to the local church. When a Christian commits or covenants with a particular local church, he or she takes ownership of the discipleship of every member, "that there may be no division in the body, but that the members *may have the same care for one another*" (1 Cor. 12:25). He or she will suffer together with those who suffer; he or she will rejoice with those who are honored (v. 26). To submit ourselves to the whole body and every member means that we not only give *of* ourselves, it means we give ourselves to the body.

4) The biblical commands to submit to our overseers require it. Just as submitting to the apostolic church means submitting concretely to a local church, so submitting to a local church will involve submitting to actual individuals in the body. Sometimes this will mean submitting to another member, as when a brother or sister calls upon us to turn away from sin. Jesus said, "If your brother sins against you, go and tell him his fault, between you and him alone. If he listens to you, you have gained your brother" (Matt. 18:15). Every member of the body can exercise this authority over every other member in the body precisely because it's Christ's authority that finally rules in the congregation, and every instance of rule is merely a representation of his.

At the same time, certain individuals in the congregation will and should be recognized for the fact that their lives present a commendable example to every believer. Over time they have demonstrated the fact that their lives are above reproach, that they are "one-woman men," sober-minded, self-controlled, respectable, hospitable, able to teach, not drunkards, not violent but gentle, not quarrelsome, not lovers of money (1 Tim. 3:2–3). They have demonstrated the ability to shepherd or pastor their families, their "little church," as Luther called it, which gives credibility to the fact that they might shepherd the "big church" (see 1 Tim. 3:4–5). They have demonstrated these things over time. They are not recent converts (1 Tim. 3:6). As part of submitting to the church,

Christians should submit to these overseers, elders, or pastors.[64] Paul describes them as having "oversight" (Acts 20:28). Peter tells the congregation to "be subject" to the elders (1 Pet. 5:5). The author of Hebrews tells the church, "Obey your leaders and submit to them, for they are keeping watch over your souls, as those who will have to give an account" (Heb. 13:17a). Doing so blesses the one who submits. The author continues, "Let them do this with joy and not with groaning, for that would be of no advantage to you" (v. 17b). Apparently, submitting to our leaders is to our advantage.

Is the authority of church pastors and elders predicated on the authority Jesus handed the apostolic church in Matthew 16? Obviously, the Roman Catholic Church and perhaps others would say that it is, but I'm not so sure. The authority of Matthew 16 is the effectual power to bind and loose on earth, and it's an authority that's to be exercised by the entire church. By "effectual," I mean that it achieves what it commands. If the church says that an individual is excluded, he is excluded. Yet neither in this passage nor in any other do we see a connection between this organizational charter and the office of elder or overseer.

The authority of an elder or pastor is more organic. It's something that's recognized and affirmed by the congregation. Truly, Jesus gives pastors and teachers to the congregation as good gifts, just like he gave apostles and prophets (Eph. 4:8–11), but nowhere are we told that pastors and teachers are used to establish the foundation of the church, as we are told about apostles and prophets (Eph. 2:20). Therefore, where Rome describes the bishop as of the essence (*esse*) of the church, Protestants typically say that pastors and teachers are not of the essence. Christ has given them for the benefit of the church (*bene esse*). As such, their authority is not effectual. They cannot command or formally require a member or even the church to do something, as an apostle can.[65] Church members are commanded to obey them, but that obedience is to extend no further than where the Bible prescribes because the authority is Jesus', not the pastor's. In other words, Jesus can command me to submit to you, but you cannot command me to submit to you.

A pastor, for example, cannot command a Christian man to marry a particular Christian woman. A pastor cannot even effectually command him not to marry a non-Christian woman. However, a pastor can instruct a Christian man not to marry a non-Christian woman, in light of the Scriptures (2 Cor. 6:14). Indeed, he must; and, indeed, the Christian should submit, because his pastor is instructing him out of the Scriptures. Nevertheless, there is no passage in

---

[64]Since the three titles of overseer or bishop (*episcopos*), elder (*presbuteros*), and shepherd/pastor (*poimain*) are used interchangeably in the New Testament, I understand them to refer to the same office. See, for instance, Acts 20:17 and 20:28; 1 Pet. 5:1–2; or compare 1 Tim. 3:1 and Titus 1:5.

[65]See Acts 16:18; 1 Cor. 5:3; 2 Cor. 2:10; 8:8; Phil. 4:8; 2 Thess. 4:4, 6, 10.

Scripture that tells me that an elder or overseer, one or many, bears the effectual authority of Matthew 16 to bind and loose for disobedience. The church, of course, can. It can unilaterally exclude someone from membership.

As we compare the church's authority with the elder's authority, we can employ the age-old distinction between authority of counsel and authority of command. The elders have the authority of counsel; the church has the authority of command.[66] Interestingly, Paul's interactions with Philemon present a place where he could have invoked the authority of command, but he has instead set a good example for pastors by invoking the authority of counsel. He says to Philemon, "Though I am bold enough in Christ to command you to do what is required, yet for love's sake I prefer to appeal to you" (Philem. 8–9).

No doubt, Presbyterians, Anglicans, and others will disagree with me on this point since they regard the church as present in the session or as present in the bishop, but here is where I commend the congregational model as more consistent with the New Testament and as a guard against abuses of authority, since the authority of command is spread over the entire congregation.

In short, the New Testament command to submit to our overseers requires us to submit to a local church, even if on a slightly different basis from that presented in Matthew 16. Surely all these matters work in concert.

5) The nature of our salvation requires it. At a couple of places above I have employed phrases or analogies that we are now in a position to bring to the surface more clearly. I have said that the local church is to embody the life of the eschatological church, that we are to put flesh on our professions by joining the local church, and that submitting to a local church is how we submit to Christ. All these ideas depend on the underlying point that a relationship exists between our faith and our deeds, and that relationship finds an expression in the difference between the universal church and the local church. Our faith is an eschatological faith. It is given by heaven. And that eschatological faith, if it's true, will put on deeds. Likewise, our membership in the universal church is an eschatological membership. It too is given by heaven, and that eschatological membership, if it's true, will put on an earthly membership. The universal church is to the local church as faith is to deeds. Indeed, there is a reason why Protestant and Catholic differences over the church are closely bound together with their differences of faith and deeds. The Roman Catholic Church fuses the eschatological church and the visible church on earth, just as it fuses faith and deeds.

A parallel relationship abides between the declaratory righteousness we have in Christ and the works of righteousness we pursue. The first is given

---

[66]Some would say that an authority of counsel is not authority at all, e.g., James Bannerman, *The Church of Christ*, vol. 2 (Carlisle, PA: Banner of Truth, 1974), 239–40.

by heaven; the second we do. A man who claims to be righteous in Christ yet makes no effort to pursue a life of righteousness is, at best, self-deceived. Likewise, a woman who claims to love all Christians everywhere but does not love her Christian sister is likewise self-deceived. Both are hypocrites. They are nominal Christians—Christians in name only—because their profession does not translate into action or reality. They claim a positional status before the throne of God, but nothing in their lives commends the reality of that status, as if God were a fool who could be mocked (Gal. 6:7). Their faith is without works, which, James tells us, is a dead faith. It's meaningless. It's hot air, even if they think that they really, really mean it. The kingdom of Christ is about reality—a new reality, not the illusory old one.

So too with one who claims to belong to the church without belonging to a church. I fear that he looks very much like a nominal Christian and a hypocrite. The apostolic church on earth was given the authority to bind and loose. What else can we conclude about someone who professes to belong to the church but will not submit to an apostolic church on earth? As the apostle John puts it, "He who does not love his brother whom he has seen cannot love God whom he has not seen" (1 John 4:20).

Christ loves his people, and he means to change and grow them. He does this by asserting his authority over them, because Christ's authority is the power of creation, the power of life. Christ's authority is the license given him by the Father to author, shape, order, build, and generally enact all the demands of his generous and compassionate love as he pleases. Astoundingly, he handed this authority to the first twelve men he saved, and he told them to hand that authority on to others, who in turn were to hand it on to still others, and others, and others. Christian life and growth occur upon the humming energy field of the church's authority, because that authority energizes life. If we pull ourselves out from under the umbrellas of the local church's authority, we remove ourselves from God's ordained means of growth.

Most well-trained Protestants will probably respond to these statements by saying, "No, it's submission to the Word that counts. The Word, not the church, is what grows the church." That objection is partially correct. Submission to Christ's Word converts and grows the Christian, because conformity to Christ is the goal, not conformity to the church, per se. But it is the church that speaks the Word, and it is the church where each believer has the occasion to submit to the Word.

For instance, the Word commands us to forgive as we have been forgiven. That's an authoritative pronouncement from Christ. If we refuse to forgive a brother, then, it's the church that will act on Christ's behalf, first in exhorting and then in disciplining us for our failure to repent. The church might, in one way or another, be mistaken in any given exercise of authority. Still, Christ left the church in charge, because it's through our practice of submitting to other believers that we enact our obedience to Christ. Children obey God by obeying their parents, and this grows them. On slightly other terms and within different bounds, Christians obey God by obeying their fellow believers and the church as a whole, and this *grows* us. We submit to one another, as Paul puts it, out of reverence for Christ (Eph. 5:21).

Paul's image of the physical body illustrates this precisely. As the foot submits to the hand, insofar as the foot has something to gain from the differently gifted hand, the whole body grows (1 Corinthians 12). As each member submits to the teaching of the pastors and teachers, the whole body grows (Eph. 4:11–12). As each member submits to other members by outdoing one another in showing honor, the whole body grows (Rom. 12:10). Our personal discipleship with Christ and our love for other people should rest in the same hand as our church membership. Growth in the love of the gospel and church membership should work together, like content and form work together. Church membership—our submission to the local church—is what Christ intends in order that our discipleship take shape and grow.

In short, the nature of our salvation and the relationship between faith and deeds require Christians to submit to the local church. Submitting to a local church, or what we typically speak of as "joining a local church," is faith putting on deeds. To use another analogy, it's a word putting on flesh. A Christian must choose to join a church, just as a Christian must choose to submit to Christ, but having chosen Christ, a Christian has no choice but to choose a church to join.

6) *The nature of our new identity requires it.* Opponents of regenerate church membership often criticize the practice for its voluntarism, that is, the idea that a Christian must join a church voluntarily. After all, Anabaptists, Baptists, and others who went the way of the Radical Reformation advocated believer's baptism and regenerate church membership over against infant baptism. The concern about voluntarism is that it leads to individualism, free agency, and a diminishment of the church as God's corporate people.

Since I am a Baptist and a congregationalist by conviction, I believe the criticism is, in part, misplaced. At the same time, it may be that some advocates of regenerate church membership, along the way, have leaned too far toward voluntaristic assumptions about life in the local church. What's seldom picked up in the old confessions, whether free church or Reformed, is the notion that the Christian life *must* be lived through the local church because Christ has made us members of his body. The old confessions sometimes refer to Christ's command to unite with local churches, but what they miss is the fact that the command emerges out of our new identity. Christ commands us to join a local body because we already *are* members of his body. The imperative follows the indicative. The structure of Ephesians 2 presents this argument. The first half describes our reconciliation with God through Christ (2:1–10). The second half then explains the immediate implication of our reconciliation with God. We are reconciled with all those who likewise belong to God: Christ has created in himself "one new man in place of the two" (Eph. 2:15). Those who were formerly divided are now "fellow citizens with the saints and members of the household of God" (Eph. 2:19). Since we belong, we must belong. Faith must put on deeds.

By this same token, saying that Christians should belong to a local church merely because it's advantageous for living the Christian life, or in Calvin's words, "the external means or aids by which God invites us into the society of Christ and holds us therein," misses the point that the church body is now part and parcel of a Christian's identity.[67] An adopted son attends the family dinner with his new brothers and sisters not just because it's good for him but because that's what he *is*—a member of the family.

THE WEIGHTINESS OF LOCAL CHURCH MEMBERSHIP

Today, we don't believe that authority belongs to the church; it belongs to the consumer who asserts his rule through his presence and pocketbook. Instead of calling consumers to submit to the lordship of Christ, the church does all it can to cater to the consumer. The preacher pulls up a stool and plays the comedian. The minister of music closes his eyes, leans back, and lays into a guitar riff. The church "audience" is delighted—for a while.

One of the chief tragedies of evangelicalism today is that it has lost sight of the wonderful, life-giving force of authority. We've been carried away by culture. More than we realize, we view ourselves as independent agents charged with determining how best to grow, serve, and love in the faith. Yes, we may listen to others, defer to others, and accept guidance from others, but in the final analysis we view ourselves as our own coaches, portfolio managers, guides, judges, and the captains of our own ships in a manner that is more cultural than biblical. In short, an underdeveloped theology conspires with our anti-authority and individualistic instincts to deceive us into claiming that we love all Christians everywhere equally while excusing ourselves from loving any of those Christians specifically, especially submissively. Unsurprisingly, churches are shallow, Christians are weak, and God's people look like the world.

But what if local churches were to recover the understanding that each stands as a proxy for Christ? Each church is his representative on earth. Con-

---

[67]See Kevin Vanhoozer, "Evangelicalism and the Church: The Company of the Gospel," in *The Futures of Evangelicalism: Issues and Prospects*, ed. Craig Bartholomew, Robin Parry, and Andrew West (Grand Rapids: Kregel, 2003). Cf. Michael Sandel, *Liberalism and the Limits of Justice* (New York: Cambridge University Press, 1982).

sider, then, the weightiness of accepting members. Consider the weightiness of saying goodbye to those who move to another city; much more the weightiness of excluding them. If churches were to undertake such considerations, receiving members would be treated more like an adoption. "Are the child's papers in order? Have all the necessary questions been asked by both sides of the adoption? How can we best serve and protect this child?" Saying goodbye to members as they depart for another city would feel like saying goodbye to a precious son as he leaves home. "Let us know when you arrive safely. Let us know if you need money. Find good friends. Remain steady in what we've taught you. We love you."

Step 7: How then can we formally define local church membership and discipline? As the forming or breaking of a covenant between a Christian and a church.

Defining Church Membership and Discipline

This brings us to our definitions of church membership and discipline. Consider these definitions in the context of what we said that love is: the lover's affirmation of and affection for the beloved and the beloved's good in the Holy. It's a love that leads to the activities of glory seeking and holiness seeking. It wants to see the holy and affirm it wherever it lies waiting to be acknowledged. Yet not only does it seek out the holy in order to affirm it, but it wants to see it increase and grow in the life of the beloved. Therefore, this love will exercise all the authority Christ has given it to author even more life and glory in the object of its love.

DEFINING MEMBERSHIP

With these ideas in mind, let's start with a one-sentence definition of church membership. *Church membership is (1) a covenant of union between a particular church and a Christian, a covenant that consists of (2) the church's affirmation of the Christian's gospel profession, (3) the church's promise to give oversight to the Christian, and (4) the Christian's promise to gather with the church and submit to its oversight.*

Notice that several elements are present. First, a church body *affirms* an individual's profession of faith and baptism as credible. Next, it promises *to give oversight* to that individual's faith. The individual then *submits* his or her life to the service and authority of this particular body and its leaders. This entire exchange can be summarized with the word *covenant*. Both church and Christian give themselves (not just give of themselves) to the other, albeit in different capacities. Principally, the church body says to the individual, "We recognize your profession of faith, baptism, and discipleship to Christ as valid. Therefore, we publicly affirm and acknowledge you as belonging to Christ and the oversight of our fellowship. We will give ourselves to the growth and celebration of Christ's holy love in you." Principally, the individual says to the church body, "Insofar as I recognize you as a faithful, gospel-declaring church, I submit my presence and my discipleship to your love and oversight. I give myself to the growth and celebration of holy love in you."

Affirmation. Speaking in terms of the church's affirmation of someone's faith means that church does not create faith but only affirms it. It affirms the holy. Salvation does not derive from unity with the bishop or the Eucharist, as in Roman Catholic or Orthodox sacramental conceptions of church member-ship. Churches have the authority only to affirm faith, not to give it. Salvation is by grace alone through faith alone. Contrary to the older Roman Catholic Church's teaching, there is salvation outside the visible, institutional church.

Another way to say this would be that the church's authority is both medi-ated and declarative. It's not absolute or *ex opere operato*. All authority in the church ultimately belongs to Christ the king, and individual Christians will ultimately give an account to him, not to the pope or the pastor. And, as we have already seen, the church does not have the authority to keep one whom Christ has united to himself from itself. In that sense, I don't like Calvin's description (and Cyprian's) of the church as a mother, even if Calvin means it in a purely instrumental fashion. The church's authority to unite an individual to itself is nothing more than the authority to affirm what Christ has made him or her. We might as well say that an ambassador or a White House press secretary mothers his leader's decisions or actions. The metaphors of representative or ambassador better describe the role that the church plays in this context rather than that of mother. Strikingly, however, God does use fallible and often fool-ish churches and leaders to represent his authority in giving an affirmation or denial on earth as a foreshadowing of what will be ultimately affirmed or denied in heaven. Whereas in Genesis 1 God pronounced that his creation was good, now the church, standing in for Christ on earth, publicly affirms God's new creation as good.

Some authors today critique the idea of church membership as a bounded set because it reminds them of the standard-setting Pharisees, and they don't want to say that joining a church means passing some bar or living up to some standard. That instinct is partly right. I assume churches *could* view membership in the same spirit as the apostles' wrongheaded question, "Who is the greatest in the kingdom of heaven?" (Matt. 18:1). At the same time Jesus himself presents a kind of standard: a person must profess Jesus' name and present the basic posture of humbling oneself like a little child (vv. 3–5). We are not looking to affirm people who are perfect. No, we must be willing to forgive them seventy times seven times (vv. 21–22). But they must understand the gospel and demonstrate the fruit of repentance, including the ability to forgive others (vv. 23–35).

Giving oversight. The church's affirmation is not a onetime event to be followed up with indifference and neglect, like the false shepherds of Israel who let the sheep wander off into the hills. It's not about simply affirming doctrinal content and hopping over the boundary. Rather, the church's love should be a persevering, enduring love, one that longs to keep its members gathered beneath its wings. It's also an instructive and authoritative love, one that burns to author growth and holiness in an individual's life, that he or she might increasingly image the Savior, encouraging the individual from one degree of glory to the next (2 Cor. 3:18). Jesus charges the church to teach disciples everything he has commanded.

Submission. Speaking in terms of the individual's submission to the church body, aside from being biblical, will help us avoid another extreme—the foolhardy idea that, since faith does not depend on the church, a Christian can get along just fine without belonging to a local church. Speaking of submission (not just of relationship) is the true guard against modern individualism. Christians are obligated to submit to a local church and its leaders by virtue of their membership in the universal body of Christ, in the same way Christians are obligated to pursue a life of righteousness by virtue of the alien righteousness they have been granted in Christ. A man should not claim to belong to *the* church without belonging to *a* church. In that sense, speaking of church membership as voluntary, though technically correct, doesn't quite do the matter justice. This is one reason that the language of *submission* is good. Joining a local church, like pursuing a life of righteousness, is a matter of necessary obedience to Christ. It's about an ongoing relationship, not a onetime event. There is a Protestant spin we can give to the Catholic phrase, "There is no salvation outside the (visible, institutional) church." The authority of the church is mediated. But the Christian who demonstrates an inability to submit to divinely decreed human mediators demonstrates what appears to be an inability to submit to Christ the king.

To put it more positively, an individual submits to a church like a young, unformed player submits to his coach's discipline and drills, or a young pianist submits to the teacher's scales and lessons. It's like the dirt presenting itself to Adam saying, "Plow me, cultivate me, bring forth a harvest from me." That is what we do with our hearts when we submit them to the church's authority— we ask to be *authored* upon for the sake of the Holy, and this submission gives way to exercising authority in the lives of others. We give our hands, feet, and breath to working in their lives—tilling, weeding, and planting seeds.

A covenant. Though we might speak of committing to or joining a church, a Christian does not simply commit to or join a church. To merely commit is the action of one who retains ultimate sovereignty over his life but chooses, for whatever reasons, to enter into some type of contract. The idea of *covenant*, on the other hand, certainly involves the activity of making a commitment, but it involves more. A covenant articulates and formalizes a relationship that already exists. It explains how the very identities of each party in the relationship are changed by that relationship, and then it gives expression to the responsibilities, obligations, entitlements, prerogatives, and freedoms of that relationship. A commitment creates something out of nothing. A covenant explicitly affirms what, in a sense, already exists. A commitment can be rescinded without a change to one's public identity. A covenant cannot. We will pick up this idea of a covenant in the next chapter.

DEFINING CHURCH DISCIPLINE

Bound up in the covenant of church membership is the idea of church discipline. It's the other side of the coin. What is church discipline? In the broadest terms, it's what constitutes a significant part of Christian discipleship. Notice that the words *discipline* and *disciple* share a common root; both words are about education. More specifically, a church disciplines its members for the sake of discipling them. That is, it disciplines them to educate them in the way of Christ's righteousness to help them conform to his image. Just as education involves both formation and correction, so church discipline involves both formation and correction. Teachers teach and teachers correct. That's how students grow. Churches, likewise, teach and correct. That's how church members grow in their discipleship to Christ. An undisciplined church membership is an undiscipled church membership. It will be weak and flabby, foolish and unchaste.

Our concern here is specifically with corrective church discipline. If we compare church membership to a marriage covenant—like the covenant God made with the nation of Israel—then corrective church discipline begins informally with the threat of divorce in response to unfaithfulness. Formal church discipline is, then, the divorce itself. It's excluding someone from the church body. To use the education analogy, church discipline begins informally with correction and the threat of a failing grade. It occurs formally when the teacher fails and expels the student who is utterly noncompliant and recalcitrant.

To define it more specifically, *corrective church discipline occurs any time sin is corrected within the church body, and it occurs most fully when the church body announces that the covenant between church and member is already broken because the member has proven to be unsubmissive in his or her discipleship to Christ. By this token, the church withdraws its affirmation of the individual's faith, announces that it will cease giving oversight, and releases the individual back into the world.*

Every church disciplines its members formatively. That is, every church, even the unhealthy ones, teaches its members something. However, most churches fail to discipline their members correctively, either personally and informally or as an act of formal church discipline. This formal act is also known as excommunication, because it excludes an individual from the recognized communion of the church. A church that teaches its members but never corrects them is like a teacher that gives every student an A+ grade, whether the student turns in good work or bad. Christians will learn and grow for a time apart from corrective church discipline, but eventually the lines between good work and bad will become hazy in the body as a whole because everyone is receiving an A+ grade. In time, fewer and fewer Christians will do good work at all, because good work is always harder and takes more self-sacrifice (see 1 Cor. 9:24–27). That's why the undisciplined church becomes fat and flabby. Eventually, it's difficult to see the difference between the church and the world.

Corrective church discipline is the church's response to the unholy within itself. It's what that Bible says should happen when a member chooses to love a particular sin over and above Christ. To speak in the language of authority, the member has reverted to following his or her own rule, just like Adam and Eve did in Genesis 3. The church offers the member several remonstrations concerning the consequences of unrepentant sin, yet the member essentially says (at least with his or her actions), "I don't care. I love this sin. I love my autonomy—being a law unto myself. I refuse to abandon it, even if the King says otherwise in his Word." The individual may still, ironically, profess to be a Christ follower and a citizen of Christ's kingdom, but the profession sounds fraudulent, so the church corporately determines to withhold the bread and cup of Communion. The individual is ex-Communion-ed. If the believer continues in unrepentant sin, the covenant between body and member formally ends as an expression of the fact that the individual's belonging to the new covenant of Christ appears to be false.

MEMBERSHIP AND DISCIPLINE AN IMPLICATION OF GOSPEL LOVE

If love is "the lover's affirmation of and affection for the beloved and the beloved's good in the holy," then it's almost difficult to understand why Christians would ever oppose the idea of church membership and discipline. If Christians love Christ, they will want to affirm his presence wherever it shows up. They will want to protect it, display it, and see it grow. "Do you belong to our Savior? Let us affirm you, oversee you, serve you, encourage you." Church membership is a clear implication of gospel love, and Christ has handed the church a charter to do exactly that.

Church discipline, too, is a clear implication of God-centered gospel love. It's an inevitable and loving tool in a world where Christ's kingdom has been inaugurated but not consummated. If God's love was centered on man, then discipline would be cruel, and to those who remain convinced of Satan's God-toppling lie (Gen. 3:5), it will always sound that way. Yet for the holiness-seeking church, church discipline is the refusal to call the unholy "holy." It's a way of removing an affirmation so that self-deception no longer reigns. In radical defiance of the wisdom of this world, it helps to clarify exactly what love is.

Step 8: This covenant between a Christian and a local church does not remove a Christian's responsibilities to other Christians, but it does give a Christian more responsibility over the members of his or her church.

A Church and Other Churches

After explaining my definition of church membership to a friend, he asked the simple question, "So what's the difference between my relationship with a Christian who belongs to my church and one who does not?" That is a great question, and a second question follows: how should a church interact with a Christian under the authority of another local church?

PERSONAL OBLIGATIONS

Suppose I have two friends: Shane, a fellow member of my local church, and Doug, a member of a different local church. Do my biblical obligations to Shane and Doug, as a Christian to Christians, differ because one is a member of my local church and one is not? Surely I am called, occasion permitting, to encourage, love, serve, carry the burdens of, forgive, rebuke, give money to, and pray for each. They, in turn, are obligated to me, occasion permitting, in the same ways. Paul commends the example of the Macedonians, for instance, for giving so generously to the church in Jerusalem (2 Cor. 8:1–5). I don't believe there's much disagreement between Christians about this much. Everybody sees the one-another commands in Scripture and concedes that we should love, serve, and encourage other Christians because we all belong to one body in Christ. But do my biblical responsibilities toward the two men differ in any way whatsoever because one is a member of my local church and the other is not?

Shane and I have both formally submitted our life and discipleship to a particular group of Christians (consisting of elders, deacons, and laypeople) to whom Doug has not submitted. That means that a particular group of Christians has affirmed and taken responsibility for my faith and Shane's faith in a way that they have not affirmed and taken responsibility for Doug's faith. It means that Shane and I have covenanted to oversee one another's discipleship in a way that we have not covenanted with Doug—even though we love Doug and are committed to him in many ways as a fellow Christian. It's not that we're not one in Christ with Doug. It's just that, on this earth, no one church has the infinite resources capable of responsibly overseeing every pilgrim. For the sake of responsibly stewarding our resources and time, I agree to help oversee one body, while you agree to help oversee another. It's a team effort. We're all playing for the same team, but that team meets in a number of locations with a number of coaches.

The practice of church discipline presents one concrete illustration of how our commitments to one another differ. As members of the same church, Shane is accountable to me, and I to Shane, in a way neither of us is to Doug. Should Doug begin engaging in a lifestyle of sin, I would no doubt bear some level of obligation to rebuke him as a Christian brother, perhaps severely. Depending on the circumstances of his sin, I might even say, "Doug, given your unrepentant lifestyle decisions, I'm not sure why you continue to call yourself a Christian." Yet that's the limit. As one Christian to another, that's all I can do. My powers and responsibilities go this far and no farther. Should Shane begin engaging in a lifestyle of unrepentant sin, the Bible grants me an even greater level of responsibility and authority.

I would be called to participate together with my local church in enacting a public ceremony that bears all the symbolic meaning that Shane's baptism bore but indicates that Shane has moved in the opposite direction. Just as Shane's baptism symbolized his reconciliation with Christ and his admittance into the fellowship of Christ's universal church, so our local church's collective act of discipline or excommunication would symbolize his estrangement from Christ and his removal from the fellowship of Christ's universal church. Like baptism, it's a public act enacted locally that bears meaning universally. The responsibility and authority do not belong to me as an individual, but I share them with the entire congregation with whom Shane and I have an especial commitment. As we have seen, Jesus has given the local church a power that he does not give to lone individuals—the power to bind some things and to loose others on earth (Matt. 18:18; cf. 16:19).

CHURCH OBLIGATIONS

How then should churches view Christians who belong to other churches? For instance, should my church respect the affirmation that Doug's church gave to Doug? Can he receive the Lord's Supper at our church? If he is a baptized member of another gospel-preaching local church in good standing, yes.[68] If church member Doug is visiting our church, we should receive him as a brother, and we should do so not simply because he professes faith but because another

---

[68] For my discussion of how this pertains to the Lord's Supper and "fencing the table," see chap. 6.

congregation that gives oversight to this brother affirms him in the faith. It vouches for him.

This is what we see in the New Testament. Paul tells Philemon to receive Onesimus as a brother (Philem. 17), and Paul seems to intend for the church that meets in Philemon's house to take notice of whether he does (Philem. 2). John rejoices because the church of Gaius lovingly received the workers John's church had sent (3 John 3–8), and he scorns Diotrephes for not giving a welcome to the brothers (3 John 10). The boundary line of affirmation, oversight, and submission practiced by one local church hardly means that a church can be closed off to the members of other churches. In fact, it's just the opposite. It should respect the authority of all other gospel-believing churches, and it should receive their members, just like a family should receive guests.

At the same time, this reception must be temporary. The longer a member stays away from his home church, the less capable that home church becomes of giving meaningful oversight. Eventually, a church that has been welcoming someone from another church should encourage the individual to return to the place and people to whom he has committed or to transfer his membership; that is, he should come under the oversight of the new church. Either way, the individual should be living in submission to the one body of Christ by submitting to one particular manifestation of it.

By the same token, one church should respect and heed another church's act of discipline. Should Doug undergo the discipline of his church, my church should respect the authority of that church. This is what we find in the Scriptures. The apostle John tells another church, "If anyone comes to you and does not bring this teaching, do not receive him into your house [probably meaning *church*] or give him any greeting" (2 John 10). John may not be referring to a disciplined individual, per se, but he is referring to a teacher who does not carry the apostolic gospel and, in that sense, is under the discipline of every apostolic church. Such an individual should not be welcomed or received by a local church.

That does not mean that an individual who has been unfairly treated and disciplined by one church should be shunned by every local church. Nothing prevents a church from doing a little of its own due diligence. Indeed, every church should, in order to properly steward its authority.

At the same time, we must emphasize the fact that churches today need to recapture the respect and deference they owe to other congregations that also belong to Christ's body. For instance, when a baptized Christian leaves one church and presents him- or herself for membership in another church, the receiving church potentially reinforces an individualistic conception of Christianity by showing no interest in the previous church's affirmation of the individual. It would be wrong to require people to show the prospective new church their licensure or ID or accreditation from the previous church, the way we might ask to see the badge of a plainclothes police officer. After all, every local church has the authority to grant such licensure. Still, a church that fails to ask a baptized Christian about previous church affiliations may be implicitly communicating that Christians are all free agents, free to come and go as they please.

In sum, every local church should adopt a posture of openness and love as well as deference and respect toward other churches and their members, since all are together participating in the one body of Christ. Perhaps few churches have better exemplified such posture than the churches of Macedonia, whom Paul found "begging us earnestly for the favor of taking part in the relief of the saints" in spite of their "extreme poverty" (2 Cor. 8:4).

At the same time, the covenant of union between a Christian and a local church means that we acquire more responsibility—both formally and informally—for the members of our own church than for the members of others. This is what families do, of course, in caring for their children. It's not that I as a father don't care for another family's children, or that I wouldn't give myself sacrificially to them should the occasion require it. Yet God has made me the unique steward of my children, which means that I should pour more time and love into them than another's. It also means that I am charged with instructing and disciplining them in a way others are not.

Conclusion

In 1 Corinthians 5, Paul calls on the Corinthian church members to protect the gospel by no longer identifying themselves with the man committing a sin that even non-Christians would question. They are the people in the city of Corinth who publicly "assemble in the name of our Lord Jesus" by the authority of Christ's charter. Therefore, they are responsible on Jesus' behalf to ensure that this man is not allowed to publicly identify himself with Jesus. They should heed the charter by breaking his connection to their corporate name. They should withdraw their affirmation and oversight. They should exclude him. They should remove him from membership. His profession of faith no longer appears credible because his life decisions have the appearance of someone on the path to damnation. Paul cannot know for certain that this man is not a Christian, but the church still needs to speak for Jesus. Since the man is unrepentantly acting like a non-Christian, Paul, in love, exhorts them to treat him like one by removing him. Paul's goal, clearly, goes beyond holding God's people together. He's interested in marking off God's people for the sake of Christians in the church, the Corinthian public at large, the name of Christ, and this man—for the sake of preserving and protecting the gospel.

Paul knows that a symbiotic relationship exists between the church's form and content, between its structure and its gospel. You cannot bump matters of church structure into the category of "peripheral and unimportant" and expect to preserve the gospel in the face of hypocrites and heretics. Certainly churches need to "renew their centers" and to articulate doctrine rightly in order to preserve it. But churches also need boundaries, structures, and authority. I don't just mean doctrinal boundaries signed by the leaders of evangelicalism's various societies and movements or boundaries that a seminary might lay down. I mean the boundaries that belong around the biblical institution of local churches. This is the tool that Christ has given the church on earth to enforce such statements of faith and vibrant doctrinal centers, as Satan employs hypocrites and heretics to destroy the church.

When a seminary moves toward unorthodoxy, for instance, the fault does not finally lie with the seminary; it lies with whichever churches the straying professors attended.[69] Theologian Carl Trueman gets it just right when he says:

> The . . . problem with the way evangelicalism now functions is that it has weakened the church. Because it requires the marginalizing of ecclesiastical distinctives such as views on baptism and church government, evangelicalism and its institutions cannot, in theory, replace the church. Furthermore, the whole problem of accountability is a hardy perennial for parachurch organizations, from seminaries to academic fellowships like the Evangelical Theological Society. The problem is that, in practice, evangelical institutions come to supplant the church, even though they are not designed to fulfill that role. For some they become the key theaters of action, the forums in which little fish can be big shots, and the deviant and heretical can flourish without proper accountability. For others they become the primary centers of Christian identity, the reason why they become evangelicals first, and Presbyterian or Baptist or Pentecostal only second.[70]

It is the local church, not unaccountable organizations and financially motivated publishing houses, that are called to discipline such members, no matter how many academic degrees those members hold or books they have published. The same is true whenever pastors, bishops, movements, or whole denominations move toward unorthodoxy. Paul makes this remarkably clear in Galatians 1. He chastises not the false teachers but the churches themselves for listening to a false gospel. It's the members of the church who will finally have to stand before God and give an account for whether they tolerated a false gospel. A recent illustration of this occurred when a number of local churches belonging to the Episcopal Church of America (ECUSA) voted as congregations

---

[69]This point comes from Mark Dever.
[70]Carl Trueman, "Confessions of a Bog-Standard Evangelical," in *Reformation 21: The Online Magazine of the Alliance of Confessing Evangelicals*, issue 28 (January 2008), http://www.reformation21.org/Counterpoints/Counterpoints/373/vobId__6997/.

to secede from the ECUSA and unite themselves to several Anglican bishops in Africa.

We began the chapter with Kevin Vanhoozer's "mere ecclesiology." We can appreciate the pulsing gospel heart of his proposal, as well as the evangelical impulse to affirm the essentials and not divide over nonessentials, but the formula isn't as simple as gospel = essential; polity = nonessential, especially when it's the nonessentials that God means to use to protect the essentials. Sturdy concrete structures are not as important as human beings, but in a hurricane they are pretty important, and we want our loved ones inside those structures. As such, we need to make our ecclesiology one or two steps less *mere* by encouraging leaders and members of every polity to see once again the significance of their polity.

What we haven't yet done in our argument for membership is to consider a little more carefully the very thing that Vanhoozer's essay does so well, namely, explain how the church on earth is an implication of the gospel. Our focus has been on the institutional side of things—the charter. In order to get the whole picture, we need to spend a little more time considering the church's pulsing gospel heart and how the gospel fits together with this charter. That requires us to consider the biblical idea of covenant, which we turn to now.

CHAPTER FIVE

THE COVENANT OF LOVE

"Love is a burning thing, and it makes a fiery ring."
—*Johnny Cash*

Main Question: What exactly is this commitment or "covenant" of local church membership?

Main Answer: The commitment believers make to one another to form a local church is a covenant-like commitment. Since Christ has identified them with him through his new covenant, and since he has authorized them to identify themselves with him through his charter, they covenant together in such a fashion that his name is protected and their good is promoted.

For several years now, a friend of mine, Josh, has wanted to be a missionary to a restricted-access nation in the Middle East, yet over the last year Josh's love has dramatically grown for the local church in Washington DC, of which we are both members. He's become more committed to what God is doing through these people, and that has affected how Josh has been thinking through his desire for overseas missions. Recently Josh described to me the evolution of his thoughts on the matter. Since I had already begun writing this book, I stopped him mid-sentence, grabbed a pen, and asked him to start over so that I could take down his words. Here's what he said:

> I've always thought that since I had a desire to go to the Farsi-speaking group, it must be God's plan for my life. But since being at this church, and thinking about the ways that God is glorified in submission as we see it modeled in children and parents, husbands and wives, church members and elders, I have begun to consider the possibility that God might be more glorified and my sanctification served by submitting my individual desires and plan for missions to the church's vision for missions—even though that might mean going to a different people group and a different context.

I expect that some evangelicals would respond to my friend, "Josh, if God is calling you to those people, he's calling you to those people. Are you going to deny him like Jonah did?" Other evangelicals, who might have a less mystical understanding of calling, perhaps would more simply say, "Josh, I don't see why it's the church's business to tell you where to go."

I agree that the church cannot tell him where he must go, and I certainly have no intention of wading into a theology of ministerial calling here. Still, it's worth observing the posture of Josh's heart and the woof of his thinking. His understanding of the Christian life is congregation-centered and congregation-shaped. His life and gifts belong to the Lord, not himself, and he doesn't assume he has a perfect read on the Lord's intentions for his life. Rather, he knows he needs help. He understands from Scripture that God has placed other Christians around and over him for doing the work of the ministry together, and sometimes this might mean not doing what he originally planned to do. He does not perceive himself to be a superstar free agent, signing deals with this or that team of Christians in order to best enhance his own spiritual package. He is more like a son speaking up at family dinnertime, asking for counsel from those who love him. He is like a husband or wife who wouldn't dare make a life-impacting decision without doing so with and through the other. He is like a subject of a king, who wouldn't glibly presume to have immediate access to the king's mind without consulting with some of the king's ministers. He is like the hand or foot of a body, which wouldn't think to say to the rest of the body, "I don't need you." Could it be that the person who says, "Josh, forget what the church says," has capitulated far more than he realizes to our individualistic culture?

What if the church to which Josh is thinking about submitting doesn't have a vision for missions? What if the church has a few ornery and seemingly unregenerate old deacons who run the show? What if the church cannot be trusted for any number of reasons? What if the church responds to Josh's desire to do missions like J. R. Ryland supposedly responded to William Carey when Carey said he wanted to take the gospel to India: "Young man, sit down; when God pleases to convert the heathen, he will do it without your aid and mine"? Is this a vision for missions to which Josh should submit? Certainly not. It's not biblical. We can probably imagine a vast number of circumstances in which Josh's ability to submit trustingly to the church's vision for mission could be complicated, requiring careful balances and much wisdom, just like every wife who is called to submit to a sinful husband and every citizen who is called to submit to unjust rulers. Yet the biblical reality remains. Josh is not a free agent in a professional sports league. He is the member of a household, a marriage, a holy nation, a body. That's his identity, so he is thinking through life and ministry decisions in light of who he is biblically.

I can envision some situations in which Josh should slowly, reluctantly, and with the fear of God in his heart, decide to reject the church's counsel because, as best he can discern, it appears to be foolish and unbiblical. I can imagine other situations in which Josh might decide to put his hopes on hold and first devote himself for several years to helping an unhealthy church develop a healthy vision for missions, and then, with that work well underway, go, as sent with glad hearts by the church. I can picture still other situations in which Josh might persuade a church to send a team to his restricted-access nation, or in which they might persuade him to go to another.

In whatever scenario, the point is that Josh knows he should receive the church's counsel in light of the connection between his identity and the church's identity. He understands that he is identified with the church and the church with him, because both are identified with Christ. Therefore, he has ownership in this church. Its successes and failures are his, and his successes and failures belong to the church.

Step 1: We can answer the question of what a "local church covenant" is by considering the relationship between Christ's "charter" (described in chapter 4) and his new covenant.

A Charter and a Covenant?

In chapter 4 we saw that Christ has given his church a commission or a charter that holds it together, marks it off, and protects the gospel. But we skipped a step. Christ gave this apostolic charter to *the church.* Wouldn't that suggest that the church exists prior to the charter? The church universal is not created by the charter but by a covenant, Christ's new covenant. My friend Josh, like every Christian, belongs to the church universal by virtue of Christ's new covenant. This leaves us asking, how does the new covenant relate to the charter? And is the new covenant the same thing as the covenant of membership?

Let's consider the New Testament storyline once more. All this talk about "covenants" and "charters" might seem complicated, but this is the theological challenge we're faced with as we attempt to understand how the Bible's "kingdom" language works together with its "covenant" language as pertains to the local church. Christ came declaring a kingdom, telling people to repent. He meant that he came to rule and bless everyone who would follow. Along the way, he commissioned twelve men to build a church, a society of people who declare allegiance to him, and he gave these men a charter, which they in turn entrusted to the entire church. Then Christ did something more, something in a sense more personal. He held out a covenant—an oath that he sealed with his blood. The covenant promised to forgive sins and to grant the Spirit so Christ's people would follow. After all, those whom he called were still at enmity with him and one another, and they didn't have the power to change. This covenant, amazingly, offered effectual pardon and change.

Today, Christ plants churches with both his charter and his new covenant. To fully understand the existence of the local church and its membership, we need to understand both and how they relate together. Furthermore, we need to understand how these two things yield a local church covenant. Nowhere in the New Testament is the phrase *local church membership* or *local church covenant* mentioned, but these ideas can be clearly inferred. Christians should make such a covenant-like commitment to a body of believers as an indication of, first, their belonging to the new covenant and, second, their submission to Christ's rule. It's required, just like deeds are required of those who profess faith.

Step 2: Church membership involves identifying ourselves with Christ and Christ's people. The work of mutual identification occurs through covenants.

What's Your Name?

At the heart of church membership is the idea of identity. Church membership is about uniting our individual names to Christ's name through uniting our names to his people. It's in this corporate fashion that he identifies with us as individuals, and we with him. Other facets of membership such as accountability and assurance then emerge out of this foundational idea. I am accountable to my father as a child, for instance, because he identifies me as his.

A person's name establishes his or her identity and distinguishes him or her from others. From kindergarten through twelfth grade, my teachers began every academic year by calling roll. Which names belonged to which faces? When God unites an individual to himself, he gives that person a new identity, a new name, because that person is a new creation. The individual has been born again. At several places in Scripture, God even changes certain individuals' names to picture the new identity he gives to all his people—Abram to Abraham, Jacob to Israel, Simon to Peter, Saul to Paul, or all of us today, in a sense, to Christ-ian.[1]

But God doesn't merely give converts a new personal identity; he invites them into a family, a body, a covenant community of holy love. He gives them a new corporate and public identity. When a family adopts a child, the child is given the family name, the name shared by father, mother, sister, and brother. So it is with Christian conversion and adoption. God adopts us as individuals into a family, because he intends to identify himself not with just you or me but with an entire family of children.

---

[1] With regard to Abraham and Israel, I am not trying to argue that they were "born again" in a John 3 sense (though I believe they were). I am simply saying that their being renamed typologically represents or foreshadows the New Testament idea of being born again.

Not only does our new personal identity come in conjunction with our new corporate identity, but our corporate membership publicly affirms our new personal identity. When the human race calls out, "Who here belongs to God?" the church has been authorized to answer, "We do," which in turn affords every member the privilege of saying, "I do." The renaming ceremony is a family event amidst many witnesses—"We baptize you in the name of the Father, Son, and Holy Spirit" (Matt. 28:19–20; 1 Tim. 5:9).[2]

The citizens of liberal democracies often insist upon the distinction between their public and private rights and responsibilities, but there is no neat and clear distinction between the public and the private—or rather, the corporate and the individual—for the Christian. When a person becomes a Christian, his private life and actions begin to represent both Christ and Christ's body whether he means them to or not. He is a member of a family and so he wears the family name—in everything. For example, I might commit a crime all by myself, but if I'm caught, my actions will bring disrepute on my entire family. Likewise, a Christian's life reflects and represents the church, just as the church's life reflects and represents Christ.

- That's why Luke could say that Saul was "ravaging the church" by going house to house and dragging its individual members off to prison (Acts 8:3). *The individuals being persecuted are identified as representatives of the local church in Jerusalem.*

- Christ could speak of Saul's persecution against individual Christians and against the church as persecution against "me" (Acts 9:4). *Christ identifies himself as a representative for his people, whether corporately or individually considered.* (We saw the same in Matthew [18:5; 25:40, 45]).

- Paul could refer to a Christian's sleeping with a prostitute as uniting the members of Christ to a prostitute (1 Cor. 6:15). *The sinning individual is identified as a representative at least for Christ and maybe for the church ("members of Christ").*

- Paul warns us that by "sinning against your brothers and wounding their conscience when it is weak, you sin against Christ" (1 Cor. 8:12). *The individual being sinned against is identified as a representative for Christ.*

- Paul could say that "if one member suffers, all suffer together; if one member is honored, all rejoice together" (1 Cor. 12:26). *The individual members of a church are identified as representatives for one another.*

---

[2]See W. W. J. Van Oene, "Before Many Witnesses," in J. Geertsema, et al., *Before Many Witnesses* (Winnipeg, Manitoba: 1249 Plessis Road, 1975), 9–13, for a meditation on the corporate nature of our confession. As Van Oene puts it, "At your public profession of faith you are not standing as an individual person, but as a member of the Body. . . . Your profession of faith is, so to speak, a community affair."

Notice what's happening in each of these illustrations: one name is substituted for another name or names, like the radio advertisement I recently heard for a Broadway show: "*Time* magazine calls it, 'Outstanding!'" Did *Time* really say "Outstanding!" or did a magazine staff writer say this? A writer did, and the review was probably published with the writer's byline at the top or bottom of the article, but the staff writer's reviews could properly be ascribed by an outside party to the magazine itself. The same is true of a Christian's relation to both his or her church and to Christ. A Christian speaks and acts on behalf of his church and of Christ.[3] Many of the metaphors for the church, such as body and family, point to the same conclusion.

Local churches have been given a charter to bind and loose, include and exclude, exactly because a Christian does represent Christ. Non-Christians in society don't have to understand a biblical theology of headship in order to have their opinions of Jesus impacted by the crass behavior of Christians in the office on Monday morning. When someone starts calling himself a Christian, non-Christians will associate him with Christ. For this reason, churches should take great care when affirming someone as a Christian through baptism and the Lord's Supper. Doing so gives them licensure, as it were, to publicly represent Christ.

Surely, the significance of names and being identified with a larger body is not unique to Christians and churches. The chief official of the king of Babylon gave Daniel and three Hebrew boys new names to establish their Babylonian identity (Dan. 1:7). Citizens of a nation take on the name of the nation. Converts to Islam adopt a new name that indicates their new loyalties. Sports fans emblazon the names of their favorite teams on their jackets and shirts. In general, the name of something establishes its associations, loyalties, and more.

That brings us back to a point made early in chapter 3: the question, "What holds people together?" is not enough for church leaders. This question must be complemented by the question of what marks a people off and identifies them with God. God means to do both, and he does it by giving his people a covenant of holy love and placing his name upon them. Abraham and his descendants were marked off by the covenant sign of circumcision. The people of God in the wilderness and in the land of Israel were marked off by dietary restrictions, cleanliness laws, the Ten Commandments, various annual festivals, and the covenant sign of the Sabbath. The New Testament church is to be marked off and identified with Christ by its love and holiness as well as by the covenant signs of baptism and the Lord's Supper. At every stage of redemptive history,

---

[3]These relationships between Christian, church, and Christ are not symmetrical. We aspire to represent him on earth for who he is in his sinlessness, whereas he represents us before the Father in heaven, not for who we are in our sinfulness, but according to who he is in his sinlessness!

God marks off his people with his presence and name, which he gives to those with whom he makes a covenant of holy love.

Step 3: In the Old Testament, God broadly used covenants to identify a people with himself and establish his kingdom.

A Formal Covenant of Love

It's not uncommon in our days to hear couples plead their love for one another in order to justify sexual activity outside of marriage, or even cohabitation. The excuse typically runs something like this: "We don't need an arbitrary certificate to affirm our love. Our love is what counts, not the legal recognition of the fact."

I suppose God could have used the same excuse when declaring his love for Abraham, the nation of Israel, or King David; and perhaps he could have allowed the nation to reciprocate in kind. But he didn't. Instead, he presented Abraham, Israel, and David with a covenant, a formal oath (Genesis 15, 17; Exodus 24; 2 Samuel 7). In fact, since the "wedding" performed at Sinai was with a generation that fell under God's judgment and died in the wilderness, he asked the nation to "renew their vows" at Moab before entering the Promised Land.[4] God wanted the covenant, its stipulations and promises, to be clear.

As with the couple pleading their preexisting love to justify cohabitation, covenants in the Bible do not produce relationships.[5] They merely affirm a relationship that already exists and give further structure to those relationships.[6] God had a relationship with Noah before presenting him with a covenant; just so with Abraham, Israel, and David.

If that's true, the question becomes, what's wrong with the cohabiting couple's excuse? Or in the case of God and Israel, why would God insist on formalizing his love relationship with Israel through a covenant? We can answer that question in two ways reminiscent of our discussion of holy love—broadly and specifically. Broadly speaking, God uses covenants in order to establish his kingdom or rule among a people identified with himself. They are the mechanisms by which his holy love boomerangs outward and draws his people into a

---

[4]For a discussion of the relationship between the covenant as it was articulated at Sinai (or Horeb) and then again at Moab, see Gary Millar, *Now Choose Life: Theology and Ethics in Deuteronomy*, New Studies in Biblical Theology, ed. D. A. Carson (Downers Grove, IL: InterVarsity, n.d.), 82; also, Dumbrell, *Covenant and Creation: A Theology of the Old Testament Covenants*, Biblical and Theological Classics Library (Kent, UK: Paternoster, 1997), 114.

[5]T. D. Alexander, *From Paradise to the Promised Land: An Introduction to the Main Themes of the Pentateuch* (Grand Rapids: Baker, 1995), 166.

[6]Paul Williamson, *Sealed with an Oath: Covenant in God's Unfolding Purpose* (Downers Grove, IL: InterVarsity, 2007), 75–76; also, Bruce Waltke with Cathi J. Fredericks, *Genesis: A Commentary* (Grand Rapids: Zondervan, 2001), 136.

loving conformity to his character. Covenants are about relationships, kingdoms are about rule, and God is interested in combining both. God is interested in relationships but relationships of a particular kind; namely, those wherein his rule is displayed.

Specifically speaking, God uses covenants to do eleven things: to identify a people with himself, to distinguish them from the world, to call them to righteousness, to make them his witness, to display and share in his glory, to identify a people with one another, to act as a testimony for them, to assign responsibilities to every party, to render accountability, to protect his people, and to provide clarity in all these matters. I will ultimately argue that God uses local church membership to do all these things—broadly, to establish his kingdom on earth; specifically, to identify a people with himself for all these purposes. Love affectionately unites the lover with the beloved, causing him to give himself to her with a shared identity. It is the covenant of local church membership that aspires to such a definition. We begin by considering the broad reason why God uses covenants, namely, to establish his kingdom among a people identified with himself.

KINGDOM THROUGH COVENANT

The word *covenant* is never used in Genesis 1 and 2, perhaps because sin had not entered the world and no disruption in the relationship between God and Adam had occurred that would have required a formal covenant. Still, the structure and nature of the relationship between God and Adam bears all the characteristics of what covenantal relationships would eventually bear—two designated parties in a formally defined relationship with variously prescribed obligations and privileges. It was to be a relationship of holy love, in which God affectionately united his name and image to Adam, desiring that Adam would do the same. Old Testament scholar Peter Gentry uses the phrase "kingdom through covenant" to describe God's prototypical relationship with Adam in the garden.

Adam rebelled. He broke the covenant. Yet God graciously inaugurated a new plan for accomplishing his creation purposes through the promise of Adam's seed. Adam's line eventually came to Noah who, after the un-creation and re-creation of the flood, received the same mandate as Adam to be fruitful and multiply (Gen. 9:1). Yet Noah's descendants, like Adam's, did no better and were eventually scattered over the earth.

ABRAHAMIC COVENANT

God then called Abraham and gave him two commands: "go" and "be a blessing" (Gen. 12:1–2)—not unlike Jesus' command to "go and make disciples" (Matt. 28:19–20). Amidst those two commands God made several promises to

Abraham. He promised to make him a great nation; to bless him and make his name great; to draw a line between those who bless him and those who dishonor him, blessing one group and cursing the other; and to bless all the families of the earth through him (Gen. 12:2–3).[7] Again, it was an offer of holy love to unite his name to Abraham's and to share all his glory with him.

What's striking about God's promise to make Abraham a great nation, Gentry observes, is the Hebrew word used here for nation, *gôy*. The term *gôy* is typically used in the Old Testament for Gentile nations and has a basic meaning of an organized community with a governmental, political, and social structure. (Other nations are described in this passage with a term meaning clans or families, *mišpāhâ*.) That's significant because almost everywhere else in the Old Testament, Abraham's descendants, the nation of Israel, are described with another term suggestive of kinship or family relations, *'am*. Why the exception here? Gentry infers:

> Genesis 12 presents us with a political structure brought into being by the word of God, with God at the center and God as the governmental head and ruler of that community. In other words, we have the Kingdom of God brought into being by covenant (between God and Abram). The author's choice of terms emphasizes that the family of Abram is a real kingdom with eternal power and significance, while the so called kingdoms of this world have no lasting power or significance.[8]

God means to establish his kingdom among a people whom he will identify with himself through a covenant. That covenant, of course, is eventually formalized in Genesis 15 and 17. Gentry further observes that the word in Hellenistic Greek that best describes such a structure is *polis*, or *city*, a term that carried governmental and administrative associations. This helps us to understand what the author to the Hebrews means when he tells us that Abraham was "looking forward to the city that has foundations, whose designer and builder is God" (Heb. 11:10), an entity that he also calls the "assembly of the firstborn" (Heb. 12:22–23).

MOSAIC COVENANT

We learn in the first chapter of Exodus that God had begun to deliver on his promise to make Abraham a great nation by giving him many descendants, even though its godly administration was not yet up and running. In fact, Pharaoh's oppressive administration over the Israelites indicated that something more was needed, something that would eventually be supplied with the Mosaic and Davidic covenants. God begins to administrate the blessings of the Abrahamic

---

[7]Peter J. Gentry, "The Covenant at Sinai," in *The Southern Baptist Journal of Theology*, vol. 12 (Fall 2008): 39.
[8]Ibid., 40.

covenant, then, by giving the nation of Israel the Mosaic covenant.[9] This covenant explains his will for their lives in terms of how they were to relate to him, the surrounding nations, and creation.[10] After reminding them that he carried them on eagles' wings out of Egpyt, he promises, "If you will indeed obey my voice and keep my covenant, you shall be my treasured possession among all peoples, for all the earth is mine; and you shall be to me a kingdom of priests and a holy nation" (Ex. 19:5–6). It was an offer to set his holy love upon them. Israel, by obeying this covenant, would be "the agent used by God to achieve the wider purposes which the Abrahamic covenant entails."[11] They would be blessed with a great name as his "treasured possession," and they would be a blessing to others as a "kingdom of priests."

Like Adam, Israel was created to rule, but its dominion was supposed to redefine authority for a world that had perverted it. Its rule, grounded in submission to God, was intended to create life and hope in the nations by mediating God's character and glory to them.[12] Once again, God was establishing his kingdom among an identifiable people through a covenant.

DAVIDIC COVENANT

The covenant given to David was then set within the context of the two preceding covenants. Specifically, it gave further clarity to the Mosaic covenant, and it moved the Abrahamic covenant closer to fulfillment.[13] The occupant of David's throne was expected to preeminently embody the values of Sinai, thereby reflecting the kingship of God as God's vice-regent (Deut. 17:18–20).[14] David was also put to work marking out the borders of the land, so that a permanent residence for God's presence might be built.[15] In all this, the king of Israel bore a special relationship with God such that the "son of David" was the "son of God" (Ps. 2:7; cf. 45:6; 89:26–28). Not only that, but the king of Israel had a unique role in relation to God's covenant with Israel. He was the covenant mediator, representing God as covenant Lord to the people

---

[9]Ibid., 41. See also, Stephen G. Dempster, *Dominion and Dynasty: A Theology of the Hebrew Bible*, New Studies in Biblical Theology, ed. D. A. Carson (Downers Grove, IL: InterVarsity, 2001), 174.

[10]Dempster, "Dominion and Dynasty," 172.

[11]William Dumbrell, *Covenant and Creation*, 89; cf. Craig A. Blaising and Darrell L. Bock, *Progressive Dispensationalism* (Grand Rapids: Baker, 1993), 141–42; Andreas J. Köstenberger and Peter T. O'Brien, *Salvation to the Ends of the Earth: A Biblical Theology of Mission*, New Studies in Biblical Theology; Graeme Goldsworthy, *According to Plan: The Unfolding Revelation of God in the Bible* (Downers Grove, IL: InterVarsity, 1991), 141.

[12]See Dempster, *Dominion and Dynasty*, 101–2, quoted in Gentry, "The Covenant at Sinai," 47. I was tempted to quote Dempster on the point of Israel "redefining dominion," but he uses the word *service*, as evangelicals commonly do, to describe what they perceive as a redeemed rule. Whereas I agree the motive of service should be imported into a redeemed concept of authority (e.g., Mark 10:45), I don't believe it's strong enough to capture all that God intended for Adam (or pictured in Christ) through their respective dominions, such as the element of command or judgment.

[13]Dumbrell, *Covenant and Creation*, 127; Blaising and Bock, *Progressive Dispensationalism*, 168–69.

[14]Dumbrell, *Covenant and Creation*, 150–52.

[15]Ibid., 151, 162–63.

but also representing the people to God, embodying them and their cause before him.[16]

God's work of establishing a kingdom for himself progressed as redemption history moved from the Abrahamic to the Mosaic to the Davidic covenants, each building on the last.[17] The Abrahamic promises of a great nation and a great name that, in turn, bless other nations was finally to be realized through the Davidic son. The son of David alone could establish God's kingdom through covenant: "In this important sense, the Davidic king becomes the mediator of covenant blessing, tied back to Abraham, ultimately tied back to Adam, as the covenant head of the human race."[18]

Step 4: In the New Testament, he sent his Son to establish a better, effectual covenant. This new covenant, which unites us to Christ representationally, by the Spirit, and by faith, is the foundation of the church.

An Effectual Covenant of Love

Of course, David and his sons failed to keep God's covenants, as did Israel, Abraham, and Adam before them. Each was only a type or a shadow.

THE SON OF DAVID, THE NEW ISRAEL, THE SEED OF ABRAHAM, THE LAST ADAM

On the very first pages of the New Testament, however, we learn that Christ is this Davidic son who mediates a new covenant of God's holy love. He is "the son of David, the son of Abraham" (Matt. 1:1), and "the offspring . . . to whom the promise had been made" (Gal. 3:19, 16). Indeed, "all the promises of God find their Yes in him" (2 Cor. 1:20). He is the true Israel (Matt. 2:15), and he is the king of Israel (Matt. 27:42; John 12:13). He is the one whom great David called "my Lord" (Ps. 110:1; Matt. 22:4; Acts 2:34; Heb. 1:13), and who came to declare the inauguration of God's kingdom (Mark 1:15).

Christ also, in holy love for the Father, fulfilled the conditions of all three covenants. In his circumcision, he kept the requirements of the Abrahamic covenant.[19] He was the one Son of David who did not need to be disciplined (just

---

[16]O. Palmer Robertson, *The Christ of the Covenants* (Phillipsburg, NJ: P&R, 1980), 235; Stephen J. Wellum, "Baptism and the Relationship between the Covenants," in *Believer's Baptism: Sign of the New Covenant in Christ*, ed. Thomas R. Schreiner and Shawn D. Wright, NAC Studies in Bible and Theology (Nashville: Broadman, 2006), 39.

[17]Blaising and Bock, *Progressive Dispensationalism*, 172–73; Robertson, *Christ of the Covenants*, 185–90, 268.

[18]Wellum, "Baptism and the Relationship between the Covenants," 39.

[19]As Wellum states, "In this regard, Luke 2:21 is important. Jesus' circumcision is not a minor event; it marks the fulfillment of circumcision in its purpose of preserving a line of descent from Abraham to Christ." Baptism and the Relationship between the Covenants," 69.

compare the exilic and post-exilic versions of the Davidic covenant—2 Samuel 7 and 1 Chron. 17:3ff.) and pleased the Father perfectly (see Heb. 1:5, 8–9, 13). Yet he underwent discipline nonetheless and so fulfilled the stipulations of the Mosaic covenant through the "covenant in my blood." Jesus used this phrase in the Upper Room with his disciples principally to refer to his inauguration of a new covenant, yet one cannot hear those words without hearing the old covenant faintly ringing in the background, since his work would cancel the debt incurred under the old covenant (Rom. 3:25–26; Col. 1:13; Heb. 9:15; 10:10).[20]

Yet Christ is not only the Son of David, the new Israel, and the seed of Abraham, but he is the last Adam (1 Cor. 15:22, 45; cf. Luke 3:23–38). Where Adam failed to image the Father perfectly (as did Abraham, Israel, and David), Jesus was the perfect image and perfect son (2 Cor. 4:4; Col. 1:15; cf. Heb. 1:3).[21] He inaugurated a whole new creation, symbolized in his ministry by his healings, his raising of the dead, and his feeding of the masses, then accomplished in his own resurrection as the "firstfruits" (1 Cor. 15:23). Just as death came to the world through the first federal head, life and promise comes to the world through the second (Rom. 5:12–19).[22]

It's in light of who Jesus is that he could offer a better covenant (Heb. 7:22; 8:6). He is the God-man who was able to provide an effective sacrifice and covenant.[23] This brings us to the foundation of the church.

WHAT IS THE CHURCH?

What is the church? The many metaphors for the church in the New Testament provide a rich source of identification and description: temple, vineyard, bride, community, gathering, body, household, sheep, family—the list is long.[24] Very often, works of ecclesiology will privilege one metaphor above the others in order to define the essence of the church. Moreover, certain metaphors will come in vogue for a time, only to be replaced by another a decade or two later. The Roman Catholic Church, for instance, has moved back and forth between *people of God* and *body of Christ*, each one bring-

---

[20]D. A. Carson calls Jesus' use of this phrase the antitype to the type of Exodus 24:8. *Matthew*, Expositor's Bible Commentary, vol. 8, ed. Frank E. Gaebelein and J. D. Douglas (Grand Rapids: Zondervan, 1984), 537.

[21]See G. K. Beale, *The Temple and the Church's Mission: A Biblical Theology of the Dwelling Place of God*, New Studies in Biblical Theology, 169–76.

[22]*Federal headship* can be defined as the actions or decisions of one individual standing in for, or representing, the many, just as a vote of a representative on the floor of the U.S. Congress "enacts" or "binds" or "represents" the vote of his or her constituents. For further description and discussion of this view, see Louis Berkhof, *Systematic Theology* (Carlisle, PA: Banner of Truth, 1958), 242–43; Millard J. Erickson, *Christian Theology*, 2nd ed. (Grand Rapids: Baker, 1998), 651–52. A slightly more extended engagement with the view can be found in Henri Blocher, *Original Sin: Illuminating the Riddle*, New Studies in Biblical Theology, 70–81, 96–99, 116, 129ff.

[23]Wellum, "Baptism and the Relationship between the Covenants," 55, 57.

[24]For a fairly exhaustive list of images for the church, see Paul S. Minear, *Images of the New Testament Church* (Philadelphia: Westminster, 1960).

ing with it a host of polity implications and potential misuses.[25] A popular approach these days among both Catholic and Protestant writers is to argue for a Trinitarian church by privileging the three metaphors: people of God, body of Christ, and temple of the Spirit. The Trinitarian emphasis is good, but why these three metaphors instead of, say, household of God, bride of Christ, and temple of the Spirit? Or another set? It's hard to know, hermeneutically, how we can justify picking one set of metaphors above the others as the most important ones.

Another approach to defining the church is to consider the fact that the storyline of the entire Bible is driven by God's work of establishing his kingdom through covenant. Instead of randomly picking our favorite metaphor, therefore, I would propose that we begin our definition of the church with the person and work of Christ, as the church has long done. He is the God-man who has come as last Adam, Abraham's seed, the new Israel, and son of David. According to God's plan and by the Spirit's power, he has fulfilled God's covenants and so won all their blessings and promises. He has inherited the earth, like Adam. His name has been made great and become a blessing to the earth, like Abraham. He has won the promised rest, like Israel. His throne is an everlasting throne, like David's. But then, most remarkably and graciously, this God-man has declared a new covenant for all who repent and believe.

Shortly after giving his disciples the keys of the kingdom, he took them to an upper room and gave them a cup saying, "This cup that is poured out for you is the new covenant in my blood," and he commanded them to continue to "do this in remembrance of me." He was alluding backward to God's promise through Jeremiah that he would "put my law within them," that he would "be their God . . . from the least of them to the greatest," and that he would "forgive their iniquity" (Jer. 31:33–34; Heb. 8:6–13). He was alluding forward to the death he was about to undergo.

So Christ came declaring a kingdom, but then he did something a little more personal. The king went to his death as a personal substitute for sinners. He offered a new covenant and sealed it with his blood. With this act, he joined a people to himself as fellow heirs and vice-regents. They too would inherit the earth like Adam, bear a great name and be a blessing like Abraham, enter God's rest like Israel, and rule together with Christ like David. What is the church? It is the new-covenant people of Christ. It's the people of his holy love. It's the people who are united to him and share his identity, because he identified himself with them in his incarnation, baptism, death, and resurrection. He exchanged his life and righteousness for theirs. Whereas once Adam was our covenantal

---

[25]Veli-Matti Kärkkäinen, *An Introduction to Ecclesiology: Ecumenical, Historical and Global Perspectives* (Downers Grove: InterVarsity, 2002), 26–38.

head, now Christ is our covenantal head. We start our definition of the church, then, with Christ's covenant.

However, almost as quickly as we say that the church is the covenant people of Christ, we must also say that it is the kingdom people of Christ. After all, Christ purchased them *for* his kingdom and gave them its keys. He shared his identity with them so that the church might share in the rule of a kingdom with him. Theologians commonly recognize that the person and work of Christ cannot be separated. Christ could only do the work he did because of who he is—the God-man. The same is true for the church. The church can only do the work it's called to do on account of who it is. That's why Peter calls us a royal priesthood (1 Pet. 2:9). The title communicates both who we are and what we do. We are made Christ's fellow priests and kings so that we might mediate the Father's glory as we push out the borders of Christ's domain.

By beginning with Christ's person and work, we build our doctrine of the church on the covenantal and kingdom structures of the entire canon rather than by arbitrarily privileging one metaphor over another. It keeps us from saying philosophically speculative things such as, "the church is the continuation of the incarnation," based on an over-reaching understanding of the body metaphor; or "we are Christ's mystical bride" based on an over-exuberant understanding of the bride metaphor; or "Christ the head is not complete without his body, and together they form *one total Christ*" based on an inability to see the body metaphor within the context of Davidic headship. These are some of the prominent errors in the history of the doctrine of the church.

At the same time, beginning with Christ's person and work allows each metaphor to be given full play in reflecting the church's manifold splendor. These covenantal and kingdom people do bear attributes of a body, a flock, a family, a vine, a bulwark of truth, a temple, a nation with "borders" and laws, and so forth.[26] The church is united to Christ's person and work like Eve is to Adam. She shared his name (wo-man) so that she could be a helper to his work (Eph. 5:22–32). But the husband-wife analogy isn't enough. The church is united to God like a son is to a father, that is, a son of ancient Israel who would have looked like his father and followed in his father's professional footsteps—and received his inheritance (Matt. 5:9, 45; Gal. 4:4–7). That's not all: the church is united to Christ as a people are to its king. The king rules over all, but the king represents them and they him, and all share in the citizenship and symbols and

---

[26]Perhaps an illustration here would be helpful. A husband and wife might have many ways to describe the nature of their relationship: friends, lovers, partners, fellow travelers, soul mates, coworkers, and so forth. Suppose one was then asked to define the nature of marriage: "What is marriage?" Should we privilege one of the names/descriptions over another? As in, "A marriage, fundamentally, is friendship," or, "A marriage, fundamentally, is the act of sexual union." None of these names or descriptions quite captures the whole of the thing. It would be better to define the nature of marriage as "a lifelong covenant between two people," or something along those lines. Then, we can allow each of those names or descriptions to be given full play in enhancing and coloring in that foundational definition.

pageantry and glory of the kingdom. We could keep going. Some metaphors are more central than others, but it's impossible (and hermeneutically irresponsible) to finally privilege any one metaphor. All of them work together to describe the people chosen by God and purchased by the Son in the new covenant of his blood by the power of the Spirit.

How then do we put covenant and kingdom together? Think about it like this. A king defeats another king and occupies his land, yet the populace remains defiant, as if their old king still reigned. The new king now rules over all in one sense, yet his rule remains limited in another, extending to the hearts of only those who affirm him as king. In response to the widespread rebellion, the king promises to one day punish all who remain defiant, but he also promises clemency and pardon to all who swear allegiance to him. Not only that, he promises to provide coins to pay the taxes that will be levied upon the population. The analogy is not perfect, but what is Christ's kingdom? It's the rule he bears by having thrown out the old king, as well as the rule he bears in the hearts of those who have repented. His new covenant is this promise of clemency, pardon, and sin forgiven. It's also the Holy Spirit–given ability to live out this new allegiance (to pay the taxes). The covenant is what makes us Christians, or upstanding citizens of this kingdom.

THREEFOLD UNION

Exactly how does this covenant unite the church to Christ? We can speak of our union with him in at least three ways, each of which has significant implications for our corporate life.

First, this covenant unites us to Christ representationally (Rom. 5:12–21). There is a formal commitment or oath whereby we take on his identity and work, like a wife taking her husband's name, or an adopted son taking his father's, or an immigrant becoming a citizen. It's a covenant of marriage because the bridegroom loves his bride exclusively and dearly. It's a covenant of adoption because the Father and Son want to share the Son's inheritance with many brothers and sisters. It's a covenant of a body politic because the king bears authority over the whole. A shared identity means that everybody shares everything, but not in such a way that overlooks the asymmetries between king and nation, father and son, husband and wife, and so forth.

Christ takes our guilt, while we acquire his righteousness and all the blessings that come with it. He takes our burdens and sorrows, while we acquire his glory and comfort. He receives our diligent labor, while we receive his commission and charge. He takes our weakness, while we acquire his strength. Our representational union with Christ is extensive. It extends to his total human experience in all he has done for us (Rom. 6:1ff.; Gal. 2:20; Col. 2:20–3:4).

Thus, we share in his life, death, burial, resurrection, ascension, rule, and reign.[27] Indeed, it's good to be a member of his family! Being "in Christ," says theologian Sinclair Ferguson, "means that all he has done for me representatively becomes mine actually."[28] To say that the church is the body of Christ, then, is not to say that we are his ontological or mystical body. It's to speak federally or covenantally, as we would speak of a body politic. Our congressman votes for us because he represents us. King David spoke for God's people because he represented them. The fact that Christ is the "head of the body" means that he is the covenant mediator and the federal head of the church (1 Cor. 11:3; Eph. 1:22; 4:15; 5:23; Col. 1:18; 2:10, 19).

Second, this covenant unites us to Christ spiritually, because we have been given his Spirit (1 Cor. 12:13; cf. Rom. 8:9–11; 1 Cor. 6:17–19; 1 John 3:24; 4:13). The Spirit regenerates, seals, deposits, gifts, perseveres, and glorifies those who belong to Christ. Hence, Christ's covenant is effective. It effects what it promises. It gives what it asks for. The church is Trinitarian indeed because the covenant work of Christ is grounded in the Father's election and applied by the Spirit.

Third, the covenant unites the church to Christ by faith (John 2:11; 3:16; Rom. 10:14; Gal. 2:16; Phil. 1:29). We get into Christ by faith. Christ's new covenant may be unilateral and effectual, but its effects operate within the context of a compatibilist rendering of divine sovereignty and human freedom. The covenant gives what it asks for, and it asks for a human decision. An individual must repent of sin and put his or her trust in Christ. We must *choose* Christ with the faculty of will he has given to us. Therefore, the author to the Hebrews still warns his readers not to "profane the blood of the covenant" by which they have been set apart for salvation (Heb. 10:29; cf. 6:4–6; 10:26–27). Jesus effectively purchases a people for himself, but members of the visible church can "deny the Master who bought them" (2 Pet. 2:1). An individual is united to Christ by faith.

Christians indeed share a "political union" beneath one king by virtue of Matthew 16:18–19, as we considered in chapter 4—a political union that should be given expression in the church "on earth." Yet it should be evident from the foregoing conversation on the Old Testament covenants and the new covenant that the new covenant yields elements of this political unity or citizenship, as well. The governmental and political associations of the nation (*gôy*) promised to Abram, which took one particular form in the "nation-state" under David and Solomon, find a reconstituted form in the citizens of Christ's rule—church

---

[27]Thanks to Steve Wellum for this point.
[28]Sinclair B. Ferguson, *The Holy Spirit*, Contours of Christian Theology, ed. Gerald Bray (Downers Grove, IL: InterVarsity, 1996), 109; see also Robert Letham, *The Work of Christ*, Contours of Christian Theology, ed. Gerald Bray (Downers Grove, IL: InterVarsity, 1993), 75–87.

members! Local churches, in fact, are less analogous to clubs or societies than they are to brought-forward-in-time embassies of Christ's final "nation-state"—a kingdom "not of this world" (John 18:36).

IMPLICATIONS OF THIS THREEFOLD UNION

Manifold implications for the church can be drawn from the threefold union to Christ. First, the fact that the church shares Christ's identity means that the members of the church share an identity with one another. That means we also share with one another all the things that are constituent of identity, such as work, relationships, joys, and sorrows. As I said before, this loving union is extensive. If one part mourns, we all mourn. If one part rejoices, we all rejoice. If one part sins, we all fail. In our lives together, we share responsibility, culpability, victory, and opportunity, because we represent one another as we represent Christ. That's what it means to be members of a family, citizens of a nation, bricks in a temple. The successes and failures of every member are mine, even the ones I may not have personally met. That doesn't mean all differences between members of the body are obliterated, just as the difference between creator Christ and creature Christian are not obliterated. The fact that we all represent one identity—Christ's—is meaningful precisely because we are different. Christian life necessarily has a congregational shape.

Second, the fact that we share the identity of Christ means that our doctrine of church membership does not depend on pure voluntarism, decisionism, or consumerism. Christians must choose to join a church as a matter of human responsibility and freedom, but they really have no choice about whether to join a church as a matter of the relationships between faith and deeds. To remain aloof from a local church is to "profane the covenant" (Heb. 10:26–29).

Third, the fact that we are united to Christ by faith means that entrance into and participation in the church occurs without the voluntary cooperation of the individual. Each must choose to join, choose to stay, and can choose to go. The covenant of grace is unilateral because Christ effectively conquers exactly what he means to conquer, but Christ still calls for a decision. The church has the right to declare someone a true believer while simultaneously recognizing that its stamp of approval is contingent upon the believer's persevering to the end (Matt. 10:22; 18:15–17; Rev. 2:7, 17, 26). Such is the nature of the church's declaratory authority. What would happen if we were to deprive church membership of its voluntaristic element, as the Church of Rome and others attempt to do? We would create a vast space for nominal Christianity and hypocrisy, whereby the church unilaterally declares individuals as belonging to itself, based either on birth or an adulthood conversion, but then, downplaying the processes of human decision making, it neglects to call for perseverance in the faith.

Fourth, the Spirit was given to the church not so that the church could throw off all constraints of polity and adapt its organizational structure to whatever environment it finds itself in, as so many today argue. Rather, Christ has given his Spirit to the church so that he might accomplish the kingdom rule of his covenant in the lives of people—to regenerate, sanctify, seal, gift, make a deposit, and persevere. He has given him to make his covenant effectual. He has given him for the sake of faith and obedience. Whereas unregenerate ethnic Israel could not keep the laws of the nation-state, the regenerate church is learning to keep the laws of Christ's "state" (kingdom) through the Spirit.

The fact that we have the Spirit has further institutional implications, but it doesn't mean that we can throw off all human hierarchies and authorities except when they are missiologically conducive to a certain context. Paul responds to just this point when he tells the Corinthians, "Without us you have become kings!" (1 Cor. 4:8). A king is a sovereign upon whom no one else can lay an authoritative claim. To make biblical church structure entirely a matter of con-textual expediency and pragmatism is to declare every Christian a self-sovereign who voluntarily contracts together for a particular job (or mission) and remains bound only as long as he or she chooses. This *is* pure voluntarism. It has lost sight of the covenantal identity that Christians share, an identity that's more significant than the blood they share with biological mother, brother, and sister (Matt. 12:50). Notice, then, that defining the church entirely by its mission, insofar as this downplays our shared identity in the covenantal work of Christ, can lead right back to individualism and autonomy.

What institutional implications does the Spirit's effectual work have for the church? First, a church's gatherings should be orderly (1 Corinthians 14). Second, a church's leaders will become leaders, at least in part by virtue of their Holy Spirit–given character and gifts. Their lives are above reproach, and they are able to teach. The leaders are leaders, at least in part because of qualities that can be publicly recognized and affirmed by the congregation rather than because of something mystical. Third, every exercise of authority, whether a pastoral exercise of counsel or an apostolic exercise of command, appeals to the individual's will. It aspires to command what the believer wants, believing that the Holy Spirit is powerful precisely in the area of reordering desires. Paul tells Philemon, "I am bold enough in Christ to command you to do what is required, yet for love's sake I prefer to appeal to you" (Philem. 8–9).

Both pastoral and apostolic authority should always appeal to the new covenant, Holy Spirit–given realities within an individual. This is what we do as pastors whenever we call upon the new man over and against the old man. Of course, at times the church will have to make decisions that contravene an individual's will. Certainly this is the case in an act of discipline when the church formally announces that it has no reason to believe an individual has the Holy

Spirit. And there will be other times when the church must make decisions that not everyone agrees with. In general, however, I believe we must say that the institutional authorities of the Christian church, by virtue of the new covenant, should expect (not insist) that their commands and counsel will progressively align to the desires of believers.

For any theologians, let me put it like this: An over-realized eschatology would expect church authority and the desires of its members to perfectly align, leading to a lack of structure and accountability. An under-realized eschatology would expect just the opposite, leading to authoritarianism and a heavy reliance on command. A properly balanced inaugurated eschatology will aim for the difficult and often elusive middle, knowing that Christians are simultaneously justified and sinful, capable of both self-deceit and genuine faith.

Step 5: The "covenant" of local church membership is what results when Christ's charter draws together and marks off Christ's new covenant people.

A Local Church Covenant

At the end of the last chapter, I said that a *covenant of union* between a particular church and a Christian consists of affirmation, oversight, and submission. The church covenants to affirm and oversee the Christian, while the Christian covenants to submit to the church's oversight. To be clear, I'm not talking about a written document that churches sometimes refer to as their "covenant." I'm talking about the reality behind such a document: the covenant-like agreement between the members of a church. Should we assume that this covenant-like commitment, this local church covenant, is the same thing as the new covenant? What is a local church covenant in relationship to Christ's new covenant? After all, the word is not used of local churches anywhere in Scripture.

WHERE THE CHARTER AND COVENANT COLLIDE

The new covenant and the covenant-like commitment, or local church covenant, that I make with the other members of my church *are not* the same thing. Rather, this commitment is right where Christ's charter and new covenant collide. It is the charter that yields church membership, yet the church itself is a creation of Christ's new covenant. We can see this collision, as it were, in the church's two ordinances. On the one hand, the local church practices baptism, as commanded by Christ in the *charter* of Matthew 16, 18, and 28. On the other hand, the local church practices the Lord's Supper, as commanded when Jesus promised a *new covenant* in Matthew 26. If we bring these two things together, we have the two marks of church membership. Church members are simply those marked off by baptism and the Lord's Supper in a local congregation. That's the church. Still, observing the collision doesn't answer how the covenant and charter work together to yield a local church covenant or local church membership.

It is important to recognize that the new covenant comes first. The charter doesn't create Christ's eschatological and heavenly body; the new covenant does. Matthew 16 (charter) might come before Matthew 26 (promise of a new covenant), but in both places Christ was getting things ready for the birth of the church at Pentecost, the moment at which the heavenly powers of the new covenant first exploded on earth. The covenant is prior to the charter because the universal church exists prior to the local church.[29] Salvation precedes church membership.

Then Christ gives the people of this eschatological and heavenly body a key that can be used wherever two or three of them deliberately and consistently gather on earth in his name. It's up to them to bind and loose. This means that the local church—and local church membership—doesn't exist until human beings corporately and publicly say so. The existence of a church on earth is always the direct result of human actions of a public nature. People must do it visibly and aloud. Certainly it's the case that divine action and human action are necessary in the existence of the universal church as well; an individual must repent and believe in order to join Christ's universal body. But there remains a significant difference. Joining a local body requires the agreement of more than one. It requires at least two or three people coming together to say, "Let us submit to one another. Affirm my profession and keep watch over my soul on behalf of Christ. I, together with the others, will do the same for you. All of us together then will speak for Christ." Christ has given this collection of people the authority to do just this. It would be presumptuous for human beings to agree to speak together on behalf of the risen Christ had it not been for the fact that Christ had given them authority to do so. It's this agreement or commitment to bind and loose one another that constitutes a local church covenant. *The covenant of membership between Christians is nothing more or less than the existence of the local church—the visible church on earth.*

Imagine for a second that Christ had not given his people this charter. Imagine, in other words, that Christ decided to stake both the gospel and his reputation on the right of every individual on the planet to independently declare, "I'm one of his!" Who would ensure the safety of each sheep? Who would call them to account? Who would preserve the gospel from generation

---

[29] I don't mean to give priority to the universal church over the local church in the same sense that a Roman Catholic will. A Roman Catholic will define the universal church as the visible institution on earth, which then gives birth to many local churches. I have defined the universal church instead as Christ's heavenly and eschatological body that we belong to upon conversion. Our baptism into a local church merely affirms the primary membership. Miroslav Volf presents a good discussion of this matter in *After Our Likeness: The Church as the Image of the Trinity* (Grand Rapids: Eerdmans, 1998), 139–41.

to generation? Who would teach us about all that Christ commanded us to do? Who would keep Christ's people from descending into utter chaos?

Praise God he has given us, his heavenly and eschatological body, the authority to gather from place to place as the one holy, catholic, and apostolic church on earth. He has determined to protect his sheep, preserve his gospel, and proclaim this good news by authorizing a covenant between individual Christians so that they can affirm one another and set one another apart to the apostolic gospel (see Gal. 1:6–9).

The local church covenant is the very life and existence of the local church. The local church exists when Christians commit to giving one another authority over themselves, and they do so expressly because Christ instructed his people to bind and loose, baptize and teach, in his charter.

A COVENANT MORE THAN A COMMITMENT

Why would we refer to membership as a "covenant" if it's not, in fact, the same thing as the new covenant? Isn't it sufficient to simply call it a "commitment," and isn't calling it a "covenant" confusing, since they are different things? Perhaps, and, like *Trinity* or *penal substitution*, it's not found in the Bible, so nothing requires us to use it. Still, like *Trinity* and *penal substitution*, it helpfully captures the essence of the thing itself. It explains what church membership is—a kind of covenant between a people who already belong together by virtue of the new covenant and the apostolic charter.

This action certainly involves a commitment, but it's more than a commitment. It's a bending or bowing of the whole person around these other people in love. I place my discipleship to Christ under them, and they under me and the others because we love one another with the affection of Christ. We intend to unite and give ourselves to one another.

When my wife-to-be and I went to premarital counseling, the pastor told us that the covenant of marriage was not to be "one more piece in the pie of our lives," as if to say one slice of the pie was marriage, another slice was work, another slice was friendships, and so forth. Rather, we were to begin viewing the whole of life together through the other person. We were one flesh, which means each of us in marriage should view all the pieces through the lens of our togetherness. I am committed to my wife, but my relationship with her involves more than that. My very identity changes. My whole person is now bent or bowed around her and our shared fellowship. A church covenant is certainly not the same thing as a marriage covenant. There are plenty of differences. But there is this similar dynamic: it involves a commitment of the whole person in such a dramatic fashion that it bends our very identity.

This doesn't mean that our identity bends around *this* local church as opposed to *that* local church. Here is one place where the analogy with marriage does not work. My covenant with my wife is exclusive. A Christian's identity, however, is ultimately bent around Christ and all of Christ's people. After all, our union with Christ is extensive. However, we cannot express our submission to Christ and his people by submitting to all Christians everywhere, at least not in any meaningful sense. Imagine trying to pray for every Christian on earth by name, much less serve each or ask each one to discipline us should our life begin to stray from the narrow path. This bending of our person must be expressed somewhere among some people, and it happens in a local church body.

If we view discipleship to Christ in every area of life through the lens of our local church, we will attempt to pray for every member by name, serve all in one way or another, and ask all collectively to discipline us if we begin to stray from the narrow path. We will aspire to weep with those who weep and rejoice with those who rejoice, and we will expect all to aspire to the same with us. Furthermore, we will want our church to help us think through our work in the marketplace, our involvement in the public square, our marriage, our friendships with non-Christian neighbors, and so on.

Consider the resources we avail ourselves of as we call upon the strengths of the entire body to aid us in extending Christ's rule into our own little corner of the nations, wherever that happens to be. The diverse gifts, talents, strengths, and prayers of the whole body will author life in us and in our ministries—our attempts to extend Christ's rule—as we submit to its authority.

Step 6: As with the covenants of the Old Testament, the covenantal commitment shared by the members of the local church serves nine specific purposes.

The Work of a Covenant

Yet, the argument for describing local church membership as a kind of covenant is stronger than a nice-sounding analogy afforded by my premarital counseling. In fact, it rests on the pattern of the covenantal commitment by God's people throughout Scripture. There has always been an inside and an outside to God's people. The garden of Eden had an inside and an outside, as did Noah's Ark, the Israelites in Goshen, the night of the Passover, the wilderness, and the Promised Land. At every stage God's people were marked off by one covenant or another.

We have seen that God uses covenants to establish his kingdom among a people he means to identify with himself, yet to better understand the commitment Christians make to one another when they gather together, we should drill a little deeper. Specifically, God uses covenants in Scripture to do at least nine things: identify a people with himself, distinguish them from the world, call them to righteousness, be his witness, display and share in his glory, identify a people with one another, act as a testimony and standard of accountability, assign responsibilities to every party, and protect his people. We characterize the commitment shared between Christians in a local church as a "covenant" because Christians who formally gather together in Christ's name do so with these nine purposes in mind, both for his glory and their own good.

1) A covenant identifies a people with God. God formally and publicly identifies himself with a people through covenants. Sometimes he will change their names, as he did with Abram and Jacob. More remarkably, perhaps, he will identify himself by their names, as when he identifies himself as the God of Abraham, Isaac, and Jacob (Ex. 3:6, 15–16; 4:5). The same God who in his magnificence is known among his people as infinite and without antecedent or predicate—I AM—also condescends to be known by their names.

When God presents a covenant to the nation of Israel, he identifies precisely whom he makes this covenant with: "Hear, O Israel, the statues and the rules that I speak in your hearing today" (Deut. 5:1); "Hear, O Israel: The LORD our God, the LORD is one" (Deut. 6:4). God is not making an oath with everyone—not the Egyptians or the Canaanites. He is making it with Israel.

By the same token, how many times did God say to the Israelites something to the effect of, "I will take you to be my people, and I will be your God" (Ex. 6:7)?[30] How many times did he declare himself jealous[31] and warn them not to make covenants with other nations (see Ex. 34:12–15; Deut. 7:2)? How many times did he promise judgment upon the nations, not just for explicit sin against him, but for their ill treatment of his bride, Israel? Indeed, the various metaphors used to describe his relationship with Israel indicate this close identification between God and his people: son, bride-virgin, vine, flock, house, heritage, portion, and more.

God's identification with David through the Davidic covenant is evident, among other places, through the mercy he extends to later worse kings "for the sake of my servant David."[32] More amazing, though, must be God's promise to David's son: "I will be to him a father, and he shall be to me a son" (2 Sam. 7:14; cf. Pss. 2:7; 45:6; 89:26–28).

At every step along the way in the Old Testament, God dwells with those on whom he places his name.[33] He dwells with those within his covenant, while he abandons those who break his covenant, which is why the analogy between

---

[30]Here are a number of the places in the Pentateuch where God refers to himself as the "LORD your God" when speaking to the nation of Israel: Ex. 15:26; 16:12; 20:3, 5; Lev. 11:44, 45; 18:2, 4, 30; 19:2–4, 10, 12, 25, 31, 34, 36; 20:7, 24; 22:33, 23:22, 43; 24:22; 25:17, 38, 55; 26:1, 12–13; Num. 10:10; 15:41; Deut. 4:1; 5:6, 9; 11:2, 28; 13:18; 29:6.

[31]In the Pentateuch alone: Ex. 20:5; Deut. 4:24; 5:9; 6:15; 32:21. God even describes his name as "Jealous" in Ex. 34:14.

[32]1 Kings 11:13, 32, 34; 2 Kings 19:34; Isa. 37:35.

[33]E.g., Gen. 26:3, 24; 28:15; Ex. 3:12; 25:8; 29:45–46; Deut. 12:11.

adultery and idolatry is pertinent at so many levels (e.g., Jeremiah 2, 3; Ezekiel 16; Hosea 2).[34] The most significant symbol of his covenantal presence in the Old Testament, of course, is his temple (2 Sam. 7:1–12; 1 Kings 8:13).

As in the Old Testament, God means to identify a New Testament people with himself under a new covenant. The promise was present from the get-go: "I will be their God, and they shall be my people," God says concerning these new-covenant people (Jer. 31:33; Ezek. 36:28; Heb. 8:10). The people of God in the New Testament are then identified with God because they are united to Christ, who bears the very identity of God himself. Initiation into the local church means being baptized "in the name of the Father and of the Son and of the Holy Spirit" (Matt. 28:19). In fact, so closely does the beloved Son identify himself with these people that, when the resurrected Christ confronts Saul for persecuting Christians, he doesn't ask Saul why he's persecuting his *people*, but he says, "Saul, Saul, why are you persecuting me?" (Acts 9:4).

Unsurprisingly, just about every New Testament epistle opens with some reference to the recipients' identification with God: "To all those in Rome who are loved by God" (Rom. 1:7); "To the church of God that is in Corinth" (1 Cor. 1:2); "To those who are called, beloved in God the Father and kept for Jesus Christ" (Jude 1). The local church is where God means to publicly identify a people with himself on earth.

Notice, then, what's going on here. God identifies with his New Testament people through the new covenant of Christ. He places his name on every individual united to Christ by this covenant. But who, then, has the authority to claim such an identification? It's not us all by ourselves. It's those who belong to the church on earth—the local church in Rome, Corinth, and so on. God identifies himself with new-covenant believers whenever and wherever the charter is put to use. He identifies himself with any group of Christians who gather together and submit their lives to one another in a local church covenant. Godly authority or rule is the operation of love. Love reaches out and acts, and it acts through life-authoring or authoritative actions. The new-covenant love of Christ gets put into action through the authority of Christ's charter. When a man discovers that he belongs to the love of Christ in the gospel, he hands himself over to the authority of Christ as it's exercised through the local church. In short, the local church is where God lovingly identifies himself with repentant sinners. The covenant of local church membership signifies it.

Joining a church is a momentous and awesome thing. It signifies the fact that you have entered a kind of marriage between Christ and his people and been adopted into the family of God. It signifies the fact that you have changed

---

[34]See Raymond Ortlund, *God's Unfaithful Wife: A Biblical Theology of Spiritual Adultery*, New Studies in Biblical Theology.

your name, your primary associations, and your primary influences, and it's the place on earth where you do these things. The local church is where you identify yourself with the people on whom God has placed his royal name. God no longer dwells in a temple of stones and cedar; he dwells in a temple of bodies and spirits (1 Cor. 3:16; 2 Cor. 6:16; Eph. 2:21; 1 Pet. 2:5). It's in the presence of the local church that you enjoy this reality.

2) A covenant distinguishes God's people from the world. God also formally and publicly distinguishes his people from all other people through covenants.[35] God identifies with his people so that he can distinguish them. Now, does God distinguish his people from the nations before any covenantal wedding vows are spoken? Before the Sinai covenant is established with all Israel, God tells Pharaoh, "I will put a division between my people and your people" with the plague of flies (Ex. 8:23). He tells Moses that he "will make a distinction between the livestock of Israel and the livestock of Egypt" (Ex. 9:4). Just so with the plague of hail (Ex. 9:26) and with the final plague, the death of the firstborn, "that you may know that the LORD makes a distinction between Egypt and Israel" (Ex. 11:7). Yet God's distinguishing love for Israel over Egypt is then formally expressed as distinguishing love for Israel over all the nations of the earth:

> You yourselves have seen what I did to the Egyptians, and how I bore you on eagles' wings and brought you to myself. Now therefore, if you will indeed obey my voice and keep my covenant, you shall be my treasured possession among all peoples, for all the earth is mine; and you shall be to me a kingdom of priests and a holy nation. (Ex. 19:4–6a)

God's love and activity of love preceded the Sinai covenant: "You your-selves have seen . . . ," yet the covenant then provides a public articulation of the nature of this love, the promise of Israel's unique place in God's love, and his stipulations for remaining in that love: "Now therefore, if you will indeed obey my voice and keep my covenant."[36] God gives his covenant to those he discriminately chooses, as he does with David (e.g., Ps. 89:3; cf. Deut. 7:6ff.).

The various signs of the covenants, such as circumcision and Sabbath, distinguished God's people from the surrounding nations. Also, the command-ments and God's special presence distinguished God's people, as can be seen when God threatens to remove his presence when his people worship the golden calf. Moses pleads in response:

---

[35] See Mark Dever's meditation on God's distinguishing of his people in Exodus in *The Message of the Old Testament: Promises Made* (Wheaton, IL: Crossway, 2006), 93–99. Also his meditation on Leviticus in the same volume, 111–22.

[36] Some dispute exists over whether v. 5 refers to the Abrahamic or Mosaic covenant.

> If your presence will not go with me, do not bring us up from here. For how shall it
> be known that I have found favor in your sight, I and your people? Is it not in your
> going with us, so that we are distinct, I and your people, from every other people on
> the face of the earth? (Ex. 33:15–16)

Once again, God's presence, which is tied to his covenant, made the people distinct. Being excluded—cast out—from his presence would make them indistinct.

Likewise, God pictures judgment throughout the Old Testament as scattering his people among the nations thereby making them indistinct from all other peoples.[37] The prophets then employ the language of "divorce"—a covenant ending—to describe this activity of exile (Isa. 50:1; Jer. 3:8; cf. Jer. 31:32).

As in the Old Testament, God intends for his new-covenant people to be distinct from the world. The continuity between the Old Testament and the New is unmistakable on this point, even if the signs and boundary markers have changed. The church's call to be distinct permeates every book.[38] In Matthew, Jesus tells his followers to be distinct like salt and bright like light (Matt. 5:13–17). In Mark, he divides humanity into those who are for him and those who are against him (Mark 10:40). In Luke, he disowns Israel and its religious leaders because they do not bear fruit, and he calls for a people who do bear fruit (Luke 13:6–9). In John, Jesus says that he and the Father will make their home with whoever keeps his word (John 14:23). In Acts, the entire story line is pushed forward as the line of demarcation between those who have been baptized in the Spirit and those who haven't extends outward from Jerusalem, to Samaria, to the Gentile nations.[39] In Romans a clear demarcation is drawn between those who have been buried with Christ in baptism, who should walk by his Spirit, and those who haven't (Rom. 6:1–14; 8:1–11). In 1 Corinthians, Paul asks, "Do you not know that you are God's temple and that God's Spirit dwells in you?" and says, "For God's temple is holy, and you are that temple" (1 Cor. 3:16, 17b). We could extend this list through every book of the New Testament. It should not be surprising, therefore, that God repeats his Old Testament command to his New Testament people, "You shall be holy, for I am holy" (Lev. 11:45; 1 Pet. 1:16).

The continuity between Old Testament and New on this point of distinctness can also be seen as Old Testament covenantal images are applied to the church. No longer is Israel God's holy nation, royal priesthood, vine, flock,

---

[37]Lev. 26:33; Deut. 4:27; 28:64; 1 Kings 14:15; Neh. 1:8; Jer. 9:15–16; 13:15–27; Ezek. 12:14–15.

[38]See Kent E. Brower and Andy Johnson, eds., *Holiness and Ecclesiology in the New Testament* (Grand Rapids: Eerdmans, 2007) for a book-by-book examination through the New Testament on the theme of the church as holy.

[39]See David W. Pao, *Acts and the Isaianic New Exodus*, in the Biblical Studies Library (Grand Rapids: Baker, 2002).

bride, people, and temple; it's the church. Peter even describes the church as a "chosen race" (1 Pet. 2:9), which is especially striking. Apparently, the bond that unites and distinguishes the members of a church is stronger and closer than the physical bonds of Hebrew blood. How could that be? The church is united to Christ, the distinctly beloved Son.

One of the most vivid instances of Old Testament–New Testament continuity occurs when Paul reaches back to the cleanliness and ritual purity laws from the Pentateuch, holds them up in his hand, and says in essence to the Corinthians, "Church, be distinct like this!" He writes:

> Do not be unequally yoked with unbelievers. For what partnership has righteousness with lawlessness? Or what fellowship has light with darkness? What accord has Christ with Belial? Or what portion does a believer share with an unbeliever? What agreement has the temple of God with idols? For we are the temple of the living God; as God said, "I will make my dwelling among them and walk among them, and I will be their God, and they shall be my people. Therefore go out from their midst, and be separate from them, says the Lord, and touch no unclean thing; then I will welcome you, and I will be a father to you, and you shall be sons and daughters to me, says the Lord Almighty." Since we have these promises, beloved, let us cleanse ourselves from every defilement of body and spirit, bringing holiness to completion in the fear of God. (2 Cor. 6:14–7:1)

Paul envisions quite the line distinguishing God's people in Corinth from the larger Corinthian population. No partnership. No fellowship. No accord. No portion. No agreement. Instead, go out. Be separate. Cleanse yourselves. Bring holiness to completion.

He is not talking geography; he is talking identity. He's not telling them to refrain from befriending non-Christians or living among them. He's affirming the church in its separate identity as the covenantal people among whom God dwells. They are the "temple of the living God." Therefore, they must not enter into any partnership, fellowship, or accord with unbelievers that would tempt those unbelievers to think they belong to God, or tempt those believers to think they belong to the world. Yes, moral implications follow, but everything starts with an affirmation of their new identities. This New Testament church should be just as "set apart unto God," as kosher-eating, Sabbath-keeping, Canaan-inhabiting, male-circumcising, ethnic Israel.

We might wonder where this passage has disappeared to in the last few decades of evangelical ecclesiology. There's no whiff of "belonging before believing" here. We use 2 Corinthians 6:14 to persuade the teens in the youth group not to date non-Christians at school, and that's about it.

It's not as if Paul is unmindful of the points of discontinuity between the old covenant and the new. He has already spent an entire chapter explaining those discontinuities (2 Corinthians 3), followed by two more chapters emphasizing the outward missional thrust of the new covenant (2 Corinthians 4–5), which he concludes by calling himself an ambassador on behalf of a reconciling God (5:19–20). He even uses the first half of chapter 6 to explain the extravagant lengths to which he would go to "make many rich" in the gospel (6:1–10). Then, in the second half of chapter 6, Paul tells the church to "go out" and "be separate." Apparently, Paul sees no contradiction between the call to be an ambassador of reconciliation and the call to exclude unbelievers from the church. Mission and holiness are not opposed to one another; they work together. It's no wonder that Jesus said that salt that loses its saltiness is useless, like light hidden under a bowl (Matt. 5:13–16).

In my mind, two questions follow from Paul's exhortation. First, do Christians and church leaders today see the biblical connection between the church's holy distinctness and its witness? Second, how does Paul intend for his readers "to bring holiness to completion"? Does he mean for us to start our own colleges or magazines? Write more books? Affirm the center? Begin conferences? Establish denominations? Figure out the perfect formula for relating Christ to culture? Each might play a supplementary and salubrious role, but let's not miss Paul's primary point, for if we do, we can forget the rest. Paul knows that Jesus assigned only one institution on earth with the authority to discipline its membership, to maintain its distinctiveness, and to bring holiness to completion—the local church.

In light of these matters, consider again what it means to join a church. It's not about going with the flow or following the crowd. It's not about making an entrance into society, so that we'll be one of the respected adults. It's just the opposite. It's about identifying ourselves with a group that has committed to being outcasts and to going against the stream. It's like joining up with a group of traveling pilgrims in your hometown, or joining a group of minority language speakers in your own country. Our membership in the new covenant *makes* us distinct, but how do we enact a life of being distinct? We unite our identity to the local church. We covenant together with it, which is good news. It means we're not left to swim upstream all by ourselves. Committing to swim upstream is no casual commitment, and gratefully we have a group that has covenanted to do it with us.

3) A covenant provides the grounds for personal and corporate righteousness. God also uses covenants in Scripture to tell his people how to live. They explain what the righteous life looks like. Moses therefore instructed the Israelites entering the Promised Land to teach their children that keeping God's commands would be their righteousness: "You shall say to your son, '. . . it will be righteousness for us, if we are careful to do all this commandment before the LORD our God, as he has commanded us'" (Deut. 6:21, 25)

The Abrahamic covenant was also interested in Abraham's righteousness, but Abraham was credited with righteousness according to what he believed: "He believed the LORD, and he counted it to him as righteousness" (Gen. 15:6). Paul, of course, picked up this line of thought to help explain a Christian's righteousness in Christ through the new covenant, a "ministry of righteousness" (2 Cor. 3:9). Christ is perfectly righteous, and his righteousness will be counted "to us who believe in him who raised from the dead Jesus our Lord, who was delivered up for our trespasses and raised for our justification" (Rom. 4:23–25). In short, he is our righteousness (1 Cor. 1:30), and through him we become "the righteousness of God" (2 Cor. 5:21).

I referred earlier to the criticism that some make against the Reformed doctrine of Christ's imputed righteousness, as if it were merely a legal fiction.[40] The critique fails to understand what covenants *do*. The righteousness I have as a Christian I have not because it floated "like a gas" across the courtroom, but because the identity we now share with Christ in the new covenant means that we now share all assets and liabilities, just as my wife and I did upon the commencement of our marriage covenant. The good news for Christians, of course, is that our liabilities become his, and his assets become ours.

The new covenant is also interested in seeing that Christians "put on" this righteousness and show obedience to God's law. What guides the Christian into righteousness is beholding the image of Christ and being transformed into that same image. This is the very point Paul makes in his discussion of the new covenant (2 Cor. 3:18; also, Rom. 8:29; 1 Cor. 15:49; Col. 3:9–10). The apostle John makes ethical righteousness the line between church and world: "By this it is evident who are the children of God, and who are the children of the devil: whoever does not practice righteousness is not of God, nor is the one who does not love his brother" (1 John 3:10).

In light of our covenantal call to righteousness, what does it mean to join a church? Does it mean we show up at a church saying, "I meet the qualifications; I measure up"? Yes and no. Yes, because Jesus said that our righteousness must surpass that of the Pharisees (Matt. 5:20). The good news is that we Christians have Christ's righteousness, signified in our baptism. When presenting ourselves for membership in a church, we need his righteousness covering us. But no, we have not perfected the life of righteousness. We have only begun. "Blessed are those who hunger and thirst for righteousness," Jesus also said (Matt. 5:6). The church is the assembly of the repentant. It's a society (or better, an embassy) that has turned around and begun swimming upstream, not a people who have reached the destination. These people *want* righteousness. They fight for it. They plead with God for more of it. They humble themselves before others by

---

[40]See 110 n. 60.

asking for help in pursuing it. A church does not ask a man to defeat lust before it baptizes him, but it should ask him to stop living with a woman not his wife. Christians do sin, but there's a difference as to their position in heaven and a difference in their posture on earth. They fight against it.

Again, consider what this means for joining a church. Joining a church doesn't mean we come with a certificate of merit in our hand, nor does it mean we come expecting a concert where we'll be content to watch others perform. It means we are willing to sign our life over because we know we must ally with a band of brothers and sisters in waging war against the enemy of the world, the flesh, and the Devil.

The local church is a group of people who possess Christ's righteousness, and therefore it's a group that has pledged their lives to fight together for the divine revolution. They've signed an oath. They've made a pact. They've established a covenant. All for one and one for all. Abandoning the covenant means that discipline will follow, as with a deserter from the army. That's the covenant of church membership.

4) A covenant establishes an earthly witness for God. Covenants, insofar as they help to identify God with a distinct people, allowed both Israel and the nations to know who was playing the role of God's witness.[41] God promised to make his name great among the nations and that he would be a blessing to the nations (Gen. 12:2–3), a promise that was eventually tied to his covenant with Abraham (Genesis 15, 17). Though it's not clear that Abimelech knew that God had given Abraham a covenant, the reader of Genesis will clearly view Abimelech's testimony in this light: "God is with you in all that you do" (Gen. 21:22).

Before the people of Israel entered the Promised Land, Moses reminded them of their witness both to the nations and itself through obedience to the stipulations of God's covenant:

> Keep [these statues and rules] and do them, for that will be your wisdom and your understanding in the sight of the peoples, who, when they hear all these statutes, will say, "Surely this great nation is a wise and understanding people." For what great nation is there that has a god so near to it as the LORD our God is to us, whenever we call upon him? And what great nation is there, that has statutes and rules so righteous as all this law that I set before you today? (Deut. 4:6–8)

As bad kings and false prophets began to mislead Israel later in its history, God used his true prophets to invoke the covenants once more and lay claim to who truly spoke for God and who did not. Elijah on Mount Carmel invoked

---

[41]See Christopher J. H. Wright, *The Mission of God: Unlocking the Bible's Grand Narrative* (Downers Grove, IL: InterVarsity, 2006), esp. 87–92; 324–56.

God's covenantal identification with Abraham as well as his own participation in giving witness to that covenantal identification: "O LORD, God of Abraham, Isaac and Israel, let it be known today that you are God in Israel and that I am your servant and have done all these things at your command" (1 Kings 18:36 NIV).

By this same token, God became very concerned about the poor witness or "anti-evangelism" his people did by disobeying his covenant. The prophet Jeremiah explained how the nations would respond to the destruction of Jerusalem following God's judgment:

Many nations will pass by this city, and every man will say to his neighbor, "Why has the LORD dealt thus with this great city?" And they will answer, "Because they have forsaken the covenant of the LORD their God and worshiped other gods and served them." (Jer. 22:8–9; also, Deut. 29:25–26)[42]

As he did with Abraham, God covenants with David in order to make David's name great (2 Sam. 7:9). It's a covenant that God promises to establish "forever" (7:13, 16), an "everlasting covenant," that David might be a "witness to the peoples" (Isa. 55:3, 4).

Jesus is this Son of David who provides a perfect witness to God. He is God's Word and God's image (John 1:1; Col. 1:15). He communicates God without error. Yet Christ unites a people to himself by a new covenant and gives them a charter that authorizes them to act as his witnesses to the end of the earth (Matt. 28:19–20; Acts 1:8). He sends them, just as he was sent (John 20:21). Repeatedly, therefore, Paul tells the churches to walk worthily of the name they represent (Eph. 4:1; Col. 1:10; 2 Thess. 2:12). Churches represent him. They should act like it.

The current trend among many theologians and church leaders to emphasize the missionary nature of the church can become reductionistic. In other words, it reduces the church to its function, like reducing a person's identity to that of his or her job, and only one of those jobs, at that. Still, the missional-church stream of literature rightly calls attention to how central the work of witness or mission should be to the church's identity. As we have already seen, the church's person and work are inseparable, just as the incarnational Christ's person and work are inseparable. Christ came as the incarnate God-man to save a people. Disciples of Christ, likewise, exist, in part, to be fishers of men (Matt. 4:19).

I am especially grateful for the emphasis some missional writers give to the witness of the corporate body. One author writes, "In North America, what might it mean for the church to be such a city on a hill? to be salt? to be

---

[42]See also Deut. 31:28; Isa. 30:8ff.; Jer. 18:13–17.

a light to the world? It means, first of all, that the inner, communal life of the church matters for mission."[43] In other words, the witness of the church does not merely consist in the fact that it *goes*; it consists in the fact that it has a distinct corporate life. Its witness consists in the fact that it's distinct in holiness, love, and unity. So Jesus promises, "By this all people will know that you are my disciples, if you have love for one another" (John 13:35). The church's internal work of holiness and love amongst its members is inextricably tied to its outward work of witness. We must display Christ in our corporate life in order to display Christ in our individual lives. The church, Mark Dever has said, is Jesus' "evangelism plan," because it alone displays the wisdom of God. Paul puts it like this: "Through the church the manifold wisdom of God might now be made known to the rulers and authorities in the heavenly places" (Eph. 3:10). Only an all-wise God could take a group of people who were once at war with him and one another and convert them into an assembly of love. Let all the cosmos look on and marvel!

In light of the church's work of witness, what does it mean to belong to a church? It means that Christians belong to a church not simply to have their spiritual needs met or to be edified. Rather, belonging to a church means committing to live in a particular way and to work toward a particular end. It involves our time, our money, and indeed, our whole person, because the commitment is rooted in our new identity. A businessman or lawyer or doctor in the West today will devote an eighty-hour work week to pursuing his professional ambitions, often because he finds worth, justification, and identity in the labor. Becoming a Christian means that Christ is now the primary source of our worth, justification, and identity, which means that we're free to pour out our lives for the witnessing work of Christ's people—both the internal work of love in the church and its external work of mission. Christ does command us to regularly gather for preaching and practicing the ordinances "as a church." At the same time, belonging to a church equips us to realize that being a Christian is better likened to the weekday's labor, not the weekend's rest.

5) A covenant promises the gift of God's glory to his people. God shares his glory with his covenantal people in the Old Testament. Just as God's relationship with Israel existed prior to the covenant established with all Israel at Sinai (though subsequent to the Abrahamic covenant; see Ex. 2:24; 6:4–5), so too does he grant Israel glimpses of his glory prior to establishing that covenant (Ex. 16:7, 10; cf. Ex. 14:4, 17–18). Nonetheless, it's in the processes of establishing his covenant with all Israel that Israel encounters the greatest demonstrations of his glory (Ex. 24:16–17; 40:34–35; Lev. 9:6, 23), particularly for Moses (Ex.

---

[43]Darrell Guder, ed., *Missional Church: A Vision for the Sending of the Church in North America* (Grand Rapids: Eerdmans, 1998), 128.

33:18ff.). God's glory then remained with the ark of the covenant until it filled the temple (1 Kings 8:11), his most pronounced covenantal dwelling place.

David acknowledges that God's glory will be known among the nations because of God's covenant with Abraham, Isaac, and Jacob (1 Chron. 16:10, 15–22, 24, 28–29; also Ps. 105:8ff.). David also exults that God would share his own glory with the covenantal king (Ps. 21:5)

Sadly, the people of Israel "exchanged the glory" of their covenantal Lord for the glory of idols (Ps. 106:20; Jer. 2:11), to which God ultimately responded by removing his glory from his covenantal dwelling place, the temple (Ezek. 10:4, 18–19). So great had Israel's transgression become, and so closely was his name tied to theirs, that he determined to "vindicate his name" before the nations through a new act of salvation and a new covenant (Ezek. 36:22–32; cf. Rom. 3:25–26).

Remarkably, God promised once more to share his glory through a new covenant (e.g., Isa. 60:1–2, 19; Jer. 13:11; 33:9; cf. Ps. 73:24; Isa. 28:5), a ministry that Paul said exceeds in glory everything that preceded it (2 Cor. 3:7–11; cf. Heb. 3:3). God's glory would fill a new temple (Ezek. 43:2–5; 44:4; Hag. 2:7, 9). It would be shared with his bride, as every nation beholds the royal righteousness and divine beauty of God's people (Isa. 62:2–4).

Christ then came manifesting the glory of God (John 1:14; 8:50; 12:16; 13:31–32; 17:4), and gave his disciples the glory the Father had given to him (17:22). Just as Adam was crowned with God's glory in creation, so the church, astoundingly, will share in Christ's glory (1 Thess. 2:12; 2 Thess. 2:14; 1 Pet. 1:7; 5:4, 10; 2 Pet. 1:3). Paul therefore instructs the church to be glory seekers and to do everything for God's glory (Rom. 2:7; 1 Cor. 10:31), and he promises that they will be transformed from one degree of glory to another as they behold the glory of God in the face of Christ (2 Cor. 3:18; 4:6).

What does it mean to join a church? Joining a church is not about entertainment, even if the services have a worship band and a dynamic preacher. It's about signing up for a team, coming to practice, disciplining the mind and body, encouraging the teammates, sometimes getting harangued by the coach, dreaming of the prize, and giving your all, all in the grand project of attaining the trophy—God's glory, a glory that he remarkably shares with his children.

6) A covenant identifies God's people with one another. Old Testament covenants not only identified God with his people, but they permitted the people of Israel to identify with one another. Interestingly, here is where God's covenants with Israel simultaneously employed familial metaphors and transcended them. Through God's covenant with Abraham, Israel shared a common father, and one Israelite could refer to another Israelite as "brother," indicating this shared family identity. Yet, as the distinction between Abraham's sons Ishmael and Isaac would indicate, covenantal identity simultaneously transcended biological ancestry (see Rom. 9:6–8; Gal. 4:21–31). Two Israelites, in other words, were brothers, yes, but they were also something more, something even tighter, more united, more "one" than biological brothers. Of course, this makes sense insofar as every individual Israelite was principally identified with the Lord. To be identified with the Lord is to be identified with all who are identified with the Lord. And if God is God, only a moment's thought reveals why such an identification is even stronger than the identification of biological ties. God is ultimate; biology is not.

The corporate identification afforded by Israel's covenants was particularly manifest through the persons and work of priests, kings, and prophets. Israel's high priest offered sacrifices once a year for the entire nation (see Leviticus 16). The Davidic king, the son of God, ultimately embodied the sonship of the entire nation. The suffering prophet personified the unbelief or grief of the entire nation (e.g., Lamentations 3). Through the representative work of these three offices, every Israelite shared something far more significant than skin color, a family tree, cultural customs and mores, shared hobbies, a sports jersey, or anything else that humans typically rely upon to establish community, social cohesion, and a shared identity. They shared one salvation, one inheritance, one belief, one baptism, one divine covenant Lord.

Christ then came as representative prophet, priest, and king. He spoke to God's people on behalf of God, he suffered in their place, and he became the new federal head of a new chosen nation. Now, all those united to Christ share in his identity, and this means that Christians share the same identity with one another. The earliest Christians, therefore, referred to one another as "brothers."

Again, what does it mean to join a church? Joining a church is not just one more step in the spiritual disciplines regimen—something you do to grow as an individual Christian. As we said in the last chapter, attending church is more like attending the family dinner table. It's where your brothers and sisters are.

7) A covenant establishes a testimony for the purposes of mutual account-ability among God's people. Not only did God's covenants articulate who among the nations was God's witness, but they also acted as a public witness, testimony, or record for Israel itself. So Moses commanded the Levites, "Take this Book of the Law and put it by the side of the ark of the covenant of the LORD your God, that it may be there for a witness against you" (Deut. 31:26). Marital vows, one can say by analogy, serve to mark off a couple before all others, but they also provide a record of what they promise to one another. That is, vows offer both an outward and an inward witness or testimony.

This testimony then became the standard for which the parties of the covenant hold one another accountable. The Sinai covenant, for instance, established that the Israelites would obviously be held accountable by God (e.g., Deut. 29:1; 28). The Davidic covenant promised that David's son would be punished for disobedience (2 Sam. 7:14). The covenants enabled Israelites to keep one another accountable. God called Israelites to respond decisively to disobedience even among one's closest family members:

> If your brother, the son of your mother, or your son or your daughter or the wife you embrace or your friend who is as your own soul entices you secretly, saying, "Let us go and serve other gods,"…you shall not yield to him or listen to him…nor shall you conceal him. But you shall kill him. Your hand shall be first against him to put him to death, and afterward the hand of all the people. (Deut. 13:6–9; also, 21:18–21)

Why such a radical demand? Quite simply, God's marital vows require faithfulness; God's love requires loyalty: "For the Lord your God is testing you, to know whether you love the Lord your God with all your heart and with all your soul" (Deut. 13:3; also, 6:5). Though the law that requires a person's death has certainly passed with Christ's inauguration of the new covenant, one should not assume that the loyalty Jesus requires of his people is any less radical (see Luke 14:26).

It's not surprising, therefore, that the New Testament repeatedly emphasizes caring for the members of the church seemingly more than caring for outsiders. Jesus divides the sheep from the goats based on whether one has cared for the least of his brothers (Matt. 25:31–46). Paul tells the churches of Galatia to do good to everyone, but "especially to those who are of the household of faith" (Gal. 6:10). Peter commands his Christian readers to show hospitality to one another (1 Pet. 4:9; also Rom. 12:13). Paul even equips the church to exercise a kind of moral care for insiders that it does not apply to outsiders. He says to the Corinthians, "For what have I to do with judging outsiders? Is it not those inside the church whom you are to judge?" (1 Cor. 5:12). He also instructs them to approach the Lord's Supper always mindful of "discerning the body" (11:29).

Someone might object to this last point, saying that surely our love for our enemies and outsiders demonstrates a higher form of love than the love we show for insiders or family members. However, love for fellow church members *is* love for those who were once enemies.[44] Before salvation came we were enemies of God and one another. The love that's shared within a church is powerful precisely because it shows us the other side of God's transformative love for his enemies. It shows us the result—a bunch of former enemies not just getting along but giving themselves to one another.

Again and again Christians are told to help keep one another out of harm's way and to bear one another's burdens: "Brothers, if anyone is caught in any

---

[44]See D. A. Carson, *Love in Hard Places* (Wheaton, IL: Crossway, 2002), 56.

transgression, you who are spiritual should restore him in a spirit of gentleness. Keep watch on yourself, lest you too be tempted. Bear one another's burdens, and so fulfill the law of Christ" (Gal. 6:1–2; also 1 Cor. 4:21; Jude 22–23). Again and again, the strong are instructed to help keep the weak from stumbling (Rom. 14:20–21; 15:1; 1 Cor. 8:13).

The love of Christian accountability best occurs under the authority of the local church, where the ordinances can be distributed in a disciplined manner. In that sense, a local church covenant acts as a kind of testimony. When I join a church, I agree that you will help to oversee my discipleship to Christ, and I will help to oversee yours. Should one of us fail in either discipleship or oversight, we can both return to the original commitment as a point of reference. "Didn't you commit to caring for my soul?" For centuries many churches have even employed formal "church covenants" to act as such a testimony. Such written covenants offer a more articulate version of how Christians agree to live together when submitting to the oversight of a church.

What's the lesson for what it means to belong to a church? Belonging to a church isn't like membership in a wholesale food store such as Price Club or Costco, where membership allows us to purchase whatever discounted items we want. Rather, it means committing to a group of people who will call me to account. It means taking responsibility for others concerning the deepest matters that can be shared between two humans and making ourselves vulnerable in the process.

8) A covenant assigns responsibilities to the parties of the covenant. Covenants also assign responsibilities to the various parties involved. Under the old covenant, for instance, God instructed Israel to circumcise their hearts (Deut. 10:16). They were responsible, it seems, to produce soft hearts that loved God and obeyed his commands. Under the new covenant, on the other hand, God would assume that responsibility (Deut. 30:6; Jer. 31:33; Ezek. 36:26). He would grant them hearts that loved and obeyed him.

In addition to the *what* of responsibility, a covenant establishes *for whom* parties are responsible. In his covenant with David, for instance, God reminds David that he had made David "prince over my people Israel" (2 Sam. 7:8). David wasn't responsible for the Philistines or for their worship. He was responsible for Israel and its worship. God's anger was aroused, then, precisely when Israel's kings and priests misled the sheep for whom they were responsible: "Woe to the shepherds who destroy and scatter the sheep of my pasture! . . . You have scattered my flock and have driven them away, and you have not attended to them" (Jer. 23:1–2; also Ezek. 34:1–10; cf. Deut. 17:18–20).

A covenant tells the parties of an agreement *who* is responsible for *what*. What's striking in the New Testament is that the whole church is often assigned responsibility for matters of dispute, discipline, and doctrine. In Matthew 18, the entire church is called in to adjudicate a dispute between Christians that cannot be resolved privately. In 1 Corinthians 5, the entire church is called in to discipline a member who refuses to repent of his sin. In Galatians 1, the entire church is called to account for the fact that it has tolerated a false teacher. In 2 Corinthians 2:6–8, the church is told to restore a repentant sinner from the discipline originally placed on him by the majority.

Elders have oversight of the body and so maintain the prerogative of leadership. Still, it cannot be denied that, whatever one's polity, every Christian—every church member—is responsible to redress matters of dispute, participate in the preliminaries of discipline through admonition and rebuke, and defend the apostle's doctrine.

Belonging to a church means taking ownership of other people and their discipleship to Christ. It means receiving the Lord's assignment to proclaim, display, and protect the gospel. It means receiving the very keys of the kingdom given by Christ. When we join a church, we find ourselves authorized to bind and loose eternal souls upon the earth as they will be bound in heaven. No president or general, no civil rights leader or movie starlet has received such authority. The ordinary church member, by virtue of his or her connection to the body, has authority untold—the authority to declare who among humanity will live for eternity and who will die, who is a son of the King and who is not. When we join a church, we not only receive the "benefits of membership," but we receive a charge and trust of the highest order. Is it not astonishing, therefore, how lightly Christians today view church membership?

9) A covenant protects God's people. God's Old Testament covenants afforded protection for the individual Israelite from both natural and social harm, including the abuses of authority. Though it would be inappropriate to say that his covenants contained a "bill of rights," we could say that it effected a similar result, namely, protection from tyranny, whether a tyranny of a majority or minority.

We have also considered God's hatred of injustice. It's hardly surprising, then, to see the covenantal provisions made for widows, orphans, and the needy generally.[45] Likewise, Israel was the only ancient Near Eastern country with laws protecting the stranger and alien (Ex. 23:9, Deut. 10:19). Judges were commanded to deal impartially between aliens and Israelites (Deut. 1:16; 24:17). Cities of refuge were open to aliens and native-born alike (Num. 35:15; Josh. 20:9). Sojourners were often classed with widows, orphans, and the poor as deserving the community's provision and just treatment (Ex. 22:21–24; Deut. 24:17–18).

These are some examples of how God's covenant with Israel provided protection for both those in and around it. The larger, more profound point, however, is that, whereas contemporary people fear authoritative structures,

---

[45]Ex. 22:21–25; Lev. 19:14; 25:25, 35–55; Deut. 24:17; 27:18–19.

God provided these authoritative covenantal structures precisely because humans abuse authority. Members of the covenant received greater protection than nonmembers, but both did. By the same token, members of the covenant who disobeyed put themselves in harm's way, including the harm of oppression: "You shall be only oppressed and crushed continually" (Deut. 28:33; see also, 28; 29:18–20; 30:15–20). The protections that come with prosperity were also promised to obedient covenant members: "Keep the words of this covenant and do them, that you may prosper in all that you do" (Deut. 29:9).

The new covenant likewise affords multiple layers of protection. First, it provides protection from the wrath of God because sin is forgiven. Second, it protects the soul against those who can harm only the body. All the protections promised in the Psalms essentially become the Christian's, albeit in a reconstituted form. Third, it protects us from ourselves and our inability to fulfill the requirements of the old covenant. Fourth, it protects the Christian from the enslavement of sin, since sin no longer has mastery over him or her. Fifth, it welcomes Christians into a domain where authority is exercised to create rather than to steal, to build rather than to tear down, which means that Christians can know the protection of God's people (Matt. 20:25; 1 Pet. 5:3).

Finally, what does it mean to belong to a church? It means identifying oneself with God's Son and the Son's people and so being afforded all the protection of his name.

CLARITY

One word that perhaps sums up all nine reasons for formalizing the love between God and his people through a covenant is the word *clarity*. God has always been very clear about those with whom he identifies himself, those he distinguishes, and his witnesses, as well as who is responsible for what, who holds whom accountable, and so forth. Most important of all, he wants his image to be *clearly* displayed in his people. Another way of saying it would be that he wants to *define* all these things for his people and for the world. For the church's part, these nine covenantal benefits clarify the nature of their commitment to one another, both for his glory and their good.

Think again about the couple that cohabits but does not join their lives together through the covenant of marriage. They don't want to identify their names with one another. She doesn't want his, and he doesn't want hers. They don't want to commit to distinguishing one another as their lifelong one and only. They don't want to give public record of their oneness, because there really is no oneness. They certainly don't want to be called to account by one another or others.

In other words, there is no love, or at least their love is sadly deficient. What is love? It's an affirmation of and affection for the beloved's good according to the prescriptions of God. It's the desire to identify with another for the other's progress toward the Holy One. Yet this is the very thing that the cohabiting couple denies in their refusal to covenant their lives together.

Turning to what I'm calling the covenant of local church membership—again, not as a written document but as the agreement itself—it's important to remember that the new covenant comes first. All nine matters above are properties of the new covenant. God identifies himself with his new-covenant believers. He distinguishes them, instructs them in righteousness, elects them to be his witnesses, grants them his glory, and so forth. This covenant is made with all Christians everywhere. Yet there needs to be some place on earth where these things are put into practice. Where does it happen? It happens wherever two or more Christians commit to regularly gathering together in Christ's name to exercise the power of the keys. It is this commitment that I'm calling a covenant, a covenant that both protects his name and facilitates believers' good. By this token, these nine purposes are reasons for submitting to a local church. Submitting to a local church:

1) Identifies us with Christ.
2) Distinguishes us from the world.
3) Guides us into the righteousness of Christ by presenting a standard of personal and corporate righteousness.
4) Acts as a witness to non-Christians.
5) Glorifies God and enables us to enjoy his glory.
6) Identifies us with Christ's people.
7) Assists us in living the Christian life through the accountability of brothers and sisters in the faith.
8) Makes us responsible for specific believers.
9) Protects us from the world, the flesh, and the Devil.

There is probably a better way to systematize what the covenants of the Bible do, as well as to present reasons to join a local church. Nonetheless, I hope the manner in which I have done so at least sends us in the right direction.

Step 7: The covenant commitment of the local church makes the invisible new covenant visible. It's an earthly symbol, sign, or analogy of this wonderful heavenly reality.

The Invisible Made Visible

Another way to explain our membership in or covenant with a local church is to say that it makes the invisible visible—it defines the gospel love of God for the world. The new covenant of Christ embraces an individual silently and invisibly. You cannot see, hear, or smell a person being united to Christ and receiving his Spirit and doing so by faith. It's the strongest, most real union in the world, but its visibility pales in comparison to other forms of union. We can see the jerseys that unite a football team. We can hear the vows spoken by bride and groom. We can smell the blood that would have united one Israelite and another. But we cannot see, hear, or smell the bonds that unite an individual and God, much less the bonds of union between members of the heavenly and eschatological body called "the church," even though these bonds are eternal and unbreakable.

Christ intended for this covenant to show up on earth. He wanted it to be seen, heard, and smelled. He wanted his gospel love to be defined. Of course, doing just that isn't so easy, because the new covenant is a multifaceted thing. It involves the forgiveness of sin. It involves faith and obedience in the lordship of Christ as enabled by the Spirit. It involves a union between God and man, as well as between man and man. So how do we picture it, and do so in a way that's mindful of the threat of false profession?

Christ gave an institutional charter to the church exactly for this purpose— to help picture and define his new-covenant love for the world. Submission to the local church begins with baptism: "Repent and be baptized every one of you in the name of Jesus Christ for the forgiveness of your sins, and you will receive the gift of the Holy Spirit" (Acts 2:38). In baptism, we picture his new-covenant work of death and resurrection, but we also picture the fact that we have died to our old identity and are taking on a new one. Death to the old man, life to the new man.

Submission to the local church continues with the Lord's Supper. The night before he went to the cross, Jesus gave his disciples a cup saying, "This cup that is poured out for you is the new covenant in my blood," and he commanded them to continue to "do this in remembrance of me" (Luke 22:19–20). The repeated celebration of this meal also pictures the new covenant.

Baptism and the Lord's Supper, then, present the borders and boundaries of church membership. They are pictures of the new covenant because they depict the forgiveness of sins through the death and resurrection of Christ, because they are distributed by the authority of Christ the king, and because they should be distributed to those who acknowledge Christ as king. It is here, at the membership borders of the local church, that the world sees, hears, and even smells this covenant. It's where this covenant is enacted and symbolized. Baptism and the Lord's Supper are to church members what names are to people. They are identity markers that tell us something about the realities they picture. It's the members of the church who are the true pictures of the forgiveness, love, and authority of the new covenant.

HOW THE CHURCH DEFINES LOVE

Following the storyline of the Gospels, everything begins with Jesus coming to declare his kingdom. The world had been in rebellion, yet the Father had a plan to save and use a people for his creation's purposes: proclaiming his glory through obedience to his rule. My friend Josh, whom I mentioned earlier, was one such rebel, living life for his own fame. But Christ established his kingdom rule in Josh's heart by saving Josh through his new covenant. Through his life, death, and resurrection, Christ united Josh to himself representationally so that everything that is Christ's became Josh's and everything that is Josh's became Christ's. Josh was actually given a whole new identity. He also united Josh to himself by his Spirit so that Josh could walk in a new and genuine obedience. He united Josh to himself by faith, to which Josh must respond and act. Yet the Lord's new covenant did something more: it united Josh to all the people that share Christ's name, which means that Josh's new love for affirming and responding to his Savior will be demonstrated in affirming and responding to the Savior's people, indeed, Josh's people. Something is now inside of Josh that makes him a glory seeker and a holiness seeker. He wants everyone in the world to know when and where on earth this magnificent love of God shows up.

To accomplish this purpose of proclaiming, displaying, and protecting this precious gospel of God's love, Josh gathers with several brothers and sisters who appear to have credible professions, and together they make a covenant, based on the authority of a charter that Christ actually left for such occasions. Together, each one says to the others, "I've heard your profession of faith. It sounds credible, so let me extend to you the hand of fellowship and call you 'brother' or 'sister.' Also, I will submit my discipleship to Christ to you, trusting that you, as a brother or sister, will faithfully teach, oversee, and discipline my faith, while I will do the same for you. Together we will proclaim, display, and protect Christ's gospel. Together, we will define his love for the world." Notice what this covenant of membership does: it identifies them with Christ, distinguishes them from the world, helps guide them into the righteousness of Christ, creates a society that acts as a witness to non-Christians, identifies them with one another, makes them responsible for one another, acts as a testimony, protects them from the world, and glorifies God.

What should Josh do if he has a vision for missions and the other covenant members have another? If Josh has truly taken ownership for their discipleship and trusts that they have taken ownership of his, he won't lightly dismiss the church and its vision. He won't say, "This is between me and God. Forget about them." Saying as much would not only defy the requirements of the charter, but it would communicate a significant misunderstanding of Christ's new covenant. Josh belongs to a body, a temple, a flock, a vine, and a people. Each of these metaphors doesn't just describe the universal church; each actually characterizes the relationships in Josh's local church. The threads of his faith and discipleship are interwoven with theirs. Thankfully, he knows better than to just leave, take off, and do his own thing. Like a parent or a dutiful son, he knows to be patient, to pray, and to abide in love for their sake and for his own. Maybe he will go to the country he has always wanted go to. Maybe he will go to another. Maybe he will remain at home for a time, and then go. What's assured is that God will honor Josh's submission and faithfulness to the body, whatever form it actually takes, yielding fruit in his own life and in theirs. Among other things, Josh's submission to the church in this matter will help define love for the world. Love isn't doing our own thing. It's being one with a people for the glory of God.

Turning to the Practical

No doubt, applying these ideas and doctrines in any given context takes much wisdom and discernment. As we noted earlier, the doctrine of the church is, perhaps, more political than any other doctrine because it more directly involves hierarchies and real live actors in its formulations. For this reason, it's worthwhile to continue thinking through some of the practical ramifications of our doctrines of membership and discipline.

PART 3

LOVE LIVED

CHAPTER SIX

THE AFFIRMATION AND WITNESS OF LOVE

"We did it all for the glory of love."
—*Peter Cetera*

Main Questions: How should a church responsibly affirm, oversee, and remove members? Should it account for cultural differences in these activities?

Main Answers: To a limited measure, churches should account for culture differences, particularly in terms of a society's complexity and bearing toward Christianity. At the same time, churches should uniformly affirm, oversee, and remove members with a continual mind for its work of giving witness to Christ's holy name.

The bank-robbing, train-highjacking exploits of the man who would become Missouri's most notorious and beloved bandit, Jesse James, began when James was a member of the Mount Olivet Baptist Church in Kearney, Missouri. It seems that James was baptized into church membership in 1866, the same year as the robbery of the Clay County Savings Association in Liberty, Missouri, with which he was associated. An innocent bystander was shot dead. James was also associated with the 1867 bank robbery in Richmond, Missouri, in which the town's mayor and several others were killed, as well as an 1868 robbery in Russellville, Kentucky, which resulted in another man's murder.

Two decades later James's neighbor W. H. Price offered an overly gracious appraisal of these years: "I think he was baptized, and for a year or two he acted as if he was a sincere and true Christian. In his early years, and after he came out of the army, he was quiet, affable, and gentle in his actions."[1]

In 1869, Mount Olivet Baptist Church began deliberating over whether Brother Jesse should be excommunicated from its membership, yet, according to one unverified report, the church was concerned that Jesse would burn down the church building if they voted to exclude him. Two deacons were commissioned to address the matter with James at his mother's farmhouse, where he was known to be staying. The two deacons, apparently, were never able to make their visit. Instead, James himself attended the church's September 1869

---

[1]Ted P. Yeatman, *Frank and Jesse James: The Story Behind the Legend* (Nashville: Cumberland, 2000), 91.

business meeting and removed himself from membership "because he believed himself unworthy."[2] The church was all too happy to consent.

Three months later, in December, James and his posse robbed the Daviess County Savings Association in Gallatin, Missouri. James shot and killed the cashier, Captain John Sheets. The incident brought James into the broader public's eye for the first time when his name was printed in the newspapers. Over a decade of turpitude and infamy would follow.

How to Build a Church

Did Mount Olivet Church do the right thing by allowing James to resign? Should they have excommunicated him anyway? What does all this talk about love, authority, charters, and covenants say about all the colorful characters God brings to the church's doorstep?

Most stories about members joining and leaving churches aren't as exotic as that of Jesse James. Christian Bob shows up one day and says he believes in Jesus. The church says hello to Bob over chicken casserole in the fellowship hall. If it's a megachurch, it says hello with a glossy membership packet. Either way, Bob joins. He attends somewhat regularly. Maybe two or three people get to know him. Maybe he volunteers once in a while. Then his job calls him to another city, and Bob moves on.

We join churches like we join the gym or an athletic club. When things are going well, we show up regularly. When they're not, we take a few weeks or months off. We tell ourselves that it's okay because life moves in seasons. Of course, it helps if we have a "workout buddy." We can push each other, and it's a good partnership as long as our buddy isn't too zealous. If membership gets too expensive or time-consuming, we can always quit.

But God really did mean for the local church to define his holy love for the world—not just for the individual Christian but for the whole church body, together in its corporate life. What does such a church look like from the standpoint of membership and discipline? In this chapter we'll consider the church's responsibilities: how should churches take in, oversee, and remove members? In the final chapter we'll consider the members' responsibilities: what does our covenanting submission require? The goal in these final chapters is to take out our hammers and saws and get a little more practical. How do we go about building the church?

The first question we need to consider is that of cultural difference. Will a gospel-centered church in Baltimore practice membership and discipline in the same manner as gospel-centered churches in Bangkok or Bishkek? From there

---

[2]T. J. Stiles, *Jesse James: Last Rebel of the Civil War* (New York: Alfred A. Knopf, 2002), 203.

we will move through the church membership process—how a church takes in members, oversees them, and then says goodbye.

Step 1: Many people today exaggerate the importance of cultural difference; still, we should pay some attention to cultural differences. This measured approach to cultural differences can be illustrated by three churches in three different nations.

Cultural Difference

One of the principle themes of our era, the era of postmodernity, is cultural difference and particularity. The academy especially makes much of our differences and devotes book after book to contending that some of those differences are untranslatable since human beings are inescapably embedded in their contexts and cannot see beyond them.

In Christian circles, too, we can fixate on how people from other cultures are different, on the difficulties of communicating across cultural and ethnic lines, on the need to contextualize. Missiologists have even developed a graded scale for classifying the contextualization of a church that has been planted by cross-cultural missionaries.[3] They may consider questions such as: Have the people written their own songs or just translated Western ones? Have the locals been allowed to use the "external forms" of their traditional religion, such as placing the Bible in a Koran stand? The biblical foundation for thinking through matters of contextualization comes from the apostle Paul, who showed sensitivity to anthropological realities, saying that he would be "all things to all people, that by all means I might save some" (1 Cor. 9:22).

What has struck me both traveling and living abroad, however, is how similar human beings everywhere are. Different cultures have different idols, but we're all idolatrous to the core. Different ethnicities have different mechanisms for self-justification, but we all spend every day doing it. Different nationalities have different ways of passing the blame, but all do it. Different economic groups may love different treasures, but every man loves the world. For all the time we spend talking about the differences of Adam's sons, scattered in confused communication ever since the Tower of Babel, they're all still sons of Adam. If we as postmoderns had a more holy view of God, we might talk less about cultural particularity and more about our pathetic and predictable similarity.

Just recently, I had the privilege of spending a couple of weeks teaching local pastors in South Africa. At one point a young Khosa (indigenous South African

---

[3]See Timothy C. Tennent, *Theology in the Context of World Christianity* (Grand Rapids: Zondervan, 2007), 193–220.

tribe) pastor-apprentice raised his hand and asked, "How do I fight against caring what people think of me as a pastor?" I am unable as an American to get inside his skin and feel all the social pressures of his family, his tribe, and even his ancestors, all of whom play a much larger role in this young man's sense of self than the average American may experience. His entire worldview is probably more shaped than my own by something Africans call *ubuntu*, which is the Zulu word for "humanness." It communicates the idea that we become more human through other humans. At the same time, how familiar his question sounded! I believe we would be hard-pressed to find a pastor in the United States who never struggles with this young man's problem. An American pastor may experience "fear of man" differently than a Khosa pastor. He will probably give less thought to his ancestors, for instance. But both will experience it, and both are called to repent by fearing God more than man.

Let me advise the reader to look elsewhere for more careful thoughts about these matters. For my part, I would encourage Christians to approach the question of cultural differences with two postures. First, be sensitive. Be able to listen and learn, and expect that some flexibility will be required. In formulating a doctrine of the church, we must especially be mindful of the social dimension of human beings, since belonging to a church means belonging to an authoritative structure. People's various background experiences will dramatically affect their ability to be pastored and loved by elders and a congregation.

Second, we need to be at least a little suspicious about all the talk of our vast differences. Christians should remember that the academy and the world have a vested spiritual interest in blocking the channels of gospel communication and in disobeying the Word of God. It shouldn't surprise us when the philosophies of the world, speaking with the urbane and tweed-jacketed tone of a literature professor, tell us that our concepts about God's being, the gospel of penal substitution, or the practice of church membership are modern, Western, Platonic, oppressive, or something along these lines. There may be occasional merit to aspects of such critiques, but we must also maintain the ability to respond, "Yes, that is what you *would* say," given our knowledge of the world's spiritual commitments. I'm not saying that a Christian's commitments are perfect either, but that's all the more reason to submit to God's Word as best we can. Not only did the apostle Paul adapt some aspects of his method from culture to culture, but he also predicted that the attacks against the gospel would vary from culture to culture (1 Cor. 1:20–25).

Also, let me again throw a little suspicion on the absolute distinction evangelicals sometimes place between form and content or methods and message. It's the distinction we make whenever we talk about using new methods to teach the old message or the need for Christians to keep Ramadan while in Muslim countries in order to be regarded as holy people. As clean and tidy as the distinction may sound to our brains, neither reality nor the Bible allows for such a neat separation. In reality, form and content always affect one another. In the Bible, prescriptions are given for both. For instance, Paul tells us that he has "renounced disgraceful, underhanded ways" and commends himself only through an "open statement of the truth" (2 Cor. 4:2). That's a methodological statement, and it's an important one because these methods inherently commend the message. Similarly, Jesus enumerates several precise steps for how to confront disputes within the church (Matt. 18:15–17), a methodological prescription that derives from the very nature of the gospel itself.

That does not mean that the Bible allows for no flexibility on methods or forms as we move from place to place. Some forms, such as whether to use microphones, are best left to considerations of prudence. Will using microphones help everyone to hear? We need to pay attention to what the Bible says for both form and content, and then, with that in mind, seek to sensitively apply all of it in any given context.

Three Nations, Three Churches

Will a gospel-centered church in Baltimore practice membership and discipline in the same manner as gospel-centered churches in Bangkok or Bishkek? The answer must be yes and no.

Let's compare three different churches, one in central Asia, one on the Persian Gulf, and one in South America.

CENTRAL ASIA

This church has no name or building, and it is not registered with the city because the government would shut it down if it knew of its existence. It meets in a member's home in a central Asian city in which almost everyone is Muslim. It has eight to ten members and can never be allowed to grow beyond twenty or so. When the numbers begin to creep toward twenty, the group will have to divide, because the member's homes are not big enough to accommodate more people and because they need to fly under the radar screen of the city authorities, the Muslim clerics, and sometimes the neighborhood council.

The church gathers every Sunday with its two elders, "Frank" and "Hanz," in order to pray, sing, and learn from the Bible. Both men converted within the last decade and learned most of what they know about the Bible from two or three missionaries, though one of them was able to spend several months in the nation's capital taking a Bible course. Several other house churches meet in this same city, but every member joined this church not by transferring from one of those churches but by conversion and baptism. On any given Sunday, guests, neighbors, or relatives will show up, but those who have not been baptized will not be invited to partake of the Lord's Supper. Of course, there is little incentive for those guests to partake of the meal. In a culture that's utterly hostile to Christianity like this one, nobody will pretend to be a member. There's no social gain to church membership, because it's so costly. In fact, followers of Jesus will lose their family, social, religious, and much of their ethnic identity.

Someone becomes a member upon baptism, yet the baptism always follows several weeks of interviews with the elders and the church. When an individual first makes a profession of faith, Frank and Hanz will question him in order to make sure he understands the gospel and is repentant. If it is a woman making the profession, one of the mature women in the church will be included in the conversations. The person will be asked to make his or her profession before the whole church, at which time the members will ask questions, even though new believers are never strangers to the existing believers but are usually their friends, colleagues, or family members. The elders lead the discussion, but they encourage everyone to participate since that serves to clarify everyone's understanding of the gospel. The congregation never votes to admit someone to membership, but eventually a consensus will arise about whether the one under consideration is a believer or needs to do more growing.

In a Muslim community such as this, it's expected that conversion changes people's lives, and so the church looks for evidence of conversion. It doesn't expect everything about the convert to be cleaned up, but it does want to see the beginnings of the life of faith, particularly the willingness to identify as a follower of Jesus. As a final step, the church will give its affirmation through baptism, which officially welcomes the individual into its assembly. Of course, baptisms are logistically difficult to execute in central Asia. Sometimes baptisms will be conducted in a pond or river some distance from the city, although occasionally they will be done in the wading pool of a wealthy member. (I had the privilege of witnessing one in a wealthier individual's wading pool.)

The members of this particular church certainly love and recognize the members of other churches in their city—they are such a beleaguered few. At the same time, they recognize that Christ calls them to live out their love and submission to his body concretely, so they primarily pour themselves into one another. They encourage one another in doing evangelism. They support one another financially when someone's child ends up in the hospital. They put money together to send an elder to a ministerial training session several hundred miles away in the capital.

It's not that they would never do such things for the members of other churches, but they do understand that their primary obligation is to one another. They will not exercise the authority of binding or loosing the members of other churches whatsoever. They do not unite individuals to other churches. They are obligated to gather regularly with one another, not the others. And they would not exercise discipline on the member of another church.

On one occasion, an elder was having trouble with his family to such an extent that it required the other elder to intervene in a way he would not have done with a leader or a member in another congregation. Thankfully, repentance was immediate, and the process of discipline stopped. At the same time, when excommunication does occur by a church in this city, the entire network of churches will be notified so that the unrepentant one cannot bounce from one group to another. The churches are independent, but they are not autonomous. They are partnered together in the gospel and interdependent.

In short, there are no membership classes, other than the weekly gathering and the discipleship that occurs throughout the week, which is more common in less literate societies. There is no written membership role, because everyone knows who is in and who is out. There is no visit to the pastor's office for an interview; the pastors are not paid much, nor do most even have offices. There is no congregational vote or elder-led edict on new members; no one would be united to a community of this size over the strong objections of several individuals anyway. Doing so would, by definition, sow division in the church. It is incumbent upon any dissenters either to let go of their objections or to demonstrate why their objections are compelling. Consensus is easy to recognize in a group of fifteen or twenty.

I believe we can view this little congregation in central Asia as something of a biblical baseline. It could improve upon some aspects of its membership and discipline practices, such as articulating a more concise statement of faith or church covenant. With time, Lord willing, it will. In churches like these, statements of faith and covenants often consist of several memorized verses that are recited every time the Lord's Supper is taken. However, given its context, it is fulfilling the New Testament criteria of biblical church membership. It is accomplishing what Christ intends for the local church—the proclamation, display, and protection of the gospel through the lives of its marked-off members. It's manifestly clear who the members are, even though no membership list exists. Everyone knows who has repented and believed and who hasn't, because everyone was present at the baptisms of anyone who joined after them. The line between church and world is clear, and the Communion table is guarded to help it remain clear. Professions of faith are carefully considered in order to ensure their credibility. Discipline is practiced in order to maintain purity in the church and out of concern for each member's spiritual health. Every member submits to the oversight of the entire church, including the elders, and every member understands his or her obligation to support the discipleship of every other member. The name and fame of Christ is being protected and burnished, which is the goal.

For our purposes, it's important to observe the contextual factors at play:

- the church's size;
- the hostility of the political, religious, and social environment, and the adversity that comes at every level;
- the lack of culturally nominal Christians—all are first-generation followers of Christ;
- the lack of social incentive to baptize minors (and the obvious disincentives to do so);
- the lack of denominational divisions;
- the relative lack of heretical offshoots (yet);
- the scarcity of economic resources;
- the low transience;
- the fact that every member is not just a new believer but a new believer in a nation, city, neighborhood, and home with no remembered or recent (the last six hundred years at least) Christian tradition.

The members of this church are not living in a Judeo-Christian society, not even a secularized one. As far as they are concerned, the split between Rome and Constantinople never happened, nor did the Protestant Reformation. It's all new for them. It's Christianity in the first century in more ways than one. Following an Easter Day raid a couple of years ago, the church was required to take the security measure of destroying all their materials except their Bibles. I was recently told that their principle concern these days is "to encourage one another in the faith and to keep their leaders out of jail."

It's these very contextual factors that simplify the process of church membership. If the heart of membership is identifying people with Christ and Christ's people, then factors like small congregations, low transience, the complete absence of cultural Christianity, and persecution strongly serve to clarify who is identified with Christ's people and who is not. As one individual told me, "Figuring out who is in and who is out is relatively easy." The greater challenge for them lies with teaching the members of the church about their new obligations to one another, as well as the purpose of church discipline. Of course, these lessons aren't so much membership matters as they are Christian life matters. The Christian life and church membership almost perfectly overlap for these blessed saints. They are the same thing.

So it should be with us.

THE PERSIAN GULF

What if we mix up some of the contextual factors? Suppose, for instance, we boarded an airplane and flew an untold number of miles to the United Arab Emirates, where one of my best friends from seminary, John, pastors the United Christian Church of Dubai (UCCD) in the UAE's most populous city, Dubai. Like the central Asian church, this one is set in a Muslim nation, but UCCD exists by permission of the local sheikh as an incentive to the many international workers who help the oil-wealthy and sometimes complacent Emiratis keep the wheels of their economy in motion. In fact, nearly three-quarters of UAE's population is foreign born, the highest percentage of foreign-born residents in the world.

At the moment, UCCD is the largest English-speaking evangelical church in the country, and the only one officially recognized by the rulers. It has almost six hundred members and shares a relatively nice and commodious building with ten other congregations, each of which speaks a different language. The government has not allowed UCCD to plant other churches and has closed down one of UCCD's meeting places. Unauthorized religious gatherings are illegal. The government also forbids the conversion of Emirati citizens and, therefore, Emirati membership in the church. Hence, the church's membership consists entirely of internationals who come from roughly sixty countries and are relatively transient. Individuals will often come to Dubai for only several years before returning home.

In spite of the clear similarities of context between our central Asian church and UCCD—both being set in Muslim nations in which Christian conversion is dangerous—the challenges of membership and discipline are very different. When John arrived, UCCD bore the typical marks of an international church. Individuals had come from all around the world, representing a number of Protestant denominations. For the sake of promoting unity, therefore, previous leaders had always emphasized a lowest-common-denominator approach to matters of polity, hoping to keep the gospel central and any potential disagreements off to the side. Six hundred attended the weekly gathering, but no assessment had been made as to whether these individuals were believers, and no list existed of who the members were. All John found when his pastorate began was a telephone directory with a hundred names, fifty of whom had left. As John described it to me, "We were in disarray. We didn't know who 'we' were."

In a sense, we could say that UCCD had adopted membership and discipline practices similar to the central Asian church: no membership classes, no official membership list, no visit to the pastor's office before joining, no congregational vote or elder-led edict on new members. Yet the results here were just the opposite. It was unclear who "the church" was. It was unclear who was responsible for whom. It was unclear who was genuinely identified with Christ and who was not. As such, the gospel and its implications were blurry in the lives of those who attended the weekly gatherings, and John discovered the gospel was somewhat blurry in the minds of his congregation—hardly a way to protect and display the gospel from generation to generation.

Additionally, most attendees had a fairly low commitment to the body, in part because they had traveled to Dubai to make money as quickly as possible before returning home. There was little sense of ownership over the discipleship of others. "Mourn with those who mourn? Rejoice with those who rejoice? I'm sorry, who are you talking about? I have to get back to work." Immorality increases, of course, when Christians don't share responsibility for one another, and any Muslim onlookers will only be confirmed in their stereotype of Christianity as a loose and profligate religion.

In light of these contextual factors (high transience, low conceptions of commitment and mutual responsibility, high commitments to making money while in the country, multi-denominational backgrounds, fuzzy understanding of the gospel) John has been transitioning the church toward more structured and rigorous practices of church membership and discipline. Individuals now begin the membership process by attending five membership classes. Class one focuses on the gospel and other doctrinal basics. Class two focuses on worship, how all of life is worship and what corporate worship in particular consists of. Class three considers God's intentions for biblical church membership. Class four explains the church's approach to leadership (elders and deacons). And class five offers a primer on the spiritual disciplines.

Is UCCD asking individuals to do something extra-biblical by requiring everyone to attend these five classes before joining? Hardly. Consider what's being asked of every prospective member in each of the five classes:

- "The Bible says that these are the basics of the gospel and Christianity, at least as we understand them here. Is this what you believe?"

- "The Bible says that a Christian exists to worship Christ individually and submissively with his brothers and sisters in Christ. Is this the Christ you have submitted your life to?"

- "The Bible says that belonging to Christ's body means submitting your life to the good of a local body. Are you willing to do that?"

- "The Bible calls Christians to submit to their leaders and to serve one another. Are you willing to do that?"

- "The Bible says that a Christian is someone who talks to God and reads his Word. May we encourage you to commit to doing that, for your good and ours?"

Various contextual factors blur the gospel in the life of God's people, even in a largely Muslim state, so asking prospective members these five questions helps to clarify it once more. It forces them to slow down and ask themselves, "Is this what I really believe? Am I really committed to following Christ and loving his body as I've said I was?" We argued in chapter 4 that Christ authorized the apostolic church to exercise oversight toward believers. These classes are simply an initial step in giving such oversight. They clarify what it means to be a Christian before God and before the body. Not only that, but they demonstrate pastoral love for prospective members by letting them know who exactly they would be "marrying" by joining UCCD.

Following the five classes, prospective members are interviewed by John or another one of the elders, together with a couple others. In addition to several basic biographical questions, the prospective members are asked to provide their testimony and an explanation of the gospel. The interview provides a good opportunity to expose fogginess in their understanding of the gospel. It also helps the pastors know how to more carefully shepherd each one entering the church.

These five classes and the subsequent interview, I dare say, are a necessary (or at least a very important) part of what we have been calling "holiness seeking." They are an attempt to credibly affirm Christ's holy love with integrity rather than to flippantly assume it, thereby risking calling the unholy "holy." They are the first step toward giving meaningful oversight to a Christian's discipleship. And they are a way of calling the individual to submit to Christ by submitting to his apostolic church on earth. As such, this slightly more rigorous approach to church membership in Dubai accomplishes the same things as the slightly less institutional approach of the church in central Asia. It serves to mark off the church from the world. It clarifies who belongs to God in Christ and who does not. It helps to identify gospel love and distinguish it from something that's not gospel love.

Along these lines, UCCD has been required to discipline a number of individuals lately for pursuing false conceptions of love. One member was disciplined for marrying a non-Christian man and silently disappearing from the church. Another member was disciplined when he abandoned his wife and children. When John asked him whether he had any sense of guilt about his wife, children, or fellow church members, the man angrily denied that he had any responsibility to his church, especially to those he didn't know.

Such disciplinary actions are surely heartbreaking and difficult, but we can trust that these little pictures of present judgment help to save many from a greater judgment to come. They demonstrate love for the church, for the excluded member, for the non-Christian community, and for Christ.

SOUTH AMERICA

Here is one more example in an altogether different context that will allow us to draw out several further lessons. Igreja Batista da Graça (IBG; Grace Baptist Church) in São José dos Campos, Brazil, was planted in 1984 by two foreign missionaries and a Brazilian pastor. It's presently pastored by the native-born Guilson Carlos De Sousa Santos. IBG has approximately 130 members, most of whom are Brazilian and most of whom became Christians through the ministry of the church. (This is the church where I heard the sermon about the Father's love for the Son at Jesus' baptism, which I described in chapter 2.)

The church has always required membership interviews as a part of becoming a member, but since almost everyone joining the church since its inception has been a new convert, the membership interview is essentially an opportunity to ask for a profession of faith, to test that profession with questions, to rejoice with the young believer, and to encourage him or her in the first steps of discipleship. Also, since almost everyone has joined as a new convert the church has never held membership classes. It's never had to explain, "This is who we are in comparison to other churches you might have known." Instead, it's only offered new believer classes, with titles such as "Faith and Repentance," "The Gospel," "Conversion," "Baptism," "The Bible," and "The Church." In the minds of all the young converts, becoming a Christian is synonymous with becoming a church member, as we saw with the church in central Asia. Brazil does have a long-standing Roman Catholic tradition, to which many people nominally subscribe (almost three-quarters of Brazil's population, as opposed to about 15 percent who identify themselves as Protestant), which can play into the dynamic of evangelistic conversations, as well as certain aspects of the new believer class.

Interestingly, Igreja Batista da Graça has reached a sufficient size in the last several years so that believers from other churches have begun to take notice and decide to join. Yet that has introduced something of a quandary for the church as it considers how to wisely conduct the process of courtship between itself and prospective members. The church does not want to require baptized believers from other churches to attend the new believer class, nor does it want to fail in its obligation to responsibly oversee and shepherd even prospective members. Therefore it's asking questions such as these:

- How can we give baptized believers from other churches the opportunity to know exactly what our church believes about the gospel and all its implications before committing to us?

- How can we give these believers the opportunity to know exactly what we teach about other important and gospel-related doctrines that sometimes divide professing Christians, such as Scripture, God's tri-unity, conversion, the Spirit and his gifts, or Christ's promised return?

- How can we give these believers the opportunity to know which church obligations Christ has obligated *us* to ask of *them* as we shepherd their souls?

- How can we explain to these incoming members how the processes of decision making work in this church, both for the regular maintenance of body life and discipleship and for times of disagreement and dispute, so that there might be harmony?

- How do we prepare incoming members for what accountability to this body will look like and what they can expect if they prove unteachable and uncorrectable before the commands of Christ?

In short, IBG recognizes that Christ has given it the authority to oversee, shepherd, and instruct believers. Therefore, it wisely wants to ensure that baptized believers coming from other congregations know what the church believes about these significant matters from the beginning, rather than let people join and then discover a significant area of disagreement later on. For these reasons, IBG is planning to soon require membership classes. What are membership classes if not loving tools for promoting unity in the body?

This is particularly important for a church in Brazil at the moment due to (1) the presence of liberalism in the mainline Lutheran, Presbyterian, and Baptist churches that dominated the Protestant landscape until the 1970s, and (2) the dramatic growth since the 1970s of charismatic and Pentecostal churches that preach a false (or borderline) prosperity gospel. IBG has encountered prospective members in the last year coming from one such church or another with wrong or at least shallow conceptions of Christianity. One woman who had been a member of a charismatic church for years discovered in the process of an interview that she didn't know what the gospel is.

Step 2: In other words, churches should pay attention to how complex the culture is as well as the society's favor or disfavor toward Christianity, which requires churches to ensure that both church and Christian have the opportunity to adequately "explain" themselves.

The Significance of Context

Should a gospel-centered church in Baltimore practice membership and discipline in the same manner as gospel-centered churches in Bangkok or Bishkek? On the one hand, I think the answer is no. Let's consider just one purpose of biblical church membership, that of identification. We've been saying that Christ has authorized churches to identify believers with himself and with his people. Accomplishing this purpose might look a little different from situation to situation according to two considerations of prudence: the complexity of a society and the favor of a society.

SOCIETAL COMPLEXITY

To begin with, the larger and more complex a society becomes, the more difficult it is to identify believers with Christ and with Christ's people. It's made difficult by job transience, social mobility, church size, urban sprawl, demanding work schedules, religious pluralism, ethnic prejudice, multi-denominationalism, heretical and false-gospel churches, church-hopping, and by social factors such as individualism and consumerism. Quite simply, the bigger and more complex society becomes, the harder it is to know "who's with whom," like finding a face in a big crowd versus a small one.

Suppose a young man shows up on the doorstep of your church in the United States today saying, "I'm a Christian, please let me join." You have never seen him. You don't know his parents, friends, or colleagues. After all, he lives twenty miles from where your church meets, and he works further away still. You can ask him what churches he has attended before, but you don't know which "Jesus" and which "gospel" those churches have taught him. It might have been an easy-believism gospel, a Lordship gospel, an Emergent gospel, a kingdom gospel, a Greek Orthodox gospel, a mainline liberal gospel, or a Mormon gospel. He does tell you that on Sunday nights he will continue attending an exciting singles' ministry sponsored by another church, which gives you some indication of his commitment level to your church. Besides that, he spends all his waking moments at work, trying to stay on top of the market. What does his life look like at work? Is it any different from his non-Christian colleagues? You don't expect to ever know unless something drastic happens involving the law. Besides, there's no time to check in with him regularly. Your schedule is too full. If he does join your church, you expect to see his face floating past in the crowd on Sunday mornings, and that's about it. Maybe you will remember his name; maybe you won't.

By comparison, suppose a young man shows up on the doorstep of your church in a smallish city in central Asia saying, "I'm a Christian, please let me join." Of course, it wouldn't really be on the doorstep of a church building; it would be in his home, after the two of you shared one large dish of pilaf. You would know who he is because he has lived in the same house with its cinderblock walls and corrugated metal roof all his life, which is a two minutes' walk from your house. You would know that his parents converted from a superstitious form of folk Islam only two years ago and that for three months his father has not been paid in cash by the towel factory where he works; he's only been paid in towels, which he then sells on the street in order to set food on the family dinner table. The lack of money has not been a family concern (they're used to that) as much as finding a good way to share the gospel with the more stridently Muslim grandfather before he dies, the gospel that they first heard through you. You would know that this young man is bright, because you taught him to play chess when he was seventeen, and he beat you on the fourth game you ever played, but you would also know that he has no real job prospects due to his lack of connections with city officials. Those officials cannot be bribed with towels (not that you would recommend bribery). When he says, "I'm a Christian," you would know exactly what he means because you have been discussing the matter with him for months, even years, and no one else in his entire world ever has.

What's the difference between these two situations? The first one pictures a society that's more religiously, culturally, and economically complex. I don't know that I would say either society is preferable to the other. They both have their advantages and disadvantages, and neither of them is what's promised in glory. The point here is that it's far harder to meaningfully identify someone with Christ in the first situation. There's a lot more explaining to do from both sides. Therefore, we might summarize how churches in simple and complex societies may need to practice church membership and discipline differently with the word *explanation*. In a complex society, both sides of an agreement need to do more *explaining*, as in "When I say 'Christian,' I don't mean this, but I do mean that." I'm using this word *explain* loosely, of course. I'm not talking about something you can do in any one conversation. Rather, I'm looking for a way that we in fast-paced, pluralistic urban settings can give ourselves even a modicum of the personal information we would have for someone who grew up in our neighborhood.

My friend Robin's church in Delhi, India, a transient city of eighteen million people, tries to fill in this knowledge gap by requiring a six-month waiting period before admitting someone into membership (IBG in Brazil has the same requirement). The church decided on using this particular tool as an opportunity for the church and the Christian to get to know one another before making a covenant commitment. I'm not recommending a trial period. In fact, I can think of reasons not to use one, but I would say that different contexts might require churches to find different ways of explaining what entering the covenant of church membership through baptism and the Lord's Supper means. At the risk of sounding un-innovative, a simple solution that works in most contexts today is a membership class. Call it an "explanation class," if you want. I would also recommend many of the tools that churches one hundred years ago used, such as membership interviews, statements of faith, written church covenants, membership rolls, even letters of transfer and membership packets. All these are simple ways for the church to explain to prospective members, "This is who we are," and for them to explain to the church, "This is who I am."

Requiring careful explanations from both sides is, at the very least, a matter of prudence. It might be a matter of integrity. Certainly it's a matter of love for both parties in that it promotes transparency, instruction, and unity.

SOCIETAL FAVOR OR DISFAVOR

The same basic principles apply when we consider how one context will differ from another in terms of the society's attitude toward Christianity. Is the society at large favorable or unfavorable toward Christianity?

Consider two societies, one in which Christianity is vehemently opposed and one in which it's tolerated or even favored. When a society opposes Christianity, as in the first century or in Muslim lands today, there will be huge social disincentives for identifying oneself with a church. When it favors Christianity, as in some pockets of the United States and certainly within Christian families everywhere, conversion and membership are incentivized. And, of course, there's a broad spectrum in between favor and disfavor.

When I refer to social incentives or disincentives, I mean the approval or disapproval a person will receive from friends, family, colleagues, and the civil authorities for becoming a Christian and being baptized. A seven-year-old boy in a Christian family in Mississippi knows he will receive his parents' approval by becoming a Christian and asking to be baptized. A twenty-seven-year-old man in a Hindu community in Orissa, India, knows that he will not receive such approval. Conversion in the first scenario is incentivized. In the second it's disincentivized.

On one hand, Christians should praise God for any social incentives that point people toward Christianity. In any given situation those incentives may be part of what God is using to draw someone to himself. On the other hand, churches should exercise the prudence of taking greater care when such factors are present, because a society's favor or even tolerance toward Christianity can cloud the ability to see whether a person is responding to Christianity or to something else. Does Johnny want to be baptized because the Holy Spirit is truly at work in his heart, or because his older sister was just baptized, and we all congratulated her and took her to eat at her favorite restaurant?

If one goal of church membership is to identify individuals with Christ, then the issue of clarity is very important. When Frank baptizes someone in his central Asian church, the meaning of that baptism is clear to everyone on the outside of the church—to the dishonored Muslim parents, to the shocked Muslim neighbors, to the incensed local clerics, and to the perfidious city officials. To them, a baptism means, "He's forsaking us and choosing that false religion, Christianity. He's no longer one of us." A baptism's meaning is also quite clear to everyone on the inside of the church: "He's identifying himself with our Savior. He's one of us!" And it's quite clear to the one being baptized: "I'm putting my reputation, family, job prospects, and even my life on the line, but what else can I do? Christ alone is my Savior, and these are now my people."

We can hardly say that the meaning of baptism is this clear in the West today. Yes, being a Christian is less popular today than fifty years ago, but we're still a long way from the first century or from our Christian brothers and sisters in Muslim lands.

What's interesting is that some church leaders in the West now point to the fact that we live in a post-Christian society as a rationale for doing away with all the institutional elements of church membership, such as membership interviews, rolls, or classes. They say that these things hinder authentic community. It is probably true that there are fewer social incentives for joining a church in a post-Christian society than in a Christian one, but is the postmodern West any less complex? Is it less confused about the meaning of Christianity? My sense is that Western society is even more confused about what a Christian is. It's not that Christianity has gone away in our post-Christian society (if you want to call it that). It's that Christianity has taken on a thousand faces, like a person standing in a hall of mirrors. "Will the real Jesus step forward, please?" Even many secular Europeans who personally disavow Christianity remain members of their national churches. Such utter confusion calls for more clarity, not less.

THE DIFFERENT CHALLENGES OF OVERSIGHT

As the planet becomes increasingly urbanized and globalized, most church leaders increasingly face the same challenges when it comes to affirming credible professions of faith. But really, this is the easier challenge. So far we've only touched on the boundaries of church membership. The harder challenge is knowing how to meaningfully oversee members from month to month and year to year. How do pastors and elders give oversight to people who live thirty miles away? How does a congregation enact discipline with integrity on member number 1,281, whom it has never met? How does a young mother find an older woman to disciple her when all the older women are so busy?

I worked for several months as an interim pastor on one of the comparatively affluent Caribbean islands. The island is well known for offshore banking, which means the church was filled with bankers, accountants, and other professionals. I was only an interim pastor, so members sometimes felt free to be a little more candid with me. One day over lunch, a member of the church's finance committee complained about pastors who ask the church for lunch budgets. He was an accountant, and his firm didn't give him a lunch budget, he said. He was frugal. He usually brought a sack lunch to work.

This wasn't the only day that week in which I would have lunch with a church member for discipleship purposes. I was likely to have two to four other lunches, not to mention breakfasts and dinners. For him, a lunch like this was more of a "one-off," or at least a monthly thing. For me, such a lunch was an important tool for overseeing the souls of sheep. In a modern urban context, a pastor cannot go house to house catechizing people like Richard Baxter did in eighteenth-century England. Pastors today make breakfast and lunch appointments.

To the man's credit, I believe he paid for lunch that day, yet I did encourage him, as a member of the finance committee, to look favorably on any pastor's request for a lunch budget. I told him that's how a pastor pastors busy business-men and that he didn't want to put a pastor in the position of always having to let others pick up the tab. Don't muzzle the ox. This is *not* the advice I would give to a member of Frank or Hanz's church. Lunch budget? They can't even afford to pay their pastors.

I don't want to reduce how the church defines love for the onlooking universe simply to membership classes and pastoral lunch budgets. I'm simply making the point that, as we move from place to place and age to age, membership matters might look a little different in these kinds of ways. Anyone who has spent time pastoring knows that the work is largely mundane matters such as membership classes and figuring out how to pay for the fourth lunch that week, even if it's just fast food.

Step 3: At the same time, churches everywhere are tasked with mark-ing off a holy people, which will always be opposed by the world, the flesh, and the Devil.

The Significance of Context

We need to return to the larger point, which is that it's relatively immaterial where your church is, whether Baltimore, Bangkok, or Bishkek. Every church everywhere is tasked with marking off a people who are holy unto the Lord. Every church has been charged by Christ to affirm credible professions of faith and to oversee the professors, disciple them, and exclude them when necessary. Every church is tasked with defining God's love for the world, which means all will be opposed by the world, the flesh, and the Devil. No matter where it goes geographically or culturally, the church abides in enemy territory, an outpost despised by the lord of the land. The attack of a torch-wielding Hindu mob in Orissa is different from the subterfuge of saccharine-sweet cultural Christianity in Mississippi, but, interestingly, the church protects the gospel against both kinds of attacks by asking every prospective member the same question: "Are you sure you're really ready to take up your cross and give yourself to being identified with Christ and his body?" It protects the gospel by taking great care in uniting members to itself and by carefully overseeing souls from month to month and year to year through teaching God's Word.

A FOURTH CHURCH

The insignificance of context can also be illustrated with a fourth church, one that I briefly mentioned above. In Delhi, India, my British friend Robin pastors a multiethnic but mostly Indian church of about eighty members and twice the number of attendees. Delhi is a massive city. There are countless transplanted workers. Therefore, Robin faces some of the same problems John faces in Dubai, such as transience and a lack of commitment. But in Robin's church, the lack of commitment is a consequence of the fact that Indians feel heavily identified with the geographic region from which they come. Many Christians live in the south of India, but they will move northward to Delhi for work. When they do, they maintain a strong sense of identification with their home church in the south and so never join the Delhi congregation or give a portion of their income to it. Instead, they send their tithe to their parents' church down south.

The congregation in Delhi is not beset by the same kind of individualism that characterizes many churches in the West. In fact, people in this caste-driven society maintain a strong sense of connection with more traditional forms of identity, such as family, class, and region. Poverty has sent them elsewhere in search of employment, but the social fabric, presently, remains strong. It's this very social fabric, however, that hinders individuals from taking ownership of the body of Christ where they actually live and breathe. It causes them to forsake loving the brothers and sisters whom they see.

The point is that whether a society is individualistic, family-centric, or regionalistic, people identify themselves with Christ and his people reluctantly, because it goes against our sinful nature. That reluctance is universal. It's a condition of the fall itself. When Jesus called us to forsake our family members, let the dead bury their own dead, sell everything, and take up our crosses and follow him, he was invading every culture, every nation, every sociological group, and every era of history and calling us to participate in a new history and a new creation. In this new history and creation, everything that defined "me" in the old creation is now up for grabs. It's not that I—to use myself as an example—will no longer see the world through male, Caucasian, American, Leeman-family, and (most significantly) sinful eyes. It's that all the cultural encrustations attached to each of those categories are no longer determinative. They no longer bind me. I have been crucified with Christ. I have been born again. I am a new creation. Christ alone has the authority to utterly determine *me* from start to finish. I will always think as a male, in one sense, but I can now take my maleness and Americanness and everything else that defines me and put them at his feet. "What will you have me do with these, Lord? Define maleness for me. Help me wisely steward my American citizenship." This is why Paul could say that in the kingdom there is neither male nor female, slave nor free, Jew nor Greek. Christ determines who we are, because that's an identity that will stretch out over eternity.

The new identity is not just a new individual identity; it's a new corporate or family identity. Hence, Christ gives the local church the authority to bind us. Strange, isn't it? Yet it's within the local church on earth that this new Christian identity—individual and corporate—finds its fullest expression in the here and now. It's within the membership of a local church that we must "put on" the love and holiness that causes us to image the Creator himself (see Paul's instructions for local churches in Colossians 3, especially verses 9 to 17). This means the most amazing thing: I now share a closer unity with Priya, a woman at my church with Zambian citizenship who was born of Indian descent, than I share with my blood brother, at least by virtue of the fact that he's my blood brother, a relationship that ends at death. Church membership in Baltimore, Bangkok, and Bishkek is all about affirming this eternal fact and putting flesh on it in everyday life: baptism and the Lord's Supper mark off people like Priya and me; the teaching ministry of the church disciples us, and then we get to work living out the loving unity of Christ. This is true no matter where the church is located. Church membership affirms individual Christians as God's people, and then it holds them up as a witness for the world.

WHAT A CHURCH IS DOING BY ACCEPTING MEMBERS

When we boil it down to its barest essence, church membership is a list of names affirmed by the apostolic local church for the sake of giving witness to Christ's name. Insiders and outsiders need to know who belongs to God. They need to know who is wearing Christ's jersey, or carrying his flag, or bearing his name. When a church receives someone into membership through baptism and the Lord's Supper, they are saying to the individual and to the whole world, "One of us—a Christ follower! A Christ representative. World, you have our endorsement as a church to look at this individual as a picture of what Jesus is like. Right here in this person you can witness the holiness, love, and wisdom of God" (see Eph. 3:10). It may be only a spark of God's holiness, love, and wisdom that are visible, but the fire has been kindled. What a weighty and stupendous thing church membership is.

When we boil corrective church discipline down to its barest essence, it's the threat of removing a name from the list or it's the action of actually removing it. Insiders and outsiders need to know that some actions and perhaps some individuals do not belong to God. Corrective church discipline begins with the word of rebuke, and it culminates in the act of removal. What a weighty and fearful thing church discipline is.

On a planet well supplied with pen and paper, I'm not sure why a church wouldn't write down the names of its members, other than for the threat of persecution and imprisonment. I've had conversations with church leaders who object to the idea of church membership as unbiblical. After all, there is no mention of an earthly membership roll in the New Testament. What is manifestly clear throughout the New Testament, however, is that the apostles were very interested in ensuring the right individuals were affirmed by the church and that the wrong individuals were not. The apostolic church was to bind on earth what would be bound in heaven because there is a very clear list of names in heaven, found in the book of life (Rev. 20:12–15). Some names will be on that list, and many will not. Furthermore, the church is utterly interested in affirming the presence of Christ in whomever he's found so that the church might give witness to him. In the final analysis, therefore, I suppose the issue is not whether a written list exists, so long as it's clear to everyone on the inside and the outside of the church *who exactly belongs to the church*.

By boiling down church membership and discipline to a "list of names," I don't mean for an instant to suggest that getting someone onto the list or off the list is all that matters. I want to say just the opposite: because the names on the list are there *for the purpose of representing or giving witness to Christ*, the church has an interest in overseeing, discipling, and equipping all those names toward greater and greater conformity to Christ until he comes again.

Step 4: In order to responsibly affirm members, a church should ensure that prospective members understand who they are committing to through any necessary classes, doctrinal statements, and words to guard the Lord's Table; the church should also ensure that prospective members adequately grasp the gospel.

Member Affirmation

To help churches responsibly approach the task of affirming, overseeing, and disciplining the saints, we'll spend the rest of this chapter walking through the processes of church membership and discipline from the church's side.

Something in my anti-institutional cultural genes is reluctant to call what follows a program, but I think that is what I'm offering. It is a plan for accomplishing a certain end, which is the definition of a program. Hopefully it's also just responsible, biblical Christianity. It's also a series of activities that, I believe, are useful for marking off the church from the world. The following program aims to help churches affirm individuals as Christians and then hold them up as witnesses for Christ. Some of the ideas are explicitly biblical; some can be inferred from the biblical text; and some are simply prudential ways of fulfilling the biblical mandates of marking off a people from the world. In terms of context, I'm writing principally for a contemporary, Western, urban context, yet I attempt to be mindful of other contexts.

GATHERING TO HEAR GOD'S WORD; DISPERSING TO PROCLAIM IT

Church membership begins with God's Word, because life always begins and grows as God's Spirit employs God's Word to convict of sin and to recreate life in God's image. Together, God's Word and God's Spirit created the universe. Together, God's Word and God's Spirit have inaugurated a new creation in the hearts of all those who repent and believe. Unbelievers cannot turn to Christ without hearing the Word of God preached to them, nor can they turn without the gracious work of his Spirit. Disciples are made and grown through God's Word and God's Spirit.

Christ's disciples disperse into the nations to call sinners, by faith, with the voice of Jesus and the power of his Spirit. When those sinners repent and gather together in Father, Son, and Spirit's name through baptism, there is the church. Yet the work of the church, Word, and Spirit has not finished. As the disciples have begun, so they continue. They must now teach everything that Christ commanded. They gather together primarily to hear God's Word, to worship, and to be conformed to the image of Christ by the Spirit of Christ, and then they disperse in order to call still others with the voice of Christ by the Spirit of Christ to come and worship, as well. The boomerang goes out and then comes back.

Do you want a church membership that defines God's love for the world? Then center your church on God's Word. This begins in the pulpit, yes, but his Word then needs to reverberate in conversation after conversation throughout the church, until it informs the very life and breath of the church, until it informs the hands in all their *handness*, and the ears in all their *earness*, and the feet in all their *feetness*. Then hands, ears, and feet disperse, sometimes together and sometimes apart, to proclaim this same Word and gather in still others.

NEW BELIEVERS AND MEMBERSHIP CLASSES

Christ charged the church to teach disciples everything he commanded, including what it means to be united to Christ's body. A new believer class or a membership class is a prudential tool for teaching believers about several aspects of life in the local church. Membership classes:

- Are useful for clearly teaching what a church believes about Jesus and his gospel.

- Are useful for teaching newcomers everything that a church believes, thereby promoting unity among all who join.

- Are useful for teaching newcomers how the church expects members to live toward one another. This promotes mutual care and concern.

- Can be used for distinguishing a particular church theologically and denominationally from other churches. Many church leaders these days are anxious to downplay such distinctions and differences; however, I have observed that people, especially unbelievers, appreciate such honesty. Being forthright about distinctives shows integrity. It also helps prevent arguments that might come later.

- Can be used for explaining matters of polity and how decisions are made in a particular church. Doing so promotes unity in the body. When disagreements and disputes come in the life of the body, everyone knows how they will be resolved.

Christ calls believers to submit to the authority of the local church. Therefore, I don't believe it's a biblically unwarranted imposition to make on prospective members to ask them to attend a new believer class or a membership class. In fact, it's a way of fulfilling the church's charge to teach and disciple from the very beginning of the relationship between a church and an individual.

I have heard Christians object to being required to take a membership class, yet I've never heard of new believers objecting. New believers are usually happy to learn all they can and quickly submit themselves to such opportunities. Sadly, it seems to be the older believers who object, either because they aren't accustomed to the idea, or because they object to being required to do anything. Insofar as that's the case, they are demonstrating the lack of submission that is contrary to the very heart of biblical church membership and Christianity.

Whether the introductory class is called a "new believer class" or a "membership class," the important point to understand about such classes is that they promote a shared understanding across a range of topics and, therefore, unity. In that sense, they facilitate love. Such classes are not essential, and there may be some contexts where they would be needlessly cumbersome. For instance, I can imagine a house church of twelve people in the heart of a large Western city in which a membership class might be unduly formal and awkward. Perhaps what's needed in this type of setting is a number of deliberate and planned conversations about what that church believes and what it means to be committed to that local body.

However, I would encourage church plants and house churches to have deliberate conversations from the outset that mimic the structure of a membership class, asking: What's our statement of faith? How will decisions be made? How will we hold one another accountable? With whom will we affiliate? For the sake of love and unity, answers to these questions should be built into the

DNA of a church. If a church waits until it grows from ten to fifty people to formally answer these questions, it just might discover that its fifty members don't share the same answers. I've heard of this happening more than once. Churches should be especially clear with incoming members about the practice of church discipline. Every individual who unites with the church should be told very clearly from the beginning, "We practice church discipline. We do it for these reasons. We do it in this way, and here's why."

Let me try to illustrate what such classes accomplish this way: before I got married, our premarital counseling pastor encouraged my fiancée and me to develop a family budget at the very beginning of our marriage, even if we didn't think we had that much money to shift between budget categories. Why? Because we had both been making spending decisions for years based on an implicit set of personal values. I gave a high valuation to eating out, which was reflected in my personal budget. She gave a high valuation to vacations, which was reflected in her budget. Having a budget conversation at the front end has required my wife and me to be explicit about our different values in the calm environment of shared planning—and my wife and I are only two, not ten, twelve, or two hundred. A family budget, clearly, is a matter of prudence, and so are membership or new believer classes, yet they promote unity and love.

STATEMENT OF FAITH

The same principle carries over into a church's statement of faith. A church best serves its members by being explicit about what it believes. Are statements of faith biblical? They are at least inferential in Scripture:

- Jesus was interested in the specifics of who Peter believed he was (Matt. 16:15–17).

- Paul told the Galatians to reject anyone who taught a different gospel than the one he taught (Gal. 1:6–9). Apparently, he assumed they shared understanding of what that gospel was.

- John told churches that they must believe that Jesus is the Christ, that he came in the flesh, and that he is the Son of God. He also insisted that churches have a right doctrine of sin. If anyone claimed to be without sin, he was a liar (John 3:16; 20:31; 1 John 1:8–9, 4:2, 15; 5:1, 5, 10, 13; 2 John 7, 10).

- Peter and Jude devoted entire letters to preparing the churches against teachers with false understanding of Christian life and doctrine.

- The author of Hebrews warned his readers, "Do not be led away by diverse and strange teachings" (Heb. 13:9).

- Jesus warned churches against the false teaching of the Nicolaitans and Jezebel (Rev. 2:15, 20).

- Paul said that wrong views about the eschaton would render his preaching and the Corinthians' faith useless (1 Cor. 15:12ff.).

No verse in the New Testament says, "Churches should have a statement of faith," but the Epistles uniformly teach that the churches need to hold onto right doctrine and eschew all false doctrine. Though the Epistles correct and teach doctrine in their own right, they also speak as if the churches had a shared understanding of the apostles' doctrine (see also Gal. 2:2, 7–9).

Sometimes Christians complain that statements of faith overly systematize or constrain the biblical narrative. Others like to say that they have "no creed but the Bible." Both responses, I dare say, demonstrate a lack of self-understanding. *Everyone* has a statement of faith. *Everyone* believes particular things about Scripture, God, creation, the fall, Christ's person and work, the church, and the last days. Not only that, but those personal beliefs invariably systematize Scripture. We can walk up to any Christian and ask, "Who is God?" or "What is the Bible?" or "How must we be saved?" and he will have an answer that's more than a collection of Bible verses. Admittedly, not every Christian could articulate their answers to some of these questions. To that end, a statement of faith does the wise shepherding work of helping people to do so, and then determines whether their answers line up with the beliefs of a particular church.

While the existence of a statement of faith is a matter of biblical inference, putting a statement of faith together pushes us into the realm of prudence. Accordingly, a good statement of faith attempts to balance a number of competing considerations. It aims to be comprehensive and concise, universal and particular, historical and current, careful and simple. Above all else, a statement of faith should ask Christians to affirm only what the Bible asks them to affirm. Striking these balances wisely requires some sensitivity to one's own context.

Comprehensive and concise. On the one hand, a statement of faith should provide a comprehensive summary of the main categories of Christian doctrine, since Christian doctrine is interconnected. A statement of faith might look like a numbered list, but it's more than that. It's also a spider's web, where every doctrine conditions every other doctrine.[4] Touch a spider's web in any one spot and the whole thing vibrates. Likewise, if we touch the doctrine of Christ's person, our doctrine of Christ's work will shiver with implications. If we touch

---

[4] Of course, the spiderweb analogy is not perfect. There's a reason why systematicians have given both prolegomena and the doctrine of Scripture priority for so long and why many today give the doctrine of God priority (I think good arguments can be given for both). Either way, there's no way to capture a sense of priority or foundations with the spiderweb analogy. Still, I believe the spiderweb analogy captures certain aspects of systematic theology and the connections between doctrines in a way a linear list does not.

the doctrine of God's love, everything from our gospel understanding to our church polity will shake. In light of such interconnectivity, a good statement of faith presents a unified way of looking at the Christian life and the world through the Scriptures, or, at least, a church's understanding of the Scriptures. It helps Christians see that all these matters are tied together.

On the other hand, a statement of faith should do this briefly and concisely. It should provide doctrinal pointers rather than doctrinal explanations. It might affirm "justification by faith alone," but it doesn't need to fully explain the matter. The goal is to simply allow people to know where a church stands.

Universal and particular. On the one hand, a statement of faith should affirm those things that are universal to all Christians everywhere, such as the proposition that Christ is fully God and fully man—one person with two natures.[5]

On the other hand, a statement of faith may need to respond to the doctrinal challenges relevant to a particular time or place. For example, a church in present-day South Africa that's surrounded by Pentecostal churches preaching a prosperity gospel may choose to articulate the gospel or a doctrine of the spiritual gifts in a manner that accounts for the excesses and errors of these churches. Obviously, such decisions need to be weighed carefully.

Historical and current. Statements of faith should be both historical and current. On the one hand, there's wisdom and humility in placing one's church within the broad stream of Christian theological tradition by using an older statement of faith, even at the risk of using antiquated language. Our churches do well to admit that we have not figured out the Bible on our own. Rather, we stand on the shoulders of the faithful saints who have preceded us.

On the other hand, most members more easily identify with language written in their vernacular, which may commend using a new statement. I encourage churches to look for ways to combine both considerations.

Careful and simple. On the one hand, a statement of faith should carefully articulate what a church believes, recognizing the ability of false teachers to exploit overly broad or vague language. Here is one large American church's entire doctrine of God, at least as it is stated in what I would call its "out front" statement of faith: "God is bigger and better and closer than we can imagine."

---

[5]Postmodern and globalizing trends in theology would debunk the notion that a statement of faith could offer such "universal" statements since all doctrine is embedded and perspectival. E.g., Steve Strauss offers an interesting reflection on how the historical circumstances of the Ethiopian Orthodox Church make the formulations of Chalcedon unsuitable for communicating the same meaning Western churches mean to communicate through Chalcedonian Christology. Steve Strauss, "Creeds, Confessions, and Global Theologizing: A Case Study in Comparative Christologies," in *Globalizing Theology*, ed. Craig Ott and Harold A. Netland (Grand Rapids: Baker, 2006), 140–56. Whereas I agree that all theology is embedded and incomplete, and that some measure of sensitivity to context is required in our doctrinal formulations, I also believe that we can become a little too enthusiastic about this point and overstate the significance of contextual differences. Obviously, this is a larger conversation than I can undertake here.

To its credit, the same church also has a longer, more comprehensive "behind the scenes" statement (available on request). What's wrong with this church's "out front" statement? It's certainly friendly and warm. The trouble is that everyone from a Unitarian to a Hindu could affirm it (with the right qualifications).

On the other hand, statements of faith should be simple and clear. Christians need to be able to understand what they are affirming.

Contextual. How comprehensive and how concise? How careful and how simple? To some measure, finding that right balance depends on one's context. A literate and educated congregation might require a different balance from that of an illiterate, uneducated one. Having said that, I fear that the democratic and anti-elitist impulses that resound throughout the West cause many church leaders to err toward simplicity and not require much of their congregations. As a result, we ask our contemporary college-educated churches to understand less than the writers of the New Testament Epistles asked of their readers. How comparatively educated do we expect the first readers (or hearers) of Hebrews were? Should we ask less of our churches than the author of Hebrews did?

Biblical. Above all else, a church should never bind a believer's conscience where Scripture does not bind it. Statements of faith should never go beyond the Scriptures. Furthermore, statements generally do well to ask believers to affirm only those things that have a broad degree of Scriptural attestation, rather than one or two proof-texts.

A CHURCH COVENANT

If a statement of faith articulates what a church believes, a church covenant articulates how it agrees to live together.

In the last chapter, I discussed the theological concept of a church covenant and used the word *covenant* to characterize the nature of our commitments to one another in a local church. Such a commitment between Christians and a church is the biblically commanded reality. Whether a church chooses to enflesh or articulate that commitment in something like a one-page document is a matter of prudence, yet it is a reasonable matter of prudence with all upsides and no downsides, particularly if the church makes regular use of the covenant and doesn't merely affirm it and then shut it up in a file drawer. My own church, for instance, reads our covenant aloud every time we partake of the Lord's Supper together. That means we speak those promises to one another over twelve times a year. As a result, its refrains are familiar to all of us. Still, whether God's people choose to enshrine their commitments in a written covenant, as biblical characters did at various times (e.g., Gen. 21:27; 1 Sam. 18:3; 23:18; 2 Sam. 5:3; Ezra 10:3; Neh. 9:38), must remain a matter of Christian freedom.

PASTORAL MEMBERSHIP INTERVIEW

In order to faithfully execute its biblical duties of binding and loosing, a church must ask professing believers what they believe and how they intend to live. The formality or informality of that conversation might be left to context and judgment, but the fact that it must happen in some capacity is part and parcel of the church's call to protect the gospel's witness by affirming only those who make credible professions of faith.

In light of the societal complexities that characterize most of the world today, let me raise the ante. I once joined a church by walking to the front of the building on a Sunday morning where I was asked by the pastor before the whole congregation, "So you are here to join?"

"Yes, sir," I replied.

"Do you believe Jesus is Lord and that he died for your sins?"

"Yes, sir."

This probing interview completed, he turned to the entire congregation and said, "All those in favor of affirming Jonathan as a member of the church say yea." A fantastic picture of congregationalism at work, right? Hardly. It is careless practices such as that which rob the church of its integrity and usher in nominalism and hypocrisy. (The particular church I just described no longer exists, at least not in the same form.) Church leaders would do well to consider how much care employers take before offering a job, or insurance companies take before issuing policies. Does the church not have far more at stake than any employer or insurance company? In our anonymous and busy cities, churches should take at least thirty to sixty minutes to sit down with every professing believer to ask him about his upbringing; his immediate family and its history; his conversion; his baptism; what his discipleship has looked like since conversion; what churches he has been involved in; and whether he will affirm the church's statement of faith and church covenant. But more important than any other question is this: "What is the gospel?"

Our goal in all these questions is to discern whether he meets the standard of Matthew 18:3–5. Does he profess the name of Jesus, and does his life present a basic turning from the world of sin and becoming like a child who trusts in Jesus? He need not be perfect, but he must be repentant, which is seen, for instance, in his ability to forgive others (vv. 23–35).

There is nothing in Scripture that explicitly says that such an interview or conversation must happen with an elder, but there is biblical inference for that. It's the shepherds who stand at the gate of the sheep pen to protect the sheep and to ward off the wolves. Insofar as the elders have been charged with giving oversight to all the flock, they are the ones most suitably equipped to lead the apostolic congregation in using the keys of the kingdom for binding and loosing. There are prudential reasons as well for using an elder: a membership interview establishes a personal foundation for shepherding that individual in the months and years to follow.

As with membership classes, I have heard of older Christians objecting to membership interviewers but never new Christians. It can feel strange and unwelcoming to them, maybe even counter-Christian. This is the result of churches failing to teach their members what churches are. One of the pastors I mentioned earlier in the chapter recently received an e-mail with the following critique of his church's membership process, and the membership interview specifically:

> I have never been to a church where you feel like you are required to pass the test as a Christian in order to belong to the family. The whole church experience is meant to be a loving and caring experience. The fact that not all members are announced at once obviously is going to leave the other members with questions. . . . Surely you first lovingly invite the members into the church and then, if you feel they need guidance or further mentoring to grow as Christians, you can set something up. . . . For this reason I don't understand why my wife must be put on the spot with questions asked directly to her and then, when she can't answer them, she is not lovingly let off the hook but gets a blank stare, followed by more questions. Do you know how unworthy you made her feel?

Maybe the pastor of that particular church had an unwelcoming manner. If so, he should correct this. What's clear is that the man writing the letter was never taught by his previous churches that submitting to Christ's lordship means submitting to Christ's authorized proxy on earth—the apostolic local church. There's no sense of the church's responsibility to guard the gospel, and there's no category in this man's mind for the possibility of self-deception, that people can believe they are Christians when they are not. Hence, the questions the pastor asked the man's wife offended him.

If I had to guess, he was probably embarrassed by the fact that his wife could not answer the pastor's basic questions, such as, "What is the gospel?" I assume that, because later in the letter the man wrote, "You also said that once my wife has met with a mature Christian lady a few times, we will meet again. It is as if we need to go through another trial before we can be members." It sounds as if the pastor was not sure that the man's wife was a Christian, which is why he *lovingly* encouraged her to spend some time with another Christian woman first. Even if the pastor was wrong in his assessment, does he not strengthen her faith by ensuring that she knows how to articulate the gospel? Does he not equip her for evangelism and mothering her own children? Why, other than for pride, would a Christian husband ever object to a pastor's asking that his wife be discipled by another woman? Probably he has never been taught that love centers on God, that love calls Christians to an obedient conformity to Christ, and that Christ has given us his church to accomplish these very purposes in our lives and to participate in accomplishing them in others.

What should a pastor do when someone being interviewed is unable to articulate the gospel? To begin with, he can try to tease it out with follow-up questions. A woman who was still learning English once came to my church for a membership interview. When I asked her what the gospel was, she replied, "The gospel?" as if she didn't recognize the word itself. So I simply replied, "The good news of Jesus Christ?" She then provided a decent explanation of Christ's substitutionary death and resurrection. The conversation gave me the opportunity to ensure that henceforth she knew the word *gospel*. Membership interviews provide good teaching opportunities.

When answering, people will sometimes omit a significant part of the gospel, such as the resurrection or the call to repentance. Again, follow-up questions can charitably draw out their understanding as well as be used to teach. When an individual fails to mention anything about repentance, I might say something like the following: "Suppose someone claims to believe the message that Jesus died for our sin, but after being baptized, nothing in his life changes. He continues to sleep with his girlfriend, shows no interest in loving the weak, avoids gathering with the saints, and generally lives just like a non-Christian. What would you say about him?" Most of the time, the interviewee says something like, "No way; he's missing the point." The interviewee may not know the word *repentance*, but he or she understands the basic idea.

In general, pastors and elders should exercise a significant degree of charity in such interviews. We are not seeking to affirm theologians but to affirm Christians. When the disciples asked Jesus who was the greatest in the kingdom of heaven, he replied, "Whoever humbles himself like this child is the greatest in the kingdom of heaven. Whoever receives one such child in my name receives me" (Matt. 18:4–5). In other words, we are not listening for a perfect articulation of theological truth; we are listening for the beginning of a Holy Spirit–given brokenness and humility before God. We are listening for those who are poor in spirit, who mourn their sin, who meekly know they are not entitled to Christ's forgiveness or church membership, and who hunger and thirst for Christ's righteousness (Matt. 5:3–6).

When the Spirit gives this poverty of spirit to someone, he will also lead him or her to see that Jesus is "the Christ, the Son of the living God" who "poured out [his blood] for many for the forgiveness of sins" (Matt. 16:16; 26:28). If people sitting in the interview are truly hungering for a righteousness not of themselves, but they have not yet discovered that this righteousness comes from Christ, it's not yet time to bring them into membership. It's time for further study, which the truly poor in spirit will always welcome. When they do finally come with Christ's name in their mouths, the church can rejoice to affirm them, since they are the ones who will name his name as they extend mercy, live in purity of heart, make peace, and willingly undergo persecution for righteousness' sake (Matt. 5:7–10). They are the ones who will give witness to Christ by being salt and light for his kingdom, bringing glory to the Father in heaven (Matt. 5:13–16). It is precisely here, at the gate of the sheep pen, that pastors are called to do the work of protecting the sheep and standing firm against the wolves.

Finally, a membership interview provides an opportunity for someone to formally affirm and submit to the church's statement of faith and church covenant, in whatever cultural form most clearly communicates self-identification. In most of the world today, people offer their imprimaturs with a signature. It's the most commonly recognized way of saying, "I own all the words on this piece of paper. I give myself to backing them up with my life and actions." Although there is no direct biblical warrant for churches to ask for a signature, it makes prudential sense, since we put our signature to commitments of a far less consequential nature, such as bank checks, college applications, and tax forms.

OTHER POLITY-SPECIFIC MATTERS

Upon the conclusion of a pastoral membership interview, the specific mechanisms of a church's polity swing into motion. If it's an Episcopalian polity, the overseer may welcome the newcomer to the church then and there. If it's an elder-ruled church, as in a Presbyterian polity, the one elder will bring his recommendation back to the session for a final decision. If it's an elder-led congregational polity, he might bring it to all the elders, who will consider the application and then, in turn, make a recommendation to the congregation for a final affirmation. If the church is led solely by one pastor, he will make a recommendation to the congregation for a final decision.

My understanding of Scripture would lead me to endorse an elder-led congregational model, but I'm not going to spend any time on that here. Rather, I would encourage those of every model to look for practical ways of allowing the church to participate in affirming every person entering into membership. Even the Episcopalian bishop, who believes the church is present in his own official person, knows that he is not, finally, the congregation itself. Therefore, he should desire that the congregation itself participate, as much as it's able, in the affirmation of a new member of the body, a new representative for Christ. He should want the entire congregation to see that Christ's name and fame is now at stake in this person's life and that every member of the church now has a vested interest in his discipleship and perseverance in the faith. The advantage of a congregational polity, of course, is that the entire congregation is called upon to participate in this affirmation through a vote. Even if you, as pastor, abhor the sound of the words *church vote*, you can look for some other way to help the members of your congregation take ownership of every member of the body by name—a clear implication of 1 Corinthians 12 and many other passages in the New Testament.

FENCING THE TABLE

One other matter that helps to keep the line between the church and world clear at the church's front door is called "fencing the table." Before a church serves the Lord's Supper, it should place a fence around those permitted to take the Lord's Supper. After all, Paul warns that anyone who eats or drinks the meal in an unworthy manner eats and drinks judgment on himself (1 Cor. 11:27). The Lord's Supper is a meal reserved for Christians, since the Supper is, at the very least, a way of symbolizing the fact that they have partaken of his body and blood. It's one of only two signs that Jesus gave to the church to mark itself off from the world. This means that churches should encourage non-Christians not to partake of the meal.

However, churches should fence the table even more carefully than that. If submitting to Christ through conversion should immediately translate into submitting to a local church through baptism, then the Lord's Supper is a meal reserved for baptized members of churches. For a Christian to partake of the Lord's Supper without having first submitted to the authority of some local church through baptism is to claim an authority that Jesus never gave to the lone Christian. It's to "usurp the power of the keys," to borrow Benjamin Griffith's phrase. It's to say, "Jesus may have authorized the apostolic church to bind and loose, which in turn declares some individuals as possessing the right to represent Jesus on earth and not others, but never mind all that. I know who I am! Forget the church." In short, partaking of the Lord's Supper without being a baptized member of a local church is an act of presumption and disdain for the authority of Christ himself.

As we noted earlier, local churches should exemplify a deference and respect to other gospel-believing local churches, since they too belong to the same Lord and act by his authority. They should defer to one another like an army general will, whenever possible, cordially recognize and defer to another general of equal rank. For that reason, churches can permit visitors from other churches to partake of the Lord's Supper, yet they must be members in good standing, that is, they must not be under the discipline of another church.

For all these reasons, my own church offers remarks like these every time we partake of the Lord's Supper: "If you are a member of our church or a baptized member in good standing of another local church that preaches the same gospel you have heard preached here, you are welcome to enjoy this meal with us." Fencing the table in this manner fulfills the church's responsibility before God. The rest can be left up to the conscience of each individual.

Step 5: The goal of member oversight is to present a credible witness for Christ on earth. The whole church, leaders and members, participate in this gospel-grounded, discipleship-driven care through the ministry of the Word.

Member Oversight

Thus far, we have considered the doorway into church membership. As we turn now to consider the church's responsibility to oversee the lives of those it affirms, we will discover that the bulk of church oversight is exercised as individuals care for and disciple one another.

THE GOAL OF OVERSIGHT

What's the church's goal in overseeing the lives of its members? There are a number of ways we could answer that question. We could talk about the goal of helping the members of the church persevere to the end, as Jesus does again and again in his letters to the seven churches in Revelation. We could talk about helping members define love for the world, as John in particular seems to dwell upon in his Gospel and epistles. We could talk about equipping church members for works of ministry until they reach unity, maturity, and the stature of the fullness of Christ, as Paul does in Ephesians 4, or about preparing the church as a holy and radiant bride, as he does in Ephesians 5.

Whatever passage we point to, the goal can be summarized as maintaining and growing a credible witness for Christ on earth. If that sounds too mechanistic or exploitative from the church member's standpoint, as if he's asked to do nothing more than stand around like a road sign, keep in mind that being a road sign (or image) in God's kingdom means experiencing the fullness of God's love and glory as we participate in his rule.

THE POWER OF OVERSIGHT

Yet as we hold up these pictures of an obedient people and a radiant bride, we need to immediately stop and remind ourselves of one of the key differences between Old Testament Israel and the New Testament church. Israel, too, was supposed to be a witness for God on the earth as an obedient people and a radiant bride, and they had every law you could think of to help them become this picture. The problem was that the law doesn't change hearts.

As pastors and congregations oversee one another's lives in preparation for the day of Christ's coming, this one bedrock truth must inform every act of instruction and discipline: God alone changes hearts through his gospel. That is true at conversion, and it is true at every step of growth in the Christian life.

Therefore, church overseers, like parents, should pray and strive not just for external conformity to the law but for fundamental changes in the heart. The best illustration I know of on this point comes from counselor Paul David Tripp:

> Pretend that I have an apple tree in my backyard. Each year it buds and grows apples, but when the apples mature, they are dry, wrinkled, brown and pulpy. After several years I decide that it is silly to have an apple tree and never be able to eat its fruit. So I decide that I must do something to "fix" the tree. One Saturday afternoon you look out your window to see me carrying branch cutters, a staple gun, a step ladder, and two bushels of Red Delicious apples into my backyard. You watch as I carefully cut off all the bad apples and staple beautiful red apples onto the branches of the tree. You come out and ask me what I am doing and I say proudly, "I've finally fixed my apple tree!"[6]

The difference between an oversight that's fundamentalistic, legalisitic, and authoritarian and one that's gospel driven is that the former only commands external behavior whereas the latter is concerned with behavior, but it appeals to the heart and a person's profession of belief in the gospel.

I'm not saying that we should dispense with God's law when shepherding or overseeing others, whether our children or the members of our church. The law still presents a picture of God's holy character. But the law cannot take what's stone and turn it into flesh. It cannot create the desire for obedience to itself. As the church strives together toward this picture of a radiant bride, it must continually remember that God alone has the power to change, and that God is a God of mercy and compassion.

CONGREGATIONALLY OWNED AND EXECUTED

Who then is responsible for oversight in the church? Let me, once again, risk driving us perilously close to the borders of congregationalism (I can hardly help myself!) by affirming the whole church's responsibility in the activity of oversight. By this I don't simply mean the responsibility every member has. I mean the corporate responsibility that the church as a whole possesses by virtue of Christ's charter in Matthew 16, 18, and 28. When several members cannot resolve a dispute, Jesus tells them to take it to the church (Matt. 18:17). When the teachers of the Galatian churches departed from the gospel, Paul excoriated the churches themselves (Gal. 1:6–9).

I think we can draw something out of these kinds of "congregational-ist" passages that Anglicans, Lutherans, Presbyterians, Methodists, and others should be able to affirm within the structures of their respective polities. When

---

[6]Paul David Tripp and Timothy S. Lane, *Helping Others Change Workbook*, 3rd ed. (Greensboro, NC: New Growth Press, 2008), 2–3, lesson 2.

the fearsome day of judgment comes, every member of a church will be held accountable, each for his part, if that church forsook the gospel. Bishops or elders will be more responsible than lay members (the Anglican and the Baptist might disagree on how much more). But all will be held in some measure responsible. Likewise, every member will rejoice in one another's participation in the salvation of souls through the ministry of that church. The ear will have participated differently from the hands or the feet, but each will have played a part, and each will share the celebration of what Christ's Spirit did through all.

If there's anything that churches need to recover today, it's the understanding that a church is corporately responsible for the discipleship of every member in the congregation. Because that's true, every member is responsible in some measure for every other member, even the ones we don't know: "If one member suffers, all suffer together; if one member is honored, all rejoice together" (1 Cor. 12:26). Part of growing my small selfish heart to lovingly envelop wider and wider circles of God's people is teaching it to fix itself upon my own local congregation as fully and manifestly as God enables me.

LEADER LED

At the same time, there's no doubt that Christ and the apostles gave the responsibility for oversight to the *pastors*, *elders*, or *bishops*—three words used interchangeably, the last of which means, quite literally, "overseer." I won't discuss here all the aspects of pastoral oversight. Other helpful resources are available.[7] Since we already discussed the nature of pastoral authority versus the apostolic church's authority in chapter 4, here I will make just two conventional comments and one innovative comment.

First, an elder's oversight is conducted principally through teaching and prayer. That's what the apostles set themselves apart to do in Acts 6, even when the church was being torn apart by ethnic divisions. The ability to teach is the one attribute that distinguishes an elder from a deacon in 1 Timothy 3 and Titus 1. It's not that the work of healing ethnic division or conducting acts of service is unimportant; it's simply that, in the economy of God's household, pastors and teachers equip the saints to do such work, since it's God's Word itself that brings life and growth through God's Spirit. He has set apart particular individuals for giving themselves in pronounced fashion to teaching and praying.

Second, an elder's oversight is conducted through ruling. Paul writes, "Let the elders who rule well be considered worthy of double honor" (1 Tim. 5:17). We have already considered the fact that an elder's rule does not allow him

---

[7] See Timothy Laniak's excellent biblical theology of the shepherding metaphor throughout Scripture in *Shepherds after My Own Heart* (Nottingham, UK: Inter-Varsity, 2006). For a more popular-level work, see David Dickson, *The Elder and His Work* (Phillipsburg, NJ: P&R, 2004).

to force or command church members to act in particular ways. An elder has rule so that he might lead the congregation in making good decisions, but that leadership is always contingent upon the Holy Spirit–given, willing submission of the congregation.

Both of these observations, I think, are fairly conventional, at least in some circles, but a slightly innovative proposal is this: part of ruling well means being able to account for the entire church *by name*. I don't propose this as a biblical requirement; rather, I present it as a biblical aspiration. Moses found himself unable to dutifully discharge the responsibilities of judgment on a case-by-case basis (one part of shepherding), so he appointed others who could. Jeremiah and Ezekiel criticized the shepherds of Israel for letting the sheep wander off into the hills. Jesus himself was the good shepherd who would not forsake the one for the ninety-nine and lost none of those that the Father had given him (except the one assigned to perdition). Each of these examples presents a unique redemptive-historical moment, but each also sets the pattern upon which Paul builds when he says to the elders in Ephesus, "Pay careful attention to yourselves and to all the flock, in which the Holy Spirit has made you overseers, to care for the church of God, which he obtained with his own blood" (Acts 20:28). The same idea is behind these words: "Obey your leaders and submit to them, for they are keeping watch over your souls, as those who will have to give an account" (Heb. 13:17).

I'm not suggesting that every elder must be able to account for every member's name, but the plainest way to read these two passages is to say that the elders of a church, collectively, should be able to pay careful attention to every member of the flock, because they will give an account for every member of the flock before God. By analogy, a father of five children would not be considered faithful if he fathered four well but abandoned the fifth. He would be a faithless father. He will be called to account for all five children by name. In the same way, the elders need to ensure that, one way or another, every name in the flock is being carefully shepherded.

Can't elders do this through the auspices of another leader, such as a small-group leader? I have not made up my mind on this matter, which is why I refrain from calling this a biblical requirement. The reason for my restraint is that the apostles *might* have been delegating something like a one-to-one oversight in Acts 6. It's not clear because Acts 6 is also something of a unique historical-redemptive moment. At the very least, I do want to say that every mediating step placed in between a believer and an elder—as with that nonbiblical category "small-group leader"—moves the individual one step further away from careful shepherding. As an elder, I cannot look into the patterns and circumstances of someone's life in order to offer counsel secondhand as well as I can firsthand. I can't know who the wolves are unless I (together with all the elders) know the sheep by name. This much should be self-evident. The Scriptures place no limit on the size of churches, and the church in Jerusalem numbered in the thousands (Acts 4:4), yet in Acts we see the apostles involving themselves in the details of individuals' lives (Acts 5:1–10), gathering all the disciples together (Acts 5:12; 6:2), and generally straining to give the necessary oversight. At the very least then, we must conclude that pastors of large congregations should strain and aspire to give oversight to every member by name. One simple solution is to ask Christ to give more elders to the church.

The elders of a church, both individually and collectively, should aspire to pray for every member of their church by name. Because our church's membership is so extensive, the elders and the congregation try to pray for the people on two pages of the church directory each day. When I'm short on time, I can do that in ten minutes: "Father, keep this brother from idols. Grow this sister in her evangelism. Bring this one a husband. Bring that one spiritual encouragement." If God has made you the steward of five thousand people, do you think there is no way you can pray for that many? Did you think he would give you more so that you might pray less? Why do you think he has entrusted you with so many? What do you think would happen to your church if you prayed for every member of your five-thousand-member church by name monthly (167 members a day), or every other month (84 members a day), or even twice a year (27 members a day)? What do you expect the effect on your church would be? Personally, I would expect to hear about it in glory as the great stories of the church's work are retold.

The members of the church should follow the examples of the elders by overseeing one another. The author of Hebrews writes, "Remember your leaders, those who spoke to you the word of God. Consider the outcome of their way of life, and imitate their faith" (13:7).

Churches today need to recover the understanding that the whole congregation, leaders and laity, is corporately responsible for the discipleship of every member in the congregation. Christianity should be congregationally shaped. When false teachers entered the church in Colossae and tried to lead its members toward an individualistic and zealous asceticism, Paul reminded the church that true growth comes from Christ and *through* the whole congregation. These individuals, he said, have not held "fast to the Head, from whom the whole body, nourished and knit together through its joints and ligaments, grows with a growth that is from God" (Col. 2:19). The body depends on all its parts for a divinely given growth, and it always grows together toward unity.

OTHER MINISTRIES OF THE CHURCH

How do the various ministries of the church factor into the church's corporate responsibility to give affirmation and oversight for the sake of Christ's name?

What should we make of youth ministries, singles' ministries, homeless ministries, and other niche ministries?

I worked briefly as an interim pastor at a Baptist church in Louisville, Kentucky. One evening at an elders meeting, the discussion arose about how to deal with the bourgeoning college ministry. The church building was located one block from the University of Louisville, and the church had recently decided to hire a seminary student to work as the college ministry coordinator. This non-elder, who was very winsome, turned out to be popular with the college students. The elders were considering how we should view the college ministry in relation to the whole church, as well as how we should view the college ministry coordinator in relation to the elders.

The elders had two concerns. First, they did not want college students to begin approaching the college ministry coordinator as their pastor. The elders were not trying to keep power from the coordinator; rather, they wanted to see him grow and mature into a pastor, since that's what he was training to do. The elders wanted college students to have the benefit of developing relationships with the men whom the congregation had recognized as pastors, which would serve both the students and the elders.

Second, the elders wanted to make sure the college students would be integrated into the life of the body as a whole. I remember an elder named Greg said something that helped crystallize the issue in my mind. He said, "We don't want the college ministry to form a separate wing of the church, where they meet in their own space, have their own leaders, and have very few relationships with the rest of the body." The phrase that stuck in my mind was "not a separate wing of the church." Greg's comment was based upon the biblical insight that the "whole body" grows together as it's "nourished and knit together through its joints and ligaments" with a "growth that is from God" (Col. 2:19). It was based on the biblical insight that no member or section of the body (ear, hand, foot) should cut itself off from the rest of the body. The trouble today is that too many churches seem all too happy to allow the church's oversight to devolve to a subgroup within the body, and those subgroups often gather around some point of sociological affinity like age, family status, or professional status. The college students are left to oversee one another; so are the young married couples; so are the retirees. In the process, of course, they deprive themselves of the wisdom and gifts of the whole.

Let me propose the following: youth ministries, college ministries, small-group ministries, singles' ministries, women's ministries, men's ministries, children's ministries, benevolence ministries, visitation ministries, karate ministries, motorcyclers' ministries, and other niche ministries of the church can be viewed as either *parachurch ministries* or as *ministries of the church*. These divisions are not exact, and I trust that any reader could think of some ministry configuration that will defy these two categories, but I offer them as basic models that should help us consider how these various niche ministries fit into the life of the church.

A parachurch model. A parachurch ministry is one in which Christians, who may or may not belong to the same local church, work together for some evangelistic or social welfare end. A common example is a missions organization, such as New Tribe Missions, or a university campus organization, like Campus Crusade for Christ. In the past, some parachurch ministries have made the mistake of intentionally or unintentionally discouraging the involvement of Christians in the life of the local church. For all the reasons that we have already enumerated, this is problematic. However, parachurch ministries can play a helpful role in accomplishing work for the kingdom, capable of serving both local churches and non-Christians, and I think they are often worthy of the support of local churches, at least when they don't get confused for the local church.

What I would propose is that churches should begin to view any number of ministries that operate within their walls as parachurch ministries. Youth ministries often blend members and non-members, Christians and non-Christians. Insofar as the youth ministry is used to reach non-Christians, as any parachurch ministry would, it's a useful ministry. Insofar as it allows the youth who are church members to form a separate wing of the church, it undermines their discipleship to Christ because it robs them of the wisdom and gifts of the whole body. It also blurs the line between church and world in the minds of Christians and non-Christians both.

Other outreach ministries, say, a soup kitchen, should similarly be conceived as parachurch ministries, even if these ministries are directly sponsored by the church. Aside from helping to maintain clearer lines between church and world, calling it a parachurch ministry helps the apostolic local church distinguish between the basic responsibilities that it's been given in Christ's charter and other responsibilities it might undertake from time to time in order to further Christ's witness.

Ministries to the church. Within the ordinary course of a church's life, particular needs might arise that cannot be addressed in regular gatherings. Maybe the church has quite a few single mothers, or college students, or individuals struggling with same-sex attraction. Churches obviously have different demographics. To meet these particular needs, a church might responsibly decide to begin a ministry outside of its regular gatherings that more carefully addresses and equips this subset of members. However, it would serve those subsets best by restricting its ministry to the topic that distinguishes them. It should not attempt to form a separate wing of the church for these subgroups or undertake their entire discipleship to Christ. For instance, a ministry for single mothers might give focused attention to being a single mom more than the average church member probably needs to hear. At the same time, it should probably do so with an eye toward helping single mothers integrate with the body as a whole, and helping the body as a whole know how to minister to single mothers.

Covenant Life Church in Gaithersburg, Maryland, does not conceive of its youth ministry so much as an outreach to non-Christian youth as a ministry to its own youth and their parents. It equips the parents to equip their youth, and it encourages the youth to respond in love and obedience to their parents. The youth ministry does not try to take possession of either the youths' or the parents' entire discipleship to Christ, which is the responsibility of the whole church. It simply gives the extra emphasis to the sort of topics that parents and youth need in their discipleship together.

WHOLE-CHURCH OVERSIGHT

Oversight of the whole church begins in the regular gatherings of the church. As Christians join together to be formed by the same preaching, prayers of confession, songs of praise, and gospel pictures of baptism and the Lord's Supper, they are given a common language or currency for negotiating daily life. When the temptations, tragedies, and triumphs of the week come, they have this shared language or currency to encourage and challenge one another through it all. It's here, throughout the week, that Sunday's ministry of the Word echoes back and forth between one life and another.

So the whole church's oversight begins in the gathering but then it extends to countless times of one-on-one prayer, conversations, meals, acts of service, parachurch or ministry work, and life together. On the other hand, if church gatherings last barely an hour, if the songs are shallow, if sermons last little more than twenty-five minutes, and if only ten minutes of the sermon are given to Scripture, it's no wonder that Christians believe the gathering and the preaching event are unimportant. "What's the big deal about the weekly gathering?" If we allow hour after hour of media (radio, movies, television, Internet) to *form* us throughout the week but resist any more than an hour of church on Sunday, will it not be the media that provides us all with a common language and currency? When we discover on Sunday after the sermon that someone saw the same movie last night as we did, is it more natural to talk about the movie or the sermon?

DISCIPLESHIP

The oversight of the whole church occurs as pastors and members disciple one another. Discipleship works through countless acts of love and discipline, both formative and corrective. Two men decide to meet for accountability. Two women decide to read a Christian book together. A small group meets weekly to meditate further on Sunday's sermon. An older father offers a younger father a rebuke. A young wife asks an older wife for counsel. A family offers weekly hospitality to new members and visitors of the church. A pastor gives away good books weekly. All these little actions, as they come to characterize a body's life together, begin to form and shape a people in the image of Christ.

Discipleship, like discipline, involves evaluation and correction, which is why so few Christians these days seem to avail themselves of it. Not only does our sinful flesh despise the prospect of being evaluated, but we've imbibed the philosophies of this world that tell us that no one has the right to evaluate another person. "Haven't you read your postmodern philosophy? How dare you tell that younger man that some paths are wise and other paths are foolish? Don't you know that you are sociologically embedded and unable to speak outside of your own context and perspective?" The father figure in the book of Proverbs is forbidden from speaking, thrown out on charges of intolerance and close-mindedness. When that happens, discipleship morphs into little more than mutual affirmation. Churches become nurseries of fools.

Churches sometimes turn discipleship into a program, as if the book of Proverbs or raising children could be programmed. In fairness, such programs may be helpful to a point, especially for the purposes of instruction and cultivating relationships. What's important to recognize, however, is that discipleship ultimately requires changing hearts and changing a church culture. In like manner, we know that we have successfully discipled our child when she begins to see the difference between wisdom and folly and chooses wisdom for herself, even when we are absent. Likewise, a church functions best when it cultivates a culture of discipleship, where more and more members participate in loving, comforting, challenging, and drawing one another toward the way of Christ. A culture of discipleship is one where informal church discipline is normal, and formal church discipline is practiced. Of course, the more willing members are to receive personal and private admonitions from their brothers and sisters in Christ, the rarer the formal processes of exclusion become.

Discipleship can be hard to endure. "For the moment all discipline seems painful rather than pleasant, but later it yields the peaceful fruit of righteousness to those who have been trained by it" (Heb. 12:11). It's hard to humble ourselves in the face of correction. It's hard to receive instruction from another Christian, especially the ones who are younger than us. It's hard to make schedules coordinate for the sake of meeting with other church members. It's hard to find time. It's hard to practice what's been preached. It's hard not to secretly think, "Who are you to say? What makes you so wise?" It's hard to pray; it's hard to love; and, strangely, it's hard to be loved. But discipleship is essential for growing in Christlikeness. Churches practice oversight through discipline and discipleship.

Step 6: Since a church covenant is a two-way commitment, both church and member must consent to the end of the relationship. Churches should formally discipline members who prove unrepentantly unfaithful in their discipleship to Christ.

Member Resignation and Exclusion

There are three ways to leave a church. A member passes away, resigns, or gets excluded. Let's consider the latter two, again, from the perspective of the church's responsibilities.

WHAT RESIGNATION MEANS

In the West today, individuals and families often resign their church memberships like they check out of hotels. They make sure they have all their belongings, inform the management, and then go. In fact, many church members don't do this much. People leave and tell no one. I suppose it's only because the hotels have our credit card numbers on file that we afford them that courtesy.

Insofar as this practice is widespread, churches themselves are at least partly to blame. We have not taught our members otherwise. We have not taught them that church membership enacts on earth our unity with Christ and his people in heaven. We have not taught them about the nature of church authority and Christ's command to submit to it. We have not taught them that Jesus said obedience defines love.

As such, our first concern is not to describe the right steps for resigning one's membership, though we will get to that. Rather, our first concern should be to understand what's going on when a Christian leaves a church. Because membership is a covenant between a Christian and a church, therefore, his leaving represents an ending of the covenant. His relationships with the members of the congregation may well continue, but he is no longer under their corporate oversight. The church loses its authority either to vouch for his faith or to discipline it.

If church membership truly involves giving ourselves to the other members of our church, if it means identifying ourselves with them because they, like us, are identified with Christ, and if it means that we have been charged with overseeing their discipleship for whatever length of time Christ affords us that privilege, then the departure of members should always be a bittersweet affair, like when a grown son or daughter leaves home. We rejoice for what the Lord has in store for them, but we mourn losing them because we love their presence.

THE SIGNIFICANCE OF GATHERING TOGETHER

Leaving a church, then, is not an entirely institutional matter, as if some rule could state when the covenant should be pronounced null. The relationships within a church are held together by multiple strands, the institutional strand being only one. Gathering or personal presence is another strand. We cannot keep one another accountable from four hundred miles apart as well as we can from four feet apart. We can communicate by other means if one of us moves away and begins attending another church, but we can no longer see into one another's lives with the same perspicuity. Nor can we be formed together by the same preaching, prayers, and praises if we are not gathered together in the same congregation. Each church and city and culture has a distinct personality formed by its special emphases, which leads us to acquire the language or currency of the place we settle. Certainly the whole body of Christ is enriched by a diversity of currencies or languages; however, the authoritative or institutional strands of the relationships between Christians work best when a currency and language is shared. If I know firsthand what preaching you have been sitting under, I have a better sense of the knowledge for which God himself will call you to account. I am in a better position to speak meaningfully into your life; I'm in a better position, together with our entire congregation, to affirm or deny, to bind or loose, your profession of faith on earth.

Therefore, when a person stops gathering with a church, the church's ability to meaningfully fulfill its responsibilities to affirm, oversee, and discipline a Christian decreases relative to the length of time the individual has been away. If a church has not seen a sister for a month, can it continue to affirm and oversee her faith? Probably. What if she has been gone for four months, or twelve months? At some point, the church can no longer fulfill its responsibilities to affirm and oversee one who has left, nor can a longtime absent member fulfill her responsibilities to the church. Gathering regularly with a church is an essential component of membership. What's lamentable is that Christians regularly call themselves members of churches that they haven't attended for a year, as if the word *membership* means anything at that point.

There are occasional exceptions to this principle of insisting that "members" attend. My church in Washington DC, sometimes says goodbye to members for a year or two while they travel with the U.S. State Department or the military to a foreign location where they will be unable to join a church for one reason or another. In such circumstances, our church may decide to do our best to continue discipleship through prayer and regular contact, primarily because there is no other local church to assume that responsibility for them.

Typically, however, when people leave our Washington congregation, we encourage them to join another church as soon as possible, because we know that we can no longer fulfill our Christ-assigned oversight in their life, and we want them to find some other church that can.

Two very practical implications follow from the need to gather regularly together. First, prolonged and unrepentant nonattendance is grounds for formal church discipline. In line with Matthew 18 and Hebrews 10, someone who refuses to gather with the church should be warned several times and then excluded. This process might take months, but it's necessary, even apart from the biblical commands, in order to reflect the reality of the situation. The church eventually has no choice but to say, "We can no longer credibly affirm your profession of faith and oversee your discipleship because you're not here. We don't know where you are or what you're doing." When a church does not remove longtime absentees from its membership, it's committing a kind of fraud. It's claiming something that it has no right to claim. The Bible speaks very severely to those who fail to gather regularly with the church:

> Let us consider how to stir up one another to love and good works, not neglecting to meet together, as is the habit of some, but encouraging one another, and all the more as you see the Day drawing near. For if we go on sinning deliberately after receiving the knowledge of the truth, there no longer remains a sacrifice for sins, but a fearful expectation of judgment, and a fury of fire that will consume the adversaries. (Heb. 10:24–27)

The person who neglects meeting with the saints is on his way toward God's judgment, and the dim picture of that judgment represented by church discipline is a merciful act of warning. When members stop attending a church and don't join another one, they are often sinning or on their way to sinning. There's something in their life that they don't want to be seen. There's accountability and love they would prefer to be without.

Second, when an individual or family permanently moves away, a church should encourage them to join another church as quickly as possible. If enough time has passed, it should also warn them that they will be removed from the rolls as an act of discipline. I recognize that this idea might shock many evangelicals. Yet God's love is centered on God and is shown to us by saving us from our sin and calling us to live in conformity with his beautiful character. The local church is the place on earth where we learn to do this. Therefore, we love them by insisting that they submit themselves to the fellowship of a church. When people leave the church, move away, and fail to join another church as the months and years tick by, we show love for them with the reminder that Jesus called us to know and demonstrate God's love through obedience. Not saying or doing anything to straying people is not loving! Yet our conceptions of love have been turned upside down by the fall, and we have difficulty seeing this fact—so convinced we have become that love never imposes, makes conditions, or renders judgment. But that's not true. Love does impose, make conditions, and render judgment.

An older generation of pastors were correct when they said that "it is not reasonable to dismiss [members] to the world at large."[8] Responsibly fulfilling our covenant to affirm and oversee a Christian's discipleship is only fulfilled when we see them safely shepherded into another congregation.

RESIGNATION ONLY BY MUTUAL CONSENT

Since Christ commands Christians to submit to local churches, one might reasonably ask whether they have the right to resign their membership apart from geographical relocation. Again, many earlier pastors would have answered that question negatively. Benjamin Griffith, who pastored a Baptist church in Pennsylvania from 1725 to 1768, believed that if God's Word is rightly preached and the gospel ordinances rightly administered, someone should not leave that church "although there be weakness, imperfection and frailty" that one finds objectionable. Griffith writes:

> It is therefore unreasonable to dismiss any member, from a church that is near to any one's residence, to a church more remote, upon disgust taken at the management of some particular case . . . it is unreasonable also to grant a dismission to such a member, who would demand a dismission in a peremptory manner, without giving a reason for such a demand; in either of which cases, such a dismission is not to be granted.[9]

To unilaterally leave a church at will, like one might check out of a hotel, Griffith calls "schismatic" and describes it as "a usurping of the keys, or rather stealing of them."[10] And Griffith is not unique in his views among many pastors over the centuries.

Griffith's posture strikes me as a bit authoritarian, and I don't think we should go as far as he does and say that a "dismission is not to be granted" when a member asks for one. After all, our membership in the new covenant precedes our membership in a local church covenant, which means that an individual must choose to join and stay, and can choose to go. Also, people might genuinely benefit by leaving one church and joining another due to a host of circumstances, and I'm not sure why Griffith did not take that into account unless he was trying to press a little too hard on the logic of the church's authority. Had Griffith been the father of the prodigal son, he may well have withheld

---

[8] Benjamin Griffith, "A Short Treatise Concerning a True and Orderly Gospel Church," in *Polity*, ed. Mark Dever (Washington DC: Center for Church Reform, 2001), 103.
[9] Ibid., 102.
[10] Ibid., 108–9.

the inheritance and forbade him to leave, but that's not how the parable goes. The father consented to the prodigal's departure and even blessed him with his share of the inheritance before he went. Churches should do the same when members depart, even for foolish reasons. Grant them best wishes and blessings for their journey. In such moments, our calculus should include not only the rules of institutional procedure but also the dynamics of the human heart and how it does and does not change.

Yet here's what I think Griffith gets right: there are good and bad reasons for leaving a church. Leaving because the preaching is unbiblical is a good reason. Leaving because of music preferences is less good. Leaving to find something more exciting is perhaps foolish. Griffith is also working with a correct presupposition: a church covenant ends in a proper manner only when both parties consent to ending the covenant. Entering the church requires the agreement of both parties, and so does exiting the church.[11] Not every member who tries to resign is a member in good standing or is resigning in order to join another local church, which brings us to the topic of corrective church discipline.

WHAT IS CHURCH DISCIPLINE?

What is corrective church discipline? As defined in chapter 4, church discipline is the process of correcting sin in the church body. It begins informally with personal and private entreaties toward the person in sin. If the sinner does not repent, discipline concludes formally when the sin is explained to the church and the member is excluded from the Lord's Table.[12] This is the basic outline for corrective church discipline presented by Jesus in Matthew 18:15–17.

However, there are some occasions in which the informal and private steps are skipped and the church proceeds immediately to the formal act of excluding a member from its fellowship. This is what Paul calls for in an incident described in 1 Corinthians 5. He had heard that a member of the church was sleeping with his father's wife, a sin so scandalous that it merited the man's immediate removal.

In that sense, Matthew 18 and 1 Corinthians 5 present two ends of the corrective church discipline spectrum. The former describes a slower process of addressing a dispute with a brother, first privately, then with one or two others, and then publicly. The church waits and hopes for the sinner to repent

---

[11]I argued in chapter 4 that churches have no right to bar an individual from baptism if the Holy Spirit has converted him, but that it simultaneously remains the church's prerogative to baptize since it alone has the authority of Christ's charter (see Acts 10:47–48). The same basic formula applies to a member's resignation. When a "member in good standing" decides to leave for another local congregation, I believe the church has no choice but to accept the individual's resignation. There might be reasons why such a departure is foolish, but the decision to leave for another church is not grounds for church discipline. At the same time, it remains the case that a right departure depends upon the church's consent.

[12]I'm taking the informal/formal distinction from Jay E. Adams, *Handbook of Church Discipline: A Right and Privilege of Every Church Member* (Grand Rapids: Zondervan, 1974), 27.

at each step along the way, and the entire process could take a matter of weeks or months. Not so in 1 Corinthians 5. Paul tells the church to hand the man over to Satan at their next meeting, to act immediately.

WHICH SINS? WHICH SINNERS?

The trouble is that real life seldom shows up in the pastor's office or the elders' meeting looking exactly like Matthew 18 or 1 Corinthians 5. It shows up in a variety of forms, combined with circumstances as varied as there are people on the planet. Every pastor knows how ingenious sinners can be at tangling themselves up in situations that sneer at any simple solution. How then does a church know when to discipline, and how does it know how much time to take?

Some of the older theologies enumerated lists of when it's appropriate to conduct such discipline. For instance, the Congregationalist minister John Angell James said that five kinds of offenses should be disciplined: (1) all scandalous vices and immoralities (1 Cor. 5:11–13); (2) the denial of Christian doctrine (Gal. 1:8; 2 Tim. 2:17–21; 1 Tim. 6:35; 2 John 10ff.); (3) the stirring up of division (Titus 3:10); (4) the failure to provide for one's near relatives when they are in need (1 Tim. 5:8); and (5) unreconciled enmity (Matt. 18:7).[13]

These types of biblical lists can be helpful to a point. Notice that all the sins described are serious and have an outward manifestation. They are not just private sins of the heart; there is a public dimension to them. They mislead sheep, and they mislead the world about Christianity. Yet what such a list fails to do is account for the vast multitude of sins that the Scriptures never address (e.g., being an illegal alien) or the many sins that the broader public no longer finds scandalous (like cohabitation or divorce).

At the risk of being vague, I think it's better to simply say that formal church discipline is for sin of a public, serious, and unrepentant nature. It's the appropriate course of action when an individual involved in serious sin has been privately confronted with God's commands in Scripture, but he or she refuses to let go of the sin. From all appearances, the person prizes the sin more than Jesus.

Such was the case in my first experience dealing with corrective church discipline. The situation pertained to a good friend and running partner. Both our church and I were oblivious to the fact that he was heavily involved in sexual sin, at least until he told me one day while we were having lunch together. Immediately I asked him whether he knew what the Bible said about such activity, which he did, but he said that he had made his peace with God. I urged him

---

[13]John Angell James, *Christian Fellowship or The Church Member's Guide*, ed. and abr. Gordon T. Booth, from the 10th edition of vol. 11 of the *Works of John Angell James*, 1861 (Shropshire, England: Quinta Press, 1997), 53.

to repent. Others eventually did, as well, but he told them what he told me: "God was okay with it." After several months of such conversations, the church formally removed him from its fellowship. His sin was serious and unrepentant and had a clear outward manifestation. It would mislead others both inside and outside the church about what it means to be a Christian.

The church spent several months pursuing him. We loved him. We wanted him to turn away from his sin and to know that Jesus is more valuable than anything this world affords. Still, it was clear almost immediately that he had no intention of turning away. He was resolute. Given a choice between his sin and the Word of God, he chose sin. So the church acted.

I have been involved in other such situations where the sinner was not so resolute. One man with whom I met often was quick to confess his sin and truly seemed to hate it, and sometimes he would go months abstaining from it. Then my life would get busy and weeks would pass, and it would occur to me that I had not seen or heard from him. Sure enough, I would eventually discover that he had thrown himself headlong into his vice once more. At some point, his head would pop above the surface, gasping for breath and pleading for help. With people like this, churches often need to take more time. After all, it's not just the nature of the sin that needs to be considered; it's the nature of the sinner himself. Different sinners, to put it bluntly, require different strategies. As Paul himself put it, "Admonish the idle, encourage the fainthearted, help the weak, be patient with them all" (1 Thess. 5:14). This particular brother, in some ways, fell into the category of "the weak." He needed help—continual help— almost like an older man who simply cannot walk on his own two legs without another person holding his arm. This brother couldn't afford my busy weeks. In one particular episode, his sin looked as if it could bring harm to others in a scandalous fashion. Had he followed through, the church would probably have excluded him immediately and rightly so, in my opinion. Thankfully, he heeded the warnings given and turned back.

Multiple variables factor into any one situation, so no simple formula can be given; yet in all the equations, a church and its leaders must remember this one fact: the church is called, above all else, to guard the name and glory of Christ. Church discipline, fundamentally, is about the reputation of Christ and whether the church can continue to affirm the profession of someone whose life risks maligning it. The sins and circumstances of sin will vary tremendously, but one question must always be in the forefront of our minds: "How will this sinner's sin and our response to it reflect the holy love of Christ?" That's not the same thing as asking, "What will make Christ popular?" Some of what Christ said and did offended many; and so it will be with the church. Seeing how to reflect the holy love of Christ will not always be obvious, but it should be this concern that drives us.

To that end, church discipline helps the church grow in holy reverence and in the fear of sin. Whenever a formal act of discipline occurs, members are reminded to take greater care in their own lives. The Congregationalist James gets it just right:

> The advantages of discipline are obvious. It reclaims backsliders, detects hypocrites, circulates a salutary awe through the church, adds a further incentive to watchfulness and prayer, proves beyond question the fact and consequences of human frailty, and moreover, publicly testifies against unrighteousness.[14]

PREEMPTIVE RESIGNATIONS

On a number of occasions, I've heard pastors ask whether they should accept the preemptive resignation of someone in a position to be disciplined for unrepentant sin. Suppose, for instance, a man decides to leave his wife for another woman. Individuals from the church ask the man to repent and return to his wife. He doesn't. They ask again, but this time they also warn him about the possibility of excommunication, so he resigns his membership. Case closed. He's now immune, right? Well, that's what the unrepentant sinner is saying.

Ending a covenant requires the consent of both parties. We join a church by the consent of the church, and we leave by the consent of the church. Mount Olivet Baptist Church should *not* have accepted Jesse James's resignation. They should have excommunicated him in order to faithfully fulfill the covenant they had made with him, regardless of whether he burned the church building (yes, I know, it's easy for me to say!). These days, disgruntled members typically do not threaten to burn the building, but they do threaten churches with lawsuits and a call to the newspapers. Still, Christ gave the church the authority to bind and loose, not the individual Christian. The man who continues to call himself a Christian yet attempts to avoid the church's act of discipline is guilty, in Griffith's words, of usurping the keys or, rather, of stealing them. Christ has made the church his proxy on earth exactly for such occasions, lest heretics and hypocrites presume to continue speaking for Christ.

Should churches discipline members who explicitly renounce the faith, and does it make a difference if they are living an immoral life? I don't believe a church should excommunicate someone who no longer claims to be a Christian, whether or not he or she is living an immoral life. The church should do what it does when someone dies—acknowledge the fact and delete the name from the church directory. That's all it can do. Christ has not given the church authority over the dead or over those who do not name his name. In each

---

[14]Ibid.

case, the church covenant is simply rendered moot. It's worth observing that two of the most important passages on church discipline (Matt. 18:15–17 and 1 Corinthians 5) both instruct the church on how to respond to someone who claims to be a brother.

A TOUGH TOPIC

Corrective church discipline is a tough topic, no doubt about it. Christianity is supposed to be all about love and grace, we think to ourselves, while church discipline can feel like the opposite of love and grace, and so comes the self-doubt. We wonder if it's the best course of action. Pastors wonder if they could have done more to help the individual. They wonder if they will only harden the individual toward the church. Perhaps nowhere else do we feel the presumption of acting as Christ's proxy so acutely. "Are you sure, Lord? You want *us* to exercise these keys to bind and loose?" It's easy to take the keys when we are bringing someone in, but when sending them out?

We must keep in mind that corrective church discipline is a small act of judgment on earth that dimly points to God's final judgment in heaven. It's performed with the hope that it will help bring a sinner to repentance before that final judgment comes. When we get down to it, therefore, I think church discipline is hard to do, because we treat God's final judgment so lightly. We go for days, even months, never thinking of it. We even secretly wonder if it will be so bad after all. The evil one has never stopped whispering in our ear, "You will not surely die." What's more, we love ourselves too much, and the dissonance between God's God-centered conception of love and our own man-centered conception screeches loudest in the face of church discipline. God won't really judge those outside the gospel, will he? The Dutch Reformed minister Wilhelmus à Brakel, writing in a book first published in 1700, offers a severe warning to church leaders who are tempted to think this way. His words might sound jarring to our contemporary sensibilities, but I think they are worth hearing, especially for any church leaders who, like me, think too little of that great day of accounting. Brakel gives us a glimpse of what it means to give an account for those entrusted to our care, referring to what he calls the "key of discipline":

> Take note that this key has been entrusted to you by the Lord Jesus. You are, as it were, the porters of a city. Such porters are most unfaithful who permit the entrance of an approaching enemy coming to destroy the city. You would likewise be unfaithful porters if you permit those enemies to enter and to remain within, and thus destroy the congregation which puts her trust in your faithfulness.
>
> You are the cause that the church is becoming degenerate to the core. You are responsible for all the consequences of this. As a result, God's Name is dishonored,

many people are kept from joining the church who otherwise would do so, souls are destroyed who by the use of the keys of God's kingdom would repent, and the flourishing of godliness is obstructed. You will be the cause that one member imitates the other in the commission of evil, and that the godly are oppressed and secretly must sigh over the wretched condition of the church.

Know that the Lord will bring you into judgment for all these things, and that there you will have to give an account of the manner in which you have ruled the church entrusted to you and concerning the souls over whom the Lord appointed you as an overseer. The Lord will demand the blood of all those souls who will perish due to the neglect of the use of this key. Oh, what a weighty responsibility this is, and how dreadful will God's judgment be upon all unfaithful elders! Oh, that many would never have been elders![15]

Consider how rarely churches practice corrective discipline in our time. Consider also our quest for popularity. Could it be that, more than we realize, we are like the old priests and prophets of Israel that pronounced "Peace, peace" when there was no peace? No, surely not us. We are wise. Unlike *everyone* who has come before us, we have struck the correct balance today, right?

Conclusion

Church membership and discipline help to define love for the world because they mark God's people off from the world and hold them up on display. Therefore, carefully seeing members in and out of our churches is one of the most important things we can do to build healthy churches, evangelize the world, and bring glory to God. Yet church membership is not just about the borders; it's about the life within the body, and that's where we turn last.

---

[15] Wilhelmus à Brakel, *The Christian's Reasonable Service*, vol. 2 (Ligonier, PA: Soli Deo Gloria, 1993), 185.

CHAPTER SEVEN

THE SUBMISSION AND FREEDOM OF LOVE

"If you love someone, set them free."
—*Sting*

Main Question: What does it mean to submit to a local church? Are there limits to the church's authority over the individual?

Main Answer: Submitting to the church means submitting our whole selves to the church for its good and for Christ's glory, just as Christ surrendered himself for our good and the Father's glory.

I've left the hardest matter for last. It's the part that involves you and me and everyone who claims to be a follower of Christ. It's the part where we really get down to what it means to submit to a local church. We've been talking throughout the book about membership as a kind of submission and the fact that Christianity is congregationally shaped, but what does that look like? Are we really called to surrender our freedom? That's a tough pill to swallow.

In our discussions of love, authority, and submission, we haven't yet covered what happens to our freedom. Didn't Jesus come to set us free, and isn't this what love always does—set the beloved free? It seems that freedom is a prerequisite to love. One person cannot be forced to love another. As the divine Father figure, Papa, in William Young's pop-spirituality novel *The Shack*, says, "It is not the nature of love to force a relationship but it is the nature of love to open the way."[1] How then can Christians be bound by or under the authority of a local church as part of defining love? Surely, we need to talk about the limits of the church's authority.

We have two tough questions to answer in this chapter: what does Christianity that's lived in submission to the local church look like for Christians, and how do we put limits on the church's authority so that we don't end up with plain old authoritarianism or legalistic fundamentalism? We will consider the second question first, which will require us to do just a little more theolo-

---

[1] William P. Young, *The Shack* (Newbury Park, CA: Windblown Media, 2007), 192.

gizing. But then we will move quickly toward a concrete picture of what the congregationally shaped life looks like.

Step 1: Christian freedom is not freedom from restraint, but the Spirit-given freedom to want what God wants and conform one's life to his.

Negative Freedom versus Positive Freedom

It was the fall of 1995 when I first read political philosopher Isaiah Berlin's landmark essay, "Two Concepts of Liberty." I don't think I was a Christian then, and I didn't know any theology other than the basic ideas a person acquires growing up in church. I did, however, have a basic familiarity with the Bible, thanks to two dutiful Christian parents and verses memorized in church programs. Yet, as I sat in the British Library of Political and Economic Science in London, England, hunched over a library desk, I distinctly remember being struck by the obvious theological implications of Berlin's essay for Christianity as he compared two concepts of liberty (or freedom). How disturbing these implications were!

TWO CONCEPTIONS OF FREEDOM

In the essay Berlin distinguishes negative liberty from positive liberty.[2] He defines negative liberty as the freedom we have when our ability to make decisions is unobstructed by others: "I am normally said to be free to the degree to which no man or body of men interferes with my activity."[3] It's a freedom *from*—from chains, law, coercion, obstacles, and anything that might prevent us from choosing whatever we want to choose.

Berlin defines positive liberty, on the other hand, as the freedom of self-determination or self-mastery. It's a freedom *to*—"to be conscious of myself as a thinking, willing, active being, bearing responsibility for my choices and able to explain them by reference to my own ideas and purposes."[4]

He concedes that these may not sound too different, but the key is to recognize that negative freedom focuses on what's *external*: is anything hindering our freedom from the outside? If not, we are free. Positive freedom focuses on what's *internal*: are we able to act in accordance with our reason, principle, and truth? The positive conception of freedom brings with it an implicit appeal to an internal reason, principle, law, or truth.[5]

---

[2]Berlin's two conceptions bear a clear analogy to what Christian theologians distinguish as libertarian freedom from compatibilist freedom.

[3]Isaiah Berlin, "Two Concepts of Liberty," in *Four Essays on Liberty* (Oxford: Oxford University Press, 1958), 122.

[4]Ibid., 131.

[5]Another way to draw out the contrast is to say that negative freedom relies upon a "thin" conception of truth while positive freedom relies upon some "thick" conception of truth. A thin conception aspires to make no claim

THE REAL DANGER OF POSITIVE FREEDOM

The danger of positive freedom, says Berlin, writing in the aftermath of the Holocaust and at the height of the Cold War, is that some larger social conception of the self, reason, and truth will be adopted as the individual's own. Someone living in a fascist, communist, or Roman Catholic nation will begin to think he is "free" when he acts in accordance with the fascist, communist, or Roman Catholic truths he's imbibed from the priests of propaganda. Berlin's essay, really, is a critique of the whole tradition of positive freedom and its promulgators, such as Rousseau, Herder, Kant, Hegel, and Marx.

Meanwhile, Berlin presents negative freedom and its advocates positively. Thinkers such as Hobbes, Locke, Bentham, Mill, or Tocqueville, who are probably a little more familiar to British and American students, focused less on persuading their readers about the grand truths of history and more on securing some minimum area in which the individual can act unimpeded.

Berlin's preference for negative freedom over positive makes perfect sense. The history of politics and political philosophy, I would propose, can be summarized in humanity's embracing of one form of positive liberty after another—one new messianic ruler, system, ideology, or utopia that they hope will set them free. Yet all of these prove to be idols in the end (see Daniel 2). Some of those idols are more demanding than others, such as the idols of communism and fascism, but every form of positive freedom—every idol—relies upon a system of truth that opposes God. Unique about postmodernism and contemporary forms of philosophical liberalism is the correct insight that every form of positive freedom is in fact an idol that will eventually lead to oppression and enslavement. Therefore, those who hold to these contemporary views have opted for what seems like the least threatening of solutions—negative liberty. Negative liberty, insofar as it's able, makes no claim on truth except the so-called thin truth of agreeing to disagree. It only asks not to be bothered. Don't hinder me and I won't hinder you, just so long as we agree not to step on one another's toes.

I've taken a little time to get into the weeds of Berlin's essay here because I think his distinction helps to illumine the difference between our understanding of freedom in the postmodern West and the Bible's understanding of freedom. I didn't use the language of negative freedom in chapter 1, but that's where we eventually landed: "Don't tell me what to think; just stay out of my way." Being free, finally, doesn't mean acting in accordance with the truth. It means not being restrained by parent, teacher, or pastor. In the West today, we then lay our definition of love directly on top of this negative conception of freedom. To

---

concerning life's ultimate metaphysical issues, but simply builds its ethics and political philosophy on some type of social contract between humans. Not surprisingly, the credibility of this project has been widely critiqued. A thick conception, on the other hand, explicitly grounds its political philosophy and ethics on a metaphysical foundation.

love someone is to set them free—it's to remove all constraints and judgments: "If you love me with conditions or judgments, you don't love me because you're not letting me be free." Anthony Giddens called this the "pure relationship," one that is pure or uncontaminated by any moral obligation, any sense of duty or responsibility, any long-term commitment, any call to serve or care for the other. Right in line with the culture at large, post-fundamentalist evangelicals are often some of the first to shout "legalism" and "unloving" at the slightest whiff of pastoral authority or congregational constraint. Like Papa says in *The Shack*, "It is the nature of love to open the way." Remove those restraints.

CHRISTIANITY A SYSTEM OF POSITIVE FREEDOM

What disturbed me as someone who in 1995 called himself a "Christian" but who was very much bent on living for himself: Christianity is all about positive freedom.[6] Freedom in the Bible is knowing the truth and living by it because one desires it. Jesus says it himself: "You will know the truth, and the truth will set you free" (John 8:32). The truth is that we must know and follow him: "So if the Son sets you free, you will be free indeed" (v. 36).

Jesus is a totalitarian. He's not some monarch of old who overtaxes the peasants to build his castle. He's like the old Soviet state that wanted to get inside people's heads and change the very way they think, calling submission to their doctrine "freedom." Their claim was total, and so is his. That's what Jesus means when he tells us that we must be like a seed that goes into the ground and dies, or that we must be born again, or that we must take up our cross and follow him. We become free when the truth of him becomes our internal operating principle—our affections, motivations, desires, and worship.

Paul also talks about freedom in this way. In Romans 6 to 8, he describes freedom and slavery in the categories of a positive conception of freedom. Freedom is not just about what externally constrains us but also about what internally motivates us. It's defined by our internal operating principle. This is evident in the fact that the freedom to act according to our internal motivations and desires is simultaneously described as "slavery" or "obedience." As non-Christians, Paul says, we were "enslaved to sin" (6:6, 17, 20). It had "dominion" and it "reigned" in us "to make [us] obey its passions" (6:14, 12). In speaking of the old man, Paul doesn't explicitly equate this "enslavement in sin" with a state of "freedom to sin," because his goal is not a philosophical definition of freedom and because that would diminish the meaning of freedom. The equation does become explicit when Paul turns to our new state in Christ. Through Christ, the Christian has been "set free from sin" (6:7, 22). We are "free in Christ Jesus" (8:2). But this freedom from sin and freedom in Christ are

---

[6]Berlin says as much about Christianity ("Two Concepts of Liberty," 123 n. 2; 129 n. 2).

simultaneously a form of slavery: "But now . . . you have been set free from sin and have become slaves of God" (6:22). We are to present ourselves to God as "instruments for righteousness" or "slaves to righteousness" (6:13, 19). That's what Paul means by freedom—being a slave to righteousness.

In Galatians 3 to 5, the same understanding of freedom is at work. Before Christ came, "we were held captive under the law, imprisoned" (3:23). We were hindered externally by the law (negative), which means we were hindered internally because we couldn't do what we want (positive).[7] Yet, once again we see that Christ has set us free: "For freedom Christ has set us free; stand firm therefore, and do not submit again to a yoke of slavery" (5:1; also, 4:21–31). But this freedom is not a negative freedom from restraint; it's the internal freedom to live in accord with the loving requirements of God: "For you were called to freedom, brothers. Only do not use your freedom as an opportunity for the flesh, but through love serve one another" (Gal. 5:13).

Peter, too, has this understanding of freedom: "Live as people who are free, not using your freedom as a cover-up for evil, but living as servants of God" (1 Pet. 2:16; also, 2 Pet. 2:19). To be free is to live as God's servant.

THE NEW DESIRES OF A SPIRIT-GIVEN HEART

Biblical freedom is this remarkable state in which we want what God wants. How does this happen? How are we set free to want what God wants? At one time God's righteous law imprisoned us, but now, we're to be "slaves of righteousness," and Jesus and Paul want to call that "freedom." How is that possible? It is possible because of the new covenant. The Spirit gives us new hearts. He creates new desires in us so that we desire to love God and love our neighbor (see Deut. 30:6; Jer. 31:33–34; Ezek. 36:26–27), which is to fulfill the law (Rom. 13:8–10). Both Jesus and Paul explicitly make this point.[8] Jesus sets his people free by granting them both the truth and the Spirit, creating a whole new reality within them and enabling them to keep his commandments. One must be born again by the Spirit to enter the kingdom of God (John 3:5; cf. vv. 6, 8). One can only worship God in spirit and truth (John 4:23–24). Only the Spirit gives life (John 6:63), and the Spirit must be given to guide Christ's people into all truth (John 14:17; 15:26; 16:13). The Spirit alone convicts the world of sin and righteousness and judgment (John 16:8–11). Before ascending into heaven, Jesus breathed the Spirit upon his disciples so that they might know this freedom (John 20:22; cf. 7:39). Paul, too, is quite clear that this is the work

---

[7]Whereas the negative conception of liberty excludes the positive, the positive conception incorporates the negative.

[8]Peter does not explicitly connect freedom and the work of the Spirit as clearly as Jesus and Paul, but it is evident that the same theology of the Spirit undergirds Peter's understanding of sanctification and growth in the Christian (see 1 Pet. 1:2; 2:2, 5; 3:18; 4:14).

of the Spirit who creates new realities in our hearts: "For the law of the Spirit of life has set you free in Christ Jesus from the law of sin and death" (Rom. 8:2), and "where the Spirit of the Lord is, there is freedom" (2 Cor. 3:17).

Freedom in the Bible is consistently characterized as the knowledge of truth, the desire to heed the truth, and the ability to heed the truth. It's the freedom of being able to do what God created you to do—image him in all his glory, whether we have been designed as a runner, a thinker, an engineer, or a singer. Christ alone, then, was truly free because he knew the law and he kept it, which is precisely how every son and daughter of Adam was meant to live. We are free as Christians to whatever extent we walk by the Spirit and not by the flesh (see Romans 7–8). To whatever extent we let the passions of the flesh guide us, however, we are not free. God's righteous standards will feel constraining, even enslaving.

It's understandable that Christians today have been drawn into viewing freedom almost exclusively as negative freedom, whether intuitively or articulately (theologians describe it as libertarian freedom). The members of churches, aside from being Christians, are human beings who have suffered abuse and oppression along with everyone else through the course of political history's escalator of idols. Christians are therefore rightly suspicious of (almost) every form of positive liberty. But that's exactly what Jesus offers—a system of truth, a metanarrative, a worldview, a law, a gospel, apart from which freedom is impossible.

Step 2: Since Christian freedom can only be given by the Spirit, and not the flesh, the godly use of authority in the church will not seek to coerce individuals by the flesh; it will appeal to gospel realities given by the Spirit.

Authoritarianism and the Limits of Authority

Throughout this book I have contended that the Christian life involves submitting to authority, whether the church's apostolic authority to bind and loose or a pastoral authority to "reprove, rebuke, and exhort" according to God's Word (Matt. 16:19; 2 Tim. 4:2). Yet this discussion of positive versus negative liberty should help us to understand both what's involved in submitting to the church and the limits of the church's authority. Let me draw out four lessons in particular. As I do, I employ a distinction between authority and authoritarianism. The former will be used either neutrally or positively, while the latter will be used pejoratively and understood to be sin.

1) Christian freedom is not freedom apart from the Spirit. Apart from the work of God's Spirit in someone's heart, the freedom of Christianity is not freedom. It's an imprisoning and condemning law. Remember what Christianity says: a person *must* accept the good news of Jesus' life, death, and resurrection in order to have true life (e.g., John 3:18; 14:6; cf. Heb. 10:28–29). It says that a Christian must walk in obedience to Christ (e.g., John 3:36; 8:51; 15:1ff., 14), but it also says that a person cannot accept this news and command until he has been born again by the Spirit (John 3:5–8; cf. 5:21; 6:37, 44, 65; 8:43, 47; 10:3, 16, 27). Insofar as a person does not walk by the Spirit, therefore, he is *not free* to believe and follow. That's true for the non-Christian, and it's true for the Christian insofar as he walks by the flesh.

Unbelievers hate God's love, God's gospel, and God's church because those things sounds like *unfreedom* to their unbelieving ears and unseeing eyes. It sounds like nothing more than an exclusivistic constraint on freedom. It's a stepping on their toes, which is why Isaiah Berlin and every other non-Christian lumps Christianity together with every form of positive freedom such as communism and fascism. They cannot believe it.

2) Christian authority will always feel enslaving to fallen humans. If Christian freedom is not freedom wherever the Spirit of God is not in motion, then Christian authority will always look enslaving or burdensome apart from the Spirit's new-covenant work. If this chapter were a sermon, I would say that last sentence twice because it's so important. Apart from the work of God's Spirit in the heart, a godly use of authority will almost always feel like authoritarianism.

When the church or the pastor says, "God calls us to love," the flesh of the non-Christian and the Christian alike feels burdened and oppressed because it doesn't *want* to love. It wants to love itself alone, and the command is out of sync with this internal desire.

The tricky thing is that the action of the Christian minister, which *feels* authoritarian and oppressive to a church member, may or may not be. In chapter 3 we noted that our understanding of authority in the church must be complex because the realities of both the fall and the Spirit's new creation are simultaneously present. I likened this present age to a movie screen upon which two film projectors project their light. We have difficulty discerning which images on the screen come from which projector since sometimes they overlap.

Consider some action of authority in the church, maybe a pastor instructing a younger man, or the church excluding an unrepentant sinner. In either case, the action might be a godly one or an authoritarian one. The action might be done in the Spirit for love's sake or in the flesh for power's sake. In either case, the recipient of the authoritative action will feel as if it's an authoritarian action if he or she is not in the Spirit. He or she will feel imposed upon. Therefore, when a non-Christian or an immature Christian walks away from a church, saying that it's legalistic or sinfully authoritarian, I assume that the church might be, or that the departing member simply thinks it is.

That, after all, is the nature of all discipline (Heb. 12:11). Discipline does not accord with our internal desires; indeed, it's necessary precisely because our internal desires are out of accord.

3) Godly Christian authority recognizes these limits. What does all this mean for the limits of the church's authority? Often when people talk about the limits of a church's or an elder's authority, they are referring to a matter of domains, as in, "An elder may act authoritatively in *this* domain but not in *that* one." For instance, an elder has the authority to preach the Bible, but he does not have the authority to perform appendectomies, operate air-control towers, or legislate in Congress. And let me affirm this point entirely: neither the church nor the elders have authority beyond where Scripture permits them to go.[9]

At the same time, thinking about the limits of the church's authority in terms of domains might prevent us from seeing what's really at stake between a godly use of authority and authoritarianism. The key difference lies in the hearts of those acting authoritatively, as well as in the hearts of those under authority. As we saw in chapter 6, an authoritarian heart relies on its own strength to produce change. It staples apples onto trees. A non-authoritarian heart, however, knows that only God produces change. It feeds and waters the tree, but it asks God to give the growth.

So here's lesson three: godly Christian authority recognizes the limits described in lessons one and two above. That is, godly Christian authority recognizes that it's utterly and pathetically dependent upon God the Spirit to give true freedom, true love, and true light to the sinner's eyes (based on lesson one). It also recognizes that every law, command, truth claim, or piece of good news that it places before people is, therefore, an imposition upon their fallen flesh, and their flesh will resist it (based on lesson two). That's the ubiquitous risk of Christian ministry.

The right use of Christian authority, therefore, requires a church or an individual to recognize its utter helplessness and futility apart from the Spirit of God. It's an act of faith, not an act of the flesh. Preaching, discipling, and evangelism, which are indeed authoritative actions, must therefore always be performed by faith.

We can summarize the attributes of godly authority within the context of the local church (or Christian home) as follows:

---

[9] A classic example of this occurs in Presbyterian James Bannerman's book in a chapter titled, "The Extent and Limits of Church Power," in which he limits the church's authority (1) to the spiritual domain, as opposed to the state's domain; (2) by the fact that it's derived from Christ's own authority; (3) to that which is prescribed in God's Word; and (4) to the rights of Christian conscience. James Bannerman, *The Church of Christ*, vol. 2 (Carlisle, PA: Banner of Truth, 1974), 247–48.

- Godly authority is by faith. It relies upon God to make change. It believes that God always has the power to change and that he will if he so determines.

- Godly authority exhorts the heart first and the will second. In other words, a godly authority will help people to consider what they truly desire before telling them what they must do.[10]

- Godly authority appeals to Christians on the basis of their status in the gospel, not on the strength of their flesh. A Christian pastor or counselor should not say things like, "I expect more from you" or "You're better than that." Instead, he will say, "Don't you realize that you've died and been raised with Christ? You're a new creation. Now, what should that mean?" A Christian authority will give commands (e.g., 2 Thess. 3:6, 10, 12), but these commands will be issued by virtue of membership in the gospel. It appeals to the new realities of the Spirit. The imperatives should always follow the indicatives of what Christ has given.

- Godly authority is exceedingly patient and tender, knowing that only God can give growth (1 Cor. 3:5–9). An immature Christian may need to walk a hundred steps before he arrives at maturity, but a wise pastor seldom asks for more than one step or two. Our example in this is Jesus. "Take my yoke . . . and learn from me," he says (Matt. 11:29). To take his yoke is to become a disciple. It's to learn. But he is gentle and lowly in heart, and his yoke is easy and light (11:29–30).

- Godly authority is always carefully measured or calibrated to where a person is spiritually. The godly elder and church seldom, if ever, make spiritual prescriptions without asking questions and doing the exploratory work of a good doctor.

- Yet godly authority is also willing to draw lines and make demands that it knows cannot be met. A good doctor not only asks careful questions; he identifies cancer when he sees it. Likewise, a church or an elder should not use its authority to obscure God's gospel realities but to illumine them. The power of the keys, for instance, is to be used exactly to this end.

In short, it's not enough to say that the church's or pastor's authority must be limited to certain domains. Rather, we must recognize that Christian authority—gospel authority—is of a fundamentally different nature than worldly authority since it works by the power of the Spirit, not by the power of the

---

[10]Here is where we find the strange convergence between Christian liberalism and fundamentalism. Both often prefer a libertarian conception of freedom which eschews any role for nature and desire. As a result, both tend to do ministry in the same way, only we refer to one as moralistic and the other as legalistic.

flesh. The church's or pastor's authority doesn't root in the consent of those whom it governs. Rather, it roots in the authority of Jesus himself. But it always appeals to those whom it governs so that they might consent with one mind in the Spirit. It recognizes that any action that must be coerced or manipulated is not a true act of faith and therefore is not an act of true righteousness. It refrains from coercive or manipulative action. It doesn't puff out its chest and lay down the authority card whenever it can. Rather, it engages people in love. It spends time with them and gets to know them. It appeals to the Holy Spirit within them, calling them to greater and greater holiness.

4) Authoritarianism in the church does not recognize these limits. The fourth lesson is just the opposite of the third: a church (or a Christian leader) that has been given authority by God becomes sinfully authoritarian or legalistic when it does not recognize its creaturely limits as understood in lessons one and two. It staples apples onto trees, instead of feeding and watering the trees. Specifically:

- Authoritarianism commands the flesh and makes no appeal to the spiritual new man in the gospel.

- Authoritarianism starts with the imperatives of Scripture, not the indicatives of what Christ has accomplished.

- Authoritarianism looms heavily over the will, doing all it can to make the will choose rightly, apart from a consideration of where the will has its roots planted—in the heart's desires.

- Authoritarianism requires outward conformity rather than repentance of heart. In so doing, it creates only Pharisees.

- Authoritarianism often oversteps the boundaries of where the Bible has given it permission to go. It makes prescriptions about things such as "music with a beat" or partisan politics. This type of presumption is only natural when one has already begun to think that he has the power to change others by the strength of his flesh.

- Authoritarianism is impatient and forceful. Since it does not recognize that decisions have their ultimate foundation in the heart's desires, it feels successful whenever it produces a "right" decision, whether or not that decision was forced or manipulated.

- Authoritarianism relies on its own strength, rather than leaning on the Spirit by faith (see John 3:6; 6:63).

Insofar as the authoritative actions of preaching, discipling, and evangelism are performed in the flesh, they move the actor toward authoritarianism—the use of fleshly strength to coerce and manipulate. Insofar as a pastor's heart relies upon his rhetorical powers in the pulpit, his reliance is no different from a fascist dictator's. Insofar as a pastor's heart relies upon the uprightness of his life in discipleship, his reliance is no different from the professed standards of the Soviet politburo. Insofar as a pastor's heart relies upon his intellectual abilities to persuade in evangelism, his reliance is no different from history's worst party propagandists and con men.

That's not to say that Christian ministry should jettison all rhetorical gift-edness or intellectual recourse. It's simply to say there is a difference between employing something and relying upon it. We employ things that are expendable; we rely upon things that are necessary. We employ farmers and grocers to manufacture bread, but we rely upon God to give us food, a distinction that's implicit every time we bow our heads and thank him for the meal before us. Faith, quite simply, means having the eyes to see the difference between the two. Not having faith means assuming that brain, brawn, or beauty are necessary to produce change. In each case, we're using the flesh to manipulate the flesh.

Insofar as contemporary church-growth strategies tempt church leaders to rely upon the devices of the world—style, lighting, music, rhetorical art, building design, intelligence, humor, authenticity, cultural relevance—they tempt those leaders to calculate change and productivity in precisely the same manner as every authoritarian in history has. Indeed, Hitler had political reasons for preferring the music of Beethoven and Wagner, while Lenin's social purposes were embodied in Soviet Constructivist architecture. Such churches may not strong-arm their members, but they do strong-charm or strong-mind them. Ironically, the evangelical who thinks that rock music is necessary to make his church grow is no different from the fundamentalist who says that all rock music is sin. By this token, to charge a church with pragmatism, if that's what it has fallen into, is to be far too kind.

For those in authority, including the church as a whole, Jesus and Paul's discussion of freedom means that a church can easily assume that it's acting according to biblical principles, when it's really acting in a sinfully authoritarian manner. Is that image on the screen coming from the world's film projector or Christ's? Sometimes it's easy to tell; sometimes it's not. Worldly authority can look impatient, domineering, quick to speak, manipulative, and forceful, but it can also look humorous, sophisticated, and slick. Godly authority tends to look patient, slow to speak, gentle, and careful, but it can also look strong, powerful, and assertive. Let me sum up the matter with a few more comparisons concerning the exercise of authority in or by a local church:

- Worldly authority teaches with conviction. Gospel authority listens and then teaches with even greater conviction.

- Worldly authority often involves absolutizing one earthly teacher. Gospel authority often celebrates a plurality of human teachers, because it relies upon one Teacher.

- Worldly authority enjoys hearing itself speak. A gospel authority loves to speak the Word of God.

- Worldly authority is strong. Gospel authority is even stronger with God's strength.

- Worldly authority likes to project humility, which it does by expressing doubt or a lack of certainty.[11] Gospel authority is humble, which it demonstrates every time it submits to the certainty of God's Word.

Can we see why both the pragmatism of seeker-sensitive megachurches and the professed humility of the Emergent coffeehouses are both apples that didn't fall far from the fundamentalist tree?

Step 3: When individuals find themselves under an abusive authority, they should always trust God's provision and purposes; if possible, they should flee.

Responding to Authoritarianism

There are two further lessons to be taken from this comparison of authority and authoritarianism that are of particular relevance to the individual under authority.

---

[11]Benjamin Franklin's remarks on how he attempted to cultivate humility by mimicking the phraseology of humility, with no success, are instructive for our day and age when such a high premium is placed upon *sounding humble* in religious discourse. Franklin writes, "My List of Virtues contain'd at first but twelve: but a Quaker Friend having kindly informed me that I was generally thought proud. . . . I added *Humility* to my list. . . . I cannot boast of much Success in acquiring the *Reality* of this Virtue; but I had a good deal with regard to the *Appearance* of it. . . . I even forbid myself . . . the Use of every Word or Express in the Language that imported a fix'd Opinion; such as *certainly, undoubtedly,* &c. and I adopted instead of them, I *conceive,* I *apprehend,* or I *imagine* a thing to be so or so, or it so appears to me at present. . . . In reality there is perhaps no one of our natural Passions so hard to subdue as *Pride.* Disguise it, struggle with it, beat it down, stifle it, mortify it as much as one pleases, it is still alive, and will every now and then peep out and show itself. . . . For even if I could conceive that I had completely overcome it, I should probably be proud of my Humility." Benjamin Franklin, *The Autobiography and Other Writings* (New York: Viking Penguin Books, 1984 ed.), 102–3. A writer or church leader exposes a false humility, I *apprehend,* whenever he appeals to something like postmodernism as what should ground Christian humility. No epistemology produces true humility; only the Spirit does.

FLEE AN ABUSIVE LEADER IF YOU CAN

I have known many Christians whose lives and discipleship were dramatically hurt by an oppressive father, an abusive pastor, or a legalistic church, which is why I said earlier that I was tempted to tell any church leader who already affirms the idea of authority to stop reading. I pray that nothing I have written would affirm any leader in a conscious or unconscious pattern of abuse. The best corrective is not to throw the baby out with the bathwater, as it were, but to reform the baby. That's why I have made a brief attempt at reforming our concept of authority.

Churches and church leaders, tragically, will continue to abuse the authority that God has given them until Christ returns. In so doing, they lie horribly about the very Christ they claim to serve. How would I advise a Christian suffering at the hands of an abusive church or church leader? First, I would advise him or her to escape the abusive situation if possible. Speaking to slaves Paul writes, "If you can gain your freedom, avail yourself of the opportunity" (1 Cor. 7:21).

The godly use of authority authors life. The abusive and exploitative use of authority does not, and I would counsel most people in such a church to leave it in order to protect themselves and not be guilty of supporting its work over the lives of others. Pastors should protect their sheep, not fleece them, and the ones who do will be severally judged (e.g., Ezek. 34:1–10).

Assessing whether a church or leader is truly abusive or exploitative is no easy thing. As I just said, it can be hard to discern which film projector is casting the image we are beholding, and a Christian should never trust his own heart entirely to do that work of assessment. There's wisdom in a multitude of counselors.

TRUST GOD'S PROVISION

At the same time, there are many situations in which a Christian cannot escape the abusive authority or in which the abuse is difficult but not so intolerable that the individual feels impelled to flee. Whatever the case, Christians should always remember that the kingdoms, powers, and authorities of this world are not ultimate. For that reason, Paul writes:

> Were you a slave when called? Do not be concerned about it. (But if you can gain your freedom, avail yourself of the opportunity.) For he who was called in the Lord as a slave is a freedman of the Lord. Likewise he who was free when called is a slave of Christ. You were bought with a price; do not become slaves of men. (1 Cor. 7:21–23)

This should not be understood as Paul's approbation of slavery. Rather, Paul is saying that our membership in the gospel is more important than our political state, no matter how wretched it may be in worldly terms. If that were not true, then the political freedom any human freedom fighter offered would be better news than the freedom Christ came to give. Paul's goal is to keep our eyes ultimately fixed on the gospel: "You were bought with a price." Therefore, to whatever extent a Christian suffers underneath an unjust leader, secular or sacred, he can take comfort in God's ultimate provision and authority in the gospel. We are promised that Christ has defeated all the powers and authorities in this world (Col. 2:15). Even if this victory cannot yet be seen with the eyes, this is where our faith must rest.

These last two points are probably worth a chapter—if not a book—of their own, but let me sum up the matter, perhaps unsatisfactorily, like this: just as we must view authority in this present world in a complex fashion, so our response to it must be complex. Indeed, Jesus' own response to the authorities of this world was complex. He simultaneously condemned their exploitation of power, while, in the final act, submitted himself to it because he trusted in the ultimate rule and provision of his Father in heaven.

Step 4: Philippians 2 presents the model for submission in the local church: Christ's incarnation and crucifixion.

A Biblical Portrait of Submission to the Church

It was Christ's very willingness to submit his life to the point of death that Paul uses to paint a picture of the Christian life lived in submission to the local church. In Philippians 2:1–17, Paul presents us with a portrait of the Christian's life inside the local church, and inside that portrait he embeds a second portrait of Christ's sacrificial submission. These two portraits, taken together, essentially present the argument of this entire book: God's God-centered love mercifully pours itself out to rebellious sinners in order to mark them off from the world, reform them into the obedient image of his Son, and display them before the watching universe.

At the end of Philippians 1, Paul tells the Philippians to live a life worthy of the gospel, a life in which they stand firm in one spirit and one mind. Moving into chapter 2, Paul continues with his description of a life worthy of the gospel, reminding them of the encouragement and love they have known in Christ and the Spirit. He tells them again to be of one mind (twice) as well as to share one love. He tells them to humbly consider others better than themselves, looking to others' interests and not just their own. He then explains that the "one mind" they are to share is the mind of Christ, who made himself nothing, took the form of a servant, and humbled himself by becoming obedient to death. Christ did this so that every knee would bow to him to the glory of the Father.

Paul then reminds them that they have obeyed in the past and encourages them to continue doing so as they work out their salvation, relying upon God to work for his own pleasure in them. He even gets into the nitty-gritty of what this one-mindedness and one love looks like: not complaining and grumbling toward one another. It's when they live in this distinct fashion in a crooked and twisted world that they can expect to stand out before all the world like stars in the night sky, all the while holding fast to the word of life. This is the picture of a life lived in submission to the local church. It's a life that mimics Christ's submissive love for the Father and his sacrificial love for others. It's when we love the other members of our church in this fashion that we define love for the world.

I fear that we often read this passage without the local church in view. Yet notice that Paul is writing to "the saints in Christ Jesus who are at Philippi, with the overseers and deacons" (1:1). He's writing to a local church. Therefore, when he tells them to be of one spirit, one love, and one mind, he's primarily addressing each of his readers with respect to the other members of their church. When he tells them to consider others better than themselves, he's addressing them, again, with respect to the members of their church. It's within the context of the local church that Paul is calling them to submit and become obedient to one another, just like Christ submitted and became obedient to the Father. That's not to say Christians should treat the members of other churches without such love. It is to say that this self-sacrificing love "begins at home"—under the oversight of one's own congregation and elders. He's not telling them to be of one mind and love with all Christians everywhere, though that is surely Christ's ultimate goal. He's telling them to be of one mind and love with the Christians *right there around them.*

A life lived in submission to the local church is working out our salvation by conforming our minds and hearts to this one corporate love. It's doing this with people who may not look like us and whom we don't know very well. It's interacting with them without rivalry or conceit. It's humbly counting each one as more significant than ourselves. It's looking to their interests above our own. It's not grumbling or questioning them, even when we are tempted to do so. Most importantly, it's imitating Jesus' complete self-surrender.

Step 5: Christians emulate Christ's example by submitting to one another physically, socially, affectionately, financially, vocationally, ethically, and spiritually.

The Different Aspects of Submission

Older works on church membership and discipline would sometimes enumerate the duties or responsibilities that church members owed to other church members, such as gathering with them, praying for them, and watching over them. Such lists are helpful for practical purposes, yet if Christ's submission is our model for looking to the interests of others, then we are called to do something more involved than check off a list. We are called to wrap up our identities with theirs and share in their lives. It involves giving ourselves to the church, not just giving of ourselves while remaining at a safe distance. How do we *give ourselves* to the church for Christ's glory? We involve every area of our lives. We give ourselves physically, socially, affectionately, financially, vocationally, ethically, and spiritually. We will consider these in the context of a healthy, gospel-driven, non-authoritarian church.

PUBLICLY

Christians should submit to their local churches publicly, by which I mean formally or officially. They should join a church by committing to the local body of believers. This formal or public act is symbolic of that fact that we have submitted to a whole new reality. Joining a church goes well beyond adding our name to the membership rolls.

PHYSICALLY AND GEOGRAPHICALLY

Christians should submit to their local churches physically and perhaps geographically. We submit physically by gathering regularly with the church (Acts 2:42–47; Heb. 10:25). For all the technological advances made in communications and travel, nothing substitutes for the human presence. Even the author of Hebrews affirms this in the first lines of his book. He compares God's communication to his people in the past through apostles and prophets, with the preeminent revelation of himself in the physical person of his Son. Christians should likewise submit their bodies to the presence of the members of their local church. Where the body goes, the rest of a person generally goes.

If this book were being written 150 years ago, or in some less urban areas of the world today, I might be able to conclude this point simply with the regular weekly gathering, since people's community lives through the week were more naturally integrated. In smaller and slower communities, the fellowship shared in the Sunday gathering more easily translates into times of fellowship throughout the week. When a person lives within walking distance of the church, it's easier to invite people to one's house for dinner, to watch one another's children while running errands, to pick up bread or milk for someone when going to the store. It's easier to integrate daily life when there is relative—even walkable—geographic proximity.

When I told one scholar that I was writing a book on church membership, he encouraged me to look for ways to account for the fact that we live in a commuter society in which people sometimes travel thirty miles to get to church. One obvious solution is not to live thirty miles from one's church. Living close to church is hardly a biblical requirement, but it may be prudent, even loving. Our culture's formula for home selection is simple: how do I get the most for least? But a Christian no longer belongs to himself. He belongs to Christ and Christ's people. Shouldn't his formula for home selection, therefore, look a little different? Why not instead choose a residence that will let us count others more significant than ourselves and look to the interests of others? Part of doing so includes the availability of good schools for families with children, but it should also include price and geographic proximity to the church. Will the mortgage or rent payment allow for generosity to others? Will it give others quick access to us and our hospitality? Looking for a residence within walking distance of one's church may be more realistic in an urban setting than a suburban one, but the same basic principle applies in both settings. A young mother will more likely plan playdates with other young mothers in her housing development than with mothers in another part of town. Sometimes variables such as price and geographic proximity work at cross purposes. My point is simply that a Christian should think differently about home selection from a non-Christian, principally by placing a higher premium on relationships within the church.

I have witnessed a number of people, both in my church and in others, deliberately deciding to move closer to church, within walking distance, if possible. I have known others who, when moving to a new city for work, deliberately found a healthy church to join before beginning the house search. For my family, submitting geographically to the church didn't mean moving close to the church but moving into a neighborhood where several other church families lived.

When we moved to our present city several years ago, my wife and I felt divided between purchasing a newer, nicer, less expensive home fifteen minutes from anyone in the church, and an older, less convenient, more expensive home within walking distance of these other families. I sought the counsel of several elders, who separately advised me to prioritize relationships, which we did. That resulted in our choosing a house with a rotting front porch, drafty doors, and an occasionally flooded basement for more money than a well-decorated, better-designed, more attractive home without (to my knowledge) need of immediate repairs. But how enriching it has been for our whole family to prioritize church relationships! My wife and children interact with other families from the church almost daily. I met with one brother every morning to pray and read the Bible for a year and a half and still regularly meet with others. All the church families within this neighborhood encourage one another to carry out evangelism and to take advantage of ministry opportunities in our neighborhood. For all the time I have spent in this book talking about sociological concepts like individualism, I wonder if one of the Devil's best devices for depleting the meaning of church membership isn't our cultural lust for newer and nicer homes. How many Christians have effectively limited themselves to fellowship on Sunday mornings because of where they live? This isn't a call for Christians to isolate themselves in a Christian bubble. It is a call for them to more actively build their lives together for their sakes and for the sake of reaching their communities.

SOCIALLY

One of the purposes of submitting physically and perhaps geographically to a local church is the opportunity to submit oneself socially. I don't mean to suggest that churches should only aspire to be social clubs, but they shouldn't be less than social clubs. Christians should pursue friendships in and through their local churches.

Our friends are the ones we imitate and follow. We adopt their language and life patterns. We tend to spend money where they spend money. We value what they value. We raise our children like they raise their children. We pray like they pray. We trust their counsel and heed their rebukes more easily than that of those who are not friends. There's a reason that Paul says, "Bad company ruins good morals" (1 Cor. 15:33; cf. Deut. 13:6). It's because our friends play a large role in forming who we become as we imitate one another (see James 4:4).

Indeed, this is why there is no better friendship than the friendship of the Lord, a friendship which is given to those who keep his covenant and do his commands (Ps. 25:14; John 15:14). To say he is our friend is to say that we imitate him.

To be a friend, on the other hand, is to give, just as God gives. God gives to those whom he befriends, just as Christ has befriended us through his sacrifice (John 15:13, 15). Likewise, we should befriend the members of our church by giving ourselves to them. (Thomas Aquinas, in fact, built most of his discussion of love in the language of friendship.)

The local church community should be a place where Christians participate in forming and shaping one another for good through all the interpersonal dynamics of friendship. Christian friends are surely valuable inside or outside the local church, but friends within a local church will be formed by the same ministry of the Word, giving them the opportunity to extend that ministry more carefully into one another's lives throughout the week. Friendships are a God-given vehicle through which the church's ministry of the Word travels. Church friendships, in other words, will share all the strengths of friendship generally, but they should also be characterized by an element of discipleship.

In many respects, discipleship is merely friendship with a Christward direction or purpose—that of seeing another conformed increasingly to the image of Christ as one or both give, in order for the other to receive. Indeed, Christian friendships take humility, because it requires humility to both give and receive. As God gives humility to churches, those churches should be increasingly characterized by discipleship friendships: young men befriending other young men for the sake of encouraging one another in the faith; young women doing the same with other young women; older men befriending one another and younger men; and so forth.

Sometimes people laugh at how particular phrases and mannerisms become contagious and overused within a group of friends or a church community, but that's exactly how discipleship works among imaging creatures. We watch and mimic, at least if we are humble. "Be imitators of me, as I am of Christ," Paul said to the Corinthians twice in one letter (1 Cor. 11:1; 4:16; also 2 Thess. 3:7, 9). The author of Hebrews likewise told his readers to imitate the faith of their leaders (Heb. 13:7), and John told the church to which he was writing to imitate what is good, not evil (3 John 11).

Giving oneself socially to the local church also provides Christians with the opportunity to move outside their social comfort zones in friendship— old with the young, rich with the poor, uneducated with the educated, blacks with whites, and so forth. It's one thing for members of different ethnicities to befriend one another, but it takes just a little bit more humility to seek out instruction and discipling from one another. Yet the Spirit delights to enable members of different ethnicities to stand fast in one spirit, one love, and one mind. He delights to do the same for those divided by wealth, class, education, and other traditionally divisive demographics.

In short, the friendships within a church should look the same and different from friendships within the world. When conducted without quarreling or arguing in a crooked and depraved generation, they will shine like lights in the world.

AFFECTIONATELY

One component of friendship, of course, is the sharing of affections, and one more way that Christians are called to submit to the local church is through submitting their affections to one another. What is it that gives me joy or grief? What is it that causes me to celebrate or mourn?

Fulfilling Paul's command to "count others more significant than yourselves" and to "look not only to [your] own interests" means giving more than just our body or even our friendship. Paul tells us elsewhere that we can surrender our bodies to the flames and still not give something that we should be giving—our love and affection. Hence, he instructs the church in Philippi to be of the same mind and to have one love. This one love ascends, first and foremost, to the worship of the Son and the glory of the Father, but this very desire for the Son's worship involves the Christian in desiring this same good for the members of his church. So he says to the Romans, "Love one another with brotherly affection. Outdo one another in showing honor" (Rom. 12:10). And to the Corinthians he says, "Have the same care for one another. If one member suffers, all suffer together; if one member is honored, all rejoice together" (1 Cor. 12:25).

It's difficult to conceive how a consumeristic approach to church can coexist with such love. What I fear is that the love and emotions we typically experience in the movie theater are what we strive for in our churches. Consider for a second the tears that are shed in movie theater seats. A moment of romance or tragedy occurs with which the viewer can remotely identify; in a flash, the mind and heart feel gripped, even immersed, in the sensations of empathy. Tears follow, seemingly out of nowhere; then the scene passes, the tears dry up, and all is quickly forgotten. When all is done, one is left feeling no more or less of a human for having experienced that strange rush of emotion. You are left unchanged as a person.

It's not like this when real life causes us to cry, of course. The circumstances that cause real tears to flow often change us, either for the better or the worse. Tears in a movie theater, for me at least, are a strange experience. One moment I'm fully immersed. The next moment it's as if nothing ever happened because the movie is over and the lights have been turned on. Frankly, it often leaves me feeling manipulated. My concern, again, is that Christians today, trained by the sentiments of a movie theater, are encouraged to feel and love in the same way within their churches. A heart-tugging sermon illustration, special music that spirals higher and higher with every harmonic modulation, a praise chorus that's repeated over and over, are all ways of producing tears and the pleasant sensations of joy, love, and even conviction. But how transformative those emotions are once the service ends is less clear.

Compare that with the affection Paul commands. It combines sentiment with action; delight with self-sacrifice. He tells us to put on compassion, kindness, humility, meekness, patience, forbearance, forgiveness, and above all these, love, which binds everything together in perfect unity (Col. 3:12–14). These aren't the mawkish emotions of a movie theater. He commands us to rejoice with the brother who gets a big job promotion and all the money and prestige that come with it. Can we? He commands the thirty-year-old single woman who longs for marriage to rejoice with the twenty-two-year-old woman when she marries. Can she? Can the poor man mourn with the rich man when he loses his job? Can the older woman mourn with the younger woman whose melancholy strikes her as petty and maudlin? Saying yes to these questions, rather than saying yes to selfish ambition and vain conceit, requires something more than mere sentiment. It requires a gospel-altered heart and the power of the Spirit. The single woman rejoices for the married woman and the poor man mourns with the rich man when both find all their identity and joy in Christ. They feel affirmed in his love, which they see in his sacrifice. They know that no marriage and no riches will satisfy more than Christ. They desire nothing more than his praise, so they find themselves unexpectedly warm of heart toward all those who belong to his body, and they desire the same knowledge and joy for them.

When we view the church as a place for our own spiritual enhancement, will we love like this? When we spend more time concerned about whether our gifts are being adequately used, the music meets our standard, or the preaching is sufficiently engaging, is it likely that we give ourselves to rejoicing and mourning with others? No, true rejoicing and mourning occur when we identify ourselves with another, and that's the one thing the consumer and the spectator, by definition, always hold back— them*selves*.

Fulfilling Paul's command to "count others more significant than yourselves" with "one love" means knowing the love of Christ, who did not consider equality with God something to be grasped, and then loving the way he loves.

FINANCIALLY

Christians should submit to their local churches financially. This will look different from context to context. In some contexts, it means regularly placing a check into an offering plate. In other contexts, where the economy does not allow for that kind of regularity, it might mean regularly helping other members of the church with the essentials of life. However it is done, Christians should look for ways to fulfill biblical commands such as these:

- "Share with God's people who are in need. Practice hospitality. " (Rom. 12:13 NIV; also Gal. 2:10; 1 John 3:17)

- Now concerning the collection for the saints: as I directed the churches of Galatia, so you also are to do. On the first day of every week, each of you is to put something aside and store it up, as he may prosper, so that there will be no collecting when I come. (1 Cor. 16:1–2; also Rom. 15:26)

- For they gave according to their means, as I can testify, and beyond their means, of their own accord, begging us earnestly for the favor of taking part in the relief of the saints. . . . But as you excel in everything . . . see that you excel in this act of grace also. (2 Cor. 8:3–4, 7)

- The Lord commanded that those who proclaim the gospel should get their living by the gospel. (1 Cor. 9:14; also, 9:11–13; Matt. 10:10; Luke 10:7; Gal. 6:6; 1 Tim. 5:17–18)

Most Christians recognize that we should give financially, but I propose, further, that the firstfruits of a Christian's regular giving should go to his or her local church. There are several reasons for this. First, Paul says that "one who is taught the word must share all good things with the one who teaches" (Gal. 6:6). Just as we have an obligation to support our children, we have an obligation to support the preachers of God's Word in our local church.

Second, it's one way to submit to our church's authority. Giving our first-fruits affirms and demonstrates trust for the church leaders and how they will use the money to grow the church and its outreach. Someone who claims to submit to a church and its leadership but does not give to it financially shows that his claim of submission may be hollow. The way in which people spend money, probably more than anything else except time, reveals what their hearts value and love. A man who gives little or nothing to his church is someone with a high estimation of his own dominion and sovereignty.

However, I sympathize greatly with church members who feel reluctant to give because their leaders have a poor track record in financial decisions. Personally, I would have difficulty financially supporting a church that demon-strated little concern with kingdom work, such as missions or church planting, but spent most of its money beautifying the church building or on other non-essential matters. Still, Jesus gave authority to the local church to oversee our discipleship, which includes how we spend our money and where we contribute to God's work. Somehow we need to balance the call to submit to that authority with the call to wise stewardship of the finances God gives us, even when those two callings might be at odds from time to time.

VOCATIONALLY

For some, submitting to God and the local church means leaving secular employ-ment and moving into full-time vocational ministry in a church. For every Christian, however, submitting to God and the local church means recognizing that the lives of our fellow members will stretch on for eternity, while our jobs will not.

Just as a Christian might consider choosing a residence close to where his church gathers, the same is true of secular employment. A Christian's job deci-sions fall into the realm of freedom and prudence, except in matters of biblical morality. Yet Christians should also consider how they can "count others more significant than themselves" through the job decisions they make.

I know men and women in secular employment who, for the sake of serving in their local church, have turned down promotions and more money; moved from larger, more reputable firms to smaller ones; turned down compelling job offers; and refused to move to another city. In each case the choice was made largely so as not to hinder the ability to care for the church. I have also known others who refused to work on Sundays, or have quit jobs because they were required to do so. They quit not because they are Sabbatarians, but because that's when the church gathers.

What's unfortunate is that many churches today tend to choose their elders from among successful leaders in the marketplace, giving less regard for the spiritual or biblical qualifications of those men. Some of the men whom I have most respected as elders have made sacrifices in their careers for the sake of serving the church.

I don't mean to suggest that Christian maturity necessitates making sacrifices to one's career, yet we must consider whether we value growth and upward movement in our careers in the same way that our non-Christian colleagues do. Ambition is a good thing. It's one aspect of imaging God. We Christians should be more ambitious than non-Christians because we have more to be ambitious about! However, what does being ambitious about the kingdom of God and his righteousness look like with respect to our secular jobs and our local churches? Could it be that truly loving and serving might have a palpable effect on our career track? It's hard to know, when we are not even willing to ask the question.

When Christians do enter full-time vocational ministry, they should submit even more explicitly to the oversight and affirmation of the local church. Churches, likewise, should take ownership and responsibility for Christians who aspire to enter such work. I was working in journalism when I began thinking about vocational ministry. I mentioned this to my pastor over lunch one day, and he told me that, generally speaking, a man should not enter the ministry until his internal desires line up with the church's recognition of his character and giftedness. Individuals considering vocational ministry should submit those desires to the wisdom and guidance of the local church. We cannot always see our character or our gifts as clearly as others can. I don't mean to suggest that those who feel called to the ministry should allow a church to have absolute say in whether or where they enter it. But we should generally heed the counsel of a church.

ETHICALLY

Christians should submit themselves to the authority of their local churches ethically. I certainly do not mean that they should make the church their absolute authority, any more than a child should make his or her parents an absolute authority. Rather, the Christian should look to the church for ethical instruction, guidance, counsel, accountability, and discipline, like the child does with the parent, all according to God's Word. Elders, therefore, are commanded to teach the Scriptures, which are "profitable for teaching, for reproof, for correction, and for training in righteousness" (2 Tim. 3:16), while members are charged with helping to keep one another in the way of righteousness. Paul writes, "Brothers, if anyone is caught in any transgression, you who are spiritual should restore him in a spirit of gentleness. Keep watch on yourself, lest you too be tempted. Bear one another's burdens, and so fulfill the law of Christ" (Gal. 6:1–2). Jude similarly writes, "Have mercy on those who doubt; save others by snatching them out of the fire; to others show mercy with fear, hating even the garment stained by the flesh" (Jude 22–23). The local church is the primary place where we seek to help other believers overcome their sin and where we, in turn, should open ourselves up to receive the same help.

Submitting to a local church means willingly undergoing its corrective discipline when we have been deceived by sin and wandered into error. The scores of passages in the book of Proverbs that compare the wise son and the foolish son make for an excellent members' manual:

- The wise of heart will receive commandments, but a babbling fool will come to ruin. (Prov. 10:8)

- The way of a fool is right in his own eyes, but a wise man listens to advice. (Prov. 12:15)

- A wise son hears his father's instruction, but a scoffer does not listen to rebuke. (Prov. 13:1)

- A fool takes no pleasure in understanding, but only in expressing his opinion. (Prov. 18:2)

The local church is where we practice being the wise son and help others do the same.

Specifically, we help others by instructing, counseling, and correcting them when necessary. If a brother has something against us, we seek out reconciliation before going to worship (Matt. 5:23–24). If a brother sins against us, we go and show him his fault (18:15). If he listens, we have won our brother. If he doesn't, we take two or three others back with us to him. If he doesn't listen to them, we take it to the church (Matt. 18:16–17). All this is part of what it means to submit to the local church.

I don't mean that Christians should never counsel or receive the counsel of Christians in other churches, but I do mean that Christians have a higher obligation to open up their lives to the congregation that is ultimately responsible for binding or loosing them. If we reveal deeper levels of our sin to someone outside our local church, it deprives our church of its Jesus-assigned responsibility to keep watch over our soul. It keeps us safely beyond the reach of the church's discipline and, therefore, places our soul in a danger zone. Additionally, it deprives teachers of the Word of knowing of how to preach more meaningfully to the congregation. If teachers are oblivious as to how their members are struggling morally, they will be less capable of shepherding. Also, it fools us into thinking that we are fully in charge of our own discipleship. A self-selected accountability partner outside of one's church can be easily dismissed.

SPIRITUALLY

Christians should submit to a local church spiritually. In some ways this last category is a catchall for anything that hasn't already been covered, since it sums up everything that has preceded it, but it does include three specific things. First, the local church is where Christians should go to build up one another in the faith. Second, it's where we should seek to exercise our spiritual gifts. Third, it houses the people for whom we should intercede regularly in our prayers. Jude writes, "But you, beloved, building yourselves up in your most holy faith and praying in the Holy Spirit, keep yourselves in the love of God, waiting for the mercy of our Lord Jesus Christ that leads to eternal life" (Jude 20–21). Paul observes, "To each is given the manifestation of the Spirit for the common good" (1 Cor. 12:7; also 12:4–11; also Rom. 12:4–8).

Again, I don't mean to suggest that this kind of spiritual submission and care should never be extended to Christians in other congregations. I'm simply saying that Christians should entrust their own congregation with the primary responsibility to oversee them spiritually. This is biblical, wise, and intuitive.

Our spiritual submission to the church is more active than passive. It begins passively, when we listen to the spiritual words of someone teaching God's Word (see 1 Cor. 2:13). God's Word, whether spoken through a sermon or a private rebuke, is the fount of all spiritual life—God's Word working together with God's Spirit in the Christian. Yet once the Word has been heard and received, it should convert to immediate activity in the local church. We respond to what we have heard. We begin to pray for the church, for its members and leaders, its witness and worship. We seek to build up others with our words of comfort and occasional correction (2 Cor. 1:3–7). We exercise our Spirit-given gifts. When such activity is lacking, it raises the question of whether we have truly heard the Word through the Spirit. In short, spiritual submission, even though it begins with receiving, has more to do with giving.

By dividing up our physical, social, affectionate, financial, vocational, ethical, and spiritual acts of submission separately, I don't mean to suggest that these are unrelated aspects of our person. As used here, these are merely different themes that constitute a Christian's holistic submission to and freedom in the local church. Love involves giving ourselves for the glory of God, not giving of ourselves for the glory of self. To love another is to give our whole person in all of its aspects for God's sake. It's to identify with another for God's sake. It's to submit to another for God's sake. It's to make ourselves, in some fashion, vulnerable to another, even when, for God's sake, doing so might harm us or our reputation. Love is never given without a risk or a sacrifice. It risks all in the here and now for the sake of gaining all in eternity (see Matt. 16:26).

In spite of the fact that most people want to separate love and submission, everyone knows that love and submission involve risk. We see shadows of it in the stories of childhood where the hero risks all for the happily-ever-after ending with the beautiful damsel. What's unexpected about Christianity is that its great hero doesn't risk all for a damsel but for a whore. Then he calls everyone that he saves to submit to this whore—the bride still being made ready, the church. When you get down to it, people are not afraid of submitting. They're afraid of submitting to ugliness. We love submitting to beauty. Even something such as the market for pornography reflects this fact in a dim and tragic sort of way.

Submitting to the local church is, in one sense, submitting to loving ugliness. It's submitting to loving our enemies—other sinners who have their own visions for glory that don't match our own. But this is how Christ loved us: "Just as I have loved you, you also are to love one another" (John 13:34). Christ loves us with a love that transforms the ugly into the beautiful (see Eph. 5:22–31). So should our love for our churches be.

Who can love like this? Only the one whose eyes have been opened and whose heart has been freed from the slavery of loving this world. "So if the Son sets you free, you will be free indeed" (John 8:36).

Step 6: When the church contravenes Scripture or the gospel's witness, an individual should speak and act in dissent, but only reverently and in the fear of God.

When and How to Disagree

This entire discussion has been premised on how members should submit to healthy, gospel-driven churches. But does Christ expect Christians to submit to unhealthy churches? Also, does our call to submission prevent us from ever disagreeing with our leaders? If it's permissible to disagree, when and how should we?

The first thing to keep in mind is that no earthly church is perfect, just like no government is perfect. Despite that, Christ still calls Christians to submit to their churches and citizens to their governments (Rom. 13:1). It seems that God has his purposes in calling humans to submit to other imperfect humans.

Primarily, of course, a Christian should submit to the local church because of his ultimate submission to the Scriptures. Neither the church nor any of its representatives has ultimate authority; Christ and his Word alone do. Just as Peter and John told the Jewish authorities that they must listen to God rather than men (Acts 4:19), so a Christian's conscience is ultimately bound to God and no other with regard to life in the church. "True elders," says Alexander Strauch, "do not command the consciences of their brethren, but appeal to their brethren to faithfully follow God's Word."[12]

At times, disagreements and abuses can be borne. At times they cannot, and a church's authority should be rejected. Unfortunately, there is no precise formula for determining when a Christian should do one or the other, other than that a Christian is not bound to submit to the church whenever it requires something that explicitly contradicts Scripture or implicitly contradicts the spirit of scriptural wisdom and reflects poorly on the gospel. Discerning the latter depends finally on the exercise of one's own conscience.

It is worth observing that submitting to the local church means submitting to its good and holiness. At times, this in fact means that our very submission will require us to disagree with our leaders, even rebuking them if necessary, whenever their words, actions, or leadership explicitly contradict the Scriptures or reflect poorly on the gospel. When this is the case, we express our disagreements or concerns discreetly, carefully, respectfully, and even affirmingly. We do this in meekness and with an eagerness to submit, but we do it. If, in the final analysis, submitting to the church's or the elders' authority would lead the church into something unworthy of Christ and his bride, the Bible instructs us to speak and act in dissent.[13]

---

[12] Alexander Strauch, *Biblical Eldership: An Urgent Call to Restore Biblical Church Leadership*, rev. ed. (Colorado Springs, CO: Lewis and Roth, 1995), 98.

[13] It's over this point of dissent that misunderstandings can occur between a high church conception of authority and what I'm advocating here (which is applicable to free-churches). Criticizing the Baptist or Congregational church polity, the nineteenth-century Presbyterian James Bannerman wrote, "An authority so conditioned and checked by the necessity of the consent of the parties over whom it is exercised, cannot, in the proper sense of the word, be authority at all. It is advice, or it is counsel, administered by one party to another; but it cannot be authoritative power, exercised by one party over another, when the concurrence of both is required before it can be exercised at all, and when either party refuse their concurrence at their pleasure." To some measure, I agree with him. It's true that the authority of the church does not depend on the consent of the governed because it roots in Christ's own authority. Yet leaving our understanding of church authority here will yield authoritarianism or, at least, a law little different than the law given at Sinai. It tempts church leaders to say, "My authority comes from Christ, so do what I say. End of discussion." We should also recognize the authority of God's Spirit at work in his people (Matt. 18:15–17; 1 Cor. 2:6; Gal. 1:6–9). Gospel authority always recognizes that a church's authority will prove efficacious only to the extent that God's Spirit has moved in the hearts of his people. In other words, a church's authority never goes beyond the Word, and that authority's usefulness never goes beyond the Spirit. It recognizes, as I said earlier, that any action that must be forced is not an act of faith. Therefore, gospel

When an actual charge of a moral nature needs to be made against an elder, two or three witnesses are required (1 Tim. 5:19). Presumably, Paul requires this because leaders are in the line of the fire of sinful human beings who often regard their disgruntlements as uniquely important or just.

What should church members do when they have expressed their disagreements or concerns but have been ignored? Certainly they should not gossip and begin a faction. If the disagreement can be tolerated, then they should forgive anything that needs to be forgiven, speak of the matter no further, and determine to happily support the church anyway. One absolutely must not allow resentment to build up in the heart, nor should one say something to another—even one's spouse—that would undermine the authority of the church's leadership.

When I disagree with other leaders in my congregation, I want to be careful not to undermine their authority in my wife's life. I want her to be able to sit under their preaching week after week and benefit from God's Word without a heart that's been soured by her husband's complaints. That doesn't mean I always choose to say nothing, though often I do. It does mean that, if I say something to her about the matter, I do so only when I know my words can be used to help her love the church more. In the process, I also try to direct her gaze to some fault of my own for the disagreement, such as my impatience or my lack of love. As her husband, friend, and fellow church member, my goal should always be to protect and burnish her love for Christ *and* his bride, not trample on it. Such care should extend to every member of the congregation. "If anyone against anyone" in the church has a complaint, says Paul, he should forgive (Col. 3:13; literal translation).

If the disagreement cannot be tolerated, a member may decide to leave the church, but only in such a way that does not sow division or discontent in those who remain. Furthermore, one should make the decision to leave over a disagreement only with the greatest reluctance and after having taken every prudent measure to achieve reconciliation or shared understanding. Jeremiah Burroughs, a seventeenth-century Congregationalist pastor, explained the prayerfulness and reluctance of heart that should accompany such a decision:

> Suppose there are some godly and conscientious men in a church, but there is something done in the church that they cannot believe to be the mind of Christ. After

---

authority does not ask for blind obedience; it appeals to gospel realities in the individual and asks for a voluntary obedience. The same is true of how Christ exercises his own authority. His authority does not depend on our consent, but he asks for our consent nonetheless; then he gives it, when he wills, through his Spirit. He asks us to exercise our will in obedience to him; and our submission to him is a voluntary submission. Can we therefore dissent from Christ? No, because he is God and our ultimate authority; but that's not true of the church. Christians should dissent from the authority of the church, not "at their pleasure" as Bannerman says, misrepresenting a free-church position, but whenever it contravenes the authority of Christ's Word or gospel witness. Of course, Bannerman himself admits this last point in his discussion of the limits of church authority (Bannerman, *Church of Christ*). Since, therefore, gospel authority works not in opposition to the conscience but in concert with it, and since there's always the possibility for every earthly authority to err, there must be room for dissent.

all examination, after prayer, after seeking to God, they cannot see it to be the mind of Christ, but they should sin if they should join them. They can testify to God, their own consciences witnessing for them, that they would gladly join with their church in all the ways of God's worship, but in such and such ways they cannot join with the church without sin to their own consciences. They labour to inform themselves; they go to the elders; and they go to others in all humility to show their doubts in this thing. After hearing what others have said, they depart and, in conscience to God, examine between God and their souls what was said, and they pray over these things. They pray that God would reveal these things unto them if they be his mind. Now after all this is done, if they still cannot agree, what would you have these men do? Suppose there be a hundred such men; they cannot communicate, yet they are not presently to rend from the congregation, but to wait a while to see whether God will convince them. Now if after all using every means to find a common mind, they cannot be convinced, shall these men live without the ordinances of the Lord's Supper all the days of their lives? Hath Christ so tied a member of a congregation that he must never join with another congregation, even if remaining with his church causes him to believe he sins against Christ? Truly there had need be clear warrant for this if any one shall affirm it.[14]

Compare Burroughs's attitude with our culture's attitude toward pastors and leadership, in general. How quick and casual we are to disagree with those God has placed over us. We assume that it's our right, our prerogative, and the way good government works. Let the people have their say! This might make us good democrats, but it does not make us good church members. Let us therefore render to Locke and Jefferson what are Locke's and Jefferson's, and to God what is God's. Disagreements may need to be addressed, and when they are addressed they should be done so reluctantly, discreetly, carefully, respectfully, prayerfully, and with a heavy heart. We must finally act according to our conscience, but we must do so fearfully, knowing that (1) Christ has given the church authority, and (2) we will one day be in the position of explaining to Christ why we thought it was necessary to dissent.

Step 7: Our submission to the local church can be well articulated in a written church covenant, which serves to remind a church of its covenantal commitments to one another.

---

[14]Jeremiah Burroughs, "The Difference between Independency and Presbytery," in *The Reformation of the Church: A Collection of Reformed and Puritan Documents on Church Issues*, ed. Iain H. Murray (Carlisle, PA: Banner of Truth, 1997 repr.), 287. I have attempted to simplify the language of this quotation in several places.

A Written Church Covenant

For the last several centuries, some churches have enshrined vows of submission in a written church covenant. As I said before, writing down a church covenant is a matter of biblical freedom. A number in the Old Testament voluntarily bound themselves to covenants with one another, such as Jonathan and David. In fact, we're told that "Jonathan made a covenant with David, because he loved him as his own soul" (1 Sam. 18:3). This is exactly what local church covenants should be made of.

My own church asks all incoming members to sign such a covenant, and then we stand and read this covenant aloud to one another every time we receive the Lord's Supper, which is monthly. On a monthly basis, then, we remind one another of how we aspire to give and receive care.

The following covenant—my church's covenant—begins with the indicative of what Christ has done; it begins with the gospel. Our love for one another is born out of his love for us. It reflects our hope to submit to one another physically, socially, affectionately, financially, vocationally, ethically, and spiritually:

> Having, as we trust, been brought by Divine Grace to repent and believe in the Lord Jesus Christ and to give up ourselves to Him, and having been baptized upon our profession of faith, in the name of the Father and of the Son and of the Holy Spirit, we do now, relying on His gracious aid, solemnly and joyfully renew our covenant with each other.
>
> We will work and pray for the unity of the Spirit in the bond of peace.
>
> We will walk together in brotherly love, as becomes the members of a Christian Church; exercise an affectionate care and watchfulness over each other and faithfully admonish and entreat one another as occasion may require.
>
> We will not forsake the assembling of ourselves together, nor neglect to pray for ourselves and others.
>
> We will endeavor to bring up such as may at any time be under our care, in the nurture and admonition of the Lord, and by a pure and loving example to seek the salvation of our family and friends.
>
> We will rejoice at each other's happiness, and endeavor with tenderness and sympathy to bear each other's burdens and sorrows.
>
> We will seek, by Divine aid, to live carefully in the world, denying ungodliness and worldly lusts, and remembering that, as we have been voluntarily buried by baptism and raised again from the symbolic grave, so there is on us a special obligation now to lead a new and holy life.
>
> We will work together for the continuance of a faithful evangelical ministry in this church, as we sustain its worship, ordinances, discipline, and doctrines. We will contribute cheerfully and regularly to the support of the ministry, the expenses of the church, the relief of the poor, and the spread of the Gospel through all nations.

> We will, when we move from this place, as soon as possible, unite with some other church where we can carry out the spirit of this covenant and the principles of God's Word.
>
> May the grace of the Lord Jesus Christ, and the love of God, and the fellowship of the Holy Spirit be with us all. Amen.

Reading this covenant aloud monthly reminds the members of the church that our discipleship to Christ is not an autonomous matter but a body-life matter. "The eye cannot say to the hand, 'I have no need of you,' nor again the head to the feet, 'I have no need of you'" (1 Cor. 12:21). The Christian life is not something we can do on our own, because the very nature of the Christian life requires connectedness, obedience, and sacrificial love. We grow as we help others to grow. We become free as we help others to be free.

Sometimes keeping this covenant means raking someone's lawn. Sometimes it means leading a small group. Sometimes it means biting our tongue rather than retaliating. Sometimes it means employing our Spirit-given gifts, but sometimes it means doing the things we are not very good at, because nobody else will do them. Sometimes it means voting differently from how we intended to vote because the pastor asked us to. Always it means loving.

Conclusion

Submitting to the local church is not about submitting to a distant figure in a place like Rome or Canterbury. It's not about submitting to a historical tradition of doctrinal development and epistemic surety. When Christ calls Christians to submit to local churches, he has in mind something far more involved. He means for us to love. He means for us to love the folks sitting next to us in the pew or folding chair or patch of dirt. We're to love flesh-and-blood people with names like Jeanette, Charlie and Jessie, Marco, Paul and Alice, and Beth.

Do you know Jeanette? She's the one who gets a little cranky about making sure the pews are returned to their proper order after every Sunday's gathering. And Charlie? You have to speak up with Charlie because he doesn't hear so well, but how he loves to sing Jesus' praises. Then there's Marco, who struggles with addiction. Paul and Alice—such a kind couple. You'll never hear Paul stop talking about how much he loves Alice, even though they've been married for sixty years. Finally there is Beth. She is a single mom learning to love Jesus more with every passing month. All these names and many more—we are to count them more significant than ourselves. We are to seek to have one mind and one love with them. We are to submit to the ones we like and the ones we don't like, to the mature ones and the less than mature ones.

To share one love with Jeanette, Charlie and Jessie, Marco, Paul and Alice, and Beth means to give ourselves to them for Christ's sake, not just give *of* ourselves for our own sake. We count them more significant than ourselves by binding our identity to theirs and giving them all the honor we want for ourselves—the honor of Christ. We stake our joy and sorrow in their progress in the faith, since love always hopes, always trusts, always perseveres.

As we love like this, we define Christ's love for the world.

OUTLINE OF THE BOOK

Chapter 1: The Idolatry of Love

Main Question: How do our common cultural conceptions of love today hinder our acceptance of church membership and discipline?

STEPS IN THE ARGUMENT:

1) Doing a doctrine of the church requires us to consider our cultural baggage.
2) *Individualism* has left us detached, which sent us searching for a love that makes us feel complete. We want churches to do the same.
3) *Consumerism* has caused us to focus on the desirability of the object of love, rather than on the process of loving. We view churches like products which satisfy us or not.
4) *Commitment phobia* takes commitment out of love and love becomes about what's advantageous to me. The idea of commitment is removed from our view of churches.
5) *Skepticism* removes all judgment from love, causing us to expect unconditional acceptance from churches. Pragmatism also results.
6) But what is individualism really? It's a hatred of authority. And behind the hatred of authority is a diminished God.
7) Church membership, then, begins with repentance.

Main Answer: We have made love into an idol that serves us, and so redefined love into something that never imposes judgments, conditions, or binding attachments.

Chapter 2: The Nature of Love

Main Questions: What is God's love like and why does it offend us? What's the connection between our understanding of God's love and church membership?

STEPS IN THE ARGUMENT:

1) In ways we don't expect, God's love both attracts and repels us, which means God's gospel and God's church also attract and repel us.

2) The doctrine of God's love is more complicated biblically and theologically than people realize. Theologians before Luther centered God's love upon God.

3) Many theologians since Luther have opted for a reductionistic understanding of God's love—love merely as unconditional gift. This common evangelical understanding of love today fundamentally changes the purpose of the church and the shape of church membership.

4) The Scriptures show that God's love is holy—it centers on himself.

5) The Scriptures show that God's purposes in redemption are also holy, centering on himself.

6) Therefore, we can define love as "the lover's affirmation of and affection for the beloved and the beloved's good in the Holy."

7) God's love, God's gospel, and God's church offend us because they all center on him.

8) God's love and God's judgment work in concert, not in opposition. This also is offensive.

9) A church is a church that seeks out the Holy to affirm and separate it from the unholy.

Main Answers: God's love creates and affirms us, but it does so for the purposes of winning praise to himself. The holiness or God-centeredness of God's love offends us because it brings both salvation and judgment. Church membership and discipline therefore offend us because they picture both salvation and judgment, and draw a line between them.

Chapter 3: The Rule of Love

Main Questions: What is authority? How does it relate to love? And what role does it play in the church?

STEPS IN THE ARGUMENT:

1) The idea of authority frightens us, for understandable reasons

2) Therefore, many church leaders and pastors today present us with a vision of the loving community of relationships which downplays the idea of authority.

3) Yet God is not a God of just relationships, he's a God of authority, and authority is what holds the church together.

4) What is authority and how does it relate to love? Authority is the authorization we have from God to create and give order to life.

5) What is submission and how does it relate to love? Submission is love for God and giving oneself to the pursuit of his glory.

6) At the same time, we rightly mistrust authority because sin, in its very essence, is the abuse of the authority God has given his creatures.

7) Christ's life, death, and resurrection present the world with a picture of authority redeemed, an authority which he then hands to his people.

8) The local church is where Christians enact their submission to Christ and practice his loving rule toward others.

9) The local church is a new reality, with marked-off borders and a center.

10) Yet we must always keep in mind that authority in this fallen world is both complex and mixed.

Main Answers: Authority, grounded in holy love, creates life. It creates a whole new reality that is both marked off and shaped.

Chapter 4: The Charter of Love

Main Questions: What authority does Christ give the local church and why?

STEPS IN THE ARGUMENT:

1) In this fallen world, hypocrites and heretics confuse the world about the gospel and the nature of Christ's love. Therefore, Christ authorizes the church to mark off the people of God.

2) In the Gospel of Matthew, Jesus demonstrates concern over who is identified with his name and who is not, because identifying with him is identifying with the heavenly Father.

3) In Matthew 16, 18, and 28, Jesus gave the apostles and the apostolic church the power of the keys. This authorized the church to guard the gospel, to affirm credible professions, to unite such professors to itself, to oversee their discipleship, and to exclude hypocrites.

4) Even with all its imperfections, the church represents Jesus on earth. It gives witness to his coming salvation and judgment.

5) The church, therefore, is Christ's proxy on earth.

6) The fact that the church is Christ's proxy on earth means that the Christian must submit to the church on earth, which means submitting to the local church.

7) How then can we formally define local church membership and discipline? As the forming or breaking of a covenant between a Christian and a church.

8) This covenant between a Christian and a local church does not remove a Christian's responsibilities to other Christians, but it does give a Christian more responsibility over the members of his or her church.

Main Answers: Christ authorizes the local church to proclaim and protect the gospel, to recognize or affirm those who belong to him, to unite them to itself, to oversee their discipleship, and to exclude any imposters. He gives the local church this authority in order to protect and display his gospel in a fallen world which continually misunderstands and misportrays his gospel love.

Chapter 5: The Covenant of Love

Main Question: What exactly is this commitment or "covenant" of local church membership?

STEPS IN THE ARGUMENT:

1) We can answer the question of what a "local church covenant" is by considering the relationship between Christ's "charter" (described in chapter 4) and his new covenant.

2) Church membership involves identifying ourselves with Christ and Christ's people. The work of mutual identification occurs through covenants.

3) In the Old Testament, God broadly used covenants to identify a people with himself and establish his kingdom.

4) In the New Testament, he sent his Son to establish a better, effectual covenant. This new covenant, which unites us to Christ representationally, by the Spirit, and by faith, is the foundation of the church.

5) The "covenant" of local church membership is what results when Christ's charter draws together and marks off Christ's new covenant people.

6) As with the covenants of the Old Testament, the covenantal commitment shared by the members of the local church serves nine specific purposes.

7) The covenant commitment of the local church makes the invisible new covenant visible. It's an earthly symbol, sign, or analogy of this wonderful heavenly reality.

Main Answer: The commitment believers make to one another to form a local church is a covenant-like commitment. Since Christ has identified them with him through his new covenant, and since he has authorized them to identify themselves with him through his charter, they covenant together in such a fashion that his name is protected and their good is promoted.

Chapter 6: The Affirmation and Witness of Love

Main Questions: How should a church responsibly affirm, oversee, and remove members? Should it account for cultural differences in these activities?

STEPS IN THE ARGUMENT:

1) Many people today exaggerate the importance of cultural difference; still, we should pay some attention to cultural differences. This measured approach to cultural differences can be illustrated by three churches in three different nations.

2) In other words, churches should pay attention to how complex the culture is as well as the society's favor or disfavor toward Christianity, which requires churches to ensure that both church and Christian have the opportunity to adequately "explain" themselves.

3) At the same time, churches everywhere are tasked with marking off a holy people, which will always be opposed by the world, the flesh, and the Devil.

4) In order to responsibly affirm members, a church should ensure that prospective members understand who they are committing to through any necessary classes, doctrinal statements, and words to guard the Lord's Table; the church should also ensure that prospective members adequately grasp the gospel.

5) The goal of member oversight is to present a credible witness for Christ on earth. The whole church, leaders and members, participate in this gospel-grounded, discipleship-driven care through the ministry of the Word.

6) Since a church covenant is a two-way commitment, both church and member must consent to the end of the relationship. Churches should formally discipline members who prove unrepentantly unfaithful in their discipleship to Christ.

Main Answers: To a limited measure, churches should account for culture differences, particularly in terms of a society's complexity and bearing toward Christianity. At the same time, churches should uniformly affirm, oversee, and remove members with a continual mind for its work of giving witness to Christ's holy name.

Chapter 7: The Submission and Freedom of Love

Main Question: What does it mean to submit to a local church? Are there limits to the church's authority over the individual?

STEPS IN THE ARGUMENT:

1) Christian freedom is not freedom from restraint, but the Spirit-given freedom to want what God wants and conform one's life to his.

2) Since Christian freedom can only be given by the Spirit, and not the flesh, the godly use of authority in the church will not seek to coerce individuals by the flesh; it will appeal to gospel realities given by the Spirit.

3) When individuals find themselves under an abusive authority, they should always trust God's provision and purposes; if possible, they should flee.

4) Philippians 2 presents the model for submission in the local church: Christ's incarnation and crucifixion.

5) Christians emulate Christ's example by submitting to one another physically, socially, affectionately, financially, vocationally, ethically, and spiritually.

6) When the church contravenes Scripture or the gospel's witness, an individual should speak and act in dissent, but only reverently and in the fear of God.

7) Our submission to the local church can be well articulated in a written church covenant, which serves to remind a church of its covenantal commitments to one another.

Main Answer: Submitting to the church means submitting our whole selves to the church for its good and for Christ's glory, just as Christ surrendered himself for our good and the Father's glory.

SUBJECT INDEX

SCRIPTURE INDEX

IX 9Marks

Building Healthy Churches

9Marks exists to equip church leaders with a biblical vision and practical resources for displaying God's glory to the nations through healthy churches.

To that end, we want to see churches characterized by these nine marks of health:

1   Expositional Preaching
2   Biblical Theology
3   A Biblical Understanding of the Gospel
4   A Biblical Understanding of Conversion
5   A Biblical Understanding of Evangelism
6   Biblical Church Membership
7   Biblical Church Discipline
8   Biblical Discipleship
9   Biblical Church Leadership

Find all our Crossway titles
and other resources at
www.9Marks.org